The Irish World Wide
History, Heritage, Identity

Volume 3 **The Creative Migrant**

The Irish World Wide
History, Heritage, Identity

Edited by Patrick O'Sullivan

The Irish World Wide
History, Heritage, Identity

Volume 3
The Creative Migrant

Edited by Patrick O'Sullivan

Leicester University Press
Leicester, London, New York

Distributed in the USA and Canada by
ST MARTIN'S PRESS, New York

Leicester University Press
(a division of Pinter Publishers Ltd)
25 Floral Street, London, WC2E 9DS

First published in Great Britain in 1994
© Editor and contributors 1994

Distributed exclusively in the USA and Canada by St. Martin's Press, Inc., Room 400, 175 Fifth Avenue, New York, NY 10010, USA

British Library Cataloguing in Publication Data
A CIP catalogue record for this book is available from the British Library

ISBN 0 7185 1423 8

Library of Congress Cataloging-in-Publication Data
The Creative migrant/edited by Patrick O'Sullivan.
    p. cm. — (The Irish World Wide; v.3)
    Includes bibliographical references and index.
    ISBN 0–7185–1423–8
    1. National characteristics, Irish. 2. Irish—Foreign countries—Intellectual life.
3. Civilization, Modern—Irish influences. 4. Ireland—Civilization. I. O'Sullivan, Patrick. II. Series.
DA925.C66 1994
941.5—dc20   93–43963
                                                                                                                        CIP

Typeset by Saxon Graphics Ltd
Printed and bound in Great Britain by Biddles Ltd of Guildford and King's Lynn

In memory of Richard O'Keeffe

Contents

List of contributors

Bernard Canavan is a free-lance illustrator, whose work includes the covers of the six volumes of *The Irish World Wide*. He also teaches on Irish history for the Workers' Educational Association and for the University of London Extra-Mural Department, in England. He has published many articles on aspects of Irish life.

Martin J. Counihan is an interdisciplinary scientist with the Department of Adult Education, University of Southampton, England. He teaches and researches in fundamental Physics and in the History of Science. He has a special interest in early Irish history: he frequently arranges summer schools in the West of Ireland.

John P. Cullinane is a plant scientist at University College, Cork, Ireland. He is also a qualified Irish Dancing Master and adjudicator, who has judged Irish dancing competitions in seven countries and three continents. For some twenty years he has gathered the material to explore the world-wide history and development of Irish dancing.

Owen Dudley Edwards is the John Hopkins Reader in History at the University of Edinburgh, Scotland. Recent works include *The Fireworks of Oscar Wilde*, *Eamon de Valera* and *City of a Thousand Worlds: Edinburgh in Festival*.

Frank Molloy is Senior Lecturer in English at the Charles Sturt University, Wagga Wagga, New South Wales, Australia. He has published on Irish and Australian literature and Irish-Australian literary relations. He is currently working on the bibliography of Victor James Daley, the late nineteenth-century Australian poet.

James P. Myers, jun., is a Professor of English Literature at Gettysburg College, Pennsylvania, USA, where he teaches courses on Shakespeare, seventeenth-century poetry and drama and Irish literature and history.

Patrick O'Sullivan is the Editor of *The Irish World Wide* series.

Patrick J. Quinlivan studied History at Cork, London and Norrköping. He has taught in London, the Channel Islands, the Middle East, Scandinavia and Spain. While teaching in London he became interested in the story of the fenians, and made this his principal spare-time study. He is now based at the United World College of the Adriatic, Duino, Italy.

Kevin Rockett is a historian of cinema who teaches at University College, Dublin, and at the Irish Film Institute, Dublin. He is one of the co-authors of *Ireland and Cinema*.

Graeme Smith has written on Irish traditional dance music, folk music revival movements and other popular musics. His Ph.D. dissertation in ethnomusicology at Monash University, Melbourne, Australia, investigated the generation of social meaning within Irish accordion-playing styles.

Introduction to Volume 3:
The creative migrant

Patrick O'Sullivan

There is a word amongst those Greek terms from rhetoric that are once again fashionable: *oxymoron*. Sharp foolish. An oxymoron is a figure of speech that combines two apparently contradictory terms in a compressed paradox. The examples usually given are 'bitter-sweet' and 'living death'. The migration experience, we could hazard, is an oxymoronic experience.

To some modes of analysis the very title of this volume, Volume 3 of *The Irish World Wide*, is an oxymoron: the words 'creative' and 'migrant' do not go together. We have already seen, in the earlier volumes of *The Irish World Wide*, some of the personal, social, political and historical tensions within Ireland around the theme of migration, and later in the series those tensions will be further examined.

This volume is not called 'The Culture of Migration': in an interdisciplinary project cross-discipline uses of the word 'culture' are too problematic. Raymond Williams writes: 'Culture is one of the two or three most complicated words in the English language. This is so partly because of its intricate historical development, in several European languages, but mainly because it has now come to be used for important concepts in several distinct intellectual disciplines and in several distinct and incompatible systems of thought.'[1]

Broadly speaking, the word 'culture' is used in two senses within the disciplines straddled by *The Irish World Wide* series: there is the sociological or anthropological sense in which 'culture' is cumulatively those rules and meanings that guide and shape our lives without our quite knowing it; then there is the more widespread sense of the word, 'culture' as works and practices of intellectual or artistic activity. In this second sense 'culture' is stuff that you hang on your walls.

But if you have no walls . . . ?[2]

Many thinkers, like Raymond Williams (and indeed Matthew Arnold, whose title, *Culture and Anarchy*, conflates many meanings of that first word), explore the relationship between 'culture' in the sociological sense and 'culture' in the sense of artistic activity. Such thinkers are well represented in this volume. Contributors to the first two volumes of *The Irish World Wide* have already noted the development within Ireland of a 'culture' of migration, 'culture' in the sociological sense. A variety of circumstances, including war, famine and dispossession (as shown, for example, in chapters by Fitzgerald and McGurk in Volume 1, *Patterns of Migration*) forced or encouraged Irish people to leave Ireland, and in the ensuing centuries emigration became, as it were, the preferred individual solution. This volume, *The Creative Migrant*, begins to look at the effects of these migrations upon intellectual and artistic activity, that is on 'culture' in the other sense. We look at particular effects and at cumulative effects.

This volume, like every volume of *The Irish World Wide*, is a report on 'the state of the art'. It brings together examples of what is being studied from an Irish Migration Studies' perspective, and it suggests ways that more might be studied. Each chapter is thus an example of what might be done, opening up a whole area of study and comment: Molloy's chapter on the influence of Thomas Moore, for example, creates a new sub-department of Moore studies. In this volume I have again tried for a long chronology, a good spread of academic disciplines (within this volume's 'media studies' brief), and a world-wide spread of contributor and subject matter. Again I have written an Introduction that fills gaps and makes interdisciplinary connections. I have also tried to give a flavour of the discussions and the correspondence that shaped this volume.

In bringing together this volume I have not, you will see, relentlessly pursued the obvious.[3] I have sought out scholars who have found ways of bringing the study of migration into our thinking about Irish artistic and intellectual life. This theme has been little studied, or has been studied in limited ways. One of the more throw-away observations of Everett S. Lee, the theorist of migration, was that 'there are conditions in many places which push out the unorthodox and the highly creative . . .' And it has tended to be that aspect of the relationship between Irish migration and Irish artistic activity which has received attention.[4]

You may well feel that the study of Irish artistic and political life is already complex enough, without adding extra dimensions. My own view is that much Irish artistic and intellectual activity is impossible to understand without an understanding of migration. For example, I think it one of the achievements of this volume that it brings into academic discourse studies of Irish dance and of Irish music, and brings in music and dance in ways that throw light on the effects of migration on other artistic activities and intellectual processes.

This volume, then, looks at the ways in which migrants can be creative, at the arts of the intellect, of music and of the word. We look at migrants as 'consumers' and as creators of art. Here we can see the migration process already making our selections for us, creating our agenda: the migrant's arts tend to be the portable arts, the mobile arts, the social arts. This is indeed art without walls. We can try to fight this agenda, to rewrite this agenda. We may want to include discussion of the plastic, representational arts, of painting and sculpture, for example. Inevitably, as we saw in the earlier volumes of *The Irish World Wide*, our eyes are drawn to the Irish family names: we find ourselves trying to incorporate Georgia O'Keeffe or the O'Shea brothers into our patterns.[5] But, frankly, that is difficult.

Narratives

Since this is the 'media studies' volume of *The Irish World Wide* series, a major linking theme within the volume must be the nature of narratives. Throughout *The Irish World Wide* series questions have been raised about 'Irishness', sometimes in a straightforward methodological way when we looked at inclusive and exclusive definitions of 'Irish'. To be 'Irish' within the British Empire was to inhabit, maybe even to be confined within, a certain narrative space: in Volume 1, we talked about 'ethnic soldiers'. To migrate is to enter another's narrative, and very likely, within that narrative, become a 'symbolic other'. Thus, the practices that in Volume I I called 'contribution history' and 'oppression history' could be probed further by asking: to whom do those narratives belong? Many things, including, it will be seen, the ways that academic disciplines fragment reality, can hinder the development of an all-embracing narrative, a narrative that makes sense to us.

Let us concentrate, for a moment, on the arts that you will expect to see studied here, the arts of the written word. There is a familiar pattern in the great autobiographies and the biographies of the major Irish writers of the last two centuries: yes, they look at the writers's individual decision about migration, and yes, they acknowledge part of the social background, and yes, sometimes they acknowledge an individual intellectual or artistic problem. Yet there is little systematic exploration of the cumulative effects of these patterns of migration on intellectual life and artistic production.[6]

An admirable book by Norman Vance builds its exposition of Irish literary tradition round explorations of the lives and the works of five pairs of linked figures. In every case the issue of migration looms large in the life and in the work of at least one of the pair.[7] Yet that issue is not touched on.

There is, in any case, within literary criticism a tendency to leap from the particular to the universal, with little regard for what might lie between. What lies between the particular and the universal for Irish people is migration. I note, too, the difficulty that Irish literary criticism has had of late in absorbing some of the insights of newer literary theory, theory which might look at what 'lies between': reader theory, audience response theory, reception theory. What is the audience, where is the readership for these Irish arts of the word, these Irish cultural products? Vance notices the problem and comments on it a number of times. 'The modern Irish writer in effect mediates between two communities: a community of origin and the larger community which supplies the audience for his work.'[8]

That audience may be world-wide, as we shall see. And the influence of that audience on writers would need to be explored systematically. As we will see later in this Introduction, when we look at drama and poetry, each art of the word is affected differently, and the effects are not always patterned in the most obvious ways. What is needed is a genuine historical sociology of art, that would ask real questions about patronage and markets.[9]

My own method here is to make a slightly unusual use of migration theory. And, again as a sort of shorthand, as a quick way of making connections, I look to the 'Theory of Migration' of Everett S. Lee. I have discussed in earlier volumes of *The Irish World Wide* the patterns we would expect to find within migrations, the pattern of 'stream and counterstream' and the pattern of elites and masses, the bi-modal selection of migrants.[10]

'Stream and counterstream' involves not only persons but knowledge. Amongst 'stream' we will include works of art, particularly those literary works that are such a feature of Irish exports. 'Counterstream' considered as knowledge will absorb into our patterns of migration the emigrants' letters and books of advice to emigrants, still a staple of the Irish publishing industry. We would expect the pattern of elites and masses to have its own effects on artistic production.

To talk of 'elites and masses' when talking about the arts is not, I stress, to privilege one sort of artistic activity above another. It may simply be that when we think about the uses of the arts, their social or personal uses, that a community of a given size can only support a given number of poets or playwrights, just as (as we saw in Volumes 1 and 2) it can only support a certain number of accountants or doctors. It may also be that when we talk about arts created by and for elites we need to consider questions of patronage; when we talk about arts created by and for masses we need to consider mass markets.

If we overlay the one pattern upon the other, if we interweave the pattern of stream and counterstream with the pattern of elites and masses, we have a simple way of understanding the processes through which art and migration affect each other. Again, as ever, I do not want to use this theorising in any heavy-handed sort of way. But I think you should know that it was this sort of thinking that guided the selection and cultivation of chapters for this volume. And it was for this reason that I designed this volume so that it led naturally and chronologically to studies of those popular, community Irish arts: dance and music.

Alternative narratives

It is something of a truism, within 'Irish Studies', that notions of 'Irishness' have been shaped by notions of 'Englishness': in other words, that perceptions of self or nation have been shaped by the particular power relations that have developed within these islands. Some explorations of 'Irishness' have too readily accepted versions of 'Englishness' created for particular political or polemic (and historically-located) ends by specific English classes, or class fractions. Notions of 'Englishness' have not been problematised in quite the same way as notions of 'Irishness'.[11]

The problem with all such dyadic contrasts is that they, in effect, split up the repertoire of human possibilities, allocating some possibilities to one group, and insisting that such possibilities are not available to another group, on arbitrary and often suspect criteria.[12] One of the merits of Irish Migration Studies is that we can do what the migrant Irish themselves have done, and take our exploration of the possibilities of 'Irishness' out of the relationships that have developed within these islands, sometimes moving (it is true) through places and periods where attempts were made to replicate those relationships.

This volume begins with Martin J. Counihan's study of the Irish scientific tradition of rationalism, intellectual rigour, esteem for science and respect for the integrity of nature. Counihan himself acknowledges that some will express surprise at the very possibility of such a tradition: it will seem 'unIrish', but it will seem unIrish only to those who strictly define Irish possibilities within a dyadic contrast. Others, noting Counihan's ending, will legitimately see his chapter as part of 'compensation history', or of 'oppression history'.

Counihan, it may be felt, has some difficulty demonstrating continuity in a tradition that runs from the fifth century to the seventeenth. But Vivian Mercier felt able to demonstrate a continuous 'Irish comic tradition' from the earliest writings in the Irish language to twentieth-century writing in the English language:

> A sceptical reader might well ask how a writer can show continuity with a tradition of whose very existence he is hardly aware, or imitate models which he has never seen. My answer would run as follows: the oral culture of any area is far richer and more complex than its literary culture, especially where two languages and two cultures interact, as they do in Ireland; many unrecognized elements remain in suspension in such an oral culture, waiting for the right temperament to act as reagent and cause them to precipitate; when these elements are precipitated in literature, we are amazed, yet they were present in the culture all along and may have revealed themselves several times before under favourable conditions. This explanation has the merit of attributing cultural phenomena to cultural causes . . .[13]

It is a support to Mercier's argument that a strong element in the tradition he discovers is erotic comedy, unacceptable to groups dominant in Ireland during recent centuries. Another way of putting the argument would be to suppose that there is the potential within human beings to develop in all sorts of ways, given 'favourable conditions': which is the argument underlying many 'compensation history' approaches to Irish migration.

Another way to approach Counihan's chapter is to place it in the context provided by Richard Kearney's collection *The Irish Mind*. There John Moran's chapter on John Scotus Eriugena sees him as a lonely and isolated figure, when here Counihan sees Eriugena as part of the Irish scientific tradition. In Kearney's collection, chapters on Berkeley, on the Counter-Enlightenment, and on the Irish scientific tradition all begin where here Counihan breaks off.[14]

In *The Irish Mind* Herries Davies ends his exploration of 'Irish thought in science' since 1600 thus:

> This essay has focused attention upon the Irish contribution to science as one facet of Ireland's cultural heritage. There remains to be asked one question: why has Ireland chosen largely to ignore the very considerable achievements of those of her sons who have devoted themselves to science? Part of the answer may be simply that our historians have felt more comfortable in discussions of banking, battles and bishops than in dealing with problems concerning basalt, binomials and brachiopods . . .[15]

Another way of answering Herries Davies' question is, with Counihan, to explore the place of migration in those patterns. For Counihan's scientist philosophers Mercier's 'favourable conditions' could exist only outside Ireland. There are certain aspects of Counihan's chapter that might need clarifying within an interdisciplinary approach to Irish Studies and Irish Migration Studies. His remark in passing that 'Irish is not a Celtic language' may raise some eyebrows. That needs another book.[16]

A tale of *talaria*

In the General Introduction to *The Irish World Wide* series I promised that we would have the opportunity to explore readily available texts from an Irish Migration Studies' perspective. I also said that I had not encouraged, for *The Irish World Wide*, studies of anti-Irish prejudice as such. The next chapter by literary historian James P. Myers, jun., explores prejudice in a famous text: and he explores that text in ways that, for me, throw light on the problems that arise when we uncritically use such texts as sources.

There can hardly be a more widely available text than Thoreau's *Walden*. Though it attracted little attention with its first publication in 1854 it has since come to be seen as one of the seminal books of the century. It mapped out and gave a name to a corner of the American soul. That very name is so resonant within American culture that a freshman idyll and a behaviourist counterblast can appropriate the name without need of explanation. We know that it influenced the English socialists, we know that it influenced Gandhi. *Walden* can be cited by a student of Zen and called in evidence by Americans defending the environment.[17] I can assume that most university and college libraries have a copy. Before even reading the text we seem to know what it will tell us: the experiment in self-sufficiency and self-exploration by the transcendental philosopher, isolated in the woods.

It therefore comes as a surprise when we read *Walden* to find that these woods are inhabited. What is more, the woods are inhabited by Irish people. It was from the Irish Collins family that Thoreau bought some of the material to make his cabin. And, not too far away from that cabin, another Irish family, the Fields, struggled to make a living in this new land.

That in itself would be enough to interest us in a rereading of *Walden*. But, as we read, we become aware of the orchestrated structure of *Walden*, carefully analysed for us by Myers. The book leads up to and then away from the encounters with the Field family, described in the chapter called 'Baker Farm'. From this chapter Thoreau springboards into his philosophy. What is extraordinary, from our point of view, is that this key chapter, this pivotal chapter, itself leads up to a last sentence that is a statement about the nature of Irishness. I immediately have to reach for my quotation marks, for this of course is 'Irishness', something defined by another.

The key sentence, the last sentence in the key chapter, is the one quoted by Myers in his chapter title. It is a difficult sentence.[18] Thoreau has watched the depressed struggle of John Field, his ignorance of this new land, his attempt 'to catch perch with shiners' (and perhaps one day a fisherman will explain to me quite what is wrong with that). And Thoreau concludes:

> With his horizon all his own, yet he a poor man, born to be poor, with his inherited Irish poverty or poor life, his Adam's grandmother and boggy ways, not to rise in the world, he nor his posterity, till their wading, webbed, bog-trotting feet get *talaria* to their heels.[19]

As a sentence, it exemplifies the worst features of Thoreau's prose style. But, clearly, here we have a dismissive definition of 'Irishness'. How is an Irish person, or a person of Irish heritage (remember: 'nor his posterity') supposed to react to this sentence? How do you defend yourself against the charge of lacking *talaria*. Within the sentence the contrast is explicit: the Irishman and his kin will not be able to follow the transcendental philosopher, until they 'get *talaria*'. And get *talaria* 'to their heels'. What can this mean?

Near my home is a museum called Cartwright Hall. I was at a concert there last year, when my unfocused eyes rested on a piece of statuary. I focused on the statue's feet. '*Talaria!*' I cried. 'Ssh!' said the other concert-goers.

The root is the Latin word, *talus*, meaning the ankle or the ankle-bone. The plural noun *talaria* means the parts around the ankles, or garments that reach the ankles, and, used even more precisely, winged sandals fastened at the ankles. Not at the heels, as Thoreau suggests. These are the winged sandals of Mercury (Hermes), the god who is the messenger of the gods. Thoreau reaches, automatically (and, perhaps, unthinkingly), in the manner of his class, period and education, for the classical allusion, and the Latin word. Note how Myers, in his chapter here, explores an association of ideas within Thoreau's head, ideas which link Thoreau himself with Mercury.

So, what does Thoreau mean by 'get' *talaria*? Is it that, since these winged sandals are things from classical mythology, non-existing, impossible things, the Irish can *never* 'get *talaria*'? The Irish cannot follow the transcendental philosopher because of some innate deficiency, impossible to overcome? But what if *talaria* are real, possible pieces of footwear? Then we 'get *talaria*' by going to the *talaria* shop and buying them in the usual way. Which means that we are talking about matters of education and resources.

The statue in Cartwright Hall helped my thinking. For it was not a statue of Mercury: it was a statue of the human hero, Perseus. The gods had given Perseus various bits of equipment to help him find and kill the Medusa. Mercury lent his winged sandals to Perseus. *Talaria*, it seems, can be lent or borrowed.[20]

Myers shows through his careful reading of Thoreau's Journals, the raw material that was boiled down into the elaborate philosophical structure of *Walden*, that Thoreau's feelings about the Irish were more complex than a first, or second, reading of *Walden* would suggest. I said in the Introduction to Volume 2 of *The Irish World Wide* that this project can give us new heroes. One such hero for me, and a hero for Thoreau, Myers tells us, is little Johnny Riordan, walking in his rags along the railroad tracks in snow to school. A pair of *talaria* would, no doubt, have helped Johnny Riordan. If we cannot provide *talaria*, let us provide scholarships. I recall the Latin proverb, *talaria videamus*, which might be translated, 'let us get our skates on'.

Counihan has shown the Irish to be philosophers in themselves, Myers has shown us to be a cause of philosophy in others. Myers has also shown what happens when the Irish enter another's narrative: now we have a chapter that shows what happens when a narrative enters us.

I am not sure that I entirely agree with every part of the next contributor's argument: but then, throughout *The Irish World Wide* series, I have published chapters that I do not entirely agree with. Here it is, my own contribution to this volume. It can be regarded as an interdisciplinary approach to a number of issues that have perturbed me for some time: the way humorous material (jokes) is presented by theorists of humour, my dissatisfaction with comment on what in England are called 'Irish Jokes' and my wish to explore, and deconstruct, as many dyadic contrasts as possible.

There is something very heady, and intellectually exciting, about tracking down a story in a Latin source, two thousand years old, and then going to the pub, for a restful, well-earned pint, there to hear the *same* story, still alive, still finding new ways to be told. Watch how these jokes find that tension in power relationships, find a way to survive and be told. From this perspective to discover that the jokes have made an encampment in the middle of the English/Irish relationship is to discover a tautology. The defence of this approach is that it relativises the jokes: and would we want to see one Till Owlyglass or Cearbhall O'Dalaigh story lost to the human community?[21]

The stage English

The name of George Farquhar would figure largely in an exploration of the nature of 'Englishness'. Since that March of 1707, when *The Beaux' Stratagem* was advertised as by the author of *The Recruiting Officer*, and *The Recruiting Officer* was advertised as by the author of *The Beaux' Stratagem*, and Farquhar himself lay dying, you would be hard put to find a year that did not see his last two plays performed somewhere on the English-speaking stage. *The Recruiting Officer* may well have been the first play ever staged in North America, with a performance in New York in December 1732. *The Recruiting Officer* was certainly the first play performed in Australia. In June 1789 a group of convicts acted the play before an audience that included the Governor of New South Wales and officers of his garrison.[22]

The intricate ironies around that Australian performance were seized by Australian novelist Thomas Keneally to make that performance the theme of his novel *The Playmaker*. And Canadian playwright Timberlake Wertenbaker, in her turn, turned Keneally's novel into a stage play, *Our Country's Good*. A few years ago the Royal Court Theatre in London staged the two plays in tandem, Farquhar and Wertenbaker: the witty officers of the first becoming the convict actors of the second.[23]

Irish-born George Farquhar, in his last two plays, gave something enduring to English society and to that society's vision of itself, not so much through direct influence on later works but through a tone, an attitude, a kindly good-naturedness. Part of their charm and effectiveness is surely that the plays take us out of London to a nicely realised Shrewsbury and Lichfield: they take us out of genre to a world where country girls have their own sweet confidence and the old have some wisdom and dignity.

How interesting then that our next contributor, Owen Dudley Edwards, should build his study of 'The stage Irish' towards an Irish interpretation of George Farquhar. Edwards' chapter is ambitious and full of insights. Making ironic use of those theatre metaphors which are such a feature of sociology, he suggests, through his study of literature in the Irish language, that the impulse to drama is a natural, human one. That impulse becomes, in the English/Irish relationship, alienated, because seen as alien: the Irish are 'staged' by others before they have theatres of their own. And, as Edwards shows, 'Irish' will be used as a bogeyword in English polemic.

To a great extent thereafter Irish involvement in the international world of English-speaking theatre repeats Irish involvement in other elite professions. Certainly the theatre and cultural life of eighteenth-century Dublin are London-oriented, and successs (or failure) on the Dublin stage will springboard the hopeful to London.

But there is also, as Edwards suggests, an element of *infiltration* here. The art forms of the word have content as well as form, and have political use. And we can take Edwards' story a little further, and ask: where will the Irish find their own 'empty space' to explore their own preoccupations, their own stage on which to manifest their stage presence?

The key character, Dazzle, in the first successful play of Irish-born Dion Boucicault, *London Assurance*, is one of those outsiders so typical of Irish-born playwrights' 'drama of infiltration': we might hazard that he displays 'Dublin assurance' rather than the London kind.[24] In Irish theatrical history it is the plays of Boucicault's 'Irish Tryptych' that are influential: the three comedy melodramas, with their Irish settings and their aggressively Irish titles. These plays were created by and for the marketing opportunities offered by the mass Irish migrations of the nineteenth century. It was New York's Irish-American actor-manager Barney Williams who first suggested the drawing power of Boucicault's name linked to an Irish theme. After *The Colleen Bawn* Irishness was central to Boucicault's enterprise, but, it would seem, an Irish-American version of 'Irishness' rather than anything based on Boucicault's own experience. Augustin Daly, another New York theatre manager, suggested the approach of *The Shaughraun* to its subject matter: the audience wanted to laugh, not to think.[25]

There are many ways of measuring consciousness of identity or heritage in a migrant Irish community. Danaher's chapter in Volume 2 of *The Irish World Wide* suggested that Irish Studies courses in themselves were a kind of measure. The next chapter, Frank Molloy's study of the influence of Moore, offers another measure: statues. The erection of a statue or a memorial presupposes a certain amount of civic influence and organised finance. Molloy considers statues of Moore in Dublin, New York and Australia. Another measure, hinted at by Molloy, would involve a visit by, and the box office takings of, Dion Boucicault. I recall that, in September 1867, the first play performed at the newly-built Tyne Theatre and Opera House in the north-east of England was Boucicault's *Arrah-na-Pogue*, a financially profitable and politically courageous decision by the theatre's founder, the English radical, Joseph Cowen.[26]

Boucicault's Irish plays quickly achieved 'iconic' status for Irish communities throughout the world. Attendance at a performance was a statement of identity, a sacramental celebration of 'Irishness'. And Boucicault could himself give those performances and that attendance a political interpretation, demanding, in the famous (publicity-seeking?) open letter to Disraeli, the freeing of fenian prisoners, in the names of the thousands who had seen *The Shaughraun*.[27]

Boucicault not only prefigures Shaw, Synge and O'Casey, who all learnt from him and stole from him: in a very straightforward way Boucicault, and his world-wide audience, allow Shaw, Synge and O'Casey to come into being. In this world-wide view of the development of Irish theatre we have all been hauled out of the poacher pockets of Conn the Shaughraun.

Drama v. poetry

That the Irish seem to have a special talent for playwriting, the drama, the stage seems now almost a truism. The achievements of Irish playwrights and playwrights of Irish heritage in this century are glories of the European theatrical tradition. There are, no doubt, historical and sociological reasons for this: not least the decision by the cultural activists of the 'Irish Literary Revival' that theatre was important, an essential component in the creation of a national identity. And there are, as we have seen, strictly prosaic reasons, to do with elite involvement in the culture industries.

The subject matter of present-day Irish stage drama can be summarised as rural reminiscence, the new urban life in the Republic of Ireland, the present conflicts in Northern Ireland and emigration. In plays about emigration we even have studies of 'stream and counterstream'. Brian Friel's *Philadelphia, Here I Come* (stream) explores the decision to emigrate in a dialogue between the private self and the public self.[28] Dermot Bolger's *The Lament for Arthur Cleary* (counterstream) imaginatively explores the impossible possibilities of return.[29] In 1991 the first play of the adventurous Galway Youth Theatre was *Don't Forget to Write*, a play, devised and written by the company, which explicitly linked nineteenth-century and present-day/twentieth-century patterns of migration.[30] My own play, *Irish Night*, drew on interviews with Irish people and people of Irish heritage in England to explore the continuity of experience from the 1940s to the present day.[31]

I contrast the well-grounded exploration of emigration by these, and many other, stage plays with what seems, in comparison, to be a lack of interest in emigration by modern Irish poetry. My starting-point is a small book of poems by John Barry, *Yorkshire Sonnets*. The poems tell of a young man from Fermanagh who settles in Yorkshire. A sequence of fifteen 'Yorkshire Sonnets' explore that move, muse on Yorkshire's Irish connections (Patrick Brontë, of course), reflect on events in Ireland, the irony of an Irishman teaching English to Yorkshire's newer immigrants. In the background of the sonnet sequence there is the image, and the reality, of the poet digging his allotment with his Yorkshire-born children: literarily, putting down roots.[32]

One of John Barry's Yorkshire Sonnets explores what is something of an Irish migrant preoccupation, Sonnet 10, 'Accent':

> Homer ignores the language question: how
> did all those years of wandering affect
> Odysseus' Greek? He makes the Trojans too
> talk Greek, and even the same dialect.
> We don't hear of Penelope surprised
> when her returned hero comes out with some
> Phaeacian word, or old words disguised
> by strange articulation. Coming home
> was therefore so much easier. There's no place
> my speech can mingle like a tributary
> into the common stream, merge without trace.
> Some recognise the Irish still. For some
> the furrowed forehead of uncertainty
> and then the question: Where do you come from?[33]

These fine *Yorkshire Sonnets* add an extra dimension, a poet's dimension, to our understanding of the migration experience. I searched through the work of other Irish poets or poets of Irish heritage, hoping that they too would contribute, in this helpful way, to our understanding. I did find odd poems, here and there, by this writer or that. But nothing as substantial, interesting and beautiful as Barry's *Yorkshire Sonnets*. I have to report, then, that migration is not a major theme of modern Irish poetry.[34]

Why should this be? The answer, as I have already suggested, may lie within the sociology of literature rather than within literary criticism. I asked questions about audiences. What is the audience for poetry? Where is the audience for poetry. There is, I noted, a tendency for literary criticism, particularly literary comment on poetry, to leap from the particular to the universal, without much consideration of what lies between. Recent trends at the more sociological end of the critical spectrum have tended to question 'universals' and to look at what lies between particulars and universals. For the Irish what lies between the particular and the universal is migration.[35]

But maybe I ask too much of the craft of poetry. 'Poetry has commonly concerned itself with anything but "society" and "social action" as those are now conceived.'[36] Or is it simply a matter of markets? The market for stage drama is a community market. As we saw with Boucicault, and as we saw with the community-based Galway Youth Theatre, groups of people must be willing to come together, in a special place at a certain time, and they must want to see there, or make there, plays that address their community as well as their individual preoccupations. The market for poetry is much more fragmented, individualistic, universalistic: for Irish poetry in the English language the market is indeed world-wide.[37]

The melody lingers

Frank Molloy's chapter on the influence of Moore explores the sigificance of another Irish 'icon', those volumes of Moore's *Irish Melodies* that symbolically graced Irish shelves throughout the world. But the books are not only iconic objects: they are literary works, with a certain content, style and diction. Moore's *Melodies* have a way of approaching their subject matter that is skilful and ambiguous.

In a fascinating chapter that, as I have said, creates a whole new branch of Moore studies, Molloy first explores the iconic status of the *Melodies*. He then shows how in one part of the world, Australia, people of Irish heritage felt constrained to explore that heritage in the manner of Moore. 'Irishness' was a matter of style and content. It is especially interesting that Molloy has found a way of exploring the transferability of a poetic diction. 'The problem of assimilating the Australian scene into literature is a double one: it was a matter of finding both the right outlook and the right language. Of these the technical problem, the development of a diction suitable to the environment, was by far the most difficult.'[38]

It is the imitable, the parodyable aspects of Moore's style that attempt to settle in Australia. Molloy then shows further how there could be no tidy fit between

Moore's manner and that new life in the new country. I am reminded of the way another art form experienced Australia: 'it took at least two decades for colonial watercolourists to get the gum trees right, so that they did not look like English oaks or elms.'[39]

Molloy's chapter also allows us to follow the careers, outside Ireland, of two significant nineteenth-century Irish women poets, Eva Mary O'Doherty, who has entered the Irish anthologies as 'Eva of the *Nation*', and Eliza Hamilton Dunlop. And Molloy chronicles not only their careers as emigrants, but their further careers as *poets*. Eliza Hamilton's hard-won 'Moore-ish' diction is abandoned for something more sparse as she writes on the plight of Australian native peoples (aborigines), yet implicit in her work is a connection between the Irish and the Australian experience of conquest.

Again by exploring diction, Molloy recovers for Irish Migration Studies the Irish heritage of Charles Harpur, the significant nineteenth-century Australian poet. It was to Moore that Harpur, the would-be poet, first turned, taking down from the shelf that iconic volume of Moore's *Melodies*. It was only by working through and ultimately rejecting that part of his Irish literary and musical heritage that Harpur solved an Australian problem and found himself as a poet.

Fenian fever

'I met nearly all leaders of the Irish people . . . The only genuine revolutionary among these men was Michael Davitt. He belonged to a group that had advocated the use of physical force, and had lost his arm in one attempt . . . He had the clarity, the logic, and the fanaticism of the true revolutionary, and a consuming passion shone through his burning eyes.'[40]

You can make a little hobby out of collecting quotations like that. This, not unsympathetic, commentator on Ireland before independence is perhaps entitled to his assessment of Davitt's personality, though it is at odds with the picture of the man that emerges from Moody's biography. But he is not entitled to simple error, caused by an association of ideas: Davitt lost his arm to a factory machine, as an eleven-year-old child worker in a Lancashire cotton mill.[41]

For our next contributor, Patrick J. Quinlivan, such quotations cannot be an amusing hobby. This sort of material he must collect and weave together in his chosen area of study, the history of the fenians. It may appear odd to include a study of history in a volume entitled *The Creative Migrant*, but to have done anything else would have curiously isolated the kind of creativity that goes into the writing of history.

If we study identity, we study self-awareness. If we study self-awareness we study the processes through which history comes to be written. I can report, not a particularly new observation but certainly an observation confirmed by the development of *The Irish World Wide* series, that there is a world-wide interest amongst Irish people and people of Irish heritage in exploring their own history. This interest in history amongst the *émigré* Irish has, of course, itself a long history. Indeed, I sometimes think that Irish people have long before they were uttered taken the words of Sven Lindqvist to heart, 'Dig where you stand'.[42]

This Introduction has shown that, where you stand, now, there is material of interest to Irish Migration Studies: if it be only a pair of *talaria* on the side of a truck. For Quinlivan it was a plaque on a school wall, a plaque on an English school wall recalling a fenian explosion. The time has long gone when we could regard such events with the insouciance of Chesterton's *The Man who was Thursday*. And inevitably, like Quinlivan, we will find ourselves linking that Clerkenwell explosion of 1867 with the many bombs of today.[43] Yet the founding myths of many countries (the United States of America and the Republic of Ireland, to name but two) appeal to successful acts of violence.

One of the research gaps pinpointed by Roger Swift, in his historiographic chapter in Volume 2 of *The Irish World Wide*, was the study of Irish revolutionary activity, and of fenianism in particular.[44] And someone, cited by Swift, who has done much to fill that gap is Patrick J. Quinlivan.[45]

The reasons for that gap are complex, and some of the reasons, clearly, are purely political. Outside Ireland, the Irish communities are the sea through which the secret organisation swims. Where the energies of those communities can be harnessed the secret organisation can be successful, as in the *Catalpa* rescue. Yet the research gap also has to do with the processes through which the historical record is laid down. If Roy Foster has suggested that some significant figures were written out of Irish history because they were *not* fenians, Quinlivan here suggests that the fenians, in turn, have been written out of English history.[46]

All researchers make notes, as we plod along. Quinlivan has worked his decades of notes into a coherent, and charming, historiographic chapter. He thus shares with us processes that are too often hidden: the time-consuming tedium, the false trails (can we all please remember that there were at least two James Stephens?), the dead ends, the occasional discoveries, of archive-based research. There are many lessons to be learnt here by would-be researchers. Very often, when we study women, for example, or the working poor, we are studying 'secret' organisation, which standard written sources will belittle or ignore. The problems that Quinlivan encounters, as he hunts the fenians through history books, works of reference, letters and memoirs, police archives and old people's memories, have a general application to all historical research.

If, for example, we come across a word we do not understand, or whose history we need to know, we automatically reach for a standard work of reference, not thinking about the ways that class, national or political interests have shaped that work. Quinlivan made me reach down the *Oxford English Dictionary* to look up the word 'fenian', and to explore further that 1816 quotation from Walter Scott. How extraordinary — and is it significant? — that the first illustrative quotation under 'fenian' should be a parody of a forgery.[47]

Autobiography, history, identity

In *Ireland 1912–1985*, a book which brings a healthy bad temper to the discussion of twentieth-century Irish emigration, the historian J. J. Lee speaks of the 'defeatist political and professional elite, spiritual collaborators in the mass eviction process that drove more than half a million out between 1945 and 1960'.[48] Of that mass migration, Lee says, 'They were flying from nothing. And whatever about the streets of London or New York being paved with gold in the popular imagination of an earlier generation, there were few such illusions on the boat to Holyhead. The Connemara man whom Dónal Mac Amhlaoibh glimpsed at the customs in Holyhead, his suitcase empty to the world except for a solitary pair of wellingtons, harboured few fancies about the grandeur of his future estate.'[49]

Lee goes on, 'it is to the writers the historian must turn, as usual, for the larger truth. It is they, some themselves emigrants, who best convey the fetid atmosphere of the forties and fifties, the sense of pervasive, brooding hopelessness at home, the emptiness, the uncomprehending remorse, the heartbreak and heroism of many caught in the web of the "experience of abandonment" as families were sundered and communities withered.'[50]

And it is to the writers that we now turn. Donall Mac Amhlaigh, cited by Lee, is one of the autobiographers considered by our next contributor, Bernard Canavan. It was Canavan who alerted me, when I was studying the auto-biographical novels of Patrick MacGill, that we were here looking at an Irish working–class autobiographical tradition. I am grateful to Canavan for his contribution to *The Creative Migrant*. If we study identity we study self-awareness. If we study self-awareness we must study autobiography.

This is a fascinating area of study, in which the different disciplines come together in a fruitful collision. We may take as our starting-point the fact that the historian had to turn to the writers. But we recall having been warned that written memoirs are a form of oral history set down to mislead historians.[51]

Is there a way through this impasse? 'Despite the excellent theoretical work produced over the past two decades by Continental and American critics, autobiography is still largely treated by the literary establishment as a reservoir of information, which, to be sure, needs to be used with caution, but which nevertheless is felt primarily to constitute a repository of personally vouched-for insights into the author's earlier life. Only within the small circle of critics of the genre is it now a commonplace that an autobiography is likely to throw more light on the normally ageing author than on the earlier self about whom the book is ostensibly written.'[52]

The theoretical work on autobiography is fascinating, and not yet over-whelming. Indeed this is one of the few areas where our colleagues in France are respectful of the achievement of the English-speaking countries.[53] However one French scholar, Philippe Lejeune, has made a contribution with his concept of *Le pacte autobiographique*. The writer makes a pact with the reader. 'Undertaking "the sincere project to seize and understand his own life", the autobiographer, in contrast to the fiction writer, guaranteed that the writer, the narrator and the protagonist in his story were one and the same, that the events recounted had in fact been lived and to the best of his ability he was truthfully recording them.'[54]

There still are problems, not least with the tradition, by now a very strong tradition within Ireland, of the novelisation of a writer's own life: I have mentioned the example of Macgill. Indeed, it may be that novelisation is a technique for avoiding the demands of the autobiographical pact. Taking it further, here perhaps is an example of a difficulty in applying a generalised literary theory to an understanding of Irish writing which accepts the reality of emigration. It is the problem noticed by Vance. With whom, with what audience, what readership, has the Irish autobiographer made a pact?

Most, if not quite all, the major Irish writers of the nineteenth and the twentieth centuries have left us autobiographies, some of them massive. Their achievements tend to be subsumed within general studies of the European or of the English-speaking literary autobiography.[55]

Yet it is surely significant that so many of these figures spent a substantial amount of time outside Ireland. There are figures who self-consciously collect formative experience and knowledge outside Ireland and self-consciously return to Ireland: so that what is brought back to Ireland is part of 'cultural counterstream'. I think of Synge and Yeats. There are those who leave Ireland at an early age, and really have very little further involvement in events within Ireland, but whose artistic production, whose literary works become part of discourse about Ireland. I think of Thomas Moore and Shaw. Boucicault we have looked at.

There are others who leave Ireland in what really, from one perspective, looks like the standard pattern of elite migration and professional development, though the actual departure may be hung about with literary mystery or political and social significance. I think of Joyce. O'Casey and *The Plough and the Stars* controversy may seem like a special case, given O'Casey's working-class background, and the fact that he found his playwriting *métier* comparatively late in life. Yet the processes through which Joyce and O'Casey came to decide to leave Ireland may not seem too different from the processes we looked at in Volumes 1 and 2 of *The Irish World Wide*, the search for professional space and development. I have said, it may be that a community of a given size can support only so many poets or playwrights, just as it can support only so many doctors or accountants.[56]

But the arts of the word do have content, despite our century's exploration of art without content, or art without context. Much comment on autobiography has focused on literary autobiography, a literary genre, with its repertoire of devices, and its history, and seen the history of autobiography as the history of human self-awareness. Various starting-points for this self-awareness are postulated. The spread of the technology of writing is seen as important.[57] The break-up of the Roman Empire, it is suggested, shocked Augustine into that exploration of the self that distinguishes his autobiography from more static accounts of personality. Another point of origin is seen in the Renaissance, the invention or discovery of the private self.[58]

In any case, what has tended to happen is that insights derived from the study of literary biography have been generalised to the study of working-class autobiography, which is usually seen as an imitation of the more literary form. What Canavan has done for us here — and I think this is an important insight — is firmly to link the Irish working-class autobiographies he has studied with the oral tradition, the folk tradition, the story-telling tradition. These story-tellers also bring us the historical insights that J. J. Lee hoped for. Canavan thus helps us to make a conceptual bridge between, on the one hand, the theorists of literary autobiography, and the literary autobiographers themselves, and, on the other hand, the historians, particularly those, like Quinlivan, who respect oral history. This means, also, that Canavan allows us to make connections in another direction with the increasing interest amongst sociologists in auto-biography and life histories.[59] For Canavan's writers, what we might call the 'Augustinian' event is the act of emigration itself, the discovery that a life and a self need to be explored, and explained. The autobiographical pact is then made, and each one of the writers makes that pact in his own way. The pact may not be with a reader: the pact may be made with a listener.

Picturing Ireland

The most socially significant Irish person in cinema is the housekeeper in the Tom and Jerry cartoons. The most disappointing Irish person in film is Fitzcarraldo. *Fitzcarraldo*, the film itself, is extraordinary, and the lowering, taciturn performance of Klaus Kinski in the title role is mesmeric. But, as we follow our interest in the transmutations of Irish family names, we could have hoped to find in that character some Fitzgerald charm, and an Irish sense of the magic of the spoken word: a sense of magic, I am given to understand, that we share with the native peoples of the Amazon. My information comes from movies, of course.[60]

So much of what we think we know about other peoples comes from the fictional narratives of cinema. Kevin Rockett, Luke Gibbons and John Hill, the three authors of *Cinema and Ireland*, with that book brought needed good sense to the difficult study of an important twentieth-century art. If Cairns and Richards clarified our thinking about *Writing Ireland, Cinema and Ireland* clarified our thinking about picturing Ireland: I think here especially of Hill's liberating study of *film noir*'s use of Irish subject matter. And it was, somehow, no surprise to learn from *Cinema and Ireland* that the first cinema in Ireland, the Volta in Mary Street, Dublin, 1909, was one of the never-quite-successful commercial ventures of James Joyce.[61] Counterstream, indeed.

In all discussions of Ireland and cinema there is the same fear that Owen Dudley Edwards explores in his study of 'The stage Irish': the fear that what is seen on the screen or stage will have real consequences in the real world. Now, Kevin Rockett, one of the authors of *Cinema and Ireland* develops the story, looking at cinema's images of the migrant Irish. Though he does look at Australian and at English material, it is right that he concentrates on the portrayal of the Irish migrant within the American cinema.

Those who map the relationship between 'culture' in the sociological sense and 'culture' in the sense of artistic activity, have long watched the American cinema with awestruck fascination. For most of the twentieth century a huge popular culture industry has, almost automatically it would seem, transformed the hopes, fears (usually fears) and preoccupations of its audience into strong narratives and compelling images. Production costs are amortised within the home country, and the American film industry can then sell its products on at prices that raise fears of cultural imperialism on this side of the Atlantic. It helps, of course, that the language spoken on the screen is the current world language, English.

Much as Myers explores the central place of an Irish person in the philosophical narratives of Thoreau's *Walden*, Rockett now looks at the places of many Irish people in the many narratives of American cinema. If, in Edwards' study of the 'stage Irish' we saw something of a 'theatre of infiltration', here we see the Irish playing a role, an important role, in the American 'cinema of assimilation'. But it is not as simple as that, as Rockett shows, giving due attenton to that cinematic chronicler of Irish America, John Ford. In contrast to Ford's hymns to Irish–American service and loyalty, I think here of two 'Irish' figures, outside the Ford repertoire, but central to two examples of that most Fordian of genres, the western: O'Meara, played by that fine actor Rod Steiger in Fuller's 1956 *Run of the Arrow*, and Tyreen, played by that fine Irish actor Richard Harris in Peckinpah's 1965 *Major Dundee*. In both cases, difficulties with the notion of assimilation, and commitment, after the American Civil War, are made manifest, are *heard* through an exploration of the character's perceived 'Irishness'.[62]

The chimerical hope

'I am mad, or rather was for a score of years and paid the penalty too in more ways than one, not the least being reflections on my dignity for associating with a class of musicians which so many of our countrymen and co-religionists affected to despise. I'm not crazy enough however to entertain the chimerical hope that the Irish will ever accomplish anything of enduring value by their sporadic attempts at reviving an interest in the preservation of traditional Irish music in the face of both racial and national indifference . . .'[63]

So wrote Francis O'Neill, sadly, to a 'Dear Kindred Soul', in 1918. Since that time the the academic disciplines which feed into, and feed on, the study of traditional, 'folkloric' arts have blossomed, and their observations have underpinned many developments in other disciplines. Yet it has been a curiously un-nourishing interest. A technical, academic discussion would be far-ranging.[64] I think it sufficient, and fair, here to observe that, within a variety of disciplines, and from a range of intellectual impulses, what has been stressed within the academic study of traditional cultures are ideas of timelessness, or deep structures that stand outside time, and that these ideas have become linked with notions of authenticity. Words like 'decayed', 'corrupt, 'ersatz' become attached to linguistic, social and artistic practices. There is the problem of what the last contributor to this volume, Graeme Smith, calls the 'habitual past tense'.

I can acknowledge the rigour, and the intellectual excitement, of developments in fields like anthropology and folklore studies. But I have to add that this discussion is of more than academic interest to Irish people.

For Francis O'Neill's 'chimerical hope' has been realised. The Irish find themselves at the end of the twentieth century with a still living and still used and useful folk music and folk dance tradition. That this is so owes much to the efforts of O'Neill himself, who, from 1903 to 1922, published 5 compilations of Irish folk music and two books about the subject. Crucial too was O'Neill's realisation that he was dealing with the music of the migration and that Chicago was the perfect base for a compiler of folk music: 'exiles from all of Ireland's thirty-two counties can be found . . . Among Irish and Scotch music lovers, every new arrival having musical taste or talent is welcomed and introduced to the "Craft", to the mutual advantage of all concerned, and there is as much rejoicing on the discovery of a new expert as there is among astronomers on the announcement of a new asteroid or comet'.[65]

As O'Neill there makes clear, Irish music was played, and Irish dance was danced, and both were enjoyed, in Chicago and throughout the world, and were changed through exploration and learning. The Irish migrants shaped music and dance to meet new needs, musical and social needs, in new circumstances. The effects of this on dance and music are explored in our last two chapters.

First, a living embodiment of Martin Counihan's Irish scientific tradition, with its respect for nature, we have John P. Cullinane, who is a respected marine botantist as well as being a dance master, a dance adjudicator and a historian of dance. There is much in Cullinane's chapter to absorb the social scientist, particularly the sociologist of migration, and of the arts. Note, for example, how as Cullinane explores the relationship between migration and the dance, he sees effects of age and gender. What was an activity of mature men has become, primarily, an activity of young girls. This is, perhaps, a good example of a pattern noticed in the study of other migrant groups: migration displaces into the home, and on to women, problems of cultural continuity. Yet the world-wide phenomenon that is Irish dancing has attracted little academic attention.[66]

Cullinane is brought to this study by his love of the dance, and by his respect for those who, throughout the world, have kept the dance alive, and who have reshaped it for emigrants' needs. There are many links with Rockett's chapter on cinema, not least the central place of George M. Cohan, who did so much to shape Irish dance, and reshape it for the stage and the cinema. Again, this seems, at least in part, a migration effect: what were traditional, community practices in the home country become commercial practices within the migration. The consequences are complex, and interesting. Present-day Irish music and Irish musicians are comfortable within the genres of American popular music because, no doubt, earlier Irish music and Irish musicians played such a large part in developing them.[67] But, in the background, remains the wish for continuity and identity.

The notion of 'authenticity' is more difficult, and can be extraordinarily technical. As Cullinane shows it is a notion that can be used politically, and can itself lead to problematic innovations: as when, in 1900, the influential London Irish turned up at the Macroom Feis wearing their kilts. The changes over time in the permitted costumes, particularly the costumes of women and girls, deserve detailed study.

Cullinane is an 'insider', himself part of the Munster dance master tradition: and, of course, troubled by some of the ambiguities presented to a dance master by dance's place in the patterns of migration. The patterns of *The Irish World Wide* series mean that, in a beneficial juxtaposition, I can put the 'insider's' chapter on dance alongside one on music by the respectful academic 'outsider'.

The last contributor to *The Creative Migrant*, Graeme Smith, is an ethnomusicologist, based in Australia, and fascinated by this Irish interrelationship between music and migration.

With Smith we enter a Melbourne pub. We talk to two Irish accordion players. Look at the patterns of migration of his accordion players, now based in Australia, and compare their lives with the patterns we saw in Volume 1 of *The Irish World Wide*, or in Canavan's chapter in this volume. Notice how the status of O'Neill is still a matter of lively discussion amongst Irish musicians. Smith also gives due attention to the Coleman records of the 1920s and 1930s: he calls them 'cultural remittances', a powerful concept which I would absorb into my own suggestion of 'cultural counterstream'.[68]

Notice, too, that in order to have a meaningful conversation with the musicians the academic ethnomusicologist must, bravely, rethink and reconstruct academic narratives, academic ways of understanding their art. It may not, strictly speaking, be absolutely essential that you have read all six volumes of *The Irish World Wide* before you go and listen to an accordion player in an Australian pub. But, as I think our ethnomusicologist has demonstrated, it would be a good idea.

Patrick O'Sullivan
Bradford
May 1993

Notes

1. Raymond Williams, *Keywords: a Vocabulary of Culture and Society,* Fontana, London, 1976, pp. 76–7.
2. John Berger has suggested, drawing on Lévi-Strauss for support, that one of the reasons the elite culture of Western Europe privileges small to medium-sized oil paintings is precisely because such works of art can be hung on the walls of a reasonably-sized room (John Berger, *Ways of seeing*, BBC/Penguin Books, London, 1972, pp. 83–7). It may follow then that elites will undervalue art that is not made to be hung on walls, the arts of wanderers. In the same way, elites will not understand or value the experiences explored by John Berger and Jean Mohr, *A seventh man: a book of images and words about the experience of migrant workers in Europe*, Penguin, Harmondsworth, 1975, a powerful collage of comment, photograph and quotation, exploring the emotional and social realities of the migrant.
3. Indeed I have sometimes avoided the obvious. I felt, for example, that James Joyce had too firmly imposed his way of understanding the relationships between Irish migration and Irish creativity: one ground rule for the entire *Irish World Wide* series was that no chapter could be called 'Silence, exile and cunning'.

   'The very act of writing can be compared with exile in that it involves a critical scrutiny of the assumed,' writes Diana Laurenson, p. 159, 'The writer and society' in Diana Laurenson and Alan Swingewood, *The sociology of literature*, Paladin, London, 1972. She quotes Lukács and has Joyce in mind. And she observes (p. 160): 'An exiled writer is often dependent on single-figure patronage or promotion to mediate his work with the home audience and market.'
4. Everett S. Lee, 'A theory of migration', *Demography*, 3 (1), 1966, p. 56. I discuss in Volumes 1 and 2 of *The Irish World Wide* my decision to use Lee's theory, to allow us to make connections with the study of other migrating peoples. On Irish migration

and creativity see Des Hickey and Gus Smith, *A paler shade of green*, Leslie Frewin, London, 1972, an interesting book based on a series of tape-recorded interviews with writers, actors and others active in theatre and cinema. The recurring theme in the interviews is the search for career development and creative fulfilment. The title, quite apart from the unacknowledged reference to Procul Harum, suggests one standard response to migrant Irish creativity. Also relevant here is Julia Carlson, *Banned in Ireland: censorship and the Irish writer*, Routledge, London, 1990.

5. The paternal grandparents of Georgia O'Keeffe, Pierce and Catherine O'Keeffe, left County Cork in 1848, but ultimately they are but one part of her Irish, Hungarian, Dutch and supremely American heritage. Georgia O'Keeffe herself is one of the major American painters of the twentieth century. See Roxena Robinson, *Georgia O'Keeffe: a life*, Bloomsbury, London, 1990, pp. 6–7. The O'Shea brothers were the stone-carvers responsible for the extraordinary decoration of the University Museum, Oxford, built in 1855.

What might seem elements of 'celtic' design in O'Keeffe's early work, or in the O'Shea's flowers and owls, turn out on reflection to be manifestations of the nineteenth-century obsession with decorated surfaces, and it may be that the nineteenth-century rediscovery of 'celtic' design is itself, at one level, simply part of that obsession. See T. J. Edelstein (ed.), *Imagining an Irish past: the Celtic revival, 1840–1940*, the David and Alfred Smart Museum of Art, Chicago, 1992, and Jeanne Sheehy, *The rediscovery of Ireland's past: the Celtic revival, 1830–1930*, Thames and Hudson, London, 1980. The O'Sheas seem part of the further pattern, which we see in the ceramic and textile industries of the period, whereby Irish craftspeople and artisans search for ways to continue using their skills outside Ireland.

For another discussion of 'decorated surfaces' see Cullinane's discussion of permitted dress in Irish dance competitions, in Chapter 9 of this volume.

6. I have already mentioned Diana Laurenson, Hickey and Smith, and Carlson. Quite reasonably, given such approaches, the Irish writer's experience is often seen as part of a wider literary pattern. See Andrew Gurr, *Writers in exile: the identity of home in modern literature*, Harvester Press, Brighton, 1981, which uses Joyce as a starting-point to explore the writing and the lives of Katherine Mansfield (from New Zealand), V. S. Naipaul (Trinidad) and Ngugi wa Thiong'o (Kenya).

7. Norman Vance, *Irish literature: tradition, identity, and difference*, Basil Blackwell, Oxford, 1990. The five pairs are James Ussher and Wentworth Dillon, Earl of Roscommon; William Drennan and Thomas Moore; William Carleton and Thomas D'Arcy McGee; St. John Ervine and James Joyce; John Hewitt and Seamus Heaney. These pairings work and allow Vance to make visible in the individual life points that would otherwise appear as generalised abstractions. But each of those pairings could be re-explored from an Irish migration studies' perspective. The most poignant pairings, perhaps, are those of Drennan and Moore, and Carleton and McGee. Moore left Ireland when he was not twenty years old, yet, and as we shall see below in Chapter 5, he cumulatively had immense influence on the ways that 'Irishness' would be seen and negotiated. McGee is a pivotal figure in the history of Canada. The issue of migration, strictly defined, has recently loomed large in the life of Seamus Heaney, and in discussions of his symbolic importance (see Vance, p. 252), and nowadays the poor man has to live the dreadful life of the wandering academic celebrity.

8. Vance, *Irish Literature*, p. 211.

9. The sociology of literature that has emerged is intellectually exciting but curiously arid and, to use my favourite word of the moment, un-nourishing. I discuss this in my chapter on 'Patrick MacGill: the making of a writer' in Seán Hutton and Paul Stewart, *Ireland's histories*, Routledge, London, 1991, p. 204.

10. See Everett S. Lee, my General Introduction, Volume 1, p. xvii, and my Introduction to Volume 2, pp. 13–14, *The Irish World Wide.*
11. David Cairns and Shaun Richards, near the end of *Writing Ireland: colonialism, nationalism and culture,* Manchester University Press, Manchester, 1988, move towards an exploration of this absence, quoting (p. 154) Declan Kiberd: 'The current crisis has prompted most Irish people to re-examine some of their deepest historical assumptions, but it has as yet given rise to no similar self-questioning in England.' But see, as starting-points, Robert Colls and Philip Dodd, *Englishness: politics and culture, 1880–1920,* Croom Helm, London, 1986 (which includes D. G. Boyce on 'The marginal Britons: the Irish'), and Linda Colley, *Britons: forging the nation. 1707–1837,* Yale University Press, Yale, 1992.
12. It is always useful to find a book that states a case in its most extreme form. For a lively deconstruction of the very notion of 'celt' see Malcolm Chapman, *The Celts: the construction of a myth,* Macmillan, London, 1992. Chapman makes excellent use of the thinking of social anthropologist, Edwin Ardener, on culture meeting. Ardener's thinking, from a quite different methodological and discipline base, can be seen as mirroring the thought of Said or Foucault.
13. Vivian Mercier, *The Irish comic tradition,* Oxford University Press, Oxford, 1962, p. 238.
14. Richard Kearney, ed., *The Irish mind: exploring intellectual traditions,* Wolfhound Press, Dublin, 1985, includes Dermot Moran, 'Nature, man and God in the philosophy of John Scottus Eriugena'; Harry Bracken, 'George Berkeley: the Irish Cartesian'; David Berman, 'The Irish Counter-Enlightenment'; Gordon L. Herries Davies, 'Irish thought in science'.
15. Herries Davies, 'Irish thought in science', p. 310.
16. See below, Counihan p. 40, n. 11. We, at the end of the twentieth century, are inheritors of (and products of) a nineteenth-century synthesis, which constructed 'Irish' as a subcategory of 'Celt'. This 'Celt' may be defined in contrast with some other group, for different purposes, including Irish nationalist purposes. But, meanwhile, as the twentieth century progressed, the academic disciplines which had contributed to that synthesis lost all faith in it. See Chapman, *The Celts,* particularly Chapter 2 on language.
17. I have in mind Garry Trudeau's *Doonesbury* series; B. F. Skinner, *New Walden*; Edward Carpenter and Henry Havelock Ellis; R. H. Blyth, *Zen in English literature and oriental classics,* Hokuseido Press, Tokyo, 1942, p. 391; Richard F. Fleck, 'Foreword: deep in the woods with Henry Thoreau', p. xvii, in Henry David Thoreau, *The Maine Woods,* Harper & Row Perenniel Library edition, New York, 1987.
18. The helpful article by George E. Ryan, 'Shanties and shiftlessness: the immigrant Irish of Henry Thoreau', *Éire-Ireland,* Volume 13, 1978, pp. 54–78, which Myers cites, avoids quoting this sentence. You can see why.
19. The reference to my own copy is Henry David Thoreau, *Walden,* with an Introduction by Brooks Atkinson, Crowell, New York, 1966, p. 277. But there are many editions of *Walden*: we are considering the last sentence of Chapter X, 'Baker Farm'.
20. I turned to my elder son, Dan, for further clarification. He brought me a book from his collection, *The Orchard book of Greek myths,* retold by Geraldine McCaughrean, Orchard Books, London, 1992, in which Mercury/Hermes says (p. 42) quite simply, 'I'll lend him my feathered shoes.' That is the usual story, though I note that Robert Graves, *Greek myths,* Cassell, London, 1958, pp. 237–45, has a more complex version.
    The statue of Perseus in Cartwright Hall is by Alfred Gilbert, who was

responsible for another winged creature, the statue usually called 'Eros' (but apparently meant to be the Angel of Christian Charity) in Piccadilly Circus, London. See *Reverie, myth, sensuality: Sculpture in Britain, 1889–1910*, Stoke on Trent City Museum and Art Gallery, 1992, p. 43; Richard Dorment, *Alfred Gilbert*, Yale University Press, 1985. A more famous 'Perseus' is by Benvenuto Cellini. The making of the statue is described in *The autobiography of Benvenuto Cellini*, translated by George Bull, Folio Society, London, 1966: this edition has a picture of the 'Perseus'. If you want to see *talaria*, a museum or art gallery with nineteenth-century material is bound to have something: otherwise look in your local phone book for organisations called 'Mercury-this-or-that', and then watch out for the logo.

21. For Cearbhall O'Dalaigh see James E. Doan, *Cearbhall O'Dalaigh: an Irish poet in romance and oral tradition*, Garland, New York, 1990, and for his place and Owlyglass's place in the world-wide patterns of the jokes, see my chapter, 'The Irish Joke', below.

22. This is to speak of 'plays' as they are understood within the European theatre tradition, of course, with due deference to the perception of our contributor, Owen Dudley Edwards, that 'drama' is a basic human impulse. I find it fascinating that, quite independently, Owen Dudley Edwards here finds himself constrained to repeat the exercise of J. P. Clark, the Nigerian poet, dramatist and critic, find origins for Irish/Nigerian drama in early literature and oral arts and imagine what such a drama might have been without the colonial incursions. See 'Aspects of Nigerian drama' in J. P. Clark, *The example of Shakespeare*, Longman, London, 1970. Clark also has a chapter on 'The legacy of Caliban'.

   For the performance history of the two Farquhar plays see Shirley Strum Kenny, (ed.), *The works of George Farquhar*, Clarendon Press, Oxford, 1988, Volume 2, pp. 7–17 and pp. 136–48; George Farquhar, *The recruiting officer*, edited by Peter Dixon, Manchester University Press, Manchester, 1986, p. 27. There seems to have been something of a tradition of military interest in the *The recruiting officer*, and military units would commission a performance or attend one at the end of manoeuvres. The Belfast Volunteer Corps attended a performance in 1785. The West Riding Militia, in Yorkshire, attended a perfomance in Doncaster in 1792.

23. Thomas Keneally, *The playmaker*, Hodder & Stoughton, London, 1987; Timberlake Wertenbaker, *Our country's good*, Methuen, London, 1988, revised 1991. Wertenbaker's title is taken from a prologue to *The recruiting officer* supposed to have been written in Australia by a convict bard, but it seems in reality written by a London hack. See Robert Hughes, *The fatal shore: a history of transportation of convicts to Australia, 1787–1868*, Collins Harvill, London, 1987, p. 340. Whoever did write the prologue certainly knew Farquhar's plays, for the line 'We left our country for our country's good' echoes the words of Gibbet the highwayman in Act 3, Scene 2 of *The beaux' stratagem*.

24. The English actor Donald Sinden, in the 'Foreword' to Richard Fawkes, *Dion Boucicault: a biography*, Quartet Books, London, 1979, p. xiii, recalls that in the original manuscript of *London assurance*, 'Dazzle was called Ignatius Mulfather, a good Irish name. We had never before considered the possibility of Dazzle being Irish, but the more we thought of him as Irish, the more sense he made as a character, for, quite simply, Dazzle is a leprechaun.' However, in my view, the play does not work if Dazzle is identifiably Irish.

25. Fawkes, *Boucicault*, p. 114, pp. 191–2.

26. Nigel Todd, *'The militant democracy': Joseph Cowen and Victorian radicalism*, Bewick Press, Tyne and Wear, 1991, pp. 66–7.

27. Richard Fawkes, *Boucicault*, pp. 196–7.

28. Brian Friel, *Philadelphia, here I come*, Faber, London, 1965. Talking to Irish migrants I have found that this image of the fractured self has resonances: one man observed that, after you had left Ireland, another ghostly you seemed to stay in Ireland, living (in your imagination) the life you would have lived had you not left.

29. Dermot Bolger's 'The lament for Arthur Cleary' is one of the plays that appears in a useful collection, *The crack in the emerald: new Irish plays*, selected and introduced by David Grant, Nick Hern Books, London, 1990.

    Bolger's title and his play make explicit connections with the fate of another returned Irishman, Arthur O'Leary, and his grieving widow's poem, 'The lament for Art O'Leary'. O'Leary, a Catholic and a colonel in the Austrian army, was murdered in 1773, in Cariganimma, County Cork, in a feud resulting from his refusal to sell his horse to a Protestant for £5: Catholics were not permitted to own a horse of greater value than this. See Frank O'Connor, *Kings, Lords and Commons: an anthology from the Irish*, Gill & Macmillan, Dublin, 1970 [Original edition 1959], pp. 109–19. In Bolger's play the horse becomes a motorbike.

30. *Don't forget to write* was devised and written by Rebecca Bartlett and Molly Fogarty in workshops with the Galway Youth Theatre.

31. There were successful tours in 1987 and 1988 of *Irish night*, written by Garry Lyons and Patrick O'Sullivan, with song lyrics by Patrick O'Sullivan. I have long thought that such plays are an interesting way of giving research back to the people who have 'been researched'.

32. The word 'allotment' may need explaining to readers who are not familiar with this intriguing presence on the English landscape. 'The word "allotment" is curiously abstract: a legalistic term meaning simply "a portion", but it is shorthand for a number of images, places and activities,' (David Crouch and Colin Ward, *The allotment: its landscape and culture*, Faber and Faber, London, 1988, p. 5). Allotments are little parcels of land where, for a small rent, city dwellers can grow fresh fruit and vegetables. Questions of diet and the use of leisure are nicely mixed. Such little plots are not peculiarly English: they are a feature of European life and there are connections with the Community Gardening movement in the United States and in Canada: see Crouch and Ward, *The allotment*, Chapter 8, pp. 132–55.

    But, whilst 'allotments' are not peculiarly English they are of interest to the student of 'Englishness', especially when considering that interrelationship between the rural and the urban noted in Volume 2 of *The Irish World Wide*. Note, for example, employer opposition to allotments: allotments offered workers a possible source of food and earnings outside waged work (Crouch and Ward, *The allotment*, pp. 60–1). The English allotment movement also earns a footnote in British parliamentary history and Irish political history: for, in 1886, it was the failure of the Queen's Speech to mention the provision of allotments that made Jesse Collings, MP (the apostle of allotments and small holdings) put down a motion which the Conservative government lost, leading directly to Gladstone's 'First Home Rule Government'. (Lord Eversley, *Gladstone and Ireland: the Irish policy of Parliament from 1850–1894*, Methuen, London, 1912, p. 295; p. 299).

    As well as being contributions to the poetry of the Irish migrations, John Barry's *Yorkshire sonnets* form a significant addition to a neglected genre, English allotment poetry. The English poet Charles Tomlinson (quoted in Crouch and Ward, *The allotment*, p. v.) says of the allotment:

> This
>
> is a paradise . . .
>
> for those
>
>   who labour, linger in

their watch-chained waistcoats
rolled-back sleeves –
   the ineradicable
     peasant in the dispossessed
and half-tamed Englishman.

33. John Barry, *Yorkshire sonnets*, Rivelin Press, Bradford, 1984, p. 20. Not all classical allusions are bad.
34. My original plan was to preface each volume of the *Irish World Wide* series with a poem. It was my kindly publisher who pointed out that, in my search for poems, I was wasting a lot of time on a peripheral part of the project. My search for poems was not exhaustive, but it was fairly thorough. The few poems on migration by modern poets that I did find seemed to me predictable, adding nothing to our understanding, and all suffered in the comparison with John Barry's *Yorkshire sonnets*.
35. I have in mind developments like Wolfgang Iser, *The act of reading*, Routledge and Kegan Paul, London, 1978, or Norman Holland or David Bleich.
36. J. P. Ward, *Poetry and the sociological idea*, Harvester Press, Brighton, 1981, p. 6. He goes on to list some of poetry's characteristic preoccupations: nature and identity with nature; the solitary and the egotistical; God and dead people ('entailing, very revealingly, the apostrophic mode'); time; roots; the mythic past; Eros; the hero; poetry itself. It is as if the subject matter of poetry is as limited, in its way, as the subject matter of family photograph albums. Ward's book explores the 'seemingly fundamental incompatability between poetry and the sociological idea'(p. 7): part of that incompatibility is sociology's lack of interest in poetry, including an odd lack of interest in that lack of interest.
37. Which may, indeed, explain why modern Irish poetry so often becomes a 'version of pastoral'. My friend and colleague, the Yorkshire poet, K. E. Smith, has objected (quite rightly) that here I am being less than just to the efforts of those Irish poets who, after Yeats, and after Independence/Partition, explored the nature of the 'place' they had inherited.
38. T. Inglis Moore, *Social patterns in Australian literature*, Angus & Robertson, London, 1971, pp. 110–11.
39. Robert Hughes, *The fatal shore*. p. 3.
40. M. J. Bonn, *Wandering scholar*, Cohen & West, London, 1949, p. 94. Bonn was born in Germany in 1873, and taught at numerous universities throughout the world, including the London School of Economics.
41. See T. W. Moody, *Davitt and Irish revolution*, Clarendon Press, Oxford, 1981, for the assessment of Davitt's character, pp. 550–7; for the account of the 11-year-old boy whose arm is mangled by the carding engine, in the Victoria Mill, Baxenden, Lancashire, see pp. 17–18.
42. Sven Lindqvist, 'Dig where you stand' in Paul Thompson (ed.), *Our common history: the transformation of Europe*, Pluto, London, 1982, is a brief introduction to the oral history methods that went into the making of his 1978 history of the work place, also called *Dig where you stand*.
43. The staid and useful *Modern Ireland: a bibliography on politics, planning, research and development*, compiled and edited by Michael Owen Shannon, Greenwood Press, Westport/Library Association, London, 1981, p. 61, makes the obvious connection, in its comment on Léon Ó Broin, *Revolutionary underground: the story of the Irish Republican Brotherhood, 1858–1924*, Gill and Macmillan, Dublin, 1976: 'A fascinating, recent account of the Brotherhood for the general reader, with obvious parallels to the IRA of today'.

44. Roger Swift, 'The historiography of the Irish in nineteenth-century Britain', *The Irish in the New Communities*, Volume 2, *The Irish World Wide*, edited by Patrick O'Sullivan, Leicester University Press, Leicester & London, 1992, p. 67.

45. Patrick Quinlivan and Paul Rose, *The Fenians in England, 1865–72*, Calder, London, 1982.

46. R. F. Foster, *Modern Ireland, 1600–1972*, Allen Lane, London, 1988, p. 404.

47. The *Oxford English Dictionary*'s first illustrative quotation under 'fenian' is taken from Chapter XXX of Walter Scott's 1816 *The Antiquary*, where the Antiquary himself, Jonathan Oldbuck, angrily teases Hector M'Intyre about the authenticity of 'Macpherson's English Ossian'. 'But Hector stoutly abode the storm; like many a sturdy Celt, he imagined the honour of his country and native language connected with the authenticity of these popular poems . . .' The poem that Hector chooses to 'translate' from memory tells of the confrontation between Patrick and 'the poet Oisin, or Ossian', and includes the lines quoted in the OED:

Do you compare your psalms,
To the tales of the bare-arm'd Fenians?

Then follows a little Scott-ish joke as to which part of the body might be expected to be poetically nude.
    For further discussion see Quinlivan, p. 140 below.

48. J. J. Lee, *Ireland 1912–1985: politics and society*, Cambridge University Press, Cambridge, 1989, pp. 383–4.

49. J. J. Lee, *Ireland 1912–1985*, p. 384.

50. J. J. Lee, *Ireland 1912–1985*, p. 384.

51. Trevor Lummis, *Listening to history: the authenticity of oral evidence*, Hutchinson, London, 1987, p. 81, attributes this dictum to A. J. P. Taylor.

52. Brian Finney, *The inner I: British literary autobiography of the twentieth century*, Faber, London, 1985, pp. 258–9. This echoes the observation made by the historian, Quinlivan, in Chapter 6 below. Finney is also (p. 258) highly critical of the moralising approach to texts of theorists like A. O. J. Cockshut, *The art of autobiography in nineteenth and twentieth-century England*, Yale University Press, New Haven, 1984.

53. 'The critical interest in autobiography as such was slower to develop in France than in the English-speaking countries . . .' Germaine Brée, *Narcissus absconditus: the problematic art of autobiography in contemporary France (the Zaharoff Lecture for 1977–8)*, Clarendon Press, Oxford, 1978. It may be that was because in recent decades French intellectual life embroiled itself with various theories which, from different theoretical bases, found it difficult to embrace the concept of a 'self'.

54. Brée, *Narcissus absconditus*, pp. 7–8. See also Phillipe Lejeune, *Le pacte autobiographique* Éditions du Seuil, Paris, 1975, and Philippe Lejeune, *L'autobiographie en France*, Libraire Armand Colin, Paris, 1971. Georges May, *L'autobiographie*, Presses Universitaires de France, Paris, 1979, is a useful checklist of the devices of autobiography, as is Roy Pascal, *Design and truth in autobiography*, Routledge & Kegan Paul, London, 1960.

55. Thus, Yeats, O'Casey, George Moore and Maurice O'Sullivan all appear in Pascal, Yeats and George Moore in Finney. There is nothing intrinsically wrong with this: Finney is particularly good on the autobiographical devices of Moore (*The inner I*, pp. 62–3). It is just that here we want to look at these autobiographies from an Irish Migration Studies perspective.

56. This would also be a way of absorbing the case studies of Hickey and Smith, *A Paler Shade of Green*.

57. I suspect that there is an important point there, and that we should now be thinking about 'technologies of autobiography': see Samuel Beckett, *Krapp's last tape*, Faber, London, 1959. It is intriguing, by the way, how often theorists of autobiography quote Samuel Beckett: Brée, *Narcissus absconditus* p. 3, Jerome Hamilton Buckley, *The turning key: autobiography and the subjective impulse since 1800*, Harvard University Press, Cambridge, 1984, p. 156. Buckley's is a defiantly non-structuralist study, seeking to establish the integrity of text as independent artefact and autobiography as a process of semi-fictional self-creation.

58. One theory suggests that Renaissance autobiography began with the ledgers of the merchants of Florence: one ledger was kept for tax purposes; another, less confusing, secret ledger was kept because the merchant needed to know what was really going on. See Gene Brucker, ed., *Two memoirs of Renaissance Florence: the diaries of Buonaccorso Pitti and Gregorio Dati*, translated by Julia Martines, Harper & Row, New York, 1967, p. 9–12.

59. A good starting-point for exploring the sociological interest in autobiography is *Sociology*, the Journal of the British Sociological Association, Volume 27, Number 1, February 1993, a special issue on 'Biography and autobiography in sociology'. The cover actually has 'Auto/biography in sociology', suggesting an acceptance of Liz Stanley's term 'auto/biography', which stresses the interrelation between biography and autobiography at the formal level but which further acknowledges the processes by which the self theorises, speculates and produces material relating to selves. See Liz Stanley, *The auto/biographical I: the theory and practice of feminist auto/biography*, Manchester University Press, Manchester, 1992.

   As well as Lummis, see also, Sidonie Smith and Julia Watson, eds., *De/colonizing the subject: the politics of gender in women's autobiography*, University of Minnesota Press, 1992; Shirley Dex (ed.), *Life and work history analyses: qualitative and quantitative developments*, Routledge, London, 1991; Anthony Seldon and Joanna Pappworth, *By word of mouth: élite oral history*, Methuen, London, 1983.

   As ever, when one academic discipline, at last, takes an interest in something that other disciplines have long thought important we are aware of gaps in the references and the thinking: but I think that this interest by sociology and by history in autobiography is valuable because it leads us away from a too mesmerised preoccupation with the literary genre.

60. In the 1958 Ferrer film *Green Mansions*, Anthony Perkins wins the trust of the rain forest people through his ability to *talk*. This effective cinematic scene is expanded from a few lines of observation in the original W. H. Hudson 1904 novel, *Green Mansions*: see W. H. Hudson, *South American romances*, Duckworth, London, 1930, pp. 381–2.

61. Kevin Rockett, Luke Gibbons and John Hill, *Cinema and Ireland*, Croom Helm, London, 1987. Joyce and the Volta, pp. 5–6. Chapter 6, 'Images of violence', is John Hill's exploration of *film noir* and Ireland. An interesting point of comparison with *Cinema and Ireland* is Colin McArthur, 'Scotland and cinema: the iniquity of the fathers' in Tony Bennett (ed.), *Popular fiction: technology, ideology, production, reading*, Routledge, London, 1990, which (p. 94) leaves aside the notion of 'stereotypes' to explore 'discursive positions relating to Scotland'.

62. Both films and both characters have been much analysed. See, for example, Phil Hardy, *Samuel Fuller*, Studio Vista, London, 1970, p. 7 onwards; Philip French, *Westerns*, Secker and Warburg, London, 1973, p. 89, on O'Meara; Jim Kitses, *Horizons West*, Thames & Hudson, London, 1969, pp. 141–2 on Tyreen.

63. Francis O'Neill, in a seven-page, typewritten letter to the Revd. Seamus O'Floinn, dated 15 October 1918, quoted in *Music mad: Captain Francis O'Neill and traditional Irish music*, the catalogue of an exhibition compiled by Laura Sue Fuderer, University

Libraries, University of Notre Dame, Indiana, 1990, p. 2. The Captain Francis O'Neill Collection of Irish Music is housed within the Department of Special Collections of the Thomas M. Hesburgh Library, Notre Dame. My thanks to Librarian, Laura Sue Fuderer.

64. But, to give some idea of what I mean, Edwin Ardener, in 'Social anthropology and the historicity of historical linguistics', in Edwin Ardener (ed.), *Social anthropology and language*, Tavistock, London, 1971, races through the notion of 'timelessness' in anthropology, nodding to Saussure, Evans-Pritchard, Lévi-Strauss, Leach, Jakobson, Chomsky.

65. Francis O'Neill, *Irish folk music: a fascinating hobby* . . ., Regan Printing House, Chicago, 1910, quoted in Ciarán Carson, *Irish traditional music*, Appletree, Belfast, 1986, pp. 22–3.

66. As an example of what can be done see Cynthia M. Sughrue, *The O'Shea Dancing School as a socio-cultural medium in a Boston Irish community*, Working Papers in Irish Studies, Number 85/3, Northeastern University, Boston, 1985.

67. This theme is explored systematically in Nuala O'Connor, *Bringing it all back home: the influence of Irish music*, BBC Books, London, 1991, and illustrated in the accompanying records and television series.

68. The extraordinary effects on fiddle playing within Ireland of the recordings made in America by fiddle players Michael Coleman and James Morrison are also dealt with by Carson, *Irish traditional music*, pp. 21–22, and O'Connor, *Bringing it all back home*, pp. 87–8.

1 Ireland and the scientific tradition

Martin J. Counihan

The Irish cultural tradition is exceptionally ancient and multi-faceted. Within Ireland itself it is a communal self-awareness deeply rooted in literature, history, language and toponymy, and in other parts of the world it is a cultural inheritance supporting a distinctive ethnic identity among migrants and their descendants. Even for those who are not personally of Irish origin, it is an appealing and instructive part of the cultural richness of Europe and of the world with a prominence out of all proportion to the size and population of Ireland itself.

But there is a remarkable gap. Both in Ireland and outside it, the Irish cultural tradition is a mixture of several components in varying proportions, but it is not normally seen to include features such as rationalism, intellectual rigour and esteem for science; instead Irish tradition has become associated almost proverbially with irrationalism. For example, in America in 1842 Lydia Child wrote 'not in vain is Ireland pouring itself all over the earth . . . The Irish, with their glowing hearts and reverent credulity, are needed in this cold age of intellect and skepticism'.[1] It hardly needs to be added that even today, in British popular imagination, Irishness is linked pejoratively with romanticism, superstition and intellectual underachievement.

This would not be surprising if Ireland in her early history had been isolated from the spirit of Classical and Scholastic learning, handicapped by an inadequate educational system, or diverted from rigorous thinking by religious obscurantism and superstition. However, this does not seem to have been the case. On the contrary, there is evidence for an ancient and consistent rational tradition in Ireland and among Irish scholars abroad, distinguished by critical, creative and controversial thought.

This chapter is written from the perspective of the history of science and its purpose is to describe the tradition of Irish rationalism up to about the seventeenth century. No attempt is made here to tell the sadder tale of more recent times and to explain exactly how the reputation for 'reverent credulity' was acquired: that is another story.

It must be understood at the outset that the Irish intellectual tradition embraces philosophy, theology, cosmology and what is now called 'science', or at any rate 'pure' science. Knowledge in the past was not categorised as it is today. Science and cosmology were not distanced from theology but were seamlessly woven in with it. Philosophy was the essence of universal wisdom and reason, and not the effete academic pursuit that it has now become. Although this comment is true of medieval scholarship generally, and does not reflect a uniquely Irish attitude, it is significant that we find Irish scholars foremost in supporting the integrity of knowledge. For example, John Eriugena declared that 'nobody gets to heaven except through philosophy'[2] and that 'true philosophy is true religion, and, conversely, true religion is true philosophy'.[3] He meant that Christianity is an intellectual religion, and that there should be no artificial distinctions between religiosity and rationality. So, in the title of this chapter, 'scientific' is not to be taken merely in its circumscribed modern sense but as shorthand for the cluster of connected disciplines which in the medieval world included natural philosophy, cosmology and aspects of theology.

Some readers may be surprised to learn of Ireland's distinguished and long-standing intellectual tradition. But the surprise arises from the historical circumstances which created religious and cultural barriers between Ireland and its nearest neighbour, resulting in a continuing failure, by historians of science and others, to take Irish culture seriously. This is not only a matter of a national antipathy specific to Ireland; it is also connected generally with the modern attitudes[4] which have turned words like 'medieval' and 'theological' into terms of abuse, and with a historiography emphasising conflict between faith and reason and contrasting science with Christianity in, for example, accounts of the Galileo affair[5] and of Darwinism.[6] In recent decades things have started to move in the other direction: the history of science has moved on from narrow nationalism and from the 'conflict thesis'[7] but a comprehensive revaluation of Irish science is still awaited.[8]

What follows is presented chronologically, starting with some comments about prehistory and then considering a series of individuals including Pelagius, Augustinus, Vergilius, Dicuil, John Eriugena and Bernard O'Connor. It is the similarities and affinities among them, taken together, that allow us to construct a distinctive Irish 'scientific' tradition stretching from the beginning of the Christian period if not earlier.

Prehistory

Virtually nothing is known about intellectual life in prehistoric times in Ireland, or anywhere else for that matter, but nevertheless some conclusions can be assembled from the circumstantial evidence of archaeology, language, folklore and later tradition.[9] Bronze Age Europe, at any rate in the West, was characterised by a sophisticated symbolic cosmology, the cultivation of arts such as poetry and music, and an educational system supported by a druidical caste.

Across most of Europe this culture was profoundly modified at the onset of the Iron Age with the migrations and changes associated with 'Celtic' society. Tribal names and genealogy, as well as more direct evidence from Classical literature, indicate a Celtic obsession with kingship, weaponry and patrilineal descent. This was in marked contrast with the earlier pattern of society.[10]

Like the Germanic peoples a thousand years later, the Celtic[11] peoples brought new languages and far-reaching change across a wide swath of Europe and beyond. Nevertheless, significant elements of the pre-Celtic pattern persisted in some areas of Europe. One such area, auspiciously, was a small patch of Italy south of Etruria. Another such area, the one that concerns us here, was Ireland.

This is not to say that higher culture in the West was restricted to Latium and Ireland 2,300 years ago. That would be an oversimplification. Nor is it suggested that Ireland was untouched by the Iron Age: far from it. Nevertheless it seems that in Ireland, and to a lesser extent in Britain, the old druidical culture was maintained in a purer and more cerebral form than in most other regions. In practice this meant that there was a well-established scholarly network, transcending political divisions, with centres of learning which attracted students from long distances. Caesar mentioned that Britain was an international centre for the higher training of druids.[12] In Christian times obviously there was pilgrimage, monasticism and clerical privilege, but the evidence suggests that these were features also of the pre-Christian West, and especially of Ireland where such things had not been submerged by the turbulent movements of the Iron Age.

Of the actual content of pre-Christian learning in these islands very little can be said, but its general tenor can be felt. There was clearly a devotion to protracted study and the concept of a universal (i.e. trans-ethnic) priesthood, but at the same time there was a strong emphasis on individual creativity. There was a love of wordplay, prophecy and poetic inspiration. When prehistory gives way to history, then, we should not be surprised to find Irish scholars particularly attracted by the universality and rationalism of the new Christian religion and by its emphasis on individual conscience. Also, when they encountered the Classical Hellenistic world through Christianity they may have discovered a special affinity with Neoplatonic scholarship and the tradition of Pythagorean-style brotherhood.[13]

Pelagius

We arrive on firmer ground with identifiable historical figures whose ideas and writings are preserved, and the first such figure of interest to us is Pelagius.[14] Here no attempt is made to describe the controversies that came to surround Pelagius, nor the heresy to which his name was attached, nor the details of his theology.[15] Pelagius is taken simply as a representative of the intellectual life of the British Isles in the fourth and fifth centuries. One cannot be sure whether he was born in Ireland or in Britain, but the evidence indicates that he was a 'Scot' in the sense that the word then had,[16] i.e. Pelagius came from some part of the Gaelic culture-province which then covered both Ireland and peripheral parts of Great Britain.[17]

The idea that Pelagius' philosophy might reflect his ethnic origin is not new. It was suggested some time ago that 'the fundamental doctrines of druidism, doubtlessly, were not alien to the birth of the Pelagian heresy and to the success that it obtained in its country of origin, particularly in the regions of Gaelic population'.[18] While it may be romantically appealing to link Pelagianism with druidism,[19] a strong connection is hard to establish, and our purpose here is less ambitious: simply to take Pelagius' general stance and to consider that the attitudes which distinguished him in Rome and Jerusalem are those that may have been typical of the Gaelic British Isles.

It hardly needs to be said that Pelagius lived in uncertain and violent times. In the middle of the fourth century Romanised South Britain started to be threatened by Picts, Irish and Saxons, and by the Scots whose Irish ancestors had already taken much of North Britain in the preceding centuries. In 367, when Pelagius was probably a boy, South Britain was seriously ravaged by invaders. Pelagius travelled to Rome at about the same time as the Briton Magnus Maximus briefly seized the Empire.

Pelagius was a layman, not a priest or monk, and he was an ascetic, but not to unhealthy extremes. He earned his living as a teacher, counsellor and writer, a member of the international scholarly elite sustained by the Church. He travelled far, spending time at Rome, Carthage and Jerusalem. Pelagius arrived in Rome in the 380s and remained there until 409 or 410 when the city fell to Alaric. His move to Jerusalem took place a little later, perhaps in 414.

Pelagius was excommunicated by Pope Innocent in 417. Shortly afterwards, when Zosimus succeeded to the papacy, the condemnation was rescinded; but then in 418 Zosimus reversed the reversal and excommunicated Pelagius again. Pelagius died not long afterwards. His story has the ingredients of tragedy: he was a man of intelligence, courage and rectitude, he lived out his adult life away from his homeland, but ultimately he met with great hostility and died in disgrace in a far country.

In the routine exercise of his profession Pelagius was a practical moralist. It would be anachronistic to call him a feminist, but much of his work seems to have involved the counselling and pastoral care, as it would be called today, of women. In an age when it was fashionable to regard marriage and sex as necessary evils, a view taken to extremes by his contemporary St Jerome, Pelagius had more moderate ideas, for example that young widows might be encouraged to remarry. In the context of the time his opinions were unusually liberal and pragmatic.

Pelagius wrote on nature and on people's free choice. While his opponent Jerome claimed that 'sin is an inescapable, unavoidable aspect of corporeal existence in this life',[20] Pelagius disagreed, and accepted no concept of original sin. 'Pelagius' insistence that men can be without sin is an emphatic assertion of the doctrine of creation by a just God; it is nothing more, and it is nothing less'.[21]

The idea of predestination was alien to Pelagius' way of thinking. He believed that for God, to predestine is to pre-know,[22] not to pre-ordain. In other words, God may be omniscient but nevertheless the human will is free. Divine power does not limit human freedom and responsibility. It has been said that 'if Pelagius were aware of Origen's argument that God is outside and beyond place and time, he would surely have used it to make his point still firmer'.[23] As we shall see, the notion that God is beyond space and time was central to the thinking of the Irishman John Eriugena five hundred years after Pelagius.

Overall, three particular strands of thought were characteristic of Pelagius, and it is worth listing them because they recur as common features of the Irish intellectual tradition:

Reason
Pelagius was much impressed by Greek Christianity and by aspects of Neoplatonism. In the Greek Christian Neoplatonic writings to which he often referred there was a strong emphasis on human proximity to the divine and on the importance of human reason: 'let the reason which is in you be the very law of your life'.[24]

The integrity of nature
Pelagius was insistently opposed to dualistic views that divided the universe into intrinsically good and evil sections.

Orthodoxy
Catholic orthodoxy was always very important to Pelagius, and he considered that both he and his worthy opponents were orthodox: differences of opinion are acceptable and vigorous debate is not only tolerable but performs a valuable positive function in the development of the Church.

It is important to understand that the commitment to orthodoxy is not merely a form of conservatism or an excuse for rejecting teachings that happen to be in opposition to one's own. Orthodoxy, in this context, is a positive belief about the nature of the Church as being an inclusive community, and a view that progress depends on the free but structured interchange of ideas within that community. Interestingly, St John Chrysostom testified that in Britain at the time 'men discuss the interpretation of Scripture "with differing voices, but not with differing belief "'.[25]

After Patrick

From the beginning of the fifth century ecclesiastical sources show a remarkable cultural efflorescence in Ireland. Almost certainly, Christianity occupied a pre-existing niche in society. 'The Irish monasteries were well endowed with land, and seem at times to have succeeded to the property of the old Druidical colleges.'[26] In view of the institutional continuity, it would be surprising if Irish Christianity did not preserve something of the intellectual traditions of earlier times. The travel of monks between Ireland and Britain was a continuation of a pre-Christian pattern. Christian ideals became readily associated with travel, pilgrimage, retreat and of course monasticism, withdrawing from one's homeland either in an internal sense or by voyaging abroad. In 560 the Irishman St Frediano became bishop of Lucca in Tuscany,[27] and by 563 St Columba was founding the monastery at Iona.

At about this time the Irishman Mael-Dubh founded a monastery in England at Malmesbury, the town's name preserving his. His pupil Aldhelm, later abbot, was an Anglo-Saxon and a hibernophile, whose surviving correspondence confirms the continuing importance and prevalence of travel for study from Britain to Ireland. British pupils travelled to Ireland where they could learn grammar, geometry, physics and other subjects. And later, Bede, writing of the seventh century, referred to how English boys were able to study free of charge in Ireland's schools.[28]

A revealing insight into the times is given by the *Hisperica Famina*,[29, 30] a work of verse in a curious form of florid, obscure Latin. Far removed from any mainstream literary tradition, it describes the course of a routine day in the life of a community of Latin-speaking scholars apparently residing in Ireland but not understanding the local dialect. One manuscript of the *Hisperica Famina* includes an interesting 'Pythagorean' fragment, a fortune-telling device: a circle bisected horizontally, the upper half representing the heavens and life, and containing the numbers 1, 2, 3, 4, 7, 9, 10, 11, 13, 14, 16, 17, 19, 20, 22, 23, 26 and 27. The other numbers from the range 1–30 are in the bottom semicircle, associated with the earth and death. The letters of the alphabet are listed alongside, each being linked with a particular number. The inquirer is to form a total by adding together all the numbers corresponding to the letters of his name, and also the age of the moon at the time in question, and finally taking the remainder when the total is divided by 30. A prediction of life or death follows from looking to see if the result falls in the top or the bottom half of the circle. This is striking evidence that quasi-Platonic numerology was indulged in by Irish scholars by about the eighth century and possibly very much earlier.

An important survival of scientific thinking is the work of the so-called Augustinus in a treatise 'On the Miracles of the Sacred Scriptures' written in 655 in Ireland.[31] For his time Augustinus had a remarkably rational approach to the scriptural miracles, taking the view that they could involve no new creation by God but only the manifestation of existing natural principles normally hidden. The metamorphosis of Lot's wife, therefore, as she looked back on the destruction of Sodom, was 'merely the abnormal development of the salt element which is present in every human body'. When the sun and moon miraculously stood still as described in the Book of Joshua it was simply a synchronised suspension of motions arising because nature prevents a disturbance of chronology. This was made logical by the fact, to Augustinus, that the heavenly bodies return to the same relative positions after cycles of 532 years. Augustinus also discussed the problem of the tides, and the action of the sea in separating islands from the mainland, and he pointed out that the wild animals found on islands such as Ireland — wolves, deer, foxes, badgers, hares and the like — must have been present in an earlier age before the sea separated them from Britain and the Continent.

A century later, in about 748, the Irishman Ferghil, or St Virgilius of Salzburg, was being censured for accepting the Greek idea that there exist inhabited antipodes,[32] and a second sun and moon, beneath the earth. This concept, a deduction based on natural symmetry in the cosmos, was considered dangerously bold in Virgilius' time.

At the start of the ninth century we find Dicuil, the first Irish scientific writer of whose work a substantial amount has survived. Dicuil travelled to the Carolingian court at around the turn of the century, and in 814–16 wrote an astronomical treatise dedicated to Louis the Debonnaire, who had just succeeded Charlemagne as Emperor.[33] It is fairly lengthy, in four books, in prose interspersed with verse. It deals with the calculation of the calendar, the 19-year lunar cycle,[34] the great cycle of the sun and moon,[35] and other topics such as the conjectured existence of a south polar star.[36]

Dicuil presents an interesting quantitative cosmology. The moon is said to be 500 leagues above the surface of the earth, the sun twice as far away again, and the fixed stars three times as far beyond the sun as the sun is beyond the moon. Venus is as far above the moon as the moon is above the earth, and Mercury is midway between Venus and the moon. The orbits of Mars, Jupiter and Saturn lie in that order between the sun and the fixed stars. The complete scheme is loosely credited to the ancient philosophers, in particular Pythagoras, but Dicuil was well aware of the variety of astronomical opinions that had been held before him: he mentions the notion that the sun is 18 times as far from the moon as the moon is from the earth, criticising it as a presumption unsupported by observation.

Subsequently, in 825, Dicuil produced the *De Mensura Orbis Terrae*, a book which occupies an important place in the history of geography. It was based largely on Classical authors but includes contemporary novelties such as a description of Iceland. The book ends with a most beautiful signing-off from Dicuil: 'after eight hundred and twenty-five years finished of the high lord of earth, of heaven, and the dark prison, when the wheaten seed has been sown in the country earth, at night on ending their labours the oxen are granted rest'.[37]

John Eriugena

Eriugena has been called 'the most considerable philosopher in the Western world between Augustine and Thomas Aquinas and the greatest Irish philosopher (with the possible exception of Berkeley) ever'.[38] After a long period of neglect by historians, Pierre Duhem and Henry Bett being exceptions earlier this century,[39] Eriugena's life and work have come under fresh scrutiny only during the last twenty years or so. It is now a thriving field of research with a fast-growing literature backed up by frequent scholarly conferences.[40]

John Eriugena was born in the early ninth century, and before he left Ireland in the 840s he may already have acquired a good deal of the classical education that was to develop into a mastery of Greek unrivalled in Latin Christendom. Eriugena became based at the court of Charles the Bald, in what is now France, for most of that monarch's reign; he appears to have left in about 877 to spend his remaining years in England, although this is not certain. Eriugena's work was often controversial and it may be that he was obliged to leave France because of his loss of royal protection on Charles' death. It is significant that he chose to travel not back to Ireland, which he might not have visited for forty years, but to Malmesbury, the monastery which had been founded by the Irishman Mael-Dubh two centuries earlier. Alfred the Great, who had come to the throne in Wessex in 871, admired and imitated Charlemagne's patronage of scholarship, and Malmesbury must have seemed a safe and congenial haven for the ageing Eriugena and his companions.[41]

For the present purposes it will be sufficient to mention Eriugena's commentary on Martianus Capella,[42] completed about 860, and his masterwork, the *Periphyseon* (or 'Division of Nature'), written around 865. The commentary on Martianus Capella contains many of the ideas which Eriugena was later to develop at greater length in the *Periphyseon*, a compendious work in five volumes. He had strong Neoplatonic views on the nature of man and on the importance of individual effort in the pursuit of wisdom, and an unorthodox eschatology which denied that there would be physical rewards or punishment after death. There are interesting parallels between Eriugena and Pelagius who were close together in their regard for people's individual power, free will and responsibility.[43]

In the *Periphyseon*, Eriugena quoted Aristotle, Eratosthenes,[44] Plato, Ptolemy[45] and Pythagoras and he presented a sophisticated theory of matter based on the four Empedoclean[46] elements of earth, air, fire and water.[47] Like Virgilius of Salzburg before him, Eriugena believed in the existence of an antipodean region below the Earth. He put forward a remarkable cosmological system which in a sense is Sun-centred, with the Sun's orbit equidistant between the surface of the Earth and the sphere of the fixed stars. Although the Sun rotates around the Earth, most of the planets (Mercury, Venus, Mars and Jupiter) orbit the Sun.

The dimensions of Eriugena's universe follow the Pythagorean harmony of the musical octave. There are equal distances between eight regions: the underside of the Earth, the Earth's surface where we live, the centre of the Moon, the lower orbits of the heliocentric planets, the centre of the Sun, the upper orbits of the heliocentric planets, the exceptional planet Saturn and finally the fixed stars.

Eriugena propounds an interesting theory to support the notion that most of the planets, excluding Saturn, orbit the Sun. He believed that Mercury, Venus, Mars and Jupiter show different colours which vary with time, and that this could be explained in terms of the different celestial regions traversed by those planets. Moving outwards towards the stars, different temperatures are to be associated with different regions. When the planets are closer to the Earth their colours will be reddened due to a greater natural heat, and when they are higher up towards the stars they will show a cool paleness. Saturn, always cold and white, must remain close to the stars, never falling below the Sun; it therefore orbits the earth.

John Eriugena's physical cosmology, although ingenious, has flaws. It is not based on mathematical arguments, and there is no reason to suppose that he personally made astronomical measurements. Nevertheless, Eriugena has been claimed as a precocious forerunner of Tycho Brahe[48] because, with the special exception of Saturn, Eriugena's universe is similar to Brahe's sixteenth-century system. But it is more instructive, perhaps, to compare Eriugena not with Brahe but with Copernicus,[49] and not as a mathematician but as a philosopher. Albeit technically centred on a stationary Earth, in spirit Eriugena's cosmos is heliocentric, with a Pythagorean emphasis on the primacy of the Sun, and Eriugena has no ideological requirement for the Earth to be the centre of the universe. Moreover the conventional medieval cosmos is dualistic, with an imperfect sublunar region divided from divine and immutable upper spheres and a remote heaven: but Eriugena's cosmos is unitary. Eriugena does not believe in a distinct supernatural region: all is part of divided nature.

Eriugena's cosmology is in complete harmony with his rejection of a physical heaven or hell. For Eriugena, not only is there no separate hell, but evil has no real existence in itself, being merely a negation of good. Nobody is predestined to evil. His ideas on this were developed and expounded in the context of a bitter controversy over predestination around the year 850, but were later condemned by synods at Valence and Langres.

Creation is a key concept in Eriugena's work, but creation not just as an initial act at the beginning of time but in the continuing sense. Creation gives order and reason to the universe, and we are both products and agents of divine creation. 'God's creative activity is the expression of His rational word, and so the order of the universe is wholly logical.'[50] Creation and creativity are the basis of Eriugena's analysis of the universe.

Eriugena came dangerously close to pantheism with his vision of a single universe suffused and sustained by a timeless God. All things are but thoughts in the mind of God, and God is created in everything and contains everything. We are not God, but only because we are beings constrained within the bounds of space and time, while God is above being.

In summary, Eriugena's ideas follow the same major themes as are listed above for Pelagius. He insisted on the value of human imagination and wisdom and on the rationality of nature, these being aspects of God's creative power. Christianity is to be interpreted as an essentially intellectual religion, albeit accessible to all. The integrity of nature is crucial to Eriugena; there is no separate supernature. Finally, Eriugena was an enthusiastic controversialist, although many of his contemporaries felt that he, like Pelagius, went too far. Predestination, heaven and hell, and near-pantheism have been mentioned: Eriugena also had a radical view about the nature of the Eucharist. What is of interest to us here is not whether Eriugena was right or wrong, but that he embraced debate as a way of approaching truth. Indeed, his *Periphyseon* is composed entirely in the form of a frank discussion between a Master and a Disciple.

After his death Eriugena's writings soon came to be neglected, largely because his controversialism resulted later in the official condemnation of many of the opinions ascribed to him. Although Eriugena's bold beliefs were admired by some of his more enlightened near-contemporaries, such as Pope Sylvester II, they came to be regarded as suspect in the less liberal centuries that followed.

Peter of Ireland

By the end of the first millennium the old monastic links between Ireland and the rest of Europe had ceased to be so effective or relevant, and Irish scholars no longer played a prominent part in the history of ideas, but there were still those who made significant contributions during the succeeding centuries leading up to the Renaissance. One of the most important was 'Peter of Ireland' (Petrus de Hibernia) who in 1224 was sent by the Emperor Frederick II to teach law at the newly-founded University of Naples. He steeped himself in the writings of Aristotle, newly available through translations and commentaries from the

Islamic world, and he was influenced especially by the writings of the scholar Averroës, or Ibn Rushd, of Cordoba in Spain.[51]

For Peter, Averroës' lifetime (1126–98) was still relatively recent and it is remarkable that his ideas were being transmitted, translated and taken up so rapidly in the Latin West. Peter of Ireland and his contemporaries clearly played a leading part in that process. Peter wrote three treatises on Aristotle from a radical Averroistic point of view.

Averroës integrated Islamic and Classical Greek ideas and promoted Aristotelian ideas through clear and convincing writings which had a powerful impact on thinking in the Latin West. Like John Eriugena, Averroës believed firmly that religion and philosophy must be consistent with one another and that logic is needed to arrive at deeper religious truths. Averroës, like Thomas Aquinas in the next century, believed that the existence of God can be proved by reason. Some of Averroës' later Christian followers veered towards heresy by setting reason above faith and by ascribing immortality to a collective intellect rather than the individual soul.

In the university curriculum, the seven 'liberal arts' of late antiquity (grammar, rhetoric, dialectic, arithmetic, geometry, astronomy and music) were breaking down and being replaced by a powerful new Aristotelian scheme of knowledge. There was practical knowledge, divided into the three categories of ethics, economics and politics; and there was theoretical knowledge, also divided into three categories: natural science, mathematics and metaphysics or theology. This scheme was not fixed in Peter's time: on the contrary there were many variations and the classification was a matter of continuing debate.[52]

Peter of Ireland gained a reputation as a logician and as a master of natural science. In Naples, in the early 1240s, he taught these subjects to the young Thomas Aquinas, and he obviously taught them well. While it would be absurd to give Peter the credit for Thomas' enormous impact on Christianity and Western civilisation, as if Thomas were merely Peter's agent, it would be equally mistaken to make light of Peter's influence. Peter of Ireland was an essential link in the chain that took the new Aristotelian ideas from Averroës to Thomas, changed the intellectual climate of Europe's universities, and gave a new emphasis to reason and the study of nature. Peter of Ireland is buried at the Convent of Aquila.

Bernard O'Connor

Leaving aside a few minor figures from late-mediaeval and Renaissance times, our sequence reaches its culmination with the seventeenth-century polymath Bernard O'Connor, or Connor.[53] He was born and received his initial education in Kerry.[54] O'Connor stood in two worlds: he was the last important scholar to emerge from the culture of Gaelic Ireland, but at the same time he was a keen Newtonian,[55] a sceptical scientist of the modern age.

O'Connor studied at Montpelier and Paris; he travelled in Italy, Germany and Poland, and became state physician to the Polish King John Sobieski, later publishing a celebrated *History of Poland*.[56] He travelled to Brussels in 1694, then to England. He spent time at Oxford during the summer of 1695, writing and lecturing, and then at Cambridge in 1695, on chemical and anatomical experiments. O'Connor finally moved to London where he resumed his profession as a physician and practised for the remaining two years before his early death from illness, at only 32, in 1698. O'Connor joined the Royal Society and wrote extensively on medical subjects and on curious natural phenomena such as the volcano Vesuvius.

During his time in Poland, O'Connor disputed with Polish clergy and with Sobieski about the location of the soul, which O'Connor claimed is located in the head and not in the body as a whole. He believed that death is primarily the cessation of bodily functions rather than being something caused by the departure of the soul from the body.[57] These ideas were felt to come close to heresy.

O'Connor was controversial not only as a scientist but also in his political ideas. This was perhaps inevitable for an Irish intellectual of his times: he had strong views about the upshot of the Treaty of Limerick and attracted hostility by promoting a scheme to release Ireland from the English.[58]

O'Connor's most contentious work was his *Evangelium Medici*, a book in which he applied fashionable philosophical and physical ideas to explain supernatural miracles by natural principles.[59] Predictably, he attracted a storm of opposition from the clergy. *Evangelium Medici* quotes Isaac Newton's three laws of motion, and then goes on to state three laws 'of the suspension of motion', which essentially say that Newton's laws need not always apply. 'By these three laws of suspended motion it is easily possible for the status of all bodies above nature to be explained.' O'Connor was trying to say that 'supernatural' phenomena are really natural, but obeying unusual rules. 'For want of a sufficient insight in this matter, several Divines of the latter ages, have given very gross ideas of the Miracles they have pretended to explain; and in several places where I have been I saw them, either though ignorance, or for interest, give out for Miracles, Phoenomena, that were only surprising effects of Natural Causes; which Has given so great an occasion to scepticism, and increase of deism.'

O'Connor accepted the Newtonian view that all matter is but a union of particles; motion is the only true cause of all natural effects; and the suspensions of the laws of motion are the only causes of what we call miracles. O'Connor arrived at explanations for the miracle at Cana, the Resurrection, the parting of the Red Sea, the Virgin Birth and other Biblical miracles. Bernard O'Connor had to defend himself to the Archbishop of Canterbury and he was pursued literally to the grave by the scandal of his alleged disbelief.[60]

It is irresistible to compare O'Connor's attempts to rationalise the miraculous with those of his compatriot Augustinus a millennium before, although O'Connor would almost certainly have never heard of Augustinus. O'Connor's rationalism in bringing the supernatural down to earth is reminiscent also of Eriugena, although Eriugena rather elevated nature up towards the divine. O'Connor's career was remarkably short, but it shows a sort of telescoped Pelagian tragedy with the years spent journeying abroad, never holding back from acrimonious controversy, faithful but always on the edge of theological acceptability, and vilified even after his death.

Summary

Throughout the whole of the time span surveyed above scholars from Ireland interacted creatively with those in Britain and continental Europe. There was a significant Irish input to the process which eventually led to the emergence of modern science in Europe. This had very deep foundations: from the intellectual vitality evident at the very beginning of the Christian period, it appears that systematic education, study and travel were part of a pre-Christian tradition from which Ireland and so Europe continued to benefit.

Looking at the broad sweep, we can discern a consistent tradition of Irish thought distinct from that of Western Europe as a whole but firmly rooted within it. That tradition has three particular aspects which were listed earlier in this chapter when discussing Pelagius, and which have recurred as other scholars have been discussed. One aspect is academic integrity, or 'orthodoxy' in the sense of belonging to an integral and international community in which progress follows from free, if disciplined, controversy. Another aspect is that of courageous rationalism, insisting on an integrity of knowledge: in particular science and religion are required to be subject to the same standards of reason. Finally there is naturalism, a belief in the integrity of nature, rejecting dualism in its Manichaean and later forms. The genuine Irish tradition avoids world/ spirit divisions: we have an integrated cosmos in which God works rationally through the natural world and through human will. Quoted in isolation, these three aspects of Irish intellectual tradition can appear austere and abstract, but I have tried to show how very real and influential they have been in the lives of individuals from the fourth century to the seventeenth.

If it is granted that there was a consistent Irish scientific tradition over that period of time, there remains the irresistible question of how, precisely, that continuity was effected. It would be inadequate to speak vaguely of a native psychology, or an ethnic character predisposing the Irish to particular intellectual stances. It is plausible that a concrete line of continuity existed through the Irish educational system, but this remains to be demonstrated. For the present we must content ourselves with the observation but not the explanation of the Irish scientific tradition.

Finally it should be made clear that no excessive claims can be made for Irish intellectual history. For example there is no significant tradition of mathematics, or empirical science, or innovation in medicine or technology. It is true that one is more likely to find an Irish poet and a Jewish scientist than the reverse. Nevertheless, the Irish have played a distinctive, distinguished and consistent part as champions of the integrity of nature, reason and scholarship throughout recorded history with the exception of the last three centuries. Their current reputation for 'reverent credulity' is a curious reversal which represents only the sad predicament that followed the Treaty of Limerick. There is no need to let it last.

Notes

1. Lydia Child, *Letters from New York*, I, no. 33, 8 Dec. 1842.
2. C. Lutz, *Iohannis Scotti annotationes in Marcianum*, Medieval Academy of America, Cambridge, Massachusetts, 1939, and Kraus Reprint Company, New York, 1970, p. 64.
3. J. Eriugena, *De praedestinatione*, quoted in J. J. O'Meara, *Eriugena*, Clarendon Press, Oxford, 1988, p. 28.
4. An excellent recent summary of the historiography of science is given by R. C. Olby *et al.* (eds), *Companion to the history of modern science*, Routledge, London, 1990.
5. The embroidered story of the trial of Galileo became a polemical weapon against the Catholic Church and a heroic origin-myth for modern science. For a good account, see J. M. Jauch, *The trial of Galileo Galilei*, European Organisation for Nuclear Research, CERN 64–36, 1964.
6. There is an enormous literature about how attitudes towards religion were affected by the way Darwinism was promoted. See J. H. Brooke, *Science and religion: some historical perspectives*, Cambridge University Press, Cambridge (England), 1991, and references therein.
7. The 'conflict thesis' is the view that the history of science is best understood in terms of a long struggle between science and religion. See C. A. Russell, *Cross-currents: interactions between science and faith*, Inter-Varsity Press, Leicester, 1985.
8. Incidentally there is now a fashionable 'ethnoscience' movement of historians seeking to reconstruct other traditions which have been almost overwhelmed by the success of secularised Western modern science. This applies to things like Chinese science, Islamic science, the native science of pre-Columbian America, and pre-colonial African science.
9. M. J. Counihan, 'Ethnic and linguistic origins in Europe and the British Isles' (lecture presented at the University of Calgary, October 1988), Department of Adult Education, University of Southampton, 1988.
10. In ethnic and social terms this transition is marked by a wealth of tradition and folklore. For example there is the story of Eoghan Mor, representing early-Iron Age Erainn incomers to Ireland, taking the daughter of the druid-chief of the indigenous Grecraige and begetting a future king of Munster. The story of the Sabine women is essentially the same.
11. The word 'Celtic' is used here in a restricted sense to refer to the peoples who radiated from Central Europe at the start of the Iron Age. Their origin and culture, and their relationship with the first historical peoples of Britain and Ireland, are topics of current research and controversy. The traditional picture of the 'Celts' is now believed to be wide of the mark, and indeed it is debatable what the word should be taken to signify. However, it seems likely that a proto-Celtic language was the forerunner of Gaulish and British, whereas the Gaelic language (and Latin) has pre-Celtic Bronze Age origins. Although there was a very substantial Celtic impact in Ireland, the Celtic language did not replace Gaelic there: Irish is not a Celtic language. In much the same way, later, the Germanic language of the Franks did not replace the Latin of what was to become France. See note 9.
12. K. H. Jackson, *The oldest Irish tradition: a window on the Iron Age*, Cambridge University Press, Cambridge, UK, 1964, p. 39.
13. Pythagoras (*c.* 560–480 BC) founded an ascetic community dedicated to approaching God through learning, philosophy, mathematics and contemplation. The same theme inspired followers of Plato and later Gnostic and Neoplatonic groups.
14. Pelagius (*c.* 360–420) is best known for the heresy called after him, an over-emphasis on human rather than divine autonomy, and this has unfortunately coloured later attitudes to Pelagius himself. But it takes two to make a heresy.

15. See R. F. Evans, *Pelagius: inquiries and appraisals*, Adam and Charles Black, London, 1968; and J. Ferguson, *Pelagius: a historical and theological study*, W. Heffer and Sons, Cambridge (England), 1956.
16. The word 'Scot' has changed its meaning through time. In late Roman times it was in effect a linguistic label and could be applied to the Irish, to the Gaelic-speaking peoples of north Britain, and to the short-lived Irish colonies in Wales.
17. Gaelic language marked the common culture of Ireland and much of Britain although it never reflected any political or perceived ethnic unity across that area.
18. Chevalier, *Essai sur les réveils religieux du pays de Galles*, quoted by Evans, *Pelagius*, p. 391.
19. J. W. W. Bund, *The Celtic Church in Wales*, D. Nutt, London, 1897.
20. Evans, *Pelagius*, p. 25.
21. Evans, *Pelagius*, p. 104.
22. See Romans viii: 29.
23. Ferguson, *Pelagius*, p. 138.
24. From the *Sentences of Sextus*, a second-century Greek work: H. Chadwick, *The sentences of Sextus*, Texts and Studies, New Series, V, Cambridge, 1959, S123.
25. Quoted by Ferguson, *Pelagius*, p. 37.
26. G. S. M. Walker, (ed. and trans.), *Sancti Columbani opera*, Dublin Institute for Advanced Studies (Scriptores Latini Hiberniae Vol. 2), Dublin, 1957, p. xv.
27. J. F. Kenney, *The sources for the early history of Ireland*, Vol. I (Ecclesiastical), Columbia University Press, New York, 1929, pp. 184–5.
28. Bede, *Hist. Eccl.*, iii, 27.
29. F. J. H. Jenkinson, (ed.), *The Hisperica Famina*, Cambridge University Press, Cambridge, 1908.
30. W. P. Boswell, (trans.), *Hisperica Famina: the prologue and a part of the Book of Days*, Andrew Hoyem (private printing), San Francisco, 1974.
31. Kenney, *Sources*, p. 277.
32. It was imagined that the Earth is symmetrical across the Equator, with the underside having its own continents and population separate from us. It was not clear how an antipodean population could be embraced by the Universal Church.
33. M. Esposito, *An unpublished astronomical treatise by the Irish monk Dicuil*, Proc. Roy. Irish Academy, Vol. 26, Section C, 1907, pp. 378–446 and plate xxii.
34. The lunar month not being commensurate with the solar year, longer-term cycles arise. For Irish popular knowledge of the 19-year lunar cycle, the 'duibhre', see E. Hadingham, *Early man and the cosmos*, Heinemann, London, 1983, p. 63.
35. Taking the Earth, Sun, Moon, planets and stars all together, it was believed in antiquity that the heavens returned to their exact starting-point after 'great cycle' periods. There was discussion of cycles of different lengths, and the 532-year period accepted by Augustinus was probably the shortest.
36. Like the antipodes, mentioned earlier in connection with Virgilius, the south polar star would have satisfied the idea of symmetry across the Equator.
37. J. J. Tierney, and L. Bieler (eds), *Dicuil: de mensura orbis terrae*, Dublin Institute for Advanced Studies (Scriptores Latini Hiberniae Vol. 6) Dublin, 1967; see also C. R. Beazley, *The dawn of modern geography*, London, 1897–1906; L. Bieler, *The text tradition of Dicuil's Liber de mensura orbis terrae*, Proc. Roy. Irish Academy, Vol. 64, Section C, 1965, pp. 1–32; and G. Parthey, (ed.), *Dicuil: de mensura orbis terrae*, Akademische Druck- und Verlagsanstalt, Graz, Austria, 1969.
38. J. J. O'Meara, *Eriugena*, Mercier Press, Cork, 1969.
39. P. Duhem, *Le Système du monde*, Vol. 3, Hermann et Cie., Paris, 1954 (orig. pub. 1915), pp. 53–63; H. Bett, *Johannes Scotus Erigena: a study in mediaeval philosophy*, Cambridge University Press, Cambridge (UK), 1925.

40. E.g., J. J. O'Meara, and L. Bieler (eds.), *The mind of Eriugena*, Irish University Press for the Royal Irish Academy, Dublin, 1973; Colloques Internationaux du Centre National de la Recherche Scientifique, *Jean Scot Erigene et l'histoire de la philosophie*, ed. du CNRS, Paris, 1977; III Internationalen Eriugena-Colloquiums, Freiburg im Breisgau, 1979, *Eriugena: Studien zu Seinen Quellen*, Universitätsverlag Heidelberg, 1980; J. J. O'Meara, *Eriugena*, Clarendon Press, Oxford, 1988; see also M. Manitius, *Extracts from the commentary on Martianus Capella by Johannes Eriugena*, Didaskaleion I (pp. 139–79) and II (pp. 43–61), Turin, 1912; L. Labowsky, *A new version of Scotus Eriugena's commentary on Martianus Capella*, Mediaeval and Renaissance Studies, Vol. 1, 1943, pp. 187–93; Eriugena (trans. J. J. O' Meara), *Periphyseon*, Editions Bellarmin, Montreal, 1987.

41. For some of the background to this, see K. Harrison, *The framework of Anglo-Saxon history to AD900*, Cambridge University Press, Cambridge, UK, 1976; and also K. Harrison, 'Episodes in the history of Easter cycles in Ireland' in D. Whitelock, *et al.*, *Ireland in early Medieval Europe*, Cambridge University Press, Cambridge, UK, 1982, pp. 307–19.

42. In the early fifth century Martianus Felix Capella of Carthage wrote a textbook on the seven liberal arts fancifully larded with Graeco-Roman mythology. His book remained popular across the Latin world for many centuries and transcended its own merits by serving as a framework for discussion and commentary.

43. H. Liebeschuetz, 'Western Christian thought from Boethius to Anselm' in A. H. Armstrong (ed.), *The Cambridge history of later Greek and early Medieval philosophy*, Cambridge University Press, Cambridge, UK, 1967, pp. 538–642.

44. Eriugena describes the calculation of the circumference of the Earth credited to the Stoic scholar Eratosthenes, the librarian at Alexandria.

45. Claudius Ptolemy of Alexandria, in the second century AD, devised a geocentric mathematical model of astronomy based on Aristotelian physics which was generally accepted until the time of the Renaissance.

46. The theory of the four elements, elaborated by the Sicilian Empedocles in the fifth century BC, is one of the most successful scientific theories ever. It was standard for about two thousand years.

47. P. Duhem, *Le Système du monde*, Vol. 3, p. 54.

48. In Brahe's system the Sun and Moon orbit a stationary Earth but all the other planets orbit the Sun. The similarity between Brahe and Eriugena is superficial because the latter's cosmology is qualitative rather than quantitative.

49. Nicolaus Copernicus (1473–1543) was the Renaissance astronomer who decisively rejected geocentric cosmologies and the Aristotelian paraphernalia of heavenly spheres.

50. Introduction to M. L. Uhlfelder and J. A. Potter (eds), *Periphyseon: on the division of nature*, Bobbs-Merrill Co. Inc., Indianapolis, 1976.

51. G. Sarton, *Introduction to the history of science*, Vol. II, Part II, Carnegie Institute, Washington DC, 1931, p. 949.

52. M. B. Crowe, 'Peter of Ireland's approach to metaphysics' in P. Wilpert (ed.), *Die Metaphysik im Mittelalter: ihr Ursprung und ihre Bedeutung*, Vortrage des II Internationalen Kongresses für Mittelalterliche Philosophie, Miscellanea Medievalia, 2, Gruyter and Co., Berlin, 1963, pp. 154–60.

53. In the literature O'Connor is often referred to as Connor. He was a Gaelic-speaker and there is no reason to suppose that he himself ever favoured omitting the 'O', but it was generally dropped in England at the time.

54. C. Smith, *The antient [sic] and present state of the County of Kerry*, Dublin, 1756, reprinted by Mercier Press, Cork, 1969, pp. 415–16.

55. O'Connor was dead before the philosophy inspired by Isaac Newton had reached its full popular expression, and O'Connor would certainly not have been attracted by Newton's theological and political views; but nevertheless he embraced the Newtonian scientific philosophy like most of the progressive thinkers of his generation.

56. B. O'Connor, *The history of Poland* . . ., Dan. Brown and A. Roper, London, 1698, pp. 179–84.

57. B. O'Connor, *De anima*, Oxford, Bodleian Library MS Rawl. D 1041 (13,794).

58. *Report on the manuscripts of the Marquess of Downshire*, vol. I, pt. II, HMSO, London, 1924, pp. 508–9 and p. 603. There is no information about the details of O'Connor's political proposals.

59. B. O'Connor, *Evangelium medici*, sumptibus Richardi Wellington, London, 1697.

60. W. Hayley, *A sermon preached at the funeral of B. Connor, M.D.,* . . . *with a short account of his life and death*, London, 1699.

2 'Till their . . . bog-trotting feet get *talaria*: Henry D. Thoreau and the immigrant Irish

James P. Myers, jun.

In 1939, Henry Seidel Canby briefly noted that Henry D. Thoreau 'never liked' the Irish immigrants of Concord, concluding that 'someone should write an essay on Thoreau and the Irish'.[1] Apparently heeding this advice, Frank Buckley, one year later, published such an article,[2] and in 1978 George E. Ryan authored another discussion of the subject.[3] Apart from passing comments by a few other critics,[4] Thoreau's long fascination with the Irish of Concord has not received the attention that it merits, and even in their two rather balanced discussions Buckley and Ryan concentrate more on Thoreau's economic and social evaluations than on the philosophical and literary uses to which Thoreau put his Irish acquaintances in both his *Journal* and *Walden*. It is toward correcting such an emphasis that the present study has been written.

In his *Journal* entry for 12 December 1851, Thoreau recorded his impressions of the Irishman, MacCarty, whom he employed as a surveyor's assistant. After describing how he had argued with the latter about a superstition MacCarty had learned from a doctor in New Brunswick, Thoreau concluded in exasperation that the Irishman was a 'gray-headed boy, good for nothing but to eat his dinner'.[5] Once started on the subject, he expanded his attack to denounce the Irish generally: 'Let me inquire strictly into a man's descent, and if his remotest ancestors were Erse, let me not have him to help me survey' (*J.*, 12 Dec. 1851, 3:135).

Thoreau also endorsed the generally accepted nineteenth-century Anglo-Saxon comparison of swine and Irishmen. In an 1853 letter to H. G. O. Blake, he maintained that hogs were the perfect reflection of their Irish owners.[6] And in the *Journal*, he contrasted the habitations of pigs to those of the Irish, far preferring the former over the latter: the pigs 'are comparatively clean about their lodgings, and their shed, with its litter bed, was on the whole cleaner than an Irishman's shanty' (10 June 1853, 5:241).

Coming as it does during the period when over a million destitute Irish had fled to the New World to escape the ravages of famine and pestilence, Thoreau's generalisations do not surprise us, for they reflect nineteenth-century America's prevailing hostility toward these immigrants.[7] Most of Thoreau's fellow writers in Concord shared the sentiment. Emerson, for example, called them 'shovel-handed Irish' and spoke of the 'populations of paddies' which he felt he could 'well dispense with.'[8] Hawthorne, too, expressed his dislike of the 'wild Irish'. To him, Irish children were 'always filthy of face', and he denounced Irish shanties as 'board-built and turf-buttressed hovels . . ., scattered about as if they had sprung up like mushrooms in the dells and gorges, and along the banks of the river'. He further criticised them for speaking Irish and 'nothing else'.[9]

Critic George E. Ryan reminds us, however, that 'the Irish did have a share of staunch champions, vocal advocates, among certain contemporaries and colleagues of Thoreau, Emerson and the rest'.[10] Thoreau's good friend and superintendent of Concord schools, A. Bronson Alcott, for example, observed of Irish children that they were 'a sprightly element, and a spur to the classes'.[11] Irish adults, moreover, impressed Alcott as 'at bottom one of the best nations in the world'. Ryan examines similar approval and praise of Irish immigrants by Margaret Fuller, John Greenleaf Whittier and Walt Whitman.[12]

If we are not surprised by Thoreau's attacks, we well might be by his good opinion of the Irish, for contradicting his expressions of dislike is a large number of very favourable assessments. Throughout his *Journal*, he wrote compassionately of his destitute Irish neighbours, and in a number of instances he went on to chastise the Yankee townspeople for their stinginess and flinty hearts. Trying to raise money among the people of Concord for an Irishman who was endeavouring to bring his family to the United States, for instance, Thoreau deplored their lack of charity. He wrote,

> One will never know his neighbours till he has carried a subscription paper among them. Ah! it reveals many and sad facts to stand in this relation to them. To hear the selfish and cowardly excuses some make, — that *if* they help any they must help the Irishman who lives with them, — and him they are sure never to help! Others, with whom public opinion weighs, will think of it, trusting you never will raise the sum and so they will not be called on again; who gave stingily after all. (*J.*, 12 Oct. 1853, 5:438–9)

In another case, one of his townsmen, 'notorious for meanness', endeavoured 'to get and keep a premium of four dollars which a poor Irish laborer whom he hired had gained by fifteen minutes' spading at our Agricultural Fair' (*J.*, 1 Nov. 1853, 5:472).

It is not uncommon to find Thoreau reporting in his *Journal* how employers sent out gangs of Irish labourers to perform hard, unskilled work no one else would do — particularly the clearing of trees that so smacked of vandalism to Thoreau (e.g., see 28 Sept. 1857, 10:50–1). Once, he saw 'fifteen or sixteen men, Irish mostly, at ten dollars a month, doing the work of fifty, with a Yankee overseer' (27 July 1851, 2:351). Understandably, as his language here implies, he sometimes compared the mistreatment of Irish labourers with that of Black slaves (1 Nov. 1853, 5:472). The truth is that, more often than not, Thoreau impresses the reader as far more objective than most of his contemporary commentators, who tended to express only extreme positions, one way or the other.[13] Hence, while he too criticised the Irish for their commonly denounced sins of drunkenness, dirtiness and shiftlessness, he also looked into the possible causes for many of these unfortunate excesses, and, in addition, carefully preserved several very positive illustrations of the Irish character, examples that gave the lie to the pervasive bigotry among his fellow Concordians.

Thoreau lamented that the multitudes of desperate, penniless Irishmen provided a ready pool of labourers easily exploited for brutish work. Remarking on the manufacture of potash from burned kelp, he pointed out that 'chemistry is not a splitting hairs when you have got half a dozen raw Irishmen in the laboratory' (*J.*, 25 July 1851, 2:346). The huge reserve of available labour, as we have noted, made it easy for a local businessman to get 'fifteen or sixteen men, Irish mostly' to 'do the work of fifty' (*J.*, 27 July 1851, 2:351). And that townsman ('notorious for meanness') who tried to extort from his Irish labourer the $4 the latter had won at the fair reinforced the ready-to-hand parallel between Black slavery and the exploitation of the Irish[14] — Thoreau even condemned the man 'as mean as a slaveholder!' (*J.*, 1 Nov. 1853, 5:472).

The squalid consequences of slum living also aroused his indignation. While on a trip to Hull in 1851, he witnessed a 'pleasure party' consisting of a 'large proportion of ill-dressed and ill-mannered boys of Irish extraction' (*J.*, 25 July 1851, 2:341–2). For him it was a 'sad sight to behold', particularly the spectacle of twelve-years olds 'sucking cigars!'. At first, he became so angered that he even uncharacteristically advocated that they be whipped and sent to bed. But he moderated his feeling against the children, who were after all merely victims of living in Boston's South End, redirecting it toward their parents who cruelly tried to raise their offspring in the city, where all children 'perish miserably'. He concluded the account with the generalisation that 'a true culture is more possible to the savage than to the boy . . . in a great city'.

The crude, rustic habitations of the Irish living in the vicinity of Concord offered Thoreau proof of his theory. Although, as we have seen, he often deplored the sty-like huts of the Irish, he just as frequently praised the positive influences exerted by the rural shanty on the quality of life. This paradoxical attitude comes into focus particularly in his descriptions of the Riordan hut, 'where human beings are lodged, literally, no better than pigs in a sty' (*J.*, 23 Aug. 1851, 2:419). Notwithstanding the wretched poverty everywhere evident within it, the natural setting of the Riordan cabin seems to have done its magic and produced two most remarkable children, Julia and Johnny. Accordingly, Thoreau perceived in the shanty a *natural* defence against charity and almshouses; the Riordan house suggested 'a certain wealth of nature, not poverty' (*J.*, 23 Aug. 1851, 2:420). In addition, it functioned as a wholesome locus of social warmth, for on Sundays the town Irish could escape to its sanctuary 'and stand in the doorway and so keep out the cold. One is not so cold among his brothers and sisters. What if there is less fire on the hearth, if there is more in the heart!' (*J.*, 8 Feb. 1852, 3:289). The simple rustic values of the

Riordan shanty led Thoreau to affirm that 'these Irish are not succeeding so ill after all' (*J*. 8 Feb. 1852, 3:289).

Because they were, like him in part, outsiders to Concord society who lived closer to the natural than to the artificial, Thoreau perceived grounds for praising many of Concord's rural Irish. He found in them a cluster of estimable values that revealed an overriding affinity with the 'natural'. One old unnamed Irishwoman especially attracted his enthusiasm. He described her at her 'shanty in the woods, sitting out on the hillside, bare-headed, in the rain and on the icy though thawing ground' — while he himself walked about in 'a greatcoat and under an umbrella' (*J*., 31 Dec. 1851, 3:166). Virtually undifferentiated from the revelations of nature that surrounded her, she lived in such proximity to the earth that 'she will not have to go far to be buried'; she seemed 'ready to flow down the slope with the running sand!'

As such, the old woman embodied for Thoreau the best qualities of the immigrant Irish, who were, he comments punningly, '*naturalising* themselves at a rapid rate' (my emphasis), threatening 'at last to displace the Yankees, as the latter have the Indians' (*J*., 31 Dec. 1851, 3:166). So favourably disposed was he at times that he once even happily fantasised that the town Irish, 'revelling in the genial Concord dirt' itself, should still reflect in 'their tanned and happy faces' 'my Walden wood and Fair Haven'.[15]

He was also intrigued by the evident Hibernian disposition of taking things as they come. Querying an Irishman about how many potatoes he could dig in a day, the latter replied that he did not keep an accounting: 'I scratch away, and let the day's work praise itself.' Impressed by the man's 'simple honesty', Thoreau wrote in his *Journal* that the reply marked 'the difference between the Irishman and the Yankee; the Yankee keeps an account'. He was still marvelling over the man's answer the next day: 'It was more pertinent than a scholar could have selected' (*J*., 24 and 25 Sept. 1851, 3:16–17, 19).

Canby maintained that Thoreau was fascinated by the Irish perversion of his own theory of leisure.[16] Often criticised for indolence and indifference to the Anglo-Saxon work ethic, the Irish would have attracted the interest of a man who himself objected to the economic and social busy-ness of his Yankee neighbours. More important to Thoreau were opportunities for achieving moments of meditative stillness. Notwithstanding Canby's suggestions, Thoreau clearly respected the hard-working Irish whom he met and heard of. We can see this in the number of remarks he made on the subject. As if to dispute the popular misconception of the Irish as slothful layabouts — although he himself, as in the instance of his assistant MacCarty, often associated shiftlessness with the Irish character — he pointedly stressed the tireless industriousness of Irishmen he had encountered. He meditated at length on the labours of an Irishman heroically 'wheeling home from far a large damp and rotten pine log for fuel', going on to imagine his efforts to split and dry the log before it can be used (*J*., 28 Feb. 1860, 13:169). Another exhausts himself with work and sacrifice to earn enough money to bring his family to America. Rising at 4.30 a.m., the man milks 28 cows, breakfasts 'without any milk in his tea and coffee' in order to toil 'day after day, for six and a half dollars a month'.[17] Still a third, Michael Flannery, he identified as 'the hardest-working man I know. Before sunrise and long after sunset he is taxing his unweariable muscles' (*J.*, 18 Nov. 1857, 10:187).

Despite lives of grinding drudgery, the Irish miraculously succeeded in preserving a native, childlike joy, a value Thoreau could not praise enough. There is, for example, something evocative of childlike curiosity, and wonder, too, in the glimpses he gave of Anne Karney and another Irishman looking for evidences of shamrocks in their new homeland and speculating on whether or not what Thoreau knew as the common white clover was the same (*J.*, 25 Apr. 1856, 8:311).

At least twice, he implied that their industriousness fostered in the Irish the innocent happiness he celebrated. Patrick Riordan — Thoreau had already commented on his arduous transporting of the faggots of wood he had gleaned in the neighbourhood (*J.*, 17 Feb. 1852, 3:308) — impressed Thoreau as cheerfully content to get his drinking water from a ditch by the railway.[18] More explicitly, Michael Flannery's Herculean struggles resulted 'in a singular cheerfulness. He is always in good spirits. He often overflows with his joy . . . his voice is really like that of a bird' (*J.*, 18 Nov. 1857, 10: 187).

Occasionally, however, Irish 'child-likeness' amused and baffled Thoreau. With a kind of Olympian wryness, he wrote of the terror the Irish held for all snakes and their longing for Ireland, 'where they say there is no venomous thing that can hurt you' (*J.*, 5 Aug. 1853, 5:354–5). And one February day, as he stood upon about two feet of ice 'drinking at a puddle', he

> was amused to see an Irish laborer . . . who had come down to drink, timidly tiptoeing toward me in his cowhide boots, lifting them nearly two feet at each step and fairly trembling with fear, as if the ice were already bending beneath his ponderous body and he were about to be engulfed. (*J.*, 4 Feb. 1857, 9:238)

But it was with unadulterated incredulity that he set down a further instance of this Irish mindset:

> when I came down-stairs this morning, it was raining hard and steadily, I found an Irishman sitting with his coat on his arm in the kitchen, waiting to see me. He wanted to inquire what I thought the weather would be to-day! (*J.*, 12 Aug. 1858, 11:94–5)

The undefiled perceptions and the joyful innocence of the Irish children, however, drew his inspired journalistic impulse the most.[19] Although he might view with ambivalent eye John Field's 'wrinkled and sibyl-like, crone-like infant . . . [a] young creature not knowing but it might be the last of a line of kings instead of John Field's poor starveling brat' (*J.*, 23 Aug. 1845, 1:383), his more characteristic reaction to the children was one of intense excitement and unqualified approval. He was himself filled with wonder that little Julia Riordan's promise had not been crushed under the 'squalid life' of her parents' shanty — she possessed such excellences, in fact, that even the genteel adults of Concord took 'an interest' in her (*J.*, 23 Aug. 1851, 2:419–20). But it was her brother, Johnny, who fascinated Thoreau's exploring mind the most.

In no less than three separate places in the *Journal*, Thoreau elaborated upon the character of 'little Johnny Riordan'.[20] In the most extended and exploratory of these, he stressed the abject poverty that engendered him, noting especially how Johnny refused to allow even the adversities of his pauper's rags, great distance (for a child), freezing weather and deep snow to prevent his walking along the railway tracks everyday to school, and 'there sit at the head of his bench' (*J.*, 28 Jan. 1852, 3:242, n.). Like John Field's 'sibyl-like, crone-like' infant, Johnny's face suggested to Thoreau a wisdom far beyond his five years — 'he revived to my mind the grave nobility and magnanimity of ancient heroes'; he was a boy 'who has the lore of worlds uncounted in his brain' (*J.*, 28 Jan. 1852, 3:243, n.). And although his perseverance begged comparison with such ancient heroes as 'Leonidas and his three hundred boys at the pass of Thermopylae', his heroism was far more deserving of praise: 'they dared but to die; he dares to live' — perhaps even knowing tragically that his destiny is to lead a life of economic serfdom:

I shall grow up
  And be a great man,
And shovel all day
  As hard as I can.
(*J.*, 28 Jan. 1852, 3:244, n.)

Contemplation of the boy's doomed innocence and joy drives Thoreau into a bitter attack upon social pretences and pseudo-charity. 'Our charitable institutions,' he declaims, 'are an insult to humanity, — a charity which dispenses the crumbs that fall from its overloaded tables! whose waste and whose example helped to produce that poverty!' (*J.*, 28 Jan. 1852, 3:244, n.). But he retreats from this negative tirade, finding final assurance in the present that Johnny

> is happy, is not puny, and has all the wonders of nature for his toys. Have I not faith that his tenderness will in some way be cherished and protected, as the buds of spring in the remotest wintry dell no less than in the garden and summer house?

The three journal passages on Johnny Riordan — each progressively longer and more detailed than the previous one — suggest that Thoreau might have been rewriting and revising in order to incorporate his meditation into his great prose work *Walden*. If so, it remains puzzling why he did not do so. Possibly, he recognised that his revisions had become overly sentimental, that he had not discovered the hard, chiselled prose necessary to render the material consistent with his purposes and style in *Walden*. Or possibly, he felt that much of what he said of Johnny Riordan's cheerful perseverance and natural innocence had already achieved cogent and more successful expression in his earlier portrait of the woodchopper, Alek Therien.[21]

He did, none the less, distil from the *Journal* two other passages recording his impressions of Irishmen. His sketches in *Walden* of Hugh Quoil and John Field significantly demonstrate how Thoreau reworked and integrated journal material into his work of art. But almost as importantly, perhaps, his final rendering of the two portraits reveals what in the Irish character, as he perceived it, could be made to serve his artistic purposes.

In all, four Irishmen figure importantly enough in the design of *Walden* to merit discussion here. The first two Thoreau encountered in the buying and transporting of his cabin. He acquired the original dwelling from 'James Collins, an Irishman who worked on the Fitchburg Railroad'.[22] Although reputed to be 'an uncommonly fine' cabin, Thoreau's inspection of it before its actual purchase disclosed several objectionable features. It was surrounded by a five-foot high earthen wall, 'as if it were a compost heap'; its roof boards were 'warped and made brittle by the sun'; it possessed 'a dirt floor for the most part, dank, clammy, and aguish'; its cellar was 'a sort of dust hole two feet deep'. None the less, seeing in the Irishman's shanty a good bargain, Thoreau purchased it from Collins for $4.25. The following day, as he approached to take formal possession, he met the Collins family on the road, fleeing creditors who might seek to collect, as Collins protested, 'certain indistinct but wholly unjust claims on the score of ground rent and fuel': 'One large bundle held their all, — bed, coffee-mill, looking-glass, hens, — all but the cat.'

After he disassembled the shack for removal to Walden Pond, Thoreau entrusted its carting to yet another Irishman, one Seely, who, according to 'a young Patrick', succeeded in making off with 'the still tolerable, straight, and drivable nails, staples, and spikes to his pocket', and then stood by guilelessly watching Thoreau begin the initial steps of reassembling.[23]

The Irish contrast with Thoreau's own ethics and aesthetics is pointed: (1) the Irish owner sells his sty-like shanty to Thoreau and, like a gypsy, flees down the road in the early morning to escape his creditors; and (2) the second Irishman pilfers from the materials painstakingly saved by Thoreau, who had entrusted him, moreover, to haul the same to the new location. If we take 'young Patrick' to be still a third Irishman, then we also have in the episode another hackneyed Irish role filling out the depictions of slovenliness, indebtedness and thievery, that of the informer on his own kind. These paragraphs, together with the pages where Thoreau details his transformation of the shanty into a dwelling ideally suited to his great experiment, suggest that he has rescued and vastly improved a structure associated with the worse aspects of the Irish immigrant character and succeeded certainly in translating it to a nobler purpose.

The figures of Hugh Quoil and John Field help us appreciate how carefully Thoreau adapted two Irish personalities recorded in his *Journal* to the precise demands of his great artistic work. Remarkable about Thoreau's handling of Hugh Quoil is the way he compressed four pages of his *Journal* into a single paragraph in the chapter 'Former Inhabitants; and Winter Visitors'.[24] Excised are the long passages detailing the consequences of Quoil's love of drinking — his unhealthy physical appearance, his attacks of delirium tremens, his lethargy, his mock-heroic, pathetic and somewhat drawn-out death in the dirt of the road at the foot of Brister's Hill (*J.*, 1845–7, 1:414–18). When Thoreau acknowledges these, it is by way of bare allusion and a few laconic statements. Missing also in *Walden* is the extended record of his one rather remarkable conversation with the Irishman.

To have preserved more than he did from the *Journal* would have undermined his purpose in 'Former Inhabitants'. In this section of the chapter, Thoreau provides brief, thumb-nail sketches of those who preceded him in the vicinity of his cabin. His intent is to stress the comparatively short duration of their sojourn, the impermanence of their achievements, the anonymity into which they might soon fall. Hugh Quoil, Irish veteran of Waterloo and Thoreau's immediate predecessor, rounds out the brief social spectrum of outcasts, Black slaves, drunkards and squatters who dug their cellar holes and wells, threw up their flimsy cabins and then died. Now, as Nature reclaims her desmesne, one can only detect the faintest traces of these former inhabitants — ' a dent in the earth . . . buried cellar stones . . . the well-dent'.[25] Presumably all of them failures of different sorts, these predecessors stand in thematic contrast to the hopeful newcomer Thoreau conceives himself to be. Contemplating the insignificance of human endeavour, he can only anticipate that the physical results of his experiment will succeed in enhancing 'the beauty of the landscape': 'Again, perhaps, Nature will try, with me for a first settler, and my house raised last spring to be the oldest in the hamlet.'[26]

If his use of the *Journal* passages on Hugh Quoil is remarkable for the way he pruned and trimmed them to accord with the elegiac emphasis of 'Former Inhabitants', his appropriation of the material on John Field is outstanding for the way he expanded and amplified the potential of the two pertinent journal pages to create one of the most thematically resonant episodes in *Walden* (J., 23 Aug. 1845, 1:383–4).

The Irishman who inhabits the middle of Thoreau's metaphysical myth of the unfolding of Consciousness is once again made to function as a foil for the persona of Thoreau himself, particularly the role he unfolds in this important, pivotal chapter.[27] Very possibly exploiting his reader's familiarity with the widespread commonplaces attached to the immigrant Irish, Thoreau particularises the backbreaking, paralysing serfdom imprisoning John Field and his family. His attitude is both critical and compassionate. Thus, John Field, although 'honest' and 'hard-working', is also 'shiftless'. 'He was discontented and wasted his life into the bargain.' Similarly, his bare-breasted wife toils away bravely at her stove, 'thinking to improve her condition one day'. But although her mop is never absent, 'no effects of it [are] visible any where'.[28]

Apparently, Field, his wife, 'their several children' (to say nothing of the chickens which 'stalked about the room like members of the family') were, like Thoreau, newcomers, for, escaping a rainstorm, he unexpectedly found them dwelling in a hut he had thought abandoned.[29] Field explained to Thoreau that he 'bogged' for

a neighboring farmer, turning up a meadow with a spade or bog hoe at the rate of ten dollars an acre and the use of the land with manure for one year, and his little broad-faced son worked cheerfully at his father's side the while, not knowing how poor a bargain the latter had made.[30]

Moved by their poverty and enslaving ignorance, and inspired by indications that they would like to 'improve [their] condition one day', Thoreau undertakes to help them, instructing Field in the essentials of Thoreauvian economics, but to no positive effect: 'the culture of an Irishman,' he concludes, 'is an enterprise to be undertaken with a sort of moral bog hoe.'[31] Abandoning the effort, Thoreau takes his leave, Field later joining him on the pond to fish. But even the instructional opportunities here go awry, for no matter how patiently Thoreau tries to teach him or even help him find a 'luckier' seat in the boat, poor fishing dogs the Irish bogger, while Thoreau catches 'a fair string'.

He concludes the chapter despairingly pronouncing John Field's Hibernian fate a cheerless one indeed:

> With his horizon all his own, yet he a poor man, born to be poor, with his inherited Irish poverty or poor life, his Adam's grandmother and boggy ways, not to rise in this world, he nor his posterity, till their wading webbed bog-trotting feet get *talaria* to their heels.[32]

What we have, then, in the middle of Thoreau's *magnum opus* is a portrait of an Irish labourer/farmer carefully shaped more or less in conformity with the prevailing expectations of Thoreau's audience. Certainly, commentators have expressed astonishment over Thoreau's severity with Field. Richard Bridgman, for example, finds that 'Baker Farm' reveals 'a bigotry and a megalomania in Thoreau that are difficult to credit'.[33] Supporting his assessment, Bridgman notes the telling contrast between Thoreau's puzzling offence over Field's use of worms for catching shiners which could in turn be used as bait for perch, and his later approval of a fisherman who employed the same technique to catch pickerel.[34]

More importantly, however, Thoreau centrally positions his description and short narrative to illuminate the mystical import of *Walden*: taken together, the two chapters 'The Ponds' and 'Baker Farm' function as an imagistic and thematic keystone in the work, for they stand in its exact centre, linking the earlier chapters, wherein Thoreau initiates his great experiment and search, with the later ones, in which he gives full resonant expression to the triumphant fulfilment of his mystical quest.[35]

In 'The Ponds', drifting on Walden alone during 'dark summer nights', angling for that Fish of fish, the speaker casts his line into the cosmic well of Walden and finds his heaven on earth as his consciousness expands and rises to embrace 'vast and cosmogonal themes in other spheres': 'it seemed as if I might next cast my line upward into the air, as well as downward into this element which was scarcely more dense. Thus I caught two fishes as it were with one hook.'[36]

Energised by this epiphany, Thoreau moves from the last of the first nine chapters to the first of the last group of nine, 'Baker Farm'. He is now one of the illuminated, one of the elect. As the visible sign of his transcendent consciousness, he perceives that he stands

> in the very abutment of a rainbow's arch, which filled the lower stratum of the atmosphere, tinging the grass and leaves around, and dazzling me as if I looked

through colored crystal. It was a lake of rainbow light, in which, for a short while, I lived like a dolphin.[37]

Physically, of course, it is impossible to stand within 'the abutment of a rainbow's arch', but the symbolic import should be evident enough — Thoreau's inner illumination has found its outward ratification in the natural order.

To ensure that his reader cannot ignore the significance of his achievement here, Thoreau further reinforces the scene's mythical emphasis with an analogous vignette. Walking along the railway causeway, 'I used to wonder at the halo of light around my shadow'. This phenomenon, universal and visible revelation of sanctity and cosmic awareness, encouraged Thoreau to fancy himself 'one of the elect'. Next, he subtly anticipates the narrative to follow by observing that a visitor once 'declared that the shadows of Irishmen before him had no halo about them'. Characteristically punning on the Latin etymology of the word *native*, which allows him to embrace notions of 'birth' and 'inborn' and even possibly to hint at 'rebirth', he relates that 'only natives . . . were so distinguished', i.e., set apart with haloes edging their shadows.[38]

Set thus before us in all his numinous splendour, Thoreau flees the thunderstorm and enters the sty-like shanty of John Field, immigrant Irishman.

As we have seen, the now-enlightened Seer of Walden Pond endeavours to instruct the 'honest, hard-working, but shiftless' labourer in the rudiments of Thoreauvian economics, necessary prelude to any spiritual soaring — 'I purposely talked to him as if he were a philosopher or desired to be one.' Finally conceding that he lacks the 'moral bog hoe' requisite for 'cultivating' the Irishman, he abandons the effort. The 'rainbow above the eastern woods', however, still promises him a fair evening after this set-back; so he takes his leave, but not without casting an inquisitive eye into John Field's well, the Irishman's analogue for Thoreau's cosmic well of Walden. Expectedly, he discovers there dismal reflections of mystical failure and defeat —'shallows and quicksands, and rope broken withal, and bucket irrecoverable'.[39]

In the fishing episode which concludes the chapter — symmetrically closing the circle that the brief 'cosmic' fishing narrative in 'The Ponds' had initiated — John Field confirms Thoreau's earlier estimation of him: hapless Irish immigrant that he is, the bogger remains entrapped by his 'derivative old-country mode', sadly lacking the spiritual wings essential to any transcendental flight of consciousness. Rather, John Field, with his 'Irish poverty' and 'boggy ways' is fated not 'to rise in this world, he nor his posterity, till their wading webbed bog-trotting feet get *talaria* to their heels'.

Notes

1. Henry Seidel Canby, *Thoreau*, Houghton, Mifflin Co., Boston, 1939, pp. 11 and 361.
2. Frank Buckley, 'Thoreau and the Irish', *The New England Quarterly*, 13, 1940, pp. 389–400.

3. George E. Ryan, 'Shanties and shiftlessness: the immigrant Irish of Henry Thoreau', *Éire-Ireland*, 13, 1978, pp. 54–78.

4. See, for example, Milton Meltzer and Walter Harding, *A Thoreau profile*, The Thoreau Foundation, Concord, Mass., 1976, pp. 107–8; and Mary Elkins Moller, *Thoreau in the human community*, University of Massachusetts Press, Amherst, Mass., 1980, pp. 175–81, and *passim*.

5. *The journal of Henry D. Thoreau*, ed. Bradford Torrey and Francis H. Allen, Houghton Mifflin Co., Boston, 1906; reissued, with a new foreword, by Walter Harding, Dover Publications, Inc., New York, 1962, 2 vols., 3:135. (Subsequent references to the *Journal* will be documented within the text parenthetically with the abbreviation *J.*, and the volume numbers given will follow the designated 1–14 numbering of the original journals, substituting Arabic for their Roman numerals.)

6. Thoreau to H. G. O. Blake, 19 Dec. 1853, *The correspondence of Henry David Thoreau*, ed. Walter Harding and Carl Bode, New York University Press, New York, 1958, p. 311.

7. For a discussion of anti-Irish sentiment in Massachusetts during this period, see George W. Potter, *To the Golden Door: the story of the Irish in Ireland and America*, Little, Brown, Boston, 1960, especially pp. 462–73.

8. Emerson, *The journals and miscellaneous notebooks of Ralph Waldo Emerson*, ed. Ralph Orth and Alfred R. Ferguson, Belknap Press of Harvard University Press, Cambridge, Mass., 1977, 13:112, 464, 141.

9. See Nathaniel Hawthorne, *The American notebooks*, ed. Randall Stewart, Yale University Press, New Haven, 1932, pp. 5, 7, 10, 12, for these and similar remarks.

10. Ryan, 'Shanties and shiftlessness', p. 60.

11. Cited by Ryan, 'Shanties and shiftlessness', p. 61.

12. See Ryan, 'Shanties and shiftlessness', pp. 60–4.

13. See Buckley, 'Thoreau and the Irish', p. 392

14. Canby also comments on the parallel: 'the Irish immigrants [of Concord] were also a society apart, substituting for the Negroes further south', *Thoreau*, p. 11.

15. Thoreau to Emerson, 17 Oct. 1843, *Correspondence*, p. 146.

16. Canby, *Thoreau*, p. 11.

17. Thoreau to Blake, 19 Dec. 1853, *Correspondence* p. 312.

18. Thoreau, *J.*, 14 Apr. 1852, 3:410. Conversely, when the shiftless Hugh Quoil drinks from a ditch, Thoreau roundly condemns him; see *J*, 1845–47, 1:415.

19. In contrast, his bewildered anger on beholding the cigar-smoking twelve-year old boys registered his recognition of great human potential being destroyed by parental cruelty. See Thoreau, *J.*, 25 July 1851, 2:341–2.

20. Thoreau, *J.*, 28 Nov. 1850, 2:116–18; 22 Dec. 1851, 3:149–50; and 28 Jan. 1852, 3:242–4, n.

21. See Thoreau, 'Visitors', *The variorum 'Walden'*, ed. Walter Harding, Twayne Publishers, Inc., New York, 1962, pp. 129–33. For the *Journal* material on Therien, see 14 July 1845, 1:365–7; 24 Dec. 1853, 5:23–4; and 29 Dec. 1853, 5:35–6.

22. Thoreau, 'Economy', *Walden*, ed. Harding, pp. 53–4. Of James Collins, Harding notes the following: 'there is no James Collins listed in the *Concord Vital Records*. But there is a family, now residents of Lowell, Mass., who claim to be descendants of this Collins' (p. 276, n. 113).

23. Thoreau, 'Economy', *Walden*, ed. Harding, p. 54. Possibly, Seeley is the same as the William Seley noted by Harding (*Walden*, p. 276, n. 114).

24. Thoreau, 'Former inhabitants; and winter visitors', *Walden*, ed. Harding, pp. 215–16. F. B. Sanborn says of Quoil that 'he was probably named Cahill in Ireland; he

may have been a sergeant at Waterloo — certainly not a colonel' (*Walden, or life in the woods*, Houghton, Mifflin, Boston, 1909, II, n. 160).

25. Thoreau, *The variorum 'Walden'*, p. 216.
26. Thoreau, *Walden*, ed. Harding, p. 217.
27. Thoreau, 'Baker Farm', *Walden*, ed. Harding, pp. 171–6.
28. 'Baker Farm', *Walden*, ed. Harding, p. 173.
29. In contrast with his journalistic rendering of Julia and Johnny Riordan, Thoreau develops here a description of the newest born of John Field's children: 'the wrinkled, sibyl-like, cone-headed infant . . . sat upon its father's knee as in the palaces of nobles, and looked out from its home in the midst of wet and hunger inquisitively upon the stranger, with the privilege of infancy, not knowing but it was the last of a noble line, and the hope and cynosure of the world, instead of John Field's starveling brat' ('Baker Farm', *Walden*, ed. Harding, p. 173). The child was probably the Mary Field recorded in the Vital Records of Lincoln as being born in May 1844 to 'John, Irish laborer, and Mary' (see Harding (ed.), *Walden*, p. 302, n. 12).
30. Thoreau, 'Baker Farm', *Walden*, ed. Harding, pp. 173–4.
31. Thoreau, 'Baker Farm', *Walden*, ed. Harding, p. 174. For a discussion of Thoreau's failure in his new role of teacher in this episode, see E. Arthur Robinson, 'Thoreau's buried short story', *Studies in Short Fiction*, 1, 1964, pp. 16–20; and Moller, *Thoreau in the human community*, pp. 175–81.
32. Thoreau, 'Baker Farm', *Walden*, ed. Harding, p. 176. Thoreau here alludes to the winged golden sandals, or *talaria*, given by Zeus to his son Hermes (or Mercury). One of Hermes' special powers was to serve Zeus as his herald and, more generally, as divine messenger. The winged sandals provided him with the swiftness needed to execute his tasks. In 'Baker Farm' Thoreau seems to modify the image by implying that the wings sprout from the heels, the symbolic product of spiritual evolution. More pointedly, Thoreau suggests that John Field's dull soul will never enjoy the transcendental flight promised by the *talaria*.

   Throughout *Walden*, Thoreau's association of his persona with the god Hermes merits exploration. As god of liars and thieves; as inventor of musical instruments, the musical scale and astronomy; as divine messenger, foreteller of the future and guide of the dead; and as deviser of the alphabet, Hermes provides Thoreau with a fertile cluster of associations useful in developing *Walden*'s themes. Perhaps as important as his being used by Thoreau to imply transcendental flight is Hermes' identity as seer and the herald who communicates divine judgment. Thus, at the conclusion of 'Baker Farm' Thoreau/Hermes announces the unhappy fate of John Field and his kin, actual and ethnic.
33. Richard Bridgman, *Dark Thoreau*, Lincoln University Press, Lincoln and London, 1982, p. 105.
34. See Thoreau, 'The pond in Winter', *The variorum 'Walden'*, p. 231.
35. Lawrence E., Scanlon, 'Thoreau's parable of Baker Farm', *Emerson Society Quarterly*, 47, 1967, pp. 19–21; and Stuart Woodruff, 'Thoreau as Water-Gazer: "The Ponds"', *Emerson Society Quarterly*, 47, 1967, pp. 16–17, discuss the structural and thematic centrality of these chapters. Scanlon's interpretation of Baker Farm as a 'parable of the fall of man' is especially suggestive.
36. Thoreau, 'The Ponds', *Walden*, ed. Harding, pp. 152–3.
37. Thoreau, 'Baker Farm', *Walden*, ed. Harding, p. 172.

38. Thoreau, 'Baker Farm', *Walden*, ed. Harding. Mario D'Avanzo, 'John Field's well: the Biblical context', *Massachusetts Studies in English*, 8, 1982, pp. 4–8, discusses the Biblical allusions of the well.
39. Thoreau, 'Baker Farm', *Walden* ed. Harding, p. 175. For the symbolic function of Walden as a cosmic well and of fishing as a meditation, see Woodruff, 'Thoreau as Water-Gazer'.

3 The Irish joke

Patrick O'Sullivan

The Irish joke. Yes, yes, we do. And there comes a point when anyone who thinks that humour is important (I do not say, takes humour seriously) begins to look systematically at explanations of humour.

And discovers that there is something profoundly unsatisfactory about theories of humour.[1] There is the recurring assumption that seriousness is the norm from which humour is deviation. There is the problem of under and over-prediction — one theorist, Christopher Wilson, notes that theories 'failed to describe some instances of the humorous, and with embarrassing predictive richness described many instances of the non-humorous'.[2] And then there is the starting-point for the series of thoughts presented in this chapter: the way that humorous material, funny stories, jokes are presented as evidence in a curiously casual way, without regard for their history, provenance or status as artefacts of human culture. I suggest here that, whatever theory of humour we adopt, a less casual approach to jokes is called for.

An aspect of this casualness, which causes bafflement and distress (but which ultimately raises valuable questions) is the often cackhanded way jokes are presented. One historian of comedy takes Arthur Koestler to task for Koestler's massacre of the Oedipus-Schmoedipus joke.[3] Another, with unerring leadenness, finds the worst form of the Calvin-Coolidge-is-dead-joke.[4]

Freud clearly enjoyed jokes, especially Jewish jokes, made notes of examples, and, partly as light relief from *Three Essays on the Theory of Sexuality*, presented his examples with analysis and, in his terms, consequent theory in *Jokes and Their Relation to the Unconscious*.[5] In fact, as Leach notes, most of Freud's illustrative material usually involves *puns*, though the puns are presented within a narrative.[6] Freud's analysis teases out the association of ideas and the meanings of words involved within the pun. There are problems for the translator.[7]

Some jokes, some of Freud's narratives, offer no entry point for such analysis. Freud spends two pages on the anecdote about Heine's 'Golden Calf' witticism — noting that certain elements of the narrative must occur in this form, in this sequence, otherwise Heine will not be able to make his joke. Freud continues,

> It is a pity that this fine example involves such complicated technical conditions. We can arrive at no clarification of it. So we will leave it and look for another one in which we seem to detect an internal kinship with its predecessor . . . It is one of the bath jokes which treat of the Galician Jews aversion to baths.[8]

As Ken Dodd said, 'The trouble with Freud is that he never played the Glasgow Empire on a Saturday night.'[9] For it is clear that whatever conclusion the theorist is aiming at — Freud on the unconscious, Koestler on creativity, Leach on taboo, and so on — the illustrative material, the joke, has an independent existence, a prior existence as a piece of narrative, indeed as a piece of *oral* narrative. For the most part Freud *heard* the jokes and wrote them down — even his literary anecdotes had a prior existence in the oral world.

Freud's analysis of the 'complicated technical conditions' of the Heine anecdote is an analysis of narrative. He notices, and is intrigued by, plot points, revelations, disclosures — the elements of a story and the way it is told that make the story work. If Aunt Rose had found the infant Oliver Twist the day after he was born would Fagin, Sykes and Nancy have lived happily ever after — or would they have found another doom? Dickens keeps much explanatory material from his reader, to dramatic effect — if he had, early in the narrative, simply explained Monks' malevolent interest in young Oliver would that interest appear quite so sinister?

The suggestion within this chapter is that the study of jokes as pieces of narrative might be productive, and that that study might better draw on the insights of literary criticism and related fields.[10] 'Nature, not art, makes us all story-tellers,' says Barbara Hardy.[11] This chapter tries to get past the question of the *use* made of jokes to the jokes themselves, what they are and how they work, before returning, with increased knowledge, to the question of use.[12]

Jokes: a psychological approach

Wilson ultimately feels that, despite the incongruities he has analysed, there is 'unsuspected common ground between humour theories — many seem to describe the humorous as stimulation which presents an incongruity that induces cognitive disequilibrium'. He then suggests a 'cognitive balance' model: the incongruity is 'rapidly resolved' and the end result 'is neutral — having no further implications for thought or behaviour'.[13]

This unsatisfactory 'synthesis' seems in part to derive from a too close acceptance of Berlyne's distinction between the humorous and the aesthetic.[14] What is not clear, from Wilson's analysis at this stage, is the answer to the question: When do we laugh? Do we laugh at the incongruous or do we laugh at the resolution of incongruity? Later, reporting on experimenters who have attempted to tackle this question, Wilson suggests that 'the resolution of incongruity is amusing'. 'However, amusement may be evoked in the absence of resolution.'[15] At this point it may be sufficient to suggest that Wilson, like the theorists he criticises, is trying to capture too many different sorts of human behaviour within the net of one explanation. There is the laugh of puzzlement and the laugh of discovery.

A less substantial piece of work within the disciplines of psychology offers a better way forward: Suls' 'A Two-Stage Model for the Appreciation of Jokes . . .' In essence Suls offers a flow chart analysis, borrowed from the General Problem Solver of Newell and Simon. The appreciation of a joke involves a two-stage process:

1. the perceiver finds expectations about a text disconfirmed by the ending — the punch-line;
2. the perceiver then searches for and finds a cognitive rule which makes the punch-line follow from the main part of the joke, and he reconciles the incongruous parts.

'A cognitive rule is defined as a logical proposition, a definition, or a fact of experience'. 'Humour derives from experiencing a sudden incongruity which is then made congruous.' So that, for formal jokes, Suls is presenting an explicit congruity theory — laughter is resolution. Implicit in Suls' approach is the suggestion that 'the perceiver', the person who hears the joke, has to work, and may have to invent a new 'cognitive rule' in order to resolve the joke. There is a hint that personal growth might be involved.

Note in Suls' theory the importance of the punch line. But, inevitably, elements within Suls' own illustrative material, his jokes, resist him. We find this:

> O'Riley was on trial for armed robbery. The Jury came out and announced, 'Not Guilty'. 'Wonderful', said O'Riley, 'does that mean I can keep the money?'

Suls goes through the process of finding a cognitive rule that can reconcile this incongruity. It is a long process. 'But do people go through this elaborate processing when they hear a joke and laugh? . . . We suggest that the processing works at a rapid rate.'

And this is his resolution. 'O'Riley's question points out that courts make mistakes, that legal truth and actual truth do not always correspond, and that legal truth determines consequences. In short, O'Riley can keep the money since, by law, he did not steal it.'[16]

But why is this man called O'Riley?

Jokes: a semiotic approach

Suls says of his model, 'The model involves some of the same psychological processes used in reading and listening since a person must obviously read or hear a joke to appreciate it. We emphasize this rather obvious point because some basic strategies of reading and listening are essential to the model proposed.'[17]

He seems to have the notion that reading and listening are unproblematic processes. The philosophical problems within that notion are outlined, succinctly, by Godzich in 'Caution! Reader at Work!'[18] ('Once upon a time we all thought we knew how to read . . .') and the insights of semiotics are presented in a very accessible form by Norrman and Haarberg. For our purposes it also helps that Norrman and Haarberg's book is very, very funny.

Norrman and Haarberg offer a method by which we can accurately detect and analyse what Freud calls 'internal kinship' between jokes. Commenting on the interplay between the literary branch of French structuralism and the anthropological branch, Norrman and Haarberg quote Lévi-Strauss who 'says that he attempts to show not how men think in myths but "comment les mythes se pensent dans les hommes, et à leur insu" . . .' — how myths think in men, and unbeknownst to them.[19]

It must be said, at this stage, that the ghost of Lévi-Strauss lurks deep within any theory of semiotics — and there are problems (problems which this chapter does not attempt to resolve). But for de Man these very problems give literature a privileged place within the human sciences: 'Lévi-Strauss, in order to protect the rationality of his science, had to come to the conclusion of a myth without an author . . .' However, 'Lévi-Strauss' suppression of the subject is perfectly legitimate as an attempt to protect the scientific status of ethnology; by the same token, however, it leads directly into the larger question of the ontological status of the self. From this point on, a philosophical anthropology would be inconceivable without the consideration of literature as a primary source of knowledge.'[20]

Are jokes (short, humorous, oral narratives) literature? Semiotics as such would create no hierarchy of 'texts'. Scholes begins his semiotic study with an analysis of advertisements on billboards and hoardings.[21] An aside of Riffaterre's gives the joke considerable status: '. . . the durability of even [sic] the oral joke, the first, unsigned text, reminds us that a mere [sic again] joke is an elementary form of literature, since it is as lasting, and as protected against tampering when quoted, as a more highbrow text'.[22]

Riffaterre's suggestion that jokes are 'protected against tampering' links, of course, with Freud's interest in the mechanics of anecdote, and in turn suggests a very simple way that jokes can have their own integrity, independent of a particular social presentation.

And Scholes, echoing Eco, encourages us: 'As semiotic interpreters we are not free to *make* meaning, but we are free to *find* it by following the various semantic, syntactic, and pragmatic paths that lead away from the words of the text.'[23]

Irish jokes: a racist approach

There is something profoundly unsatisfactory about much comment on 'Irish jokes'.[24] For Wilson 'Irish jokes' are a subcategory of racial humour, which itself is explained by 'consistent evidence that people deride their status, social or power subordinates behind their backs'. 'Characteristically, themes of racial humour bypass genuine ethnic features and ascribe common features of inferiority to several minority groups' — and he suggests that racial humour bolsters and defends the supremacy of the majority 'by indicating a correspondence of inferiority and minority'.[25]

Leaving aside the question of what exactly a 'genuine ethnic feature' might look like and leaving aside this very loose use of the terms 'minority' and 'majority' — Wilson is, in fact, discussing American WASP use of Negro, Irish and Jewish jokes (and Polish, Italian and Swedish jokes?) — Wilson must immediately face the problem of what he calls 'self-ridicule'. Jews enjoy telling 'Jewish jokes', Negroes enjoy telling 'anti-Negro jokes', and the Irish tell 'Irish jokes'. Wilson's analysis uses some elements of the 'licensed fool' or clown concept, and is couched entirely in terms of social relationships in the recent past or in the present.

Wilson notes in passing: 'There is a clear analogy between American racial humour and English social humour. "Punch", a geriatric English humorous magazine, sold itself in the last century and entertained its middle and upper class readership by ridiculing servants and other members of the lower classes, for their supposed stupidity, ugliness and social inadequacy.'[26] But he takes this no further.

Wilson quotes two (unpublished) papers by A. M. O'Donnell — 'O'Donnell states that the Irish ridicule themselves in the same terms as they are ridiculed by the English — as very stupid beyond the call of idiocy. There is a distinction to be drawn, though, because, according to O'Donnell, the Irish are much better than the English at deriding Gaelic intelligence.'[27] (I take this — referring back to the opening paragraph of this chapter — to mean that the Irish tell better jokes or are better at telling jokes.) Wilson finds a social class explanation — 'Lace curtain' Irish look down on 'shanty' Irish.

Much support will be found in the letters column of newspapers and journals for the assertion that 'Irish jokes' are racist in themselves — for example in *New Society*, 10 January 1980: 'The anti-Irish joke . . . is really a form of racism. Such ethnic humour tells us little about the intelligence of the Irish but tells us a great deal about the reactionary prejudices of many Anglo-Saxon Protestants.'

That particular correspondent had written to praise an article by Edmund Leach, an article which took as its starting-point 'Irish Joke Books' bought at W. H. Smith's bookshop on Charing Cross Station. Leach denies Wilson's and O'Donnell's observation that the Irish tell 'Irish jokes', but notes with approval that Jews do tell 'Jewish jokes' — 'They are an expression of international Jewish cultural solidarity, and they are often very clever. "Irish" jokes are, in every respect, just the reverse.' The stupidity of the jokes and the characters in them flatters the reader. 'The ethnic element in "Irish" jokes is thus latently racist. It would make no sense at all to substitute "Jew" for "Irishman".'[28]

At the end of this very problematic analysis Leach asserts, but in a very coded way, that the Irish do not even merit insult in their own right — 'Irish' in the joke books is code for 'Pakistani' or 'West Indian'.[29]

In the *written* forms of the jokes that Leach analyses the language is indeed ill-considered and the structure disorganised — and Leach rightly complains. But part, at least, of the problem with both Leach's and Wilson's analysis of 'Irish jokes' is that they themselves seem to be at the same time too protective and too protected. They are protective about what they call 'immigrants' or 'minorities' — that is, that part of the world's population that is not White, Anglo-Saxon and Protestant. And they are protected, in that they never seem to have heard, for example, 'WASP' or 'English' jokes, or the jokes that Australians tell about 'Pommies'.[30]

And they have not come across Vivian Mercier's account of why the Irish of the seventeenth century found English surnames irresistibly funny.[31] Their analysis is too culture specific. Within Wilson's own material more productive analyses are available — it might be thought, for instance, that, given the unavoidable intimacy of the North West European Archipelago (the British

Isles, if you will) an inter-clan teasing model might pay dividends. And that the theme of 'unavoidable intimacy' might in turn need analysing.

Jokes: a historical approach

It might be felt that what is lacking in all the approaches outlined so far is a sense of history. We read or hear a joke or anecdote and we think, I've heard this before. But where?

An admittedly very slight book, by the American historian Ray Ginger, seems to have no awareness of the fact that specific jokes or anecdotes move through history attaching themselves to appropriate historical figures, and seems to have no awareness of the history of the jokes themselves. Ginger does have sections on 'ethnic' jokes — Jewish jokes, black jokes, Norwegian/Swedish jokes, Polish, Italian, Scots and Irish jokes. Thus, Poles are dirty and stupid, Italians are cowardly, Scots are 'covetous' (he clearly means 'mean'), and the Irish are very stupid.

Ginger links the emergence of 'Irish' jokes with the arrival of great numbers of illiterate Irish peasants in North America in the 1840s and 1850s. To explain the appearance of 'Polish' jokes he postulates the existence of some very clever, but irritated, Irish jokesters — reacting to the Polish migrations.[32]

The 'Polish' jokes, of course, at once remind us of Freud and the Galician Jews. It is perfectly clear and unsurprising that jokes about dirtiness existed prior to and independently of any contact between American WASPs, Irish and Poles, and indeed prior to and independently of the existence of Poland. Similarly, jokes about cowardice, meanness and stupidity existed prior to and independently of the existence of Italy, Scotland or Ireland as the homes of identified ethnic groups, as states, or as states of mind.

Thus, concentrating on 'Irish jokes', very considerable sections of both Thompson's *Motif: Index of Folk Literature* and Propp's *Morphology of the Folktale* describe 'stupid person' jokes and stories. Norrman and Haarberg following Thompson refer to them as 'numbskull' jokes. Grotjahn, recalling his Viennese childhood, calls them 'Little Moron' jokes, linking them with 'Graf Bobby' jokes.[33]

Neuberg, in his history of popular literature in England, describes the 'jest books' of the sixteenth and seventeenth centuries (the ancestors of the books Leach found at Charing Cross Station). In unproblematic terms Neuberg shows how 'a number of European countries provided subject matter for jestbooks' — the jokes had no difficulty crossing linguistic boundaries. And Neuberg notes 'the tendency to gather groups of anecdotes round a central character, real or imaginary, and to relate them to a background familiar to the reader'. Thus a tale of Howleglas might just as well be told of Skelton (the impudent but cowardly poet) or Tarleton (the clown). There is, as Norrman and Haarberg point out, a tendency for symbols to cluster.

Howleglas (Till Eulenspiegel in continental Europe), 'whose literary origins are to be found in Marcolfus, the mythical jester at King Solomon's court', is presented within the jest books of the sixteenth century as a real person who lived in the fourteenth century. 'In the character of a Saxon peasant he delights in playing the fool by following instructions absolutely literally, or by making some witty reply.' A niggardly baker refuses him a candle to work by, saying he can sift flour by moonlight — in mock obedience Howleglas throws the flour out the window. Howleglas sides with apprentices against masters — his butts are craftsmen, employers of labour, clergymen and innkeepers.[34]

By the end of the sixteenth century some of the Howleglas stories have changed, smoothly, into 'The Pleasant Conceits of Old Hobson, The Merry Londoner'. Hobson, who was indeed a real person, a haberdasher who died in 1581, is shown tricking or catching out his thieving, skiving servants. By the same token, similar material is used by Deloney with a town and country dichotomy — the city slicker gulls the simple countryman.[35]

It might be wondered, are there similar figures within Irish folklore and literature? Is there an Irish Eulenspiegel? Luckily we now have the work of James Doan on Cearbhall O'Dalaigh, trickster and poet of Irish oral tradition. And many of the very same stories that are considered by this chapter appear in collections like Henry Glassie's *Irish Folk Tales*.[36]

Neuberg, describing the (written) sources of Howleglas and other stories, mentions Poggio Bracciolini (1380–1459), Poggio the Florentine, who, about 1420, compiled a book of humorous tales — 'the near universality of these themes seems to suggest that the culture of Europe possessed a much greater unity in the sixteenth century than it does today'. This mis-states the case, and ultimately misses the point. Thompson describes one particular 'stupid person' story that is found over large parts of Asia, Europe and in the southern part of the United States.[37]

For it is further clear that these jokes exist prior to, and, to a great extent, independently of any one particular written presentation, and are just as widespread today as they were in Poggio's time or in Hobson's time. The French tell 'stupid person' jokes about the Belgians (nicknamed 'Les Frites'), the Canadians tell them about the people of Newfoundland ('Newfies).[38] The people of Scotland tell them about the inhabitants of Forfar, an otherwise unremarkable and pleasant town to the north of Dundee.[39] The connecting theme here seems to be geographic marginality — the group round whom the stories are, or have, collected are far from the centre of metropolitan culture. This is the town and country dichotomy again.

There is a subcategory of Jewish jokes, Chelm stories, part of the oral culture of the *stetl* — 'Chelm is a legendary town, whose inhabitants are known all over the world for their stupidity'.[40] The English and the American WASPs tell these jokes about the Irish. The Irish tell them about themselves and, within Ireland, about the people of Kerry, and indeed all the creatures of Kerry.[41] Fortunately I do not now have to take this catalogue further, and I can be satisfied here with the examples that have caught my eye. For the considered work of Christie Davies is now available and can be built on.[42]

The 'stupid person' and the 'Holy Fool'

This chapter keeps the descriptive tag 'stupid person' for the jokes, and does not adopt some ready-made character name, 'Howleglas', or group name, 'the Irish', because a term of absolute transparency is required for its analysis. But it is clear by now that a character or group name is a semiotic and narrative requirement. The tautological formulation, 'The stupid person did this stupid thing', does not work and is not funny. Narrative technique requires that for 'stupid person' be substituted some name or term, *not* a synonym, and that name or term must carry with it a particular collection of associations.

At the same time the formulation, 'Howleglas did this stupid thing', will not work and is not funny. Central to the 'stupid person' joke is the suggestion not that the stupid person has misunderstood but that he *has* understood in a 'wrong' way, that is in a different way, either deliberately or by accident. And thus, either deliberately or by accident, by his misunderstanding/understanding, the stupid person has demonstrated that there *is* a different way. Inevitably some of these jokes fell into Freud's net and, with his usual perspicacity, he noted that they deserved a 'special position'. 'What they are attacking is not a person or an institution but the certainty of our knowledge itself.'[43]

It is for this reason, of course, that the *same* jokes are told about the 'Holy Fool'. I borrow the term 'Holy Fool' from histories of the Greek and Russian Orthodox Churches, within whose traditions the Holy Fool has a central place that he has not found within Western Christianity.[44]

The Holy Fool is found also in China and Japan, among the Ch'an and Zen masters: one such, Ryokwan, bears a name which means 'Great Fool'. Hyers, in *Zen and the Comic Spirit*, explores the central place of humour in Zen teaching and teaching methods, formalised in the enigmatic *koans* (test cases) and *mondos* (dialogues). 'D. T. Suzuki has argued that "Zen is the only religion or teaching that finds room for laughter." Though in relation to other religions this is, no doubt, an overstatement, in relation to Zen it is more of an understatement. For Zen does more than find room for laughter — which might, after all, mean only a very small and rarely occupied room at the back of the house. In a unique sense, the house of Zen *is* the house of laughter.'[45]

Hyers continues, 'R. H. Blyth, with his penchant for lashing comment and characterisation, has defined the essence of Zen as humour'. Indeed, Blyth, the amiable if erratic interpreter of Japanese literature and culture, makes very great claims for humour, as he defines it: '"Humour" means joyful, unsentimental pathos that arises from the paradox inherent in the nature of things.' 'Humour is laughing at all things; in Buddhist parlance seeing, "all things are empty in their self-nature" . . . and rejoicing in this truth.' Humour is a mode of apprehending reality, and there are aspects of reality that can only be apprehended humorously.

Blyth goes on: '. . . if we ask a Japanese if he himself has a sense of humour, he will say no. This is not merely modesty, but the result of a feeling that a sense of humour is too deep, too unconscious, too unintellectual a thing to be intellectually asserted.'[46]

Hyers describes 'the extensive corpus of Zen anecdotes', very often ending with the phrase 'And the monk (or master) clapped his hands and gave a loud roar of laughter'. 'Catharsis and wisdom' are achieved. We, of course, are reminded of Suls' 'Two-stage Model for the Appreciation of Jokes . . .' And there is an explicit quarrel with Wilson's suggestion that, once resolved, the joke has 'no further implications for thought or behaviour'.

The Zen masters described in the anecdotes, and the Zen masters who use the anecdotes as teaching aids, mount an assault on rigid and conventional thinking, on legalistic definitions of reality enforced by the powerful. The anecdotes are presented, in anthologies such as that compiled by Reps, with a thick veneer of pious reverence — none the less within the anecdotes can be discerned the 'stupid person' jokes analysed by this chapter.[47]

In a scathing attack on the pretensions of Zen, Arthur Koestler suggested that Zen, with its formalised techniques, is simply a way of reintroducing some spontaneity and creativity into the rigid and authoritarian Japanese culture. Similarly, Enid Welsford, in her study of *The Fool*, sees the jester/sage as precariously surviving within Islam from pre-Islamic Arab culture in such figures as Abu Daloma (the cowardly, obsequious poet) and Nasr-ed-Din.[48] Again there is the suggestion of a counterbalance within a dogmatic, authoritarian culture.

Nasr-ed-Din, or Nasrudin, and the Sufis are given even greater significance by Idries Shah. Sufism is the secret teaching within all religions. And the stories, the 'stupid person' jokes that have collected or are collected around the character of the Mulla ('Master') Nasrudin are one of the means by which this teaching is passed on. Idries Shah tells how the 'Old Villain' made Nasrudin a figure of fun, but a virtuous teacher rescued him, pouring into Nasrudin 'the Sufi power which interpenetrates the nominal significance of meaning. Henceforth all the stories about Nasrudin became works of "independent" art. They could be understood as jokes, they had a metaphysical meaning; they were infinitely complex and partook of a nature of completion and perfection which had been stolen from human consciousness by the vitiating activities of the Old Villain.'[49]

Idries Shah notes in passing that stories from the Nasrudin cycle appear in *Don Quixote* and in the *Fables* of Marie of France.[50] He analyses the Zen story of the apple, and shows that a Zen master has got hold of a Nasrudin tale, but has not got it quite right.[51] And Idries Shah tells us that, by some accounts, Nasrudin was a real person, who died in 386 (Islamic chronology) and who is buried in Turkey — where festivals in his honour are held. Such details have, for Idries Shah, mystic, symbolic meaning.

Be that as it may, the Nasrudin stories are the finest collection of 'stupid person' or 'Irish' jokes in the world. It must be emphasised again that these are the *same* stories. All the favourite stories and themes are here: searching in the wrong place, smuggling donkeys, and the mysteries of reading and writing.[52] Nasrudin is presented as exploring, sometimes by accident, sometimes in abject cowardice and sometimes in a very assertative way, the nature of power and dogmatic definitions of reality.[53]

> The King was fed up with everyone telling him lies all the time. He caused a gallows to be erected at the city gate and ordered that everyone who came to the gate should be asked a question — if the person answered truthfully he should be let pass, if he answered untruthfully he was to be hanged.
>
> Nasrudin approached the gate. 'Tell me where you are going,' said the Captain of the Guard, 'and, remember, you must answer truthfully, or else . . .'
>
> Nasrudin said, 'I am going to be hanged on that gallows . . .'

The suggestion that jokes might contain wisdom seems not in itself so extraordinary — after all Freud suggests as much, and both he and Grotjahn spend much time analysing the 'wisdom' they find in jokes like, 'A wife is like an umbrella — in the end you always get a cab'.[54] But these are examples of men coming to jokes and finding therein, as 'wisdom', something they already believed to be true, and a truth they had arrived at independently of the jokes. Jokes can be used to confirm beliefs. What is remarkable about the 'Holy Fool' jokes, the Zen anecdotes, the Nasrudin stories, is the suggestion that the wisdom they contain or express is 'new', or difficult, or uncomfortable. They upset.

Stupidity and power

The jokes clearly suffer sea changes as they move through different cultures and are welcomed with greater or lesser degrees of reverence, affection or disdain. Zen versions are presented very piously (though versions from Japanese popular culture show greater gusto), Nasrudin stories with great good humour, Howleglas stories have an element of savagery.

But there is a continuity, and we can readily build a mosaic picture of the type of personality portrayed by the stories. This personality questions authority and legalistic definitions of reality. It questions power, usually from a position of powerlessness. This personality questions power and protects itself from the powerful by using techniques such as over-literal interpretation of instructions, by understanding or misunderstanding in a very typical 'stupid person' way.

We responded to the jokes by saying, But I've heard this before. Of this personality we say, But I've seen this before — and in the real world. We look, for example, at Elkins' description of the slave personality, the 'Sambo stereotype', but, better still, the critique of Elkins' thesis by Genovese, who finds Elkins' limiting of the stereotype to one phase of slavery highly unsatisfactory: 'On close inspection the Sambo personality turns out to be neither more nor less than the slavish personality; wherever slavery has existed, Sambo has also'.[55]

But Genovese widens the argument, he does not use a legalistic definition of slavery. He quotes Frances Perroux, he quotes Marcuse's definition of slavery, 'la réduction de l'homme à l'état de chose' — the reduction of man to the status of a thing. He quotes Sartre's 'Preface' to Fanon: 'Beaten, undernourished, ill, terrified — but only up to a certain point — he has, whether he's black, yellow or white, always the same traits of character: he's a slyboots, a lazybones, and a thief, who lives on nothing and understands only violence.'[56]

This, then, is not a personality, it is a *persona*, a mask. It is perhaps not fair to read too much into what was in effect a private joke but nowhere is this persona, this attitude, better described than in Jonathan Swift's *Directions to Servants*.[57] Using the favourite Swiftian device of deadpan, but tongue-in-cheek, formality, he advises servants on the best methods to cope with the incessant demands of their masters, beginning with, 'When your Master or Lady call a Servant by Name, if that Servant be not in the Way, none of you are to answer, for then there will be no End of your Drudgery'. The *Directions* are clearly based on detailed, and irritated, observation, by an eighteenth-century gentleman, of the real behaviour of eighteenth-century servants.

Behind the Swiftian irony is the further irony — and Swift does not seem to have been aware of this — that what is being described are the various devices by which the weak, within the enforced intimacy of the master/servant relationship, defend and protect themselves. Swift describes the same pattern of behaviour that is described, with different levels of intensity, by Elkins and Genovese, Sartre and Fanon, and in the Howleglas stories. There is the same over-literal interpretation of orders, the clumsiness, the 'stupidity'. Swift suggests that there is a secret delight in getting things wrong.

In a passage that is much quoted in other contexts, Arthur Young, the eighteenth-century agriculturist, compares the fecund, child-loving Irish with the poor and lower classes of England: 'Marriage is certainly more general in Ireland than in England: I scarce ever found an unmarried farmer or cottar; but it is seen more in other classes, which with us do not marry at all; such as servants; the generality of footmen and maids, in gentlemen's families, are married, a circumstance we very rarely see in England'.[58] The status of things indeed. Imagine Jeeves with a wife and children — no, Wooster is his child. And we now see why, returning briefly to the point noted from Wilson, there should be 'a clear analogy between American racial humour and English social humour'.[59]

To talk of a personality, 'Sambo', 'Paddy', must be incorrect. To talk of a persona, a mask, is only half the story. For what the 'stupid person' jokes describe is a *relationship*, the power relationship, the relationship, using Sartre's and Fanon's terms, between 'native' and 'settler'. 'Poor settler; here is his contradiction naked, shorn of its trappings. He ought to kill those he plunders, as they say djinns do. Now, this is not possible, because he must exploit them as well.' 'For when you domesticate a member of our own species, you reduce his output, and however little you may give him, a farmyard man finishes by costing more than he brings in. For this reason the settlers are obliged to stop the breaking-in half-way; the result, neither man or animal, is the native. Beaten, under-nourished, ill, terrified — but only up to a certain point . . .' 'They're lazy: of course — it's a form of sabotage . . . their petty thefts mark the beginning of a resistance which is still unorganised.'[60]

It is a strong and disturbing vision, and sums up the unease with which the powerful regard the underdog. That unease, and the whole relationship, is caught beautifully, and with great economy, by Samuel Beckett in the characters of Pozzo and Lucky in *Waiting For Godot*.[61]

The powerful and the powerless both appear in the 'stupid person' joke. The powerless person is there, stage centre, in all his 'stupidity'. The powerful person is there, either as a discrete narrative element (the King, the Judge, the giver of orders) or by implications. He may, indeed, be the teller of the tale.

Lévi-Strauss, it will be recalled, builds his analysis on paradigms of oppositions, within which myth works to resolve contradictions. Thus the oppositions stupidity/cleverness, power/powerlessness would translate into this quadrant:

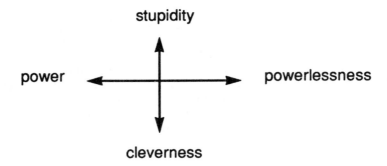

Socio-cultural, ideological norms (Gramscian 'commonsense') would have the stupid powerless and the clever powerful — as long as stupidity and power are held apart the ideology holds. But 'stupid person' jokes are a very unstable form of power. Though the jokes can be used with ideological intent, the jokes themselves explore every part of the quadrant.[62]

Now, echoing Lévi-Strauss, it is clear that jokes, or the ghosts of jokes, wander the earth, looking for a place to live, a local habitation and a name. That habitation will be within a power relationshiop. The name will be one that will, swiftly, easily within the narrative, make that relationship plain in the terms of the surrounding culture — the name is a semiotic requirement of the narrative. Ong reminds us that 'when an often-told oral story is not actually being told, all that exists of it is the potential in certain human beings to tell it'.[63] In so far as the jokes themselves have an interest in this matter it is that they have an instinct to survive — like 'Skelton', the impudent but pusillanimous poet, they will make an accommodation with the powerful.

The humour of the English/Irish relationship — the jokes that the English tell about the Irish, and vice versa — has not been intensively studied, in part, of course, because the tragedy of the relationship looms so large in the history of these islands. Mercier, as has already been suggested, touches on the subject. Snyder, many years ago, began to organise the material. Curtis, in two interesting books, has looked at the political use of stereotypes of the Irish in the nineteenth century — and Curtis's approach has been criticised by Gilley.[64]

The 'stupid person' jokes analysed by this chapter can perhaps be seen as simply a subcategory within the humour of the English/Irish relationship. What is relevant to this chapter, at this point, is how embarrassingly rich the English/Irish relationship is in those elements that will attract 'stupid person' jokes:

1. Geographic marginality, under the terms of the Act of Union;
2. a long-term, and still problematic, 'native/settler' relationship (we are reminded that Sartre suggested that the 'native' 'understands only violence'; in Suls' joke, 'O'Riley was on trial for *armed* robbery' — a detail not required by his narrative, but part of the semiotic matrix of the 'stupid person' joke);

3. part of the 'native/settler' complex is the master/servant relationship, inside Ireland and without — migrations ensure that the Irish will be skivvies and navvies to the English and to the North American WASPs.

But, wherever the jokes go, they go trailing clouds of glory. They cannot forget their heritage: Howleglas, Nasrudin, Ryokwan. That heritage cannot be forgotten, it is built into the narrative: there *is* a different way. The stories sit uneasily upon the lips of the masters: that the masters tell the jokes demonstrates the masters' unknowing. The jokes are seized with relish by the slaves: we recall that, according to Sartre, the 'native' is a 'slyboots'. The slave, in effect, says to the master: All right then, you *are* master, it's your reality — what sort of reality do you want?[65] Lurking within the 'Irish joke', like the McCarthy Gannons in the attics of Shreelane, is a critique of imperialism and imperialism's reality.

Stupidity and orality

Jokes are short humorous oral narratives, part of 'oral literature'. The 'stupid person' jokes are not simply hundreds of years old, they are thousands of years old — and their behaviour, the methods by which they survive, the uses to which they are put, the places in which they are told, is typical of 'oral literature' in a literate world.[66] As Ong says, 'Thinking of oral tradition or a heritage of oral performances, genres and styles as 'oral literature' is rather like thinking of horses as automobiles without wheels'. He suggests, diffidently, the term 'voicings' for performances of oral art forms. And, as we have seen, he believes that 'When an often-told oral story is not actually being told, all that exists of it is the potential in certain human beings to tell it'.[67] He avoids the ontological difficulties of Lévi-Strauss.

Occasionally the jokes wander in from the realm of 'oral literature', become transformed from 'voicings' to 'writings', preserved, like the inevitable fly in amber, by collectors (like Poggio), theorists (Freud or Koestler) or polemicists (like Leach). Dodd's criticism of Freud comes from one who is aware of the *orality* of his material and the particular skills that are needed to present it. Nathan's criticism of Koestler is the criticism of one who appreciates those skills.

It is lucky for us that the jokes do wander in from the convivial places, that 'voicings' become 'writings' — for without that written evidence the historical and semiotic argument would not be possible. Through the 'writings' it has been possible to demonstrate that these jokes are spread throughout history, but tend to cluster around individuals (Howleglas) or groups (Galician Jews). This chapter has used a great diversity of sources — philosophical theorists, historians of literature, joke collections for after-dinner speakers, and what we might rather grandly call field research. This diversity of sources is itself confirming evidence for the chapter's argument — the anomaly that we have in the main to study written texts in order to make a point about oral tradition is not itself a problem.

Neuburg suggests that, 'There is always an interplay between oral culture and popular literature — although in the end the printed popular literature becomes predominant. How much of the former has been lost in the process we can never know.'[68] The 'stupid person' jokes can then be regarded as an extraordinary, and extraordinarily cohesive, survival from humankind's days of orality. To that aspect this chapter finally turns.

Gilley teases out some of the realities behind national stereotypes — 'one can recognise behind the English conception of the Frenchman a French idea of the Frenchman, with a gift for clear abstract thought, and in like fashion behind the English conception of the Irish lies the Irish idea of the Irishman'. There is an interplay — each defines himself in contrast to the other.

Through the materials of popular culture, broadside ballads and the like, Gilley demonstrates that in the nineteenth century there was a stereotype of 'good-natured Paddy': an image as popular among Irishmen as among Englishmen, with a good deal of attractiveness about it. The three main virtues which Paddy claims are generosity, hospitality and courage in battle:

> His hand is rash, his heart is warm,
> But principle is still his guide,
> None more repents a deed of harm,
> And none forgives with nobler pride;
> He may be dup'd but won't be dar'd,
> Fitter to practice than to plan,
> He ably earns his own reward,
> And spends it like an Irishman.

'The key to these qualities is a quickness of spirit and spontaneity . . .' This persona we recognise from the material already presented in this chapter — this is the 'stupid person', shading into the 'Holy Fool', Zen master, Nasrudin. Gilley even confronts the issue of violence, and the differing rhetorics of violence used by the English and by the Irish — with their different traditions and experiences of each other's violence. He stresses '. . . the belligerency in which the Irish rejoiced, for Irishmen have usually fought their oppressors. Indeed, the vices which they tolerate and indulge are of the kind which oppression instils, and as these are evidence of English oppression, Irish nationalists are foolish to deny them.'[69] Here he echoes Sartre and Fanon in their analysis of oppression in other places — there is something horribly consistent about the psychodynamics of oppression.

And again we ask, but where else have we seen this stereotype, this persona, this collection of attributes? Ong, in his chapter on the psychodynamics of orality, has an interesting aside — and, inevitably, he is telling an anecdote: 'An illuminating story is told of a visitor in County Cork, Ireland, an especially oral region in a country which in every region preserves massive residual orality'. We are immediately plunged into a 'town and country' story.[70]

Ong is here making a point about the psychology of the 'oral' person, as opposed to that of the 'literate' person. His main point, well argued in a fascinating book, is that the technology of writing has restructured human consciousness — he notes, for example, that 'philosophical thinking cannot be carried on by unaided human mind but only by the human mind that has familiarized itself with and deeply interiorized the technology of writing'.[71] He does not necessarily see this orality/literacy dichotomy as having an either/or dimension in the modern world — people and cultures are not now necessarily simply either 'oral' or 'literate'.

But Ong does use the term 'verbomotor lifestyle' to distinguish those cultures which 'retain enough oral residue to remain significantly word-attentive in a person–interactive context (the oral type of context) rather than object-attentive'. He notes that, to the irritation of 'technological man', 'in primary oral cultures, even business is not business: it is fundamentally rhetoric', '. . . a series of verbal (and somatic) manoeuvers, a polite duel, a contest of wits, an operation in oral agonistic'. To 'technological', 'literate' man, 'oral' man can seem evasive and deceitful.

To help in distinguishing 'verbomotor' or 'oral' cultures Ong constructs an ideal type, an attempt to categorise the psychodynamics of orality. Oral peoples are limited by the nature of sound itself. They know only what they can recall, without the aid of texts — this in itself shapes knowledge. They are 'agonistically toned' — 'writing fosters abstractions that disengage knowledge from the arena where human beings struggle with one another', but oral peoples live face to face, attractions and antagonisms are 'kept high'.[72]

Oral peoples are 'empathetic and participatory rather than objectively distanced', they 'live in a present which keeps itself in equilibrium or homeostasis by sloughing off memories which no longer have relevance'. They are 'situational rather than abstract', 'they remain close to the living human lifeworld'.

To illustrate this last point Ong draws on Luria's work in 'cognitive development'. Luria interviewed oral, pre–literate or semi–literate, and literate individuals in a remote part of the eastern Soviet Union in the 1930s. Particularly relevant is the difficulty 'oral' people had with the syllogism — Ong notes that this is *not* to say that they could not think, or that their thinking was not governed by logic, 'But only that they would not fit their thinking into pure logical forms, which they seem to have found uninteresting'.[73]

Cumulatively we have here, yet again, a description of the 'stupid person', the 'Holy Fool', the 'Irish' persona. Is it possible to suggest that the Irish genuinely have a more 'oral' or 'verbomotor' culture than the more 'literate' English? When we put this observation into a context of power we see that literacy is yet another tool of the powerful. Kress and Hodge note, as if it were a matter of course, that 'Quite unconsciously, a community which is defined by its mastery of the written medium disvalues the resources of oral and gestural language, and hence the culture of its users'.[74]

We even have a place for 'violence' in this description of the psychodynamics of orality — oral peoples are 'agonistically toned', they live face to face, they cannot distance themselves from human struggles. The 'stupid person' is the 'oral' person.

Thus it can be seen that when the Zen Masters or the Sufis present the struggle or debate that takes place within a 'Holy Fool' anecdote as a conflict between two forms of consciousness they may be precisely right: what is being demonstrated is a conflict between two forms of consciousness, the 'new' consciousness restructured by the technology of writing, and the 'old' consciousness of humanity before the invention and interiorising of that technology.[75] In a very simple way there might be, as Idries Shah suggests, a 'secret teaching within all religions' — within most, if not all, religions there is a struggle between the 'Book' and a more immediate, agonistic approach to the human struggle, personified by the 'Holy Fool'.[76] We note the many Nasrudin stories in which he tricks or bemuses the philosophers and teachers — paraphrasing Ong, he will not fit his thinking into pure logical forms, which he finds uninteresting. He remains close to the human lifeworld.

What is particularly fascinating about the orality/literacy approach to the 'stupid person' jokes is the fact that many, very, very many, of the jokes themselves deal with the mysteries of reading and with the mysteries of writing — two sets of interrelated but clearly distinguished mysteries.[77] The jokes distinguish these mysteries through such devices as Nasrudin's bad handwriting.[78]

The problems about writing that the jokes examine are very like the objections to the technology of writing that Plato puts into the mouth of Socrates. As Ong notes, 'Texts are inherently contumacious'. The text is unresponsive — 'After absolutely total and devastating refutation, it says exactly the same thing as before'. A person can be interrogated, can explain his or her statement — a text repeats 'the same, often stupid, words which called for your question in the first place'.[79] I have suggested elsewhere that in the threatening letters sent by Irish peasants to their nineteenth-century masters there is not only *imitation* of the format and style of the official documents, writs, warrants, eviction notices, served on them by the masters — there is *parody*. One silly document is matched by another.[80]

Ong reminds us that 'We know that formal logic is the invention of Greek culture after it had interiorized the technology of alphabetic writing, and so made a permanent part of its noetic resources the kind of thinking that alphabetic writing made possible.' And Ong points out that Plato's philosophically analytic thought, 'including his critique of writing, was possible only because of the effects that writing was beginning to have on mental processes'.[81]

Indeed, it seems that at the end of a chapter on 'Irish' jokes we have wandered into the middle of Plato's quarrel with the poets — following Havelock, Ong suggested that 'Plato's entire epistemology was unwittingly a programmed rejection of the old oral, mobile, warm, personally interactive lifeworld of oral culture (represented by the poets, whom he would not allow in his Republic)'.[82] The 'stupid person' is the poet?

Coda: the semiotic matrix

It might be wondered where, in the approach of this chapter, is there a place for individual human creativity? Ong looks at this question in the light of the oral tradition.[83] Norrman and Haarberg tackle the implications for literature in Part 2 of their book, called 'Implications'. Chapter headings include: 'Is a literary work written by the author or by the readers?', 'Does a literary work write itself?', 'Independent creation versus tradition'. In this last section they almost drift, without acknowledgement, into a Jungian theory of the unconscious.[84]

The simple answer is that, at this stage, individual human creativity is a postulate not required by the argument. Whether speaking about myths as 'having a life of their own' is thought of as simply a shorthand way of referring to more complex analyses, or is thought of as saying something true about myths, is not the issue. The approach makes far better sense of the material than, for example, postulating the existence of bad-tempered but creative Irishmen in Chicago, quite independently recreating Galician Jew jokes.

It might then be wondered how it can be asserted that a joke that has moved across language and cultural boundaries is still the same joke? — or, to put it another way, how can two jokes, written down centuries apart, in two different languages and cultures, be somehow the *same* joke?

Norrman and Haarberg suggest that, 'In orally transmitted literature of this kind there is ample scope for changes towards perfection; for imperfect forms to be discarded; and for a transmitter, who may be more clever than the last teller of the story (and master the semiotic matrix of the elements more fully), to touch into life the element that was waiting for him to take it into the story, where it will strive to remain if it improves the story'.[85] By the same token an unsubtle teller of the tale may mess it up, distort the story for his own ends, or cut out elements not applicable to his ends. Or elements of the story may resist the teller, refusing to move tidily from one culture to another.

The key concept is 'semiotic matrix' — an interweave of signs, meanings and narrative devices (the very stuff that intrigued and puzzled Freud). It is the 'semiotic matrix of the elements' (Norrman and Haarberg), which includes 'complicated technical conditions' (Freud), that 'protects against tampering' (Riffaterre). Analysis of jokes in this essay has teased out elements of the semiotic matrix — if the elements from two jokes from two sources can be demonstrated to be the same then there are not two jokes, there is only one.

A simple example is called for. There is a basic 'stupid person' joke which we can call the 'First Mirror' joke. This version comes from R. H. Blyth, who says it is 'of Chinese origin'.[86]

> A husband went to the city and came home with the first mirror his town had ever seen. He placed it in a room apart and said to his young wife, 'I have brought you a present from the city — it is in the next room.' And he went off hunting, with a glow of husbandly pride.
>
> The young wife went into the next room, and quickly came out, weeping. Her mother said, 'What's the matter?' The wife said, 'My husband has grown tired of me, and has brought a new young wife back from the city.' The mother said, 'I'll see about this!' and marched into the next room.
>
> She came back, more quietly, and said, 'I can understand his getting a new young wife — but why has he brought her mother along?'

The following version was met quite independently, during the course of 'field research'.

> The time had come for a young Irishman to leave home and find work in Liverpool. Family experience prepared him — he was to take the boat to Liverpool, get in a taxi, and go to a certain address, a lodging house known to welcome the Irish.
>
> So, he went to Liverpool, came down the gangway, and asked a policeman, 'Where can I get a taxi?' 'Right along there, Paddy,' said the policeman, pointing, 'you'll find

the taxi rank there.' 'Thank you,' said the young Irishman, and walked on, thinking, 'That's funny — he knew my name.'

So, a taxi took the young man to the correct address. 'There you are, young Pat,' said the taxi-driver, 'You'll be right enough there.' 'Thank you,' said the young Irishman, and went into the house, thinking, 'That's funny — he knew my name too.'

The landlady welcomed him, and showed him to a room, saying, 'I hope you'll be comfortable here, Patrick.' 'Thank you,' said the young man, thinking, 'And *she* knows my name.'

And he went into the bathroom, where there was a small mirror hanging on the wall. 'And, by God,' he said, 'she's got a picture of me hanging on the wall!'

Envoi: So, he took the mirror off the wall, wrapped it up, and sent it home to his parents, with a note, 'Here is a recent picture of me.'

His father looked at the mirror and said, 'By God, he's *aged*!'

His mother looked over the father's shoulder and said, 'No wonder! Look at the old bag he's living with!'

It is another joke about technology. Clearly it is not naïve to suggest that the 'First Mirror' joke tells us something about the first experiences of mirrors — in terms of human culture it is a very old joke. It makes use of the town and country dichotomy and some use of the male/female power relationship.

The joke requires a mirror and a person who has never seen a mirror before — failing that, a person who for some reason fails to recognise the mirror for what it is. Stupidity alone will not do — but 'stupidity', 'Irishness', the complex of personalities and circumstances described by this chapter, will do.

It becomes harder and harder for the 'First Mirror' joke to find a home in the modern world — the demands of the semiotic matrix are too precise. There are problems with the 'Irish' version — these people seem familiar with photographs but do not recognise a mirror. The complex of meanings associated with 'Irishness' glosses over these difficulties.

Tenenbaum, recognising the difficulties, offers a 'Chelm' version which reverses the 'stupidity'/power pattern — the Chelm idiot tricks the Czar into seeing a mirror as a beautifully-painted full-length portrait.[87] This 'Emperor's Clothes' version of the tale does not work. (Acknowledge, if you will, the courage of a field researcher who deliberately tells a bad version of a joke in order to test its qualities.) The 'First Mirror' joke is clearly in great danger, and only 'Irishness' allows it to survive in the twentieth century.

Notes

1. In this chapter I am concerned only tangentially with theories of humour as such. The main elements of the established theories are summarised by Christopher P. Wilson, *Jokes: form, content, use and function*, Academic Press, London, 1979. He suggests a 'cognitive balance' synthesis (p. 21). D. H. Monro, *Argument of laughter*,

University of Notre Dame Press, Notre Dame, 1963 (original edn. 1951), concentrates on the philosophers of humour, from Hobbes to Krishna Menon. His key concept is 'inappropriateness'. Two collections offer useful starting-points for exploring the literature: Chris Powell and George E. C. Paton, *Humour in society: resistance and control*, Macmillan, Basingstoke, 1988; John Durant and Jonathan Miller (eds), *Laughing matters: a serious look at humour*, Longman, Harlow, 1988.

2. Wilson, *Jokes*, p. 24.
3. David Nathan, *The laughtermakers*, Peter Owen, London, 1971, pp. 12–13, quoting Arthur Koestler, *The act of creation*, Hutchinson, London, 1947. The joke is the one that ends, 'Oedipus-Schmoedipus, as long as he loves his mother!' See also Leo Rosten, *The joys of Yiddish*, W. H. Allen, London, 1970.
4. Wilson, *Jokes*, p. 27. This is the joke about the notoriously inactive President Coolidge:

   Interlocutor: President Coolidge is dead.

   Dorothy Parker: How can they tell?

   Wilson has her saying, 'Why I never even knew he was alive'.
5. Ernest Jones, *The life and work of Sigmund Freud*, abridged by Trilling and Marcus, Penguin, London, 1964, p. 315.
6. Edmund Leach, 'The official Irish jokesters', *New Society*, 20/27 December 1979, p. vii.
7. Sigmund Freud, *Jokes and their relation to the unconscious*, translated by Strachey, revised by Richards, Penguin, London, 1976. Freud's German title refers to *Der Witz* — Brill's 1916 translation uses the title *Wit and its relation to the unconscious*. As Strachey explains there is no tidy fit between German and English terms. Normal literary German uses *Schwank* for the type of material analysed by *this* chapter — see Henry and Mary Garland, *Oxford companion to German literature*, Oxford University Press, Oxford, 1976.
8. Freud, pp. 83–5. The Heine anecdote is not worth bothering with, but the Galician Jews are:

   Two Galician Jews meet near the bath-house.
   First Galician Jew: Have you taken a bath?
   Second Galician Jew: What? — is one missing?

9. Ken Dodd's quip has been quoted many times, and has perhaps lost its freshness. See Wilson, *Jokes*, p. 189, and Michael Billington, 'Doddy and soul', *Punch*, 5 December 1984. But Dodd made his point most appropriately in his mammoth exploration of the nature of laughter, his one-man show at the Liverpool Playhouse, April 1973. See Gus Smith, *Ken Dodd: laughter and tears*, Virgin, London, 1989, p. 181.
10. Wilson, *Jokes*, p. 30, makes a brief raid into the land of literary criticism, to capture a supporting detail for his argument — he refers to Empson and similar critics. For a critique of the philosophical assumptions behind Empson's approach see Paul de Man, 'The dead-end of formalist criticism', in *Blindness and insight*, Methuen, London, 2nd rev. edn., 1983.
11. Barbara Hardy, *Tellers and listeners: the narrative imagination*, Athlone Press, London, 1975, p. vii. She goes on, 'Narrative imagination is a common human possession'. Social work and therapy, and the disciplines that feed into them, would seem to need an interest in story-telling craft and techniques — the first contact with client or patient usually involves the telling of a story, which is then passed on as case history, or anecdote.

12. Wilson's useful but untidy book never quite grapples with this distinction, though its title suggests it might do.

13. Wilson, *Jokes*, p. 21; p. 31.

14. Wilson, *Jokes*, pp. 30–1. See also D. E. Berlyne, 'Humor and its kin' in J. H. Goldstein and P. E. McGhee (eds), *The psychology of humour*, Academic Press, New York, 1972.

15. Wilson, *Jokes*, p. 40.

16. Jerry M. Suls, 'A two-stage model for the appreciation of jokes and cartoons: an information-processing analysis' in Goldstein and McGhee, *The psychology of humour*. Suls' little essay continues to attract interest and development — see, for example, Hiram H. Brownell and Howard Gardner, 'Neuropsychological insights into humour' in Durant and Miller (eds.), *Laughing matters*, where Suls' model, with its understanding of the importance of the punch line, is used to explore cognitive problems within mental illness.

17. Suls, *Two-stage model*, p. 82.

18. Wlad Godzich, 'Introduction: Caution! Reader at work' in Paul de Man, *Blindness and insight*.

19. Ralf Norrman and Jon Haarberg, *Nature and language: a semiotic study of cucurbits in literature*, Routledge and Kegan Paul, London, 1980, p. 84. I deal, briefly, with the implications of Norrman and Haarberg's approach in the Coda to this chapter.

20. De Man, 'Dead-end of formalist criticism', p. 11; p. 19.

21. Robert Scholes, *Semiotics and interpretation*, Yale University Press, New Haven, 1982, p. 28.

22. Michael Riffaterre, *Semiotics of poetry*, Methuen, London, 1980, original edition 1978, p. 14.

23. Scholes, *Semiotics and interpretation*, p. 30.

24. 'Irish jokes': the question of definition is left till later, when it arises naturally in the argument.

25. Wilson, *Jokes*, pp. 215–16.

26. Wilson, *Jokes*, p. 216.

27. Wilson, *Jokes*, p. 217.

28. Edmund Leach, 'Official Irish jokesters', p. ix. The reader might as well begin 'The Game' now. Look back at Suls and the 'O'Riley' joke. For 'O'Riley' substitute 'Goldberg', or another family name of your choice. Is the joke still funny? If it is funny, has it changed in any way?

29. Leach, 'Official Irish jokesters', p. ix. Leach's article, as it is presented within the pages of *New Society*, contains its own internal contradictions for it is illustrated in those pages by 'Irish' jokes in cartoon form, from the cartoonist Paige. Only one of those cartoons, the nastiest one, could be interpreted, with difficulty as a 'West Indian' or 'Pakistani' joke.

    Six years earlier, in an editorial, *New Society* had already attacked 'Irish Jokes'. The ensuing correspondence is interesting in that the readers agree with *New Society* that Irish jokes are racist, cruel, etc. — but they cannot resist giving examples. *New Society*, Vol. 28, April/June 1974.

30. This joke I was told in Paris:

    An Englishman, in correct Englishman's dress of bowler hat, umbrella, and so on, was reading *The Times*, standing in the middle of Trafalgar Square, with his trousers down.

    The interlocutor approached him and said, 'Tell me, why are you reading *The Times* in the middle of Trafalgar Square with your trousers down?'

    The Englishman started, looked down, and said, 'Oh! She's gone!'

The punch-line requires the correct Belgravia Cockney drawl on 'gorn'.

Leslie Missen, *Quotable anecdotes*, Allen & Unwin, London, 1966, has a version of this joke — a Cambridge undergraduate, visiting Paris, goes for his usual morning run, clad in shorts and singlet, and ends his run with press-ups on the pavement. A young French woman approaches him, bends down and says, 'Monsieur, Madame est déjà parti'. A joke about English coldness can thus be a joke about French incomprehension, but you have to speak French to understand it. The elements of the joke are malleable, or adaptable.

On WASP jokes see Alan Dundes, *Interpreting folklore*, Indiana UP, Bloomington, 1980. For example:

How do you keep a WASP uninformed? Take away his *Reader's Digest*.

How do you keep a WASP misinformed? Give it back to him.

Dundes also has a splendid joke on the archetypal *Reader's Digest* article, p. 16. The Pommy is the ever-complaining English immigrant in Australia.

How can you tell when a planeload of Pommies has arrived at Sydney airport? The engines are switched off, but the whining continues.

31. Vivian Mercier, *The Irish comic tradition*, Oxford University Press, 1962, pp. 164–6. Briefly, English surnames are funny because:

    i.   they do not begin with Mac or O;
    ii.   they are very often monosyllables — it's like being introduced to Mr Ug or Mr Aargh;
    iii. When you learn a little English, it turns out that the English are named after incredibly prosaic things, like animals (Mr Fox, Mr Lamb) or pieces of land (Mr Hill, Mr Field).

32. *Ray Ginger's jokebook about American history*, compiled and annotated by Ray Ginger, New Viewpoints, New York, 1974: 'Ethnic jokes', pp. 29–43; Scots 'covetous', p. 30; 'Irish'/'Polish', jokes, p. 35. In fairness, Ginger's little book does collect the stories together and does begin to look at the place of humour in American history, pp. 137–8.

Here are some examples of the ways these jokes move around. Keith Hopkins, in *Conquerors and slaves, sociological studies in Roman history, Volume 1*, Cambridge University Press, Cambridge, 1978, p. 235, notes that the tale about the worried astrologer and the tyrant is told about, amongst others, Alexander the Great and the would-be Emperor Tiberius, and he analyses the appropriateness of this. Anticipating my argument, there is a further version of that tale in Idries Shah, *The exploits of the incomparable Mulla Nasrudin*, Cape, London, 1966, p. 138.

The 'pox or the gallows' anecdote is told about every pair of opposed statesmen in European history. Bennett Cerf, *Try and stop me*, Dobson, London, 1947, p. 194, very improbably, tells it about Gladstone and Disraeli. Dundes, *Interpreting folklore*, pp. 60–1, has a joke that in his experience was told about both Hitler and Governor Wallace of Alabama.

33. Stith Thompson, *Motif: index of folk-literature*, 6 Vols, Rosenkilde and Bagger, Copenhagen, 1955–8; also Helsinki, 1932–6; Bloomington, Indiana, 1932–6. See also, Stith Thompson, *The folktale*, Dryden Press, New York, 1946. V. Propp, *Morphology of the folktale*, University of Texas Press, Austin, rev. edn. 1968. Norrman and Haarberg, *Nature and language*, p. 113. Martin Grotjahn, MD, *Beyond*

laughter, McGraw-Hill, New York, 1957. Graf Bobby, 'the spirit of old Vienna', goes in for what later came to be called 'Goldwynisms' (see Cerf, *Try and stop me*, pp. 36–41), very like 'Irish Bulls'.

34. Victor E. Neuburg, *Popular literature: a history and guide*, Penguin, London, 1977, p. 39 onwards; p. 44. *The wicked tricks of Till Owlyglass*, retold by Michael Rosen, Walker, London, 1990, was for a while the favourite bedtime reading of my elder son, Daniel. My thanks to Dan for help with this part of my research programme.

35. Neuburg, *Popular literature*, p. 43.

36. James E. Doan, *Cearbhall O'Dalaigh: an Irish poet in romance and oral tradition*, Garland, New York, 1990. Henry Glassie, (ed.), *Irish folk tales*, Penguin, Harmondsworth, 1987: for example, sexual ignorance, pp. 87–9.

37. Thompson, *The folktale*, p. 190. Norrman and Haarberg also analyse this story. Since it is in Norrman and Haarberg it is, of course, about a pumpkin. Poggio's work rarely makes it into English out of the chaste obscurity of Latin — but see *The facetiae of Giovanni Francesco Poggio Bracciolini*, a new translation by Bernhardt J. Hurwood, Award, New York, 1968.

38. Belgians are called 'Les Frites', 'parce qu'ils mangent toujours les frites', as I was told by the driver of a breakdown truck, in Dijon.

    'Newfries' — Wilson acknowledges this Canadian use of 'stupid person' jokes, *Jokes*, p. 85, without comment or explanation.

    'Sikhs in India are tremendous Irish-style comic figures: their reputation for stupidity matching their uncontrollable lust . . .', Mihir Bose, 'The Clive of cricket', *New Society*, 26 May 1977, p. 381.

    It is interesting to note, in passing, that lust does not seem to be part of the semiotic matrix of the 'stupid Irishman', whilst, of course, sexual ignorance is.

39. A Forfar man was given the job of driving a lorryload of potatoes to London. He drove south and came to a large town. He stopped a passer-by and said, 'Is this London?' The passer-by said, 'No, no, this is Edinburgh — London is that way, a long way in that direction.'

    So, the Forfar man drove on, and eventually came to a large town where he stopped a passer-by and said, 'Is this London?' The passer-by said, 'No, no, (mon), this is Newcastle. London is that way, a long way in that direction.'

    So, the Forfar man drove on, and eventually came to a large town where he stopped a passer-by and said, 'Is this London?' And the passer-by said, 'No, no, this is York. London is that way, a long way in that direction.'

    So, the Forfar man drove on and eventually came to London where he stopped a passer-by and said, 'Is this London?' And the passer-by said, 'Yes.' And the Forfar man said, 'Well, where do you want these potatoes then?'

    Only the untidy intervention of the Irish Sea prevents this from being an 'Irish' joke.

40. Samuel Tenenbaum, *The wise men of Chelm*, Collier Books, London, 1969, p. 9.

41. Why do Kerry dogs have flat noses? From chasing parked cars.

42. Christie Davies, 'The Irish joke as a social phenomenon' in Durant and Miller, *Laughing matters*; Christie Davies, 'Stupidity and rationality: jokes from the iron cage' in Powell and Paton, *Humour in society*; Christie Davies. *Ethnic humour around the world: a comparative analysis*, Indiana University Press, Bloomington, 1990.

43. Freud, *Jokes*, p. 161. The example he gives is the one about going to Cracow, or is it Lemburg? — Tenenbaum, *Wise men of Chelm*, pp. 122–3, has Minsk and Pinsk. Monro (*Argument of laughter*, p. 193) is suspicious of Freud's analysis of the Cracow joke — do this joke and its like really deserve a category of their own? I think that I have demonstrated in this chapter that Freud was right and Monro was wrong.

44. G. P. Fedotov, *The Russian religious mind*, 2 Vols, Harvard University Press, Cambridge, 1966, Vol. II, pp. 316–43. In fairness, 'Holy Fool' stories are told about the early Franciscans. Inevitably, Idries Shah sees this as the product of direct Sufi influence upon Francis during the siege of Damietta — see Idries Shah, *The Sufis*, Cape, London, 1964, p. 231.

45. M. Conrad Hyers, *Zen and the comic spirit*, Rider and Company, London, 1974, pp. 32–3.

46. R. H. Blyth, *Japanese life and character in Senryu*, Hokuseido, Tokyo, 1960, p. 4; p. 5.

47. Paul Reps, *Zen flesh, Zen bones*, Penguin, London, 1971.

48. Arthur Koestler, *The lotus and the robot*, Hutchinson, London, 1960, p. 240. Enid Welsford, *The Fool: his social and literary history*, Faber and Faber, London, 1968, p. 80 onwards.

49. Idries Shah, *The Sufis*, pp. 65–6.

50. Idries Shah, *Exploits*, p. 11.

51. Idries Shah, *The Sufis*, pp. 63–4.

52. Idries Shah, 'Smuggling donkeys', *Exploits*, p. 22 — this joke moves round every troublesome border, and I have heard it told about the border between the Republic of Ireland and Northern Ireland. Donkeys tend to be modernised to bicycles — it has to be some unobtrusive, low-esteem form of transport. 'Searching in the wrong place', p. 26. 'Reading and writing', p. 124, p. 122.

53. Idries Shah, 'The subtleties of Mulla Nasrudin', *The Sufis*, pp. 56–97. 'The hanging story', p. 60.

54. Freud, *Jokes*, p. 119; Grotjahn, *Beyond laughter*, p. 156.

55. Eugene D. Genovese, 'Rebelliousness and docility in the Negro slave — a critique of Elkins' thesis', in *Red and Black: Marxian explorations in Southern and Afro-American history*, Vintage, New York, 1972.

56. Jean-Paul Sartre, 'Preface' to Frantz Fanon, *The wretched of the earth*, translator Farrington, Penguin, London, 1967. Fanon is very relevant to the argument in this section of the chapter.

57. Swift died in October 1745, the *Directions* were published in November 1745. Swift seems to have added to the work from time to time in the 1730s, until his memory failed and he laid it aside, incomplete. The Dublin publisher, Faulkner, prefaced the 1745 edition with a note that 'the Author's Design was to expose the villanies and Frauds of Servants to their Masters and Mistresses . . .' *Swift*, ed. John Hayward, Nonesuch, London, 1963, p. 596.

58. Quoted, for example, in Magnus Magnusson, *Landlord or Tenant: a view of Irish history*, Bodley Head, London, 1978, p. 52.

59. Wilson, *Jokes*, p. 216.

60. Sartre, 'Preface' to Fanon, pp. 14–15.

61. Philosophers will also be reminded of Hegel's parable of the master and the slave. 'The life-risking confrontation of master and slave is, for Hegel, the beginning of history; a journey towards the universal union of the rational with the real,' says Mary O'Brien, *The politics of reproduction*, Routledge and Kegan Paul, London, 1981, p. 69.

62. My thanks to Virginia Valentine, of Semiotic Solutions, for helping me to clarify my thinking at this stage in the argument.

63. Walter J. Ong, *Orality and literacy: the technologizing of the word*, Methuen, London, 1982, p. 11.

64. Mercier, *The Irish comic tradition*, p. 163 onwards. Edward D. Snyder, 'The wild Irish; a study of some English satires against the Irish, Scots and Welsh', *Modern Philology*, Vol. XXVII, 1920. See also J. C. Bartley, *Teague, Shenkin and Sawney: being an historical study of the earliest Irish, Welsh and Scottish characters in English plays*,

Cork University Press, Cork, 1954; L. P. Curtis, *Anglo-Saxons and Celts*, Conference on British Studies, Bridgeport, 1968, and *Apes and angels: Irishmen in Victorian caricature*, David and Charles, Newton Abbot, 1971; Sheridan Gilley, 'English attitudes to the Irish in England, 1780–1900' in Colin Holmes (ed.), *Immigrants and minorities in British society*, Allen & Unwin, London, 1978.

Gilley 'criticises Curtis's use of the term "racial", but fails to modify the substance of Curtis's analysis' says Charles Townshend, *Political violence in Ireland*, Clarendon Press, Oxford, 1983, p. 8.

65.   A hiker, pack on back, is tramping along an Irish road. He meets an old Irish couple.
Hiker: How many miles is it to Ballygobackwards?

Old Irish Man: Ah, that would be eight miles.

Old Irish Woman: Patrick, can't you see how tired he is? — make it five.

66.   There are two other sorts of stuff that behave and survive in a similar way — the material collected by Iona and Peter Opie, *The lore and language of schoolchildren*, Oxford University Press, Oxford, 1959, and 'modern urban legends' collected by, for example, J. Brunuand, *The vanishing hitch-hiker: American urban legends and their meaning*, W. W. Norton, New York, 1981.

In an essay entitled 'Projection in folklore — a plea for psychoanalytic semiotics', Dundes moves smoothly across these three different sorts of material — children's skipping rhymes, 'urban legends' (the dead granny on the roofrack), and formal jokes (Heaven's Gate).

Michael P. Carroll, 'Alligators in the sewer, dragons in the well and Freud in the toilet' *Sociological Review*, February 1984, Vol. 32, offers a Freudian interpretation of one urban legend, and a critique of Dundes.

67.   Ong, *Orality and literacy*, p. 12; p. 14; p. 11. As we develop and make use of Ong's analysis I must add a word of caution. The danger, of course, is that any of these dyadic contrasts can be used politically, ideologically. The stronger form of the orality/literacy contrast has been much criticised, and I have written, for my own purposes, an unpublished essay exploring the criticisms. Ong's book over-compacts a still active debate. See, as starting-points, the works of Goody and of Graff: Jack Goody (ed.), *Literacy in traditional societies*, Cambridge University Press, Cambridge, 1968; Jack Goody, *The interface between the written and the oral*, Cambridge University Press, Cambridge, 1987; Jack Goody, *The logic of writing and the organizing of society*, Cambridge University Press, Cambridge, 1986; Harvey J. Graff (ed.), *Literacy and social development in the West*, Cambridge University Press, 1981.

'Oral culture and its fundamental significance do not simply vanish under the attack of print, schooling, and modernization; rather, it dialectically accommodates the impact of them, one neither assimilating nor replacing the other. Too often, they are dichotomized, seen as in constant conflict with one another. Instead, in recognizing the persistence and the daily significance of oral communication, we need to study their relations: the ways in which, in some settings, one dominates or conflicts with the other, and, in others, they reciprocally support one another. A better understanding of their changing relations is required too'. (Harvey J. Graff, *The literacy myth: literacy and social structure in the nineteenth-century city*, Academic Press, New York, 1979, pp. 305–6).

I have found one account of a community deliberately eschewing education and literacy in order to preserve its life-style and culture, a study of 'travellers' of Irish descent in South Carolina, USA. See Ron Chepseiuk, 'Travellers who found a home in South Carolina', *Forthnight*, 29 April 1985, pp. 14–17.

68.   Neuburg, *Popular literature*, p. 52.

69. Gilley, 'English attitudes to the Irish', pp. 81–2; p. 105.
70. Ong, *Orality and literacy*, p. 69.
71. Ong, *Orality and literacy*, p. 173.
72. Ong, *Orality and literacy*, pp. 31–7, 'Some psychodynamics of orality'. See also Gunther Kress and Robert Hodge, *Language as ideology*, Routledge and Kegan Paul, London, 1979, on, for example, academic English, p. 134.
73. Ong, *Orality and literacy*, p. 52; A. R. Luria, *Cognitive development: its cultural and social foundations*, ed. Michael Cole, trans. Lopez-Morillas and Solotaroff, Harvard UP, Cambridge, 1976.
74. Kress and Hodge, *Language as ideology*, p. 10.
75. Reps, *Zen flesh, Zen bones*, p. 165: 'True Zen shows in everyday living, CONSCIOUSNESS in action. More than any limited awareness, it opens every inner door to our infinite nature.'
    Idries Shah, *The Sufis*, p. 76: 'Sufism is the whole, and carries with it the implications of completeness, not of the fragmentation of consciousness which the unenlightened may use in his own processes, and may call "concentration"'.
76. See, for example, the exchange between the clergy and a group of heretics — the heretics were in the end burned — at Orleans in 1022. The heretics drew a distinction between 'those who are learned in earthly things, who believe the fabrications which men have written on the skins of animals' and themselves: 'We believe in the law written within us by the Holy Spirit, and hold everything else, except what we have learnt from God, the maker of all things, empty, unnecessary, and remote from divinity'. R. I. Moore, *The birth of popular heresy*, Edward Arnold, London, 1975, p. 14.
77. The distinction will not seem mysterious to anyone who has taught literacy skills. But see, for example, J. W. Adamson, *The illiterate Anglo-Saxon*, Cambridge University Press, Cambridge, 1946, p. 38, who makes a clear distinction between the ability to read and the ability to write, 'writing being treated as a stage so far in advance of reading that only a few pupils would learn it'. And see Ong, *Orality and literacy*, p. 160; Neuburg, *Popular literature*, p. 53.
78. Idries Shah, *Exploits*, p. 124. A similar story — a neighbour asks Nasrudin to write a letter for him, to a cousin in a distant town. Nasrudin says, 'No, I can't — I've hurt my foot.'
    Or the famous 'Irish Mother's Letter to her Son' — 'Dear Son, I am writing this slowly because I know you can't read fast . . .' etc., etc.
79. Ong, *Orality and literacy*, p. 79. Ong, p. 81, also looks at a related theme: 'One of the most startling paradoxes inherent in writing is its close associations with death. The association is suggested in Plato's charge that writing is inhuman, thing-like, and that it destroys memory.' See 2 Cor. 3:6 — 'the letter kills but the spirit gives life'.
80. Patrick O'Sullivan, 'A literary difficulty in explaining Ireland: Tom Moore and Captain Rock, 1824' in Roger Swift and Sheridan Gilley (eds), *The Irish in Britain, 1815–1939*, Pinter, London, 1989, p. 268.
81. Ong, *Orality and literacy*, p. 80.
82. Ong, *Orality and literacy*, p. 80.
83. 'Of course oral cultures do not lack originality of their own kind. Narrative originality lodges not in making up new stories but in managing a particular interaction with this audience at this time — at every telling the story has to be introduced uniquely into a unique situation, for in oral cultures an audience must be brought to respond, often vigorously. But narrators also introduce new elements into old stories' (Ong, *Orality and literacy*, pp. 41–2). And see Ong, *Orality and literacy*, p. 22 onwards.

84. Norrman and Haarberg, *Nature and language*, for example, p. 152. Thus, if psychologists, like Wilson, can be criticised for unconsidered raids into the territory of the literary critic, literary critics can be criticised for their raids into psychology.
85. Norrman and Haarberg, *Nature and language*, p. 113.
86. R. H. Blyth, *Oriental humour*, Hokuseido Press, Tokyo.
87. Tenenbaum, *Wise men of Chelm*, p. 183. There is a 'First Mirror' story in Henry Glassie (ed.), *Irish folk tales*, pp. 89–90.

Acknowledgements

My thanks to those who commented on earlier versions of this chapter, within the Department of Applied Social Studies at the University of Bradford and at the Joint Annual Conference of the American Conference for Irish Studies and the Canadian Association for Irish Studies, Galway, July 1992.

4 The stage Irish

Owen Dudley Edwards

I could begin, of course, in a perfectly decent and conventional academic manner with which you are comfortably familiar, paying graceful tribute to others in the field especially when they might one day review or assess me, balancing my several judgments and conclusion and contributing enough whiff of originality to stimulate, without stifling you.

For example . . . No, on second thoughts, no examples. But look in any authorised academic journal of Hibernicity and see for yourself. There you have our *exempla prima gratissima*, of the stage Irish. Behold him, demurely ensconced behind footnotes and reservations, qualified and modified beyond reproach, making radical amendments to conservative theses, and restraining caveats to persuasive hypotheses, and exuding quiet reliability.

The most successful form of stage Irishry is that which is taken for what it mimics. Accordingly, orthodox academic Hibernian scholarship as conventionally presented is stage Irishry, and its camouflage succeeds by becoming also the reader's. Its consumption is gratifying to all parties. Truth is the casualty.

At this point you should be questioning the above, 'our first example'. Am not I, the writer, the first stage Irish person under your scrutiny in this investigation? Perhaps I am. I shall try to keep myself as your first example. Where I am analysing myself under the guise of objective scholarship, that is for you to discover. You may call it a sale of deficient produce. I may call it an additional bonus at no extra charge.

This particular exercise we have just performed is an essential part of stage Irishry, being concerned with masks and dialogue. The story-teller/playwright/performer had to assume some form of alienating expression, dress, speech formula to prevent common acquaintance with the audience impeding the absorption of the reality implicit in the fiction asserted in dramatic form. As Oscar Wilde (1854–1900) put it, 'The Truths of Metaphysics are the Truths of Masks'.[1] Or we might think of the use of mask by William Butler Yeats (1865–1939) to assert, notably in his Cuchulainn Plays, the separation of body and of soul.

But we will start with dialogue, which seems easier (and is not, since in Yeats's and Wilde's hands body and soul, mask and face, are in dialogue). And we are also starting with the assumption that a playwright in composition is in a condition of stage Irishry, whether Brendan Behan (1923–64) on the booze in front of his toadies or television–inquisitors, or Samuel Beckett (1906–91) in his intangibility and innominability, whether Wilde and Shaw let loose as aesthetic evangels in Philistine London ('he was Oscar the comic,' recalled Shaw (1856–1950), 'I was G. B. S. the clown.'), or the secretive consumptive John Millington Synge (1871–1909) alone in his Connaught bedroom listening through the crack in the floor to the ebb and flow of discourse, the complexities of syntax and speech-patterns, in the innocent gathering of post-Gaelic peasants underneath.

It is emotive language, this term 'stage Irish', usually an epithet, intended to separate the integrity of the accuser from the self-prostitution of the accused: actually its user for purposes of reproach has simply climbed on to another stage, called a pulpit. You are stage Irish, from that pulpit view; I am a national spokesman. But a pulpit is a stage, and an Irish person on a stage is not easily distinguishable from a stage Irish person. The logic of this appealed to the pioneer historian G. C. Duggan, whose *The Stage Irishman* (1937) embraced the Irish theatre over three centuries but grimly proscribed the usual outcasts normally categorised by his title, and by mine:

> It is unfortunate that the novels of [Charles] Lever [(1806–72)] and [Samuel] Lover [(1797–1868)], excellent as they are in the delineation of a genuinely humorous side to Irish life, should have led to a final deterioration on the stage of the hosts of buffoons who could only appreciate the superficialities of the novelists. To analyse such crudities would be merely a laboratory dissection. No work would be the poorer by their omission.[2]

A leading English creative authority on the varieties of stage Englishry (who had, indeed, done more to bring the stage Englishman to life in immortal prose than anyone since Dickens, possibly since Boswell), Pelham Grenville Wodehouse (1881–1975), had his own great creation Bertie Wooster receive in *The Mating Season* (1949) a bitter critique from Gussie Fink-Nottle as to distinctions between stage Irishries:

> Pat . . . prefaces his remarks at several points with the expressions 'Begorrah' and 'faith and begob'. Irishmen don't talk like that. Have you ever read Synge's *Riders to the Sea*? Well, get hold of it, and if you can show me a single character in it who says 'Faith and begob', I'll give you a shilling. Irishmen are poets. They talk about their souls and mist and so on. They say things like, 'An evening like this, it makes me wish I was back in County Clare, watchin' the cows in the tall grass.'

But, after a talk with the delectable film star Cora Pirbright, the Fink-Nottle view is changed:

> She overcame my objections entirely. We ran through the script after you had left us, and she quite brought me round to her view that there is nothing in the least degrading in this simple, wholesome form of humour. Hokum, yes, but, as she pointed out, good theatre. She is convinced that I shall go over big.[3]

It makes a difference, as Martin Luther (1483-1546) remarked, whose ox is gored — or, if you prefer, whose cow is watched in the tall grass, whose Irish bull is pregnant.

A stage absence?

'Gaelic-speaking Ireland never produced a single piece of dramatic literature in the native tongue.'[4] Thus Duggan. He meant well, but he was a little given to generalisation, especially when taking sides on an issue with implications for the Unionist-Nationalist divide in Irish politics. I recall his insistence that the Black and Tans had never been guilty of rape, which, as Conor Cruise O'Brien commented, would have made them an army unique in human history. As Sean Connery, a stage Irishman of Scottish background, learned to put it, 'never say never again'.

Our self-imprisonment in literacy makes us ignorant of the dramatic force of pre-literature. The bard declaimed his epic with the power and, so far as content enables us to judge, the variety of theatrical rendition. The complexity of ritual speaks for a theatrical culture. The Reformation when it emerged frequently outlawed theatre, seeing theatre as embodying a Roman Catholic ritual into which ancient paganism had been allowed to root. Surviving pagan festivals and superstitions do indicate a fine sense of the theatrical. Surviving scripts time and again seem dependent on dialogue of great dramatic possibility. Granted that a bellicose culture linked the bardic arts to much chauvinistic self-congratulation, the use of heroic verse with which to exhort hearers to comparable feats invited dramatic art in the telling, if not actual apportionment of roles:

> 'I'm glad the food is ready', said Conall. 'Who's carving for you?'
> 'It went to the man who is carving', said Conchobar. 'Cet mac Magach.'
> 'Is it true that you are carving the pig, Cet?' asked Conall . . . 'Get up from the pig now.'
> 'What will get it for you?' asked Cet.
> 'I have the right to challenge', said Conall. 'I give contest to you, Cet. I swear by my people's gods since I took a spear in my hand I was never a day without killing a Connachtman, or a night without raiding one, and I never slept without a Connachtman's head under my knee.'
> 'True', said Cet. 'You're a better hero than I am. But if Anluan were here he would give you contest. It is hard luck on us that he isn't here.'
> 'Oh, but he is', said Conall, taking Anluan's head from his belt; and he hit Cet on the chest with it and blood burst from his lips. So he went from the pig and Conall sat down at it.[5]

Now, did a bard deliver that in the manner of a bored supermarket clerk calling stock numbers?

The stage Irish existed before recorded history.

Epic invited dramatic narrative. But, further, the surviving poems commemorating the *Fianna* are often cast in dramatic two-part form, such as the *aighneas* (argument) and the *agallamh* (dialogue) of the magically-preserved tricentenarian Oisin and the repressively pious Saint Patrick. Oisin extols the chivalry and strength of his deceased relatives and comrades, Patrick announces that the present habitation of these heroes is in the infernal fires. The poems are variously funny, satirical, ferocious, contentious, pathetic, brutal, ribald, edifying, heroic, absurd and tragically lonely. It is an all too instructive paradigm of the confrontation of successive cultures: the Aztec and the Inca would find common ground with Oisin as they listened to the spiritual exhortations of the confessors of the Conquistadors, and the Amerindians would have understood Oisin's loyalties as they pondered the pieties of the English settlers. These things have come down to us in dramatic form, much as the miracle plays of England and Dublin have. The intention was to make great things accessible within our limited perceptions and to show how human sense of comedy can make it easier to come to terms with cosmic tragedy.

There were obvious audiences for epic or satire, patrons and comrades, young warriors and pupils; and the creators had an eye very clearly linked to audience response, intellectual, spiritual or animal as the context might be. But the earliest known stage Irish have a different audience in mind as well: Himself, in fact.

> Grant me, sweet Christ, the grace to find —
>   Son of the Living God! —
> A small hut in a lonesome spot
>   To make it my abode.
>
> A little pool but very clear
>   To stand beside the place,
> Where all men's sins are washed away
>   By sanctifying grace.[6]

And in religious poetry dramatic dialogues are sometimes very marked features, notably between the soul and the confessor, or between Death and the Sinner. Douglas Hyde (1862–1949) included in *The Religious Songs of Connaught* (1906) 'Dán an Tuir' where the protagonists are a man, a soul, Peter, Christ and Mary (whose intercession saves the all-but-damned soul).

> 'I do not know', says Peter,
> 'Does Christ recognize him?'
> 'I do not know', says Christ,
> 'Bitter alas! I do not recognize him.'
>
> Then spake the Glorious Virgin,
> And lowered herself on her white knees,
> 'Oh, my son, was it not for thee were prepared
> The heaps of embers
> To burn thy noble body?'
>
> 'O Mother, helpful, glorious,
> If it be thy will to take him to heaven,
> I let him with thee . . . '[7]

In this instance (which may be work written as late as the eighteenth or nineteenth century) the poet creates a sacred drama intended to edify its audience and remind it that Mary's intervention is efficacious in gaining mercy for sinners, but it is also 'performed' with a sense of the celestial audience noting down particulars and homologating them in due time. Puritanical criticism of the theatre existed in Catholic and Protestant circles, but the sense of performance to influence Man and to address God transcended that. The other populistic, disadvantaged, church of substantial Irish following, the Presbyterian, prided itself on its anti-ritualism, but Presbyterian sermons were their own form of sacred drama in one-person performance for simultaneous human and divine audiences. The stage Irish seldom forget that God has a box seat, whether they believe in Him or not.

Let's take a modern stage Irish witness: (Sir) William Tyrone Guthrie (1900–71), the great director and designer in British and Canadian theatre. His names testify to maternal descent from Tyrone Power (1797–1841). That original Tyrone Power made his name at Drury Lane Theatre in stage Irish roles and in several plays of his own (such as *St Patrick's Eve* (1832), *Paddy Cary, the Boy of Clogheen* (1833) and *O'Flannigan and the Fairies* (1836), toured the USA and went down with the *President* after his third sojourn. According to some reports, he afterwards made a posthumous farewell appearance at Drury Lane to take leave of his friends, which says much for the resilience of his stagecraft. His male descendants, of course, included the eponymous film actor (1914–58). But Tyrone Guthrie's paternal descent was from the preacher and philanthropist, Rev. Thomas Guthrie (1803–73), apostle of ragged schools and moderator of the Free Church of Scotland in 1862, and as the younger Guthrie put it:

> Of course, thumping the pulpit cushions is but a hair's breadth from treading the boards. And of the two great-grandparents, Doctor Guthrie, the minister, with his leonine head, his rich ringing voice, his immense renown as an orator and raconteur, was far the more theatrical figure of the two.[8]

It is meaningless to protest — though important to notice — that the elder Guthrie was Scots. The Irish not only went world-wide, but came from a wide world. Where Presbyterianism, or the Macdonald family, or the Gaelic language, or the Celtic Church were concerned, Scotland and Ulster were closer than Ulster and Munster, over the last 1500 years. Even Cuchulainn graduated from the Scottish (female-run) university of the day.

The younger Guthrie would transform the Hall of the General Assembly of the Church of Scotland in Edinburgh into a Festival Theatre in 1948 uniting the former enemies, Church and Theatre; but his stress on his Protestant great-grandfather at the expense of the Wexford-born Power may have shown less ecumenism. Yet one could not ask for a more striking exposition of theatrical descent from different Irish ethnic traditions, atypical as no doubt it was.

In any case Irish Presbyterianism and Irish Catholicism are similar in tradition-consciousness, populism, conservatism and heritage of degradation. Degradation means a step down. A stage means a step up. A stage is essential to rise above degradation. Identity seems to be an attribute discovered from others: to be Irish is an experience formulated and developed in response to persons who are not Irish and who say you are Irish. They place you on a stage, and you perform.

Curiously enough, our first major exploration of that identity, the fifth-century *Confessio of St Patrick*, places an alien performer, Patrick, before an Irish audience, and that performer's own search for identity was complicated by a pre-enslavement background of Romanised Britishness in which he sycophantically sought peer-group deference by depravity (Restoration comedy later worked on the same principle). The Irish in a sense start out not as actors in Patrick's story, but as directors: they dragged a magnificent performance out of him, found him sincerity as his key to stage success, and placed him in relation to his several audiences of God, Ireland, Britain and himself. Among other things, it is a reminder that for all of its perennial image of lamentation, Ireland first comes into written documentation as an aggressor, and in important respects the stage Irish hold that status to the end (or to the present, whichever comes first). The inherent virtues of Patrick, notably his proof of the fortitude to be drawn from humility, are not traditional stage-Irish characteristics: posterity tends to forget that Patrick was not Irish, however much his destiny shaped itself in response to Irish oppressiveness, Irish prompting and Irish needs. His most notable modern counterpart in this respect seems to have been Micheál Mac Liammóir (1899–1978), who also passed for Irish but deliberately so, English-descended and English-born Alfred Lee Willmore, Irish by adoption and acclaim. Patricius and Micheál have between them the greatest claims to stage-Irishness of all time, since they were peerless masters of their crafts while being all stage and no Irish. Mac Liammóir dramatically united their work when scripting the official pageant of the Roman Catholic Archdiocese of Dublin for its celebration of the millenary-and-a-half of Patrick's death in 1961 (proclaimed with chronological confidence in inverse proportion to its dubiety: Patrick's life-span may well be the latter part of the fifth century). Dublin report — quite possibly accurate in this instance — stated that the authoritarian Archbishop of Dublin, John Charles McQuaid (1895–1973) vetoed but one line of it: 'Patrick, this is a druid-ridden country'. McQuaid's staging was usually an achievement in negative direction, of that kind, but he had no competitors himself when in his own full performance on stage, notably in the Dublin proclamation of the Holy Year of 1950 with the Primate, flanked by his clergy and laity in full submission around him, processing up the aisle of the Dublin Pro-Cathedral to the strains of *Ecce Sacerdos Magnus*.

Irishness for Patrick seems to have been clear enough, being non-Christian, slave-owning and non-Romanised. Irishness for subsequent saints such as Columba or Colmcille had no such clear demarcations: despite subsequent legend as to his choice of exile, Columba's Scotland was an extension of Ireland, with similarity of language and literature and, as he quickly ensured, Celtic religion. Irishness became the identity of the missionaries, marked above all by its want of compromise with the non-Irish: again a feature of Irish religion in export for the next millenium and a half. The famous hagiographical account of Columba's encounter with the Loch Ness Monster, who descended at his command below the waves, is an appropriate parable for the future: the essence of being an Irish missionary was in general to take a stage stance in which any sign of concession to the home-grown opponent is a self-destructive indication of weakness. And supposedly post-religious Irish nationalist theatre is not entirely happy with the abandonment of that stance: its converse is handled severely in Brian Friel's *Dancing at Lughnasa* (1990). Hence Irish ecclesiastical administration from Celtic times to our own has tended to be *apartheid*: Irish persons and issues are the favoured votaries, others are the peripherals, the dogs permitted to take such nourishment as is allowed to fall from the children's table. Small wonder that the Scots Catholics declined to have their hierarchy restored until 1878 in fear the bishops would be nephews or protégés of the great Irish spiritual imperialist Paul Cardinal Cullen (1803–78).

A synthesis of the cases of Patrick and Columba is provided by that of St Malachy (*c.* 1094–1148). Here we have, not the missionary to benighted aliens, but the apostle to his own people, ostensibly relaxing and actually performing before an alien fan club, headed by his future biographer St Bernard of Clairvaux (1090–1153). It is the natural urge to make a good story of the problem of being misunderstood by one's own people: the cast-out-of-the-synagogue-at-Nazareth performance. Considering that the cultural apostle is all too frequently cast out of the synagogue in his native Nazareth, the temptation to stage one's wrongs in amusing but touching style is seemingly impossible to withstand. Malachy captured his audience ('You command all the affection, and all the devotion of which I am capable', wrote Bernard to him) and Malachy crowned his hold on that audience by dying in front of it. Bernard wrote of the death of Malachy to Malachy's Irish followers: 'When he lay dying he remembered you and lovingly commended you to God, and he begged even me, a person of no consequence, always to remember you . . . Even I have been stirred from my sloth and imbued with reverence by the pattern of perfection he set before me'.[9] But the personal love binding Bernard to Malachy's memory made Bernard all the more ferocious in condemning Malachy's fellow-Irish, as obstinate, lecherous, corrupt, half-pagan and above all convinced of their superiority to reformers.

This established a scenario painfully evident in the next 800-odd years and no doubt long to remain with us. The people at home learn that their reputation has, supposedly, suffered at the hands of an exile; they writhe with anger and anguish at what seems self-serving treachery. That the foreign audience has responded well to the performance, regurgitating with many simplifications its more lurid features, makes matters worse. The older community at home is close-knit, conservative, self-encapsulated; the audience which hears of it is metropolitan, sophisticated, ready to mock what looks old-fashioned. In modern times the scenario seemed to invite foreign, especially English, materialism to laugh at Irish piety; but the metropolis versus the primitives scene in the Bernardine version of Malachy's Ireland, we should remember, has piety denouncing sloth, backsliding, hedonism and paganism. The modern Irish response was to denounce the Bernards and Malachys of the day indiscriminately, and, during the heyday of the Censorship of Obscene Publications, to find any possible pretext to ban such betrayals; if the resultant books could not be banned, they might be locally burned.

Such staged betrayals might induce riot in Ireland or in Irish-America (as happened when Synge's *Playboy of the Western World* was staged in Dublin in 1907 and New York in 1911). The anger of the mob was doubtless comparable to the anger of many an Irish reader of Bernard's *Life of St Malachy*: official fury at the supposed untruth of what was being said or performed, deeper and greater shame because of the unspoken knowledge so much of it *was* true. In the case of social critics from Malachy via Bernard onwards, the performance carried with it a reformer's zeal, hence an even more unrestrained element of

lampoon in performance. And future stage-producers of stage-Irish performance would not share Bernard's decent self-denunciation. He at least cannot
be charged with implying he was holier than his audience, though he was; but
the future metropolitan hosts to stage Irishry were much more questionably
holier-than-thou. Beyond the hatred of the shame which stage Irish abroad
might induce among the home-domiciled sources, there was a note of fear:
public profanation of primitive culture before a sophisticated audience drove a
long nail into that culture's coffin. Knowledge of metropolitan ribaldry and
contempt, or even a metropolitan affectionate amusement, might inspire
defensive proscription, ostracism, commination — but all such siege defence-
works could only be temporary and the survival of old culture would grow
increasingly self-conscious. A metropolitan influence might be resisted, but as a
rule at the cost of increasingly kitsch refrigeration of the old ways. And, as
Milan Kundera remarks in *The Incredible Lightness of Being*, kitsch is an
intermediate stage between existence and oblivion. Meanwhile, in obvious
processes, the staging of Irishness, which threw the home culture on the
defensive, established on stage its own, more obvious, form of kitsch. The
offender and the offended, or the performer and the performed, froze in
counterpoint. As they grew too old to dream, they had one another to
remember.

The deeper we dig, the stronger a dramatic tradition seems to exist in all Irish
ethnic groups. We must simply stop trying to assert that to have a dramatic
tradition is to have it evolve solely as it evolved in England. In some ways the
Gaelic antecedents of theatre did develop comparably to the English: through
fairs, through jesters, through gleemen and grinners. Perhaps the Gaelic
tradition of the trickster gives us a mythological antecedent for the privileged
position such a figure enjoyed in both Gaelic and Norman courts, but he seemed
to do much the same work in both cultures: much like the Gaelic bard or the
Norman minstrel, propagandist of the chieftain and jealous defender of old
fashions.

Something quite close to dramatic presentations seem to have been made at
the fairs (notably Tailtenn in Co. Meath, Carman in Co. Kildare) by the time of
the Norman invasion, particularly in the poetic contests. The growth of
Christianity brought the dramatic personation of the protagonists to the Good
Friday and Easter narration of the gospels, and pageants on feasts such as
Corpus Christi, in summer, also figured reverent impersonation. Significantly,
in 1366 dramatic events in church festivals and vigils were formally interdicted
in the name of Christ and State by the English and the very anti-Gaelic,
Archbishop of Dublin, Thomas Minot, who ruled from 1363 to 1375. It may
have been that the business of processing in the guise of a religious figure bred a
fairly static form of acting, and this seems to persist in traditions of folk-song
also, ideally declaimed with an averted, almost masklike face. We recall that,
when the very first Abbey Theatre performances were given in the early
twentieth century, British theatre-goers were startled at the vividly statuesque
blocking with movement pared to the bone; the bones, Yeats might say, with
which they dreamed.

Our source material for Gaelic Thespianism is very deficient and inferential,
but some form of theatre evidently accompanied the more sophisticated kind

of wake. It also seems to have accompanied greater weddings in the late medieval period. When English mummer plays penetrated Ireland, they seem to have fed on live traditions in the remoter parts of Kerry: William Smith Clark notes the incidence of mummer performance in west Kerry in his invaluable *The Early Irish Stage* (1955), but (coming, as he did, from an Anglophone American background) he understandably fails to be startled at the incidence of this supposed English import so far from the metropolis. Such mumming seems to have linked up with the old (and, one fears, cruel) celebration of the hunting of the wren on the day after Christmas. It required an elaborate cast, including male and female fools (*amadán* and *óinseach*) and may reflect some faint link with the Italian *commedia dell' arte* with its own long folk origin. Kerry, after all, is much closer to the European coastline in terms of seaborne communications than it is to England. The wren production was in vigorous life in the early twentieth century and has a chapter to itself in the Irish-language Dingle-based answer to Mark Twain's Tom Sawyer and Huck Finn: *Jimín Mháire Thaidhg* (1921) by An Seabhac ('The Hawk') alias Padraig O Siochfhradha (1883–1944).[10]

The Irish-language pantomimes in the Abbey in the late-1940s seem to have drawn on a comparable mix. Clark notes the appearance of Oliver Cromwell (1599–1658) as a mummer villain after the Restoration, a role he sustained in the mid-twentieth century also but with Stalin as his counterpart in another year. (By 1950, however, the Devil was no longer brought in to carry off Cromwell: in John Charles McQuaid's Dublin that might have savoured of mockery of sacred subjects.) It might be argued that the hatred of Cromwellian proscription of the theatres would make the damnation of the late Lord Protector a most appropriate English theatre subject: but with all due deference to English tradition, Cromwell's damnation notoriously meant even more to Gaelic Ireland. It is also curious that, whatever their English antecedents, surviving texts of mummer plays (in Cork in 1685, for instance) add, to the knocking down of the 'Turkish Slasher' by St George, the knocking down of St George by St Patrick. Where it was not indigenous, mumming in Ireland seemed at least respectful of its surroundings.

The staged Irish (1)

But formal English-style theatre seems to have begun in terms much more alien and hostile to indigenous Irishry, which may explain the historiographical over-emphasis on a non-dramatic Gaelic culture. I think it reasonable to say that in the world of theatre, if Gaelic Ireland had not been to school, it met the scholars, and it seemed to meet them half-way. But where the scholars were hostile, the Irish were aggrieved. On Christmas Day 1661 a tale-bearer named John Binckes informed acting Secretary George Williamson that he had been talking with 'a person from Ireland, to discover what conspiracies are on foot there; he said Irish discontents were raised to a great height, because players were allowed to condemn the Irish on their stages'.[11] Granted Binckes's unscholarly motivation ('desires some money') his evidence nevertheless shows us how old was the suspicion attached to the stage Irish. On this showing, the rioters against Yeats's

The Countess Cathleen (1899), against Synge's *Playboy* and against Sean O'Casey's (1884–1964) *The Plough and the Stars* (1926) seem to be in a very long tradition. Dublin was certainly a much more English-dominated town in 1661 than in Yeats' time but the stakes may have been similar: the sense that the stage Irish fixed an image of Ireland in the minds of the powerful, and that the Ireland of the stage might determine the Ireland of the future. Whoever Binckes's discontented were, they imply that, from the start, theatre in Ireland was political in effect if not necessarily in content. The real hard political points might be limited to mummer and amateur festival activity (just as in the late-1940s there was more political satire in the Abbey pantomime than anywhere else on the Irish stage, with the Minister of Agriculture, James Dillon represented on stage clucking like a hen laying an egg); but formal theatre was assumed to be a political act.

   If Binckes was right, there was a perception from the first that formal theatre was power manoeuvre. Most appropriately, the very first plays we know to have been acted in Ireland were written and produced by a man who while justly called 'the father of Anglo-Irish drama'[12] might be with equal justice saluted as the Reformation in Ireland. The sixteenth-century state-appointed officials sent over to Protestantise Ireland were, for the most part, the scraping from the bottom of the venal Tudor barrel, into a good racket for money, power, pride. It is therefore a pleasure to salute, from the other side of the religious divide, the sincerity of John Bale (1495–1563), Bishop of Ossory in 1553, who breathed his hatred of Catholicism with all his heart and soul, and who wisely fled to the continent on the accession of Mary I. He sought to convert Ireland to Protestantism by staging at the Mercat Cross in Kilkenny such of his writings as *A Brefe Comedy or Enterlude of Johan Baptystes Preachynge in the Wyldernesse; openynge the craftye Assaults of the Hypocrytes with the glorious Baptysme of the Lord Jesus Christ.* His other works included *The Three Lawes* (for whose production he directed 'Let Idolatry be decked like an old witch, Sodomy like a monk of all sects, Ambition like a bishop . . . '). He lived long in the memories of the people for whose salvation he struggled so dramatically, and it is good that he has received his belated honours in our day from a fine English playwright now living in Ireland, John Arden, in his *Books of Bale* (1988).[13] But if Bale brought the Irish on stage (as a means to their conversion), we know nothing of his actors. Did he cast only his own followers, or recruit natives? Did Sodomy and Ambition have Irish accents?

   The first formally stage-Irish play was, curiously enough, the work of an English Roman Catholic, James Shirley (1596–1666). Shirley seems to have resembled most of his fellow English Catholics (headed by the landgrabbing Mary Tudor herself) in wishing firmly to distinguish their identities from those of their Gaelic co-religionists, if anything more vehemently than most of the English Protestant conquistadors. In *Saint Patrick for Ireland* Shirley exhumes Patrick as a type of British civilisation, who converted the native Irish to Christianity and, in so far as it was possible, Briticism. Patrick's very first speech, after self-introduction and statement of peaceful intentions have been received with demands from king and court that he depart, begins:

Patrick: You are inhospitable,
And have more flintie bosomes than the rocks
That bind your shores, and circle your faire Iland;
But I must not returne —

King Leogarius: How?
Chife priest Archimagus: How?
Patrick: Till I have
      Perform'd my dutie . . .

Here Patrick's proclamation seems to place him firmly within the British imperial tradition from Shakespeare's Henry V to Nelson, and Frederick in Gilbert's *Pirates of Penzance*.

Saint Patrick for Ireland ends with the foiled magician Archimagus, having furiously witnessed the banishment of the snakes he has brought on stage to destroy Patrick (a *coup de théâtre* to stage), himself descending through the trap, in the tradition of Marlowe's Faustus:

Archimagus: A fire, a dreadfull fire is underneath me
And all those fiends that were my servants here,
Look like tormentors, and all seem to strive,
Who first shall catch my falling flesh upon
Their burning pikes: There is a power above
Our gods, I see too late. I fall, I fall,
And in my last despaire, I curse you all. [14]

This is the staged Irishman with a vengeance, very much the symbol of treachery, murder, ferocity, barbarism and inevitable obsolescence. Shirley's Catholicism seems genuine enough, if necessarily muted here in the service of Lord Deputy Thomas Wentworth, Earl of Strafford (1593–1641). But Archimagus is the lineal antecedent of the Irish Popish priests to be trotted out on London and Dublin stages by zealous Protestant playwrights for many a long year. Shirley — wisely — did not try dialogue Irish-style, and his choice of pagan gods seems to argue an excessively good classical education for Archimagus: but the identification of murderous barbarism with native Irish religious leadership is well established by Spenser's *The Faerie Queen*, which had in fact supplied the name 'Archimago'. Shirley certainly holds Gaelic bards up to ignorant ridicule:

Love is a bog,
    a deep bog,
    a wide bog.
Love is a clog,
    a great clog.
    a close clog. [15]

Etc . . . Etc . . . The bog was — as Shakespeare indicates — proverbially Irish, the clog implied subjection to France. And this was dramaturgy for the official theatre, established under Wentworth's viceregal command by Ireland's first official Master of the Revels, the Scotsman John Ogilby (1600–76). Kavanagh in 1946 thought *Saint Patrick for Ireland* 'amazing . . . Shirley gave a semi-miracle play to an Anglo-Irish audience and made them like it':[16] but we must remember that Shirley appealed not to an anti-Papist colony so much as to a High Anglican court. Ireland was intended to become a deGaelicised Stuart preserve, where fine arts would flourish in a hothouse of English Cavalier culture:

> *Patrick*: This Nation
>   Shall in a fair succession thrive, and grow
>   Up the world's Academie, and disperse,
>   As the rich spring of humane and divine
>   Knowledge, cleare streames to water forraine Kingdomes,
>   Which shall be proud to owe what they possesse
>   In learning, to this great all-nursing Iland.

The myth — a myth with considerable substance — that Ireland after Christianisation became a survival capsule for captured Roman culture, was now to serve a Caroline ethos.

The hopes and fears of primitive Irish hostility to civilisation imported from Britain, were reflected in *Saint Patrick for Ireland* by the Saint's realisation that all had not yet won by the damnation, however gratifying, of the indigenous spiritual leader and the outlawry of his speckled band. The last words of the main play give us Patrick's misgivings about the representative of Ireland itself, King Leogarius:

> *Patrick* [*Aside*]:   I suspect him still
>   But feare not, our good Angels still are neer us
>   Death at the last can but untie our fraility;
>   'Twere happy for our holy faith to bleed,
>   The Blood of Martyrs in the Churche's seed.

It is a brave cry from a citadel ominously conscious of living in a state of siege, and all the more striking in the explosion of 1641 when Shirley's native fellow-Catholics rose and massacred numbers of settlers (numbers quickly exaggerated, no doubt, but numbers large enough without inflation). Ogilby and his Werburgh Street Theatre were swept away, and Shirley's Irish career was over, although, twenty years after, the Scotsman, fresh from his production of Charles II's coronation, won a life renewal of his Revels-Mastership and established in 1662 the Smock-Alley Theatre which with various vicissitudes would last until 1787: in an eerie reminder of the perpetuity of the stage Irishman *malgré lui* on the streets of Dublin, the Church of Saints Michael and John which took the theatre's site in 1815 was casually known to the working-class Catholics as 'Micky and Jacks', traditionally slang for penis and pissoir. We do not understand Catholic Ireland unless we can appreciate the comfortable coexistence of scatology and eschatology, which blended in a stage-world before private or public audiences.

The wars of Irish identity on the stage were if anything far more urgent outside of Dublin than in it: the riots against Yeats and Co. from 1899 to 1926 arose partly because for the first time in its career, Dublin was beginning to fall under Irish Catholic control and stage wars were important declarations of identity and non–identity. The stage-Irish wars in other cities came from the reverse epiphany: the Irish were penetrating cities, first London, then various urban centres throughout the English-speaking world, and the natives there did not feel easy with the new invaders. We may start at the top.

'Shakespeare', observes V. G. Kiernan, in his seminal *Shakespeare, Poet and Citizen*, 'grew up in the tradition of the old "morality" plays'.[17] And in Shakespeare's genius above all others we can see reflection and didacticism in the most powerful forms. Eugene Gladstone O'Neill (1888–1953), was the son of the Irish-American actor James O'Neill (1847–1920): the father's patriotism and his conflicting search for patrician social status united in his giving his son as second name the name of the British premier who proposed Home Rule for Ireland. The father sacrificed the hope of Shakespearean stardom to gain security in popular roles; and in a moment of dialogue between James Tyrone and Edmund, the playwright's stage version of his father and himself, Eugene captured the greatest of all stage-Irish hopes:

> Edmund (*sits down opposite his father —— contemptuously*): Yes, facts don't mean a thing, do they? What you want to believe, that's the only truth! (*Derisively.*) Shakespeare was an Irish Catholic, for example.
>
> Tyrone (*stubbornly*): So he was. The proof is in his plays.
>
> Edmund: Well he wasn't, and there's no proof of it in his plays, except to you![18]

Edmund, as Eugene's obvious unease in the writing suggests, is not as immune from the search for ethnic acceptability as he likes to imagine: and if Tyrone is absurd here, he is not wholly baseless. Shakespeare was more Welsh than the English acknowledged, and more Catholic (though not more Roman Catholic). But if Shakespeare was not an Irish Catholic, he records odd perceptions showing that he, too, had met the scholars, and some of those meetings were noted by the indefatigable pioneer W. J. Lawrence.[19] *As You Like It*, whose mock-pastoral can read like a wry comment on Spenser and Raleigh in Ireland without implying any such Shakespearean intention, includes Irish allusions which show familiarity with Gaelic sources, wheresoever derived. Rosalind alludes to the old Gaelic satiric properties capable of charming rats into destruction by the use of verse: 'I was never so berimed since Pythagoras' time, that I was an Irish rat, which I can hardly remember.'[20]

Pythagoras's doctrine of the transmigration of souls supplies the link. The awareness of magic, performance and poetry as interlinked opens up the Celtic heritage in a far more authoritative fashion than Shirley would exhibit. (This might suggest that the Pied Piper of Hamelin was also Irish. The Browning version could support a stage-Irish reading of the eponymous role.) That difficult word *Ducdame* from *As You Like It* may be a version of *tiocfaigh me*, pronounced 'tyucame', and meaning 'I will come', from the love-song 'Eibhlín a rún', a young-Lochinvar chant in which the lady tells the young man she will go with him while those in a circle around her are befooled by want of understanding of the words' meaning: Jaques says the word calls fools into a circle. The poet salutes her with a hundred thousand welcomes, as Menenius Agrippa would do in *Coriolanus*. The odd thing about this type of allusion is that it seems instinctive: Shakespeare the playwright is not reaching out in some stock joke giving common ground to his audience and himself, as thrown up with the First Gravedigger's remarks on the mad English. One might argue that if there were a case for Shakespeare being Irish, it is to be found in the *Comedy of Errors*, III. ii, when Dromio of Syracuse explains that he can find whole countries in his lady-love and his master asks;

> *Antipholus*: In what part of her body stands Ireland?

> *Dromio*: Marry, sir, in her buttocks: I found it out by the bogs.

But the classic passage is in *Henry V* where, in Kiernan's words:

> Shakespeare hints at . . . incorporation of Ireland as a partner in a coming union of the British Isles. His quartet of officers in Henry V's army includes a Captain Macmorris, a sapper. What kind of Irishman he is is left unspecified; he may be of mixed stock, like his name, or belong to one of the other three main sorts of Shakespeare's day — native Celtic, Catholic 'old English', and more recent Protestant settlers. Macmorris is sensitive on the subject, and takes offence at an innocent remark from Fluellen about his 'nation'. 'What ish my nation? Who talks of my nation?' (III.ii. 119–21). Nationality was becoming a ticklish question over much of Europe, and for Irishmen more so than most.[21]

Kiernan has solved an ancient problem. Shakespeare is in fact asserting the Irish crisis of identity. But in so doing he caters to his groundlings by festooning the part with phenomena of stage Irishness — bloodthirstiness, theocentricity, filio-pietism, rashness, zeal, plaint;

> *Macmorris*: By Chrish, la, tish ill done; the work ish give over, the trompet sound the retreat. By my hand, I swear, and my father's soul, the work ish ill done; it ish give over: I would have blow'd up the town, so Chrish save me, la, in an hour: O, tish ill done, tish ill done; by my hand, tish ill done! . . .

> It is no time to discourse, so Chrish save me: the day is hot, and the weather, and the wars, and the king, and the dukes: it is no time to discourse. The town is beseecht, and the trompet call us to the breach; and we talk, and be Chrish, do nothing: 'tis shame for us all: so God sa' me, 'tis shame to stand still; it is shame, by my hand: and there is throats to be cut, and works to be done; and there ish nothing done, so Chrish sa' me, la . . .

> Of my nation! What ish my nation? Ish a villain, and a bastard, and a knave, and a rascal — What ish my nation? Who talks of my nation? . . .

> I do not know you so good a man as myself: so Chrish save me, I will cut off your head.[22]

It is his only appearance, but he set the pattern for stage Irishmen thereafter. As Kiernan says, he could be one of three types, each type no doubt very clear in its view of its competitors for Irish identity and ready to dispute identity with any of those competitors, but capable of filling the role, and thereby encouraging the competitors to do the same. The stage-Irish identity imposed a similar pattern on antithetical persons, in that it was an identity created by an alien, a metropolitan and a more sophisticated, a wealthier and a more powerful society. Significantly, it transcended class: caste always does. Sir Lucius O'Trigger and Sir Callaghan O'Brallaghan are brothers under the uniform to Lever's Mickey Free and Lover's Handy Andy, arguably with intellect and status in inverse proportions. But as Englishness represented from Dickens's Pickwick and Weller, Wodehouse's Wooster and Jeeves, can prove, the stage Irish have no monopoly of that.

The staged Irish (2)

> Now stop your Noses, Readers, all and some,
> For here's a Tun of Midnight-work to come . . . (lines 457-8)

It may well seem a greater insult to Ireland than any uttered in stage Irish that the real politicisation of stage Irishry, to the lasting detriment of Irish self-respect, should have arisen through a personal vendetta between two literary Englishmen who purloined Ireland as a weapon in thieves' battle. John Dryden (1631–1700) and Thomas Shadwell (1640–92) pursued their vendetta in the 1680s. The Glorious Revolution of 1688–9 ejected Dryden from the Poet Laureateship and appointed Shadwell to the post. The Revolution's celebrant, Thomas Babington Macaulay (1800–59) was to defend the ejection of Dryden when writing his *History of England* but could not bring himself to mention the successor (though in private correspondence he dated the decline of the Laureateship into contempt with Shadwell's appointment). But Dryden had the last laugh as well as the first: for his *Mac Flecknoe or a Satyr Upon the Trew Blew Protestant Poet* (1682) so firmly equated Dullness with Shadwell that succeeding centuries have declined the labour of test. He threw in the above couplet to open his return to the theme in *The Second Part of Absalom and Achitophel* (1682):

> A Monstrous mass of foul corrupted matter,
> As all the Devils had spew'd to make the batter.
> When wine has given him courage to Blaspheme
> He curses God, but God before curst him . . . (lines 464-7)

The theme of *Mac Flecknoe* itself turns on Shadwell's anointment as Prince of Dullness in succession to the allegedly-Irish ex-priest Richard Flecknoe (d. 1678), hence son of Flecknoe. The poem alludes to Shadwell's residence in Ireland in 1663 by having Flecknoe give Ireland's lack of snakes as cause of Shadwell's inability to translate his malice into art:

> In thy fellonious heart though Venom lies,
> It does but touch thy Irish pen, and dyes. (lines 201-2)

Dryden knew enough to know that 'Mac' meant 'son' in Gaelic; presumably he didn't know enough to know that the English in closest proximity to 'Flecknoe' (if Gaelic) was 'the famous wet', but he seems to have managed without that information. In fact the surname seems unknown in Ireland, and one wonders if Flecknoe was indeed, as has been alleged, an Irish Jesuit. Andrew Marvell (1621–78) met him in 1645 and apparently found no Irishness in him; and Irishness would presumably have interested the future author of 'An Horatian Ode on General Cromwell's Return from Ireland'. Flecknoe himself published several unperformed plays, though he had the interesting habit of including bogus cast-lists. In one respect Flecknoe goes beyond dullness into gibbering insanity having in a treatise on the theatre extolled Charles II on the ground that 'after his happy Restauration he took such care to purge it from all vice and obscenity'. A critic who can thus term a stink a divine fragrance seems any Royal Family's answer to prayer: the rival Laureates thus kept out the ideal choice for the post.

We have to assume that after 1641 whosoever in English letters could fix an Irish label on a political opponent would do so: Dryden himself as a 'Tory' was thereby tarred by a party label derived from the Irish language, meaning a highwayman of alleged Gaelic aristocratic antecedents. Shadwell writhed under the Irish associations heaped on him by Dryden, not only with the name 'Flecknoe', but also 'for giving me the *Irish* name of *Mack*, when he knows I never saw *Ireland* till I was three and twenty years old, and was there but four months'.[23] Shadwell brought to the stage in his play *The Lancashire Witches* (1681) the pattern of an Irish priest-ruffian in Tegue O'Divelly. Shadwell's modern editor, Montague Summers, described Tegue as one of 'the two best gentlemen' in the play, but that perhaps is more of a comment on Shadwell's immersion in the perverse ethics of Restoration comedy. *The Lancashire Witches* was a scurrilous exploitation of the witch-hunting climate created by the perjury-created 'Popish Plot'. Summers describes Tegue O'Divelly as:

> a mere mock-moppet. I am afraid it was meant maliciously, but the caricature is too gross. He is lecherous and lewd, and much of his talk is scandalously profane, but I do not think he will do any harm, for he is as unreal as a pantomime head whose pasteboard cheeks and huge rolling eyes do not frighten even the littlest children.[24]

Yet, as Summers notes, in the very year of the play's first performance, Saint Oliver Plunket, the Roman Catholic Archbishop of Armagh, was executed at Tyburn, convicted on evidence as baseless as the prejudices catered for by the creation of Father Tegue O'Divelly. Shadwell brought O'Divelly back in *The Amorous Bigotte*, in 1690, when anti-Catholicism had revived.

The success of the earlier play depended in part on its success in using stage machinery to produce flying broomsticks; but the success hardened the stage-Irish tradition around O'Divelly. The satiric battle between the two English poets and their supposed Irish priests is complicated by Dryden's being aware of *The Lancashire Witches* in rehearsal and Shadwell's apparently seeing *Mac Flecknoe* in manuscript.

Granting Shadwell's provocation at Dryden's hands (to which he was no more capable of adequate response than James II, Dryden's patron, could outflank William III, Shadwell's deliverer), we may now look at Tegue O'Divelly revived in *The Amorous Bigotte*, when Shadwell's cause was won, his income secure and his enemies impoverished or outlawed. We discover Tegue in Madrid, with his devoted patroness Belliza and her sceptical daughter Elvira (who is discovered reading 'a wicked and profane Love Book'):

Tegue:	In trot it is great pitty of dee, and a great faable, by my shoul I vould have all handsome Ladies dewout indeed, and I do love to put my Eys upon dem, and maake a great faash upon dem, when I do instruct dem, indeed gra.
Elvira:	No doubt on't.
Tegue:	I do love to caast de look upon de pretty Laady indeed, vid pious meditaation, and consideration dat Heaven did maake dem sho handshom gra.
Belliza	[*an error for 'Elvira'?*]: Good holy Man, we are bound to admire the works of Heaven.
Tegue:	Vell shayd Daughter, dou dosht spake like an aable shaint, indeed gra; but I must complain upon you for dis waanity, if dou musht have some waanity, joy pridee now taake shome fitt days for dat occaasion of waanity.
Belliza:	This is a sweet preparation in procession week, to be pruning yourself, like an unclean Bird.
Tegue:	Phaat will I spaake unto you for dese spotts and blemishes upon dy swheet faash gra, arrah I vil maake you do de greaat pennance for dish.
Belliza	[*error for 'Elvira'?*]: What's the reason Father I may not wear patches?
Tegue:	Aboo, boo, boo, what am I dat dou dosht maake expostulaation, and demand a Reason of mee?
Elvira:	One that has it not about him.
Tegue:	Reashon of mee, dou dosht maake indignation and affront upon me, by my shoulwation. Am I not a Priesht, and vil I give a Reashon.
Belliza:	'Twas wickedly done to affront the good Man so.
Tegue:	Have I Converted sho many Hereticks dogs and was sho deep in our braave Plott, and had like to have bin after slain upon a Gibbet, and been a great Martyr for de Plott, and dosht dou require a Reashon of mee?[25]

The perennial English conviction that an Irish accent lies within the capabilities of any Englishman is evidently a delusion of no recent birth; but Shadwell clearly listened more attentively than most, so much so that he must have had a fine memory for his Irish months or an ecumenical exposure to native Irish voices. His Irish 's' is of course hopeless, as was Shakespeare's: the intrusive 'sh' in post-Gaelic English is pre-consonantal, not pre-vowel, and not an eclipsis of final 's'. But other forms of Shadwell stage Irish look plausible. The mingling of 'v' and 'w' sounds arise from complex rules in the pronunciation of 'bh', an aspirated labial in common Gaelic use. If we accept that 'aa' simply means the lengthening of the sound whether of 'a' as in common English 'cast' or 'a' as in 'lady', that is not bad Cork pronunciation. 'd' for 'th' is more urban Cork than rural, but it is at least native, as is the Kerry 'ph' for 'wh': they were doubtless more widespread than they are now, so Shadwell may reach the dignity of a useful though far from infallible source. 'Gra' is most impressive, being his rendering of 'a ghra', my love, exactly the word to imply over-familiar counselling and one natural in casual speech (no Castilian mother would have stood for it for a moment, priest or no priest, but we're not giving Shadwell Spanish credentials). 'Joy' sounds like a fair attempt at a Gaelic auxiliary, and 'Aboo' is presumably a perfectly accurate rendering of 'abu' meaning 'forever' — apparently it failed Shadwell to assimilate the translation when he picked up the word. And the style is not untypical of a certain kind of Irish cleric, albeit the promiscuity is most unusual (with due disrespect to distinguished exceptions). So that while it is far from an accurate rendition, it is a very fair attempt; and as a foundation for English stage Irishness, it is much less ignorant than critics might imagine. It clearly was influential: 'gra' for instance became a fixed part of stage Irishry in subsequent years.

Readers of G. K. Chesterton's *The Innocence of Father Brown* (1911), will know from the first story, 'The Blue Cross', that the priest who attacked Reason was proved by Father Brown to be no priest, for that is 'bad theology'. Our quotation suggests the pleasing thought that we may owe the deduction to Chesterton's reading of Shadwell; but at all events, Shadwell had not read Chesterton.

But what sinks the passage, and the integrity of the author, is the deliberate mockery of Oliver Plunket. Shadwell had been impoverished after the erosion of the Popish plot, and however grimy its perjurers he might still believe, if only as a good party man, that they had sworn the truth. But to glory in the death of any person in any age, above all in a death occasioned by fidelity to personal beliefs, is an ugly thing.

From an Irish Catholic point of view the idea of stage Irishness as typified by Tegue O'Divelly was that of profanation of the martyrdom of a saint, a patriot and a hero of his people. On this showing, the popular conception of stage Irishness as some sort of sacrilege or treachery takes on its own validity. Tegue O'Divelly was duly forgotten in time, although in performance he outlived his creator by nearly half a century. But his influence long survived him, and the memory of his mockery of the dead seems to have survived him also.

Perhaps the most important point is that none of the real protagonists in the story seem to have been Irish — with the possible, but not probable, exception of Richard Flecknoe. The stage Irish invited imposture.

The final irony is that there died in Dublin on 12 August 1726 Charles Shadwell, son of Thomas Shadwell. Charles Shadwell's own plays were performed at Smock-Alley in his lifetime and revived (in the case of *The Fair Quaker of Deal*) over 30 years after his death. Indeed in that same decade, the 1750s, his father's most popular play, *The Squire of Alsatia*, had its revival at Smock-Alley. Charles had come to Ireland as one of the swarm of English jobholders, but he differed from them in that he gave as well as took. Like his father he was ready enough to purloin Molière: of his five Irish plays, *The Plotting Lovers or The Dismal Squire* was lifted from a translation of *Monsieur Poceaugnac* and relocated in Dublin (Tegue O'Divelly had owed most of himself to Tartuffe). Charles Shadwell, however, genuinely cultivated the history of his land of adoption, pitching his dramaturgic tent amidst the Norman invasion of 1169–71 to stage the last native Irish High King in *Rotherick O'Connor, King of Connaught, or, the Distress'd Princess*: rather appropriately it had an epilogue 'Design'd to have been spoke by Mr Thomas Griffith, if all the Persons in the Play had been kill'd'.[26]

The surviving text leaves a very few surviving persons, but it would clearly take little further altercation to remove them. The play reads like bad Dryden rather than mediocre Thomas Shadwell. Its peculiarity is its historical basis. Commentators such as Duggan and Charles Fitz-Simon, in his 1983 *The Irish Theatre*, remind us we must not expect historical accuracy from it. The extraordinary thing is how much historical accuracy there is, or at least how much historical information. In place of the invented royal offspring and courtiers so dear to seventeenth-century drama there is evidence of the closest study. O'Connor is made out a tyrannical villain, but the Norman Strongbow is little better, and O'Connor has his own actual case against the King of Leinster off pat; if O'Connor's character here seems to conflict with the ineffectual figure of Irish nationalist historiography, Charles Shadwell's picture of him ruthlessly executing the hostage prince of Leinster is perfectly accurate. There is a decent respect for the right of the princess of Leinster to make up her own mind rather than being treated maritally as a diplomatic pawn, and to prove herself the real Irish patriot, but a historical drama needs to fill in blanks and we know nothing of the real lady's feelings when she was married off to Strongbow. Shadwell supposes an inconsolable lover for her, her father's secretary, and assigns him a name found in what was then an unpublished manuscript in Lambeth Palace — Maurice or Morice Regan, interpreter to the Leinster King. Where he got it, God knows: the manuscript, later christened 'Song of Dermot and the Earl', was not published until long after Charles Shadwell's death. One can only conjecture that he took the trouble to collect information from scholars, including possibly the manuscript's future editor Walter Harris (1686–1761). His villain, the Archbishop of Tuam, is pleasingly named Catholicus — but then he was, even if the real one died in 1201, as opposed to being stabbed by O'Connor and expiring with a cheerful

> Quite thro' you've pierc'd my Heart and I must die:
> There's all my worldly Glory thrown away;
> I've lost a Cardinal's Cap, So fare you well.

although previous to this he had been encouraging O'Connor in violent anti-Papal denunciations arising from Rome's (actual) encouragement of Norman conquest. Granted that Charles Shadwell's anti-Papist rudery is in his father's tradition, it is much close to the Mummer to-hell-with-Cromwell than a witch-hunt view halloo. Charles Shadwell remembered his father kindly, to judge by a reference to him in the Dedication of the Dublin edition of his *Collective Works* (2 vols., 1720); but his father did not remember him when making his will. Summers suggests a quarrel; but it may have been that Charles was illegitimate. In any event, Mac Shadwell had a happier Irish epiphany than Mac Flecknoe. Certainly he was more concerned with Ireland as entity rather than as epithet.

We spoke earlier of common identity between Ireland and Scotland in some areas, times and respects: we can speak of a common identity between Ireland and England, even of the stage Irishman and stage Englishman, as the office-holders come, and the educated go, and the soldiers cross, and the divines return, and the Kingdom of Ireland (to perish in Union on 1 January 1801) fashions its structures and prohibitions on religious fidelity and treachery and for the better degradation of Papists and Presbyterians worms its way still deeper into dependence on English arms with payment in Irish jobs. What gave an Irish dimension to that shifting, shifty, shiftless intelligentsia? The knowledge that the English language was not a simple inheritance, but that it stood at a frontier from whose other side questions and tricks might be rained on it; the memory of insurrections, massacres, confiscation, fear of repossession; the sight of sudden fortunes rearing themselves up as palaces and phantoms; the stench of poverty.

The theatre never confronted the true horrors and ironies of that dependence and dichotomy, although a very stage-Irish analysis in novel form took it up when Jonathan Swift (1667–1745) in his *Gulliver's Travels* explored the mingling and sundering of identities with personal mastery of English politics and personal proximity to Irish mythology. But William Congreve (1670–1729), of Yorkshire birth, found Irish education to quicken his wits, learning kill-or-be-killed in the cut-and-thrust colony's conversation; and Nahum Tate (1652–1715) learned the value of escape from reality through his Irish birth and training, such that he would give *King Lear* the happy ending preferred by all persons of taste and sensibility for a century and a half; and for Joseph Addison (1672–1719) the Chief Secretaryship for Ireland (1708–10, 1714–15) may have provided the final inspiration for oligarchic self-regarding little Senates and profusion of patriotic expression in his *Cato* (1713), long in the making though that public-spirited tragedy had been; and Sir Richard Steele (1672–1729) took an early farewell of the land of his birth and at least a cooler, more isolated view of what constituted Englishness as he would collegially define it in *Tatler*, *Spectator* and sentimental comedy — the papers for Addison's elaboration, certainly, but with Steele's own initial vision. All of them, whether born in one island or the other, knew themselves to be truly English, and frequently said it, the frequency inducing a certain hollowness in the expression. They were not stage Irish, oh no, they simply had some Irish labels on their older props, where they could not see them and their unadulterated English audience could. The best gags are sometimes the inadvertent ones.

A stage presence

Ireland's first playwright wrote his masterpiece as he coughed himself into tubercular death early in 1707. George Farquhar (1677–1707) brought drama from the leprous hedonism of Restoration comedy to a humane psychology — a leap from male chauvinism to feminism — as fully as he gave Ireland a title to motherhood of playwrights in place of a claim to have taught classics to Congreve, or to have given birth to Nahum Tate. Up to now, either the playwrights were not Irish, or the Irish were not playwrights. The author of *The Beaux' Stratagem* was both.

Conor Cruise O'Brien in 1958 decreed:

> Irishness is not primarily a question of birth or blood or language; it is the condition of being involved in the Irish situation, and usually of being mauled by it. On that definition Swift is more Irish than Goldsmith or Sheridan, although by the usual tests they are Irish and he is pure English.[27]

Farquhar, as his name indicates, was of Scots ancestry. He was episcopalian, son of a Church of Ireland clergyman who seems to have held livings (probably successively) between south Tyrone, and south-eastern Donegal; Capel Wiseman, Protestant Bishop of Dromore, was sponsor to young Farquhar until his death in 1694, but while this would not be irrelevant to the father's calling it could derive simply from friendship with the father or respect for the son. Old Farquhar, whoever his Bishop, seems to have been burned out of his living when James II arrived in Ireland to repossess that Kingdom, with ominous indication that land-titles of Protestant settlers might be questioned. Farquhar's widow in seeking economic relief was to tell Queen Anne of her husband's service at the Battle of the Boyne under Colonel Hamilton; the Colonel's name is what lends conviction to the claim. There were two Irish Williamite colonels named Hamilton at the Boyne, one of whom had organised the Protestant defence of Enniskillen against the Catholics, Jacobites and French, while the other rallied Protestant opposition to James in the surrounding countryside. The boy Farquhar almost certainly met his Colonel Hamilton inside or outside Enniskillen when the Ulster settlers faced what they took to be slaughter on the lines of the 1641 insurrection, which their horror stories round the home fires had kept so vividly burning; and then, possibly lying about his thirteen years, he followed the colonel to the Boyne. His 'only attempt at exalted verse',[28] 'On the Death of General *Schomberg* kill'd at the *Boyn*', a Pindaric Ode, abounds in elaborate analogy to Samson, the Pillars of Hercules, and the like, but

> Gods! How he stood
> All terrible in Bloud.
> Stopping the Torrent of his Foes, and Current of the Floud.

is all too consistent with an eyewitness recollection of William III's Huguenot general going down with two sabre wounds in the head, and a carbine-bullet in the neck. William III then put himself at the head of the men from Enniskillen. Ireland had mauled Farquhar.

Farquhar seems to have taken his identity as British and Irish, his Ireland being Williamite: the ode begins with mourning from the British 'Lyon' (singular, and therefore, perhaps significantly, Scottish) and the 'Hibernian Harp'. And Farquhar's first play *Love and a Bottle* (1698) begins with a beggar, crippled from war wounds, telling the hero

> A Captain will say Dam'me, and give me Six-pence; and a Parson shall whine out God bless me, and give me not a farthing . . .

This is less likely to be a comment on Farquhar's father, or on Bishop Wiseman, than on the clerics encountered by the playwright during his time in Trinity

College, Dublin, where he is credited with having offered as a discourse on Christ walking on the water 'the man that is born to be hanged will never be drowned' (a profound theological remark, properly considered, but orthodoxy was desired rather than profundity) — and where Capel Wiseman's death in 1694, the year of Farquhar's entry to Trinity, prevented any renewal of subvention. Farquhar acted for a while in Smock-Alley, retired to composition on nearly killing a colleague by failing to button a sword he wielded in Dryden's *The Indian Emperor*, and left for London with his first comedy, about a man who leaves Dublin for London (*Love and a Bottle*, Act I):

Lucinda: Are you then one of the Wise Men of the East?

Roebuck: No, Madam; but one of the Fools of the West.

Lucinda: Pray what do you mean by that?

Roebuck: An *Irish*-man, Madam, at your Service.

Lucinda: Oh horrible! an *Irish*-man! a meer Wolf-Dog, I protest.

Roebuck: Ben't [Be not] surpriz'd Child; the Wolf-Dog is as well natur'd an Annimal an any of your Country Bull-Dogs, and a much more fawning Creature, let me tell ye. (*Lays hold on her.*)

Lucinda: Pray good *Caesar*, keep off your Paws; no scraping acquaintence, for Heaven's sake. Tell us some news of your Country; I have heard the strangest Stories — that the people wear Horns and Hoofs.

Roebuck: Yes, faith, a great many wear Horns: but we had that among other laudable fashions, from London. I think it came over with your mode of wearing high Topknots; for ever since, the men and Wives bear their heads exalted alike. They were both fashions that took wonderfully.

Lucinda: Then you have Ladies among you?

Roebuck: Yes, yes, we have Ladies, and Whores; Colleges, and Playhouses; Churches, and Taverns; fine Houses, and Bawdy-Houses; in short, every thing that you can boast of, but Fops, Poets, Toads and Adders.

Lucinda: But have you no Beau's at all?

Roebuck: Yes, they come over, like the Woodcocks, once a year.

Lucinda: And have your Ladies no Springes to catch 'em in?

Roebuck: No. Madam; our own Country affords us much better wild-fowl, but they are generally stripp'd of their feathers by the Playhouse and Taverns; in both which they pretend to be Criticks; and our ignorant Nation imagines a full Wig as infallible a token of a Wit as the Lawrel.

Lucinda: Oh Lard! and here 'tis the certain sign of a Blockhead. But why no Poets in Ireland, Sir?

Roebuck: Faith, Madam, I know not, unless St. Patrick sent them a packing with other venomous Creatures out of Ireland. Nothing that carries a Sting in its Tongue can live there. But since I have described my Country, let me know a little of England, by sight of your Face.

Is the last sentence child or parent of the ancient stage-Irish allusion to an ugly face as resembling the map of Ireland? If the former, it makes a poison tongue within the velvet breath, presumably unseen, unheard and unfelt by the English audience; and many a stage-Irish sentiment let loose in London would be of similar kind.

Love and a Bottle is the precocious migrant 20-year-old showing that he too can write Restoration comedy, but the dialogue is greater than the play. The teenage veteran, who has lamented his general cut to pieces at the Boyne, and who himself fought among the Protestant frontier fighters, in defence of English order, now learns that any Irishman is an aboriginal half-animal in English eyes. The distinction, vital in Ireland, between settler and native is contemptuously obliterated in English views of Ireland. To the English, all who come from Ireland are horned and hooved devils, that is 'Tegue O' Divelly'. To the Irishman, they are horned if they are cuckolded in the moral climate imported by the Protestant settlers from London — the Protestant settlers of Dublin, as opposed to the hard, old-fashioned moralists of Protestant Ulster. The bestial imagery is a fascinating precursor of *Gulliver's Travels*: are all Irish Yahoos? Yet the imagery is also heraldic; the wolfhound had been a type of Irish heroic symbol since Cuchulainn, the human hound of Ulster, and Bran, the actual hound of Fionn and the Fianna. The lack of poets and venomous tongues in Ireland is a satirical conclusion which alone should resolve any question of Farquhar's Irishness.

But if Farquhar resented and ridiculed the English confusion of Irish Protestant and Irish Catholic, he had his own perceptions of the latter in *The Twin Rivals* (1702) by means of the servant 'Teague', the name by now generic for stage presentation of Irish Catholics (on which see the classic work on stage Irishmen, Welshmen and Scotsmen by J. O. Bartley).[29] Farquhar's Teague calls himself the grandson of 'an Irish poet', is Catholic, intermittent Jacobite, can speak French, lies when necessary but is honest about recognising it, and has the useful ambiguity both for plot and for audience of appearing much more stupid than he actually is: in fact his role in part is that of the wise servant protecting the interests of his somewhat uncomprehending master. He uses the Irish bull as a coded warning, a traditional feature of stories where the servant is from an enslaved, degraded, or oppressed ethnic group:

Footman: Then tell your Master 'tis the young Lord *Woud'be* just come his Estate by the Death of his Father and elder Brother. [*Exit*]

Elder Wou'dbe: What do I hear?

Teague: You hear that you are dead, Maishter; fere vil you please to be buried?

Elder Wou'dbe: But art thou sure it was my Brother?

Teague: Be my Shoul it was him nown self. I know'd him fery well, after his Man told me.

Elder Wou'dbe: The Business requires that I be convinc'd with my own eyes; I'll follow him, and know the Bottom on't. — Stay here till I return.

Teague: Dear Maishter, have a care upon your shelf; now they know you are dead, by my Shoul, they may kill you. (III.ii)

And Teague has ironies enough that contrast manoeuvres among the elite with the realities of class and caste:

Teague: Deel tauke me but dish ish a most shweet Business indeed; Maishters play the fool, and Servants must shuffer for it. I am Prishoner in the *Constable*'s House be me Shoule, and shent abrode to fetch some Bail for my Maishter; but foo shall bail poor *Teague* agra. (IV.ii)

The use of dialect is largely derivative, but occasionally sound. 'Maishter' seems authentic enough, especially as Teague comes from Carrickfergus and is thus Gaelic Antrim. 'Deel' is 'devil' in good post-Gaelic, 'tauke' is probably 'choke' after Ulster post-Gaelic; but Farquhar makes the usual mistake about 'sh' for 's' while missing the obvious 'Conshtable'; 'him nown' for 'his own' sounds like realistic Ulster English. Our playwright constructs in a hurry but occasionally stops to listen to the sounds of remote memories. It may be coincidence, but 'fery' suggests some acquaintance with Catholics from the Glen of Antrim, where the soft inflection associated with the parent Hebrides of so many inhabitants would have been much more obvious then and can still be heard now.

Farquhar, one might feel, had far more reason than either Shadwell, father or son, to pour scorn on the Catholic natives, who had certainly endangered his life, and may possibly have killed members of his family. But it is only in *The Beaux' Stratagem* that he shows a faint outbreak of the O' Divellys and this when he was dying of more tangible ailments. Arguably, Father Foigard is the same mixture of lechery, pimping, treachery, etc, marinated with only a little milk of human kindness:

Archer: Look'e, Sir, the Gallows or the Secret, take your Choice.

Foigard: The Gallows! upon my Shoul I hate that saam Gallow, for it is a Diseash dat is fatal to our Family . . .

But it is in keeping with the hard-bitten realism of the entire play. The persecution of priests, especially in Ireland, led them to disguises: hence the Kilkenny priest calls himself 'Foigard' ('defend the faith', a shaft more against the title given Henry VIII by the Pope and flaunted thereafter by the Protestant rulers of England, than against the priest) and pretends allegiance to an uncertainly-identified Catholic regime. The beaux from London, one of them also in disguise, come in quest of fortunes. They blackmail the priest. And the squalid intrigues into which he is drawn in self-preservation seem all too possible for a weak man whose life is forfeit once his Irish identity is smoked out and with it his legal state of treachery against England. The Restoration comedy enhancement of seduction of other men's wives by heartless rakehells is kicked away to become a remorseless if mordantly comic — black comic — dissection of marital incompatability and its imprisonment of women. Peter Kavanagh, in *The Irish Theatre*, rightly says that Farquhar is 'deadly serious here' and argues that, like Shaw, 'he has that distinctively Irish trait of dropping his most serious thoughts at their highest point, into a pool of laughter'.[30] Kavanagh's point is even more true of Wilde, because he did not apply it to Wilde: *An Ideal Husband* (1895) is a corrosive exposure of the hypocrisy of a Victorian politician whose intoxication in the rhetoric of moral reproof is so incurable that even when his friend has saved him from the consequences of his fraud he instinctively denounces that friend for having been discovered in a compromising situation whose explanation he refuses to explore. But because Wilde made his play so sparkling a vehicle for epigram and elegance, and made his instrument of justice a mocking lord (enstaging Wilde himself), the purpose is lost to sight. Shaw was more obviously didactic, but was all too often foiled of his effect because of the same genius for entertainment. Similarly Sean O'Casey (1880–1964) is casually and amazingly cited, time and again, as having defended the cause of Irish nationalism in *The Shadow of a Gunman* (1923), *Juno and the Paycock* (1924) and *The Plough and the Stars* (1926), or else with having written devastatingly witty plays about Dublin tenement life, when he was actually trying to alert humanity to its own self-destruction. Similarly Farquhar, coughing himself into his grave as he struggled to finish the play to give desperately needed economic support to his wife and daughters, inaugurated the grand march of Irish playwrights with the supreme professionalism which got *The Beaux' Stratagem* on (but not off) the stage before he died, and in doing so linked the stage-Irish heritage to pioneer feminism striking down the decades through Wilde and Shaw until in O'Casey's *Juno* it obtained its supreme and matchless realisation.

The dying Farquhar seems the fount of a thousand directions. 'Farquhar', declared the devoted Kavanagh, 'led the drama back to Shakespeare — back to life and nature.'[31] He is as big as that. But in some ways the progress could be obvious enough.

The army, for all of its self-righteousness, perhaps because of it, was one of the best ways for the socially disadvantaged (disadvantaged by being Welsh, Scots or Irish) to get ahead. Ask the Duke of Wellington if you do not believe me (i.e. little Arthur, runt of an obscure Protestant Irish litter). Among other things Farquhar typifies the attractions of the army from his days at Enniskillen and the Boyne, through his later experiences as a recruiting officer in the Earl of Orrery's regiment, 1704–6, experiences which gave him the plot of *The Recruiting Officer* (1706) and the locations of that play and of *The Beaux' Stratagem* — Shrewsbury and Litchfield respectively. Farquhar's own identity, as an Irish provincial, gave him an inherent advantage in striking sparks of fire from English provincial society. And he had seen the impact of soldiers on rural society from a boy's viewpoint as well as from that of a soldier, all the more sharpened in his concentration because the boy suddenly found himself the soldier. Farquhar established the alliance between the stage Irish and the army.

Thomas Sheridan (1719–88), father of Richard Brinsley Sheridan (1751–1816), was manager of Smock-Alley Theatre in the mid-eighteenth century, descendant of an eminent Irish ecclesiastical family (whose Gaelic founder worked on the first translation of the Bible into Irish in the early seventeenth century), and grandnephew of the private secretary to the exiled James II and of Ireland's only Protestant Jacobite Bishop. His godfather was Jonathan Swift, whom he regarded as the most beneficent influence of his life. His only original play was variously called *Captain O'Blunder* and (somewhat tactless in its singularity) *The Brave Irishman*; it premiered as 'a new Farce' on 4 February 1743, a week after its author's debut in Smock-Alley. As Esther K. Sheldon shows in her invaluable *Thomas Sheridan of Smock-Alley* (1967), the work was Molierist in derivation without being yet another rip-off, as exhibited by the Shadwells, father and son.[32] It is not only stage Irish; it is stage-conscious Irish, much as his son's *The Critic* (1779) is stage-conscious if not Irish. The idea of plays about plays, plays offstage from plays, plays inspired by plays, is thus in active germination (with due deference to such predecessors as *Hamlet*). O'Blunder's adversary Schemewell admits that he manufactures his intrigues 'By haunting playhouses', paying a particular tribute to Molière — which may be taken as innate honesty or brass neck on the author's part, as you like it. The author is as grimly conscious of the English Ireland to which he must respond as Farquhar had been: the English heroine explains her distaste for an unseen Irishman: 'Oh hideous! is he not an Irishman?' (This seems gloriously to anticipate the famous remark of Ferris, the butler, in Wodehouse's *The Small Bachelor* (1927):

'You disapprove of the Irish?'
'Yes, sir.'
'Why?'
'Because they are Irish, sir.'

But I digress.) The heroine continues: 'Why I am told they are meer Beasts and have Horns in that Country': no more than their neighbours, says the maid. The fount of Farquhar, more than Molière, seems to sparkle in the Sheridan sunlight. But if Sheridan took, he also gave. Captain O'Blunder is particularly distinguished for verbal confusions of a more complex architecture than stage Irishry to date could offer, while his impetuosity revived the gallant shade of Captain Macmorris. Both features were inescapably evident, but on different characters, in his son Richard's *The Rivals* (1775): Sir Lucius O'Trigger, and Mrs Malaprop. Curiously enough, the point, in each case, may derive from that Gaelic-English frontier where the first Sheridan had made his mark on history: explosion in lieu of exposition, *mal apropos* in place of *mot juste*, are alike the children of a shrinking vocabulary or vernacular, or excessive awareness of a neighbouring language. The younger Sheridan also seems to have developed his father's anger at English sophisticate condemnation of Ireland, and like Farquhar went on to attack that sophistication. Farquhar and Richard Brinsley Sheridan both answered derision against Irish products by making Irish products the finest in the theatre of the day, but where, after cautious imitation, Farquhar simply demolished Restoration comedy by supplanting it, Sheridan tore the sophistication asunder before its audience's eyes. For both men victory is achieved when provincial life proves superior to that of the metropolis: Farquhar makes the point by setting his own best plays in the provinces, Sheridan by the country-bred Lady Teazle's return of her diploma to the

London School for Scandal. Naturally they did not say 'Ireland': it was difficult enough to command a modest victory for the English Provinces. But Ireland was at back of it: even if Richard Sheridan left Ireland young, his art came first of all from his Irish parents. We certainly need to recognise in *The School for Scandal* (1777) a white flame of anger.

Farquhar had also quietly taught the lesson to the stage Irish of laughing at oneself: *Love and a Bottle* depends on a self-mockery neither masochistic nor narcissistic. The great centenarian Charles Macklin (1697?–1797) followed Farquhar with some diminution in that (although he certainly exceeded him in grievous bodily harm to fellow actors). Macklin was of Gaelic antecedents, with a possible Jacobite father, and a supposition of Donegal birth, as though all the Sheridan genealogy had been concentrated in one generation; his mother may have Protestantised him. He reached the London stage in 1733 and by 1741 had established himself on stage as the Shylock of his century, simultaneously re-establishing the play. He pioneered realistic performance on the English stage. Thomas Sheridan brought him to act in Dublin. His second play *A Will and No Will: Or, a Bone for the Lawyers* (1746) opened with a prologue in which the stage revealed actors 'disposed in the form of a Pit' and making 'a great Noise by Whistling and Knocking for the Farce to begin', followed by derisive discussion about Macklin and how he would speak the prologue. And then Rattle, Smart, Dullman and Snarlewit quiz an Irishman as to whether he was to 'be the Pit and say the Prologue':

Irishman: No, indeed, Sir, it is as false as the Gospel I do assure you, Sir, I never
           spoke a Pit or Prologue in my Life — but once when I was at School, you
           must know, Sir — we acted one of Terence's Tragedies there, so when the
           Play was over I spoke the Prologue to it.

Omnes: Ha! ha! ha! ha!

Smart: . . . Pray, Sir, may I crave your name?

Irishman: Yes you may indeed and welcome, Sir. My name is Laughlinbullruder-
           rymackshoughlinbulldowny, at your Service . . .[33]

Macklin's own family claimed descent from the Mac Lochlainn, kings of mid-Ulster, and, less certainly, from the Maol Seachlainn, kings of Meath, both supplying Irish High Kings and both discoverable in the name in the Prologue. Still, if he was selling his regal ancestry for a Pit guffaw, he redeemed it in *Love à La Mode* (1759) where, according to the invaluable Father Stephen J. Brown, SJ, the creation of Sir Callaghan O'Brallaghan 'was the first to bring the stage Irishman into repute'.[34] Sir Callaghan gets the girl, thus upstaging Sir Archy MacSarcasm and other ethnic representatives. Sir Callaghan owed some modelling fees to Captain O'Blunder, but then Sir Lucius is obliged to Sir Callaghan and Mrs Malaprop to Laughlinbull . . . (etc). R. B. Sheridan also turns the self-mockery trick in *The Critic*:

Sir Fretful Plagiary: . . . I sent it to the manager of COVENT-GARDEN THEATRE
    this morning.

> *Sneer*: I should have thought now, that it might have been cast (as the actors call it) better at DRURY-LANE.
>
> *Sir Fretful*: O lud! no — never send a play there while I live — harkee — [*Whispers*]
>
> *Sneer*: *Writes himself!* — I know he does —

As Sheridan's creation, Sneer clearly never speaks a truer line. Did any stage Irishman ever produce a more graceful line than Sheridan, when, reproved for taking a drink whilst contemplating the burning Drury Lane Theatre in 1809 (and with the theatre the burning of his artistic and material future), 'I suppose a man may take a glass of wine by his own fire-side?'

That particular form of authorial stage Irishry has echoes in Wilde (who had Lady Bracknell declaim on the novel satirising himself, *The Green Carnation*, in the uncut *Importance of Being Earnest*), while Shaw injected it into *The Doctor's Dilemma* where the unspeakable Louis Dubedat fills the cup of his iniquities by proclaiming himself a disciple of Bernard Shaw, to be answered by the character closest to a self-portrait:

> *Sir Patrick*: Bernard Shaw? I never heard of him. He's a Methodist preacher, I suppose.

Brendan Behan introduced a denunciation of himself into *The Hostage* (1958) — that he is already in the play (as the maidservant) he was anxious to conceal and the self-advertisement directed attention away from it. Samuel Beckett asserted the highly autobiographical character of his *Eh, Joe* (1967) by the choice of a name taken from that of a long-forgotten boxer or wrestler (and I have long forgotten which): Joe Beckett. He, too, needed the release of a laugh at himself. For this, after all, is the success or failure of the stage Irish: self-analysis, self-exploitation, self-laughter. James Joyce (1882–1941) is the most extreme case of it, obviously, and used the stage, as he used everything else including Rembrandt, with the remorselessness of a nuclear scientist. *Exiles* (1918) is probably the most appalling abuse of the theatre known to man or beast: countless worse plays have been written, but none by a person remotely approaching such genius. It is, simply, and coldly, a laboratory experiment. Joyce wishes to direct his own performance as an observer of his wife's adultery with his best friend (for which latter role candidates may apply). Purpose of the above proceedings: enablement of the artist to gain perspective for the portrait of Leopold Bloom. I would like to feel he is laughing at himself in *Exiles*: I am only certain he is laughing at me.

Joyce's disciple, Brian O'Nolan (1911–66), reversed the old Mummer tradition in his play *Faustus Kelly* (1943) by having the devil indignantly refuse to accept the souls of Irish local government officials; but his great place in the mechanics of stage-Irishry arose most inescapably from his brilliant demolition of Kitsch in a column signed with the name of the greatest kitsch figure in nineteenth-century stage Irishry, Myles na Coppaleen whom O'Nolan, a master-scholar in Gaelic, grimly proclaimed in correct grammatical form, 'Myles na gCopaleen'. In place of the great stage-Irish dialogues of Pat and Mike on the Music-Hall, or Joxer and the Captain in O'Casey's *Juno and the*

Paycock, or Mr Dooley and Mr Hennessy in the socio-political anayses of the Irish-American Finley Peter Dunne (1867–1936), or Bloom and Dedalus in *Ulysses* (all the richer there since it is done by topical classification, without speech reproduction: Ithaca), Myles presented himself as an offensively sophisticated aesthete (or any other literary satire that appealed to him) facing Neanderthal abuse from The Plain People of Ireland. It was final, mathematical, expression of stage Irishry: the one versus the all, zero versus infinity.

The original Myles was the classic lovable rogue, wooing and wowing the pit in performance and presentation from Dionysus Lardner Boucicault (1820/2–90) in *The Colleen Bawn* (1860), adapted (and happy-ended) from Gerald Griffin's (1803–40) great, tragic novel, *The Collegians* (1829). Boucicault's even more famous *The Shaughraun* (1874), with less obvious literary blasphemy about its origins, is a reminder to captious critics of stage Irishry to be very careful in what they judge: a close student of the play will see where Wilde, Shaw, Synge, Yeats, Joyce and O'Casey annexed their plenty while frequently denouncing their source. When all is said and done, it is the same stage, whatever about being the same Irish.

So it is best, after all, for us to end, not outside the stage Irish, but within them. Farquhar's most logical disciple, as far as *The Beaux' Stratagem* was concerned at least, was Oliver Goldsmith with *She Stoops to Conquer* (1773). Archer's temporary status as servant becomes Miss Hardcastle's, and the implicit feminism in Mrs Sullen's right to divorce becomes that of Miss Hardcastle's right to marry. The official stage-Irish part is greatly enhanced, from the essentially victimised, through contriving Father Foigard (as a name it is a bit like Farquhar), to the original trouble-begetter Tony Lumpkin. Tony Lumpkin is not, ostensibly, stage Irish: but he is very obviously so. He is self-portraiture when Goldsmith is considering himself as a 'gooseberry fool' (as he puts it in 'Retaliation'); and he certainly has his creator's enjoyment in appearing at his most idiotic when being at his most creative. Here, then, is the stage Irishman, disguised and fitted out for use in any other country or company, by the stage Irishman, similarly describable. But he also represents the stage Irishman as prisoner amid the classes, castes and creeds, only capable of escaping by dissolving them and inducing others to do the same. That splendid early twentieth-century expression of prose stage Irishry, the Irish R. M. series of Edith Somerville (1858–1949) and Violet Martin 'Ross' (1862–1915), hard-bitten, Unionist, Protestant, spiritualist, feministical if not feminist, where they staged every Irishman they could get their pens on, and in the centre Florence McCarthy Knox, a gentleman among stable boys and a stable boy among gentlemen, beloved, bullied and bedamned by his grandmother:

> As I listened to them both, I remembered with infinite amusement how he had told me once that'a pet name she had for him was "Tony Lumpkin", and no one but herself knew what she meant by it'.[35]

That is how the stage Irish will end — nobody will remember what was meant by them.

Notes

1. Our kindly editor, Patrick O'Sullivan, has pointed out to me that the material within this chapter is of three sorts: quotations from plays and other texts, references to other academic sources and gossip. As to the first, our editor feels that you are best served, my dear reader, if you can be helped to find your own way to pertinent matter in any standard edition of the more well-known texts: where I can, I have directed you to useful or widely available editions. Academic sources, our editor feels, should be thoroughly referenced. As to gossip, our editor feels, the least said the better.
    Thus I can tell you that my quotation from Oscar Wilde comes from *Intentions* (1891), the very end of the essay called 'The truth of masks'; I can further tell you that these words were added to the essay by Wilde at the book stage (the original essay was entitled 'Shakespeare and stage costume', *Nineteenth Century*, May, 1885) and suggest that you see *Complete works of Oscar Wilde*, with an Introduction by Vyvyan Holland, Collins, London, revised edition 1966, p. 1078, or any collection of Wilde's essays.
2. George Chester Duggan, *The stage Irishman*. Talbot Press, Dublin, 1937 (reprinted Blom, New York, 1969), pp 6–7.
3. P. G. Wodehouse, *The mating season*. Herbert Jenkins, London, 1949, p. 89: pp. 92–3.
4. Duggan, *The stage Irishman*, p 4.
5. 'Mac Datho's pig' (eighth to ninth century), translated by Frank O'Connor [Michael O'Donovan (1903–66)]: see Frank O'Connor (ed.), *Book of Ireland*, Collins, London, 1959, p. 68.
6. 'The hermitage' (*c*.900, but ascribed in its oral expression to Saint Manchan, some centuries earlier), translated by Frank O'Connor, *Kings, Lords and Commons. an anthology from the Irish*, Gill and MacMillan, Dublin, 1970, p. 5 (original edition 1959).
7. Douglas Hyde, *The religious songs of Connacht*, Irish University Press, Shannon, 1972, (original edition 1906), p. 273.
8. Tyrone Guthrie, *A life in the theatre*, Columbus, London, 1960, p. 4.
9. Bruno Scott James (trans.), *The letters of St Bernard of Clairvaux*, Burns Oates, London, 1953, pp 452–7; H. J. Lawlor (ed.), *St Bernard of Clairvaux's life of St Malachy of Armagh*, in *Translations of Christian literature. Series V. Lives of the Celtic Saints*, Society for the Promotion of Christian Knowledge, London, 1920, passim.
10. William Smith Clark, *The early Irish stage: the beginnings to 1720*, Clarendon Press, Oxford, 1955, p. 4.
11. *Calendar of State Papers, Domestic Series, Charles II, 1661–62*, Longman, Green, Longman and Roberts, London, 1861, p. 191.
12. Peter Kavanagh, *The Irish theatre*, The Kerryman, Tralee, 1946, p. 8.
13. Peter Happé, *The complete plays of John Bale. Volumes 1 & 2*, Brewer, Cambridge, 1985, 1986; Bale's *Kynge Johan* (1538) is seen as beginning the tradition of English historical drama and his work forms an important bridge between the medieval and the Elizabethan drama: thus extracts will appear in collections like Glynne Wickham (ed.), *English moral interludes*, Dent, London, 1976. John Arden, *Books of Bale: a fiction of history*, Methuen, London, 1988, is a well-researched, readable exploration.
14. John P. Turner (ed.), *A critical edition of James Shirley's 'Saint Patrick for Ireland'*, Garland, New York, 1979, pp. 101–2, p. 246 (Act 1, Scene 1; Act 5, Scene 3).

15. Turner (ed.), *Shirley's 'Saint Patrick for Ireland'*, p. 145 (Act 3, Scene 1). Later citations are from pp. 237–8 and 247–8 (both Act 5, Scene 3).
16. Kavanagh, *The Irish theatre*, p. 18.
17. V. G. Kiernan, *Shakespeare, poet and citizen*, Verso, London, 1993, p. 10.
18. See Act 4 of Eugene O'Neill, *Long day's journey into night*, Cape, London, 1956.
19. W. J. Lawrence, 'Was Shakespeare ever in Ireland? A conjectural study', *Jahrbuch der Deutschen Shakespeare-Gesellschaft*, XLII (1906), pp. 65–76.
20. One might wonder if Rosalind was ever in Ireland: Ireland and Ireland's animals seem very much on her mind. As well as her Irish rattish Pythagorean experience (*As You Like It*, III. ii) she mentions Irish wolves (V. ii). Jacques and 'Ducdame' can be found in II. v. See, for example, the Arden Edition, William Shakespeare, *As You Like It*, edited by Agnes Lathen, Methuen, London, rev. edn. 1975, pp. 69, 118, 45.
21. Kiernan, *Shakespeare*, p. 127. Captain Macmorris, an Irishman, appears, with his English, Welsh and Scottish colleagues, in *Henry V*, III. ii. It has been suggested that there was something of a fashion for such 'four nations' scenes, as theatre mirrored the expanding English state's attempts to define its 'Britishness'. In his discussion of Macmorris Alan Bliss cites a similar scene in a play by Thomas Randolph: see Alan Bliss, *Spoken English in Ireland, 1600–1740*, Dolmen, Dublin, 1979, p. 34–6.
23. Shadwell's complaint is taken from the 'Dedication' to his version of *The Tenth Satyur of Juvenal* and is quoted (Vol. 1, p. xx) in Montague Summers (ed.), *The complete works of Thomas Shadwell*, Fortune Press, London, 1927 (facsimile reprint, Blom, New York, 1968) (but note that this collection does not include *The Tenth Satyr of Juvenal*). For Dryden see James Kinsley (ed.), *The poems and fables of John Dryden*, Oxford University Press, London, 1958.
24. Summers (ed.) *Works of Shadwell*, Volume 1, p. clxxii.
25. Shadwell, *The Amorous Bigotte*, Act 1, Scene 1; see Summers (ed.), *Works of Shadwell*, Volume 5, p. 21.
26. Christopher Fitz-Simon, *The Irish theatre*. Thames and Hudson, London, 1983, p. 35. Fitz-Simon is constructive and inspirational on this, as on so much, though I differ from him slightly.
27. Conor Cruise O'Brien, 'Irishness', reprinted in *Writers and Politics*, Chatto & Windus, London, 1965.
28. Shirley Strum Kenny (ed.), *The works of George Farquhar*. 2 volumes, Clarendon Press, Oxford, 1988. Kenny's edition now replaces the faithful Charles A. Stonehill (ed.), *The complete works of George Farquhar*, Nonesuch, London, 1930. Willard Connely, *Young George Farquhar*, Cassell, London, 1949, covers the ground, however questionable some of its conclusions. Margaret Farquhar's petitions to Queen Anne (Historical MSS Comm: Portland Papers) were discovered by James R. Sutherland, who analysed them in *The Times Literary Supplement*, 1937, p. 171.
29. J. O. Bartley, *Teague, Shenkin and Sawney*, Cork University Press, Cork, 1954.
30. Kavanagh, *The Irish theatre*, p. 230.
31. Kavanagh, *The Irish theatre*, p. 232.
32. Esther K. Sheldon, *Thomas Sheridan of Smock-Alley*, Princeton University Press, Princeton, 1967.
33. Charles Macklin, *A will or no will, or, a bone for the lawyers*, William Andrews Clark Memorial Library, University of California, Los Angeles, 1967; Charles Macklin, *Love à la mode*, Oliver & Boyd, Edinburgh, 1811.
34. Stephen J. Brown, *A guide to books in Ireland, Part 1*, Hodges Figgis, Dublin, 1912, p. 167.

35. The remark is found in the story called 'Trinket's Colt': at the end of that story Mrs Knox, exasperated, affectionate, addresses Flurry as 'Tony'; See Somerville and Ross, *The complete experiences of an Irish R. M.*, Sphere, London, 1970, pp. 67, 75.

5 'The sigh of thy harp shall be sent o'er the deep': the influence of Thomas Moore in Australia

Frank Molloy

> He crossed under Tommy Moore's roguish finger. They did right to put him up over a urinal: meeting of the waters. Ought to be places for women. Running into cakeshops. Settle my hat straight. *There is not in this wide world a vallee.* Great song of Julia Morkan's.[1]

Leopold Bloom's musings on noting the statue of Thomas Moore have long amused readers of *Ulysses*. Some may even have smiled with approval at Joyce, a master of modern literature, putting in his place one whom the Victorians dared to call 'Ireland's national poet'. But the discerning reader will know that Joyce's humour was directed more at the Dublin Corporation than at the poet. Indeed, not only did Joyce greatly admire the *Irish Melodies*,[2] but such a thorough Dubliner was no doubt aware that this statue and its location in College Street had been the subject of derisory comments since its unveiling in 1857.[3] However, neither Joyce nor those familiar with Dublin statuary would have known how ill their statue compared to that of Moore in Sturt Street in the city of Ballarat, seventy miles west of Melbourne, Australia. This statue, sculptured by John Udny from Carrara in Italy, presented the poet in a natural and elegant pose, pointing to a song his audience would like him to sing.[4] It was unveiled in December 1889 in the presence of 5,000 citizens, and proclaimed as a fitting tribute to a great poet and a great Irishman. It was acknowledged as complementing the statue of Robert Burns, erected some years before, and that of William Shakespeare, soon to be added to the streetscape of Ballarat.[5]

While such adulation was understandable in Ireland throughout the nineteenth century, and even for a time in Britain, we may wonder at its surfacing twelve thousand miles away, in a country whose only mention in Moore's work was as an appropriate destination for the transported Captain Rock.[6] Discussing Moore's career on that December day in Ballarat, Sir Bryan O'Loghlen,[7] probably unwittingly, accounted for the perennial admiration Moore and his melodies engendered amongst the Irish in Australia. He alluded to 'Dear harp of my country' producing 'the finest chords of self-sacrificing patriotism, of manliness, of love, of mirth and of sadness, that thrill the human heart'.[8] The combination of advocacy for Ireland together with those uplifting sentiments that permeate many of the melodies had indeed proved very seductive to Irish migrants and their descendants who wished to maintain a cultural and emotional attachment to their native land. And the speakers's train of thought was likely to find further approval amongst the Irish in his audience when he affirmed Moore as a name to inspire the hearts and minds of all in this new land. Public support for the building of the statue, he believed, 'was an evidence of the present — and he hoped might be a happy omen for the future — unity of all our races in one nation in this happy and blessed Australian land of ours. (Cheers)'.[9] This was almost an Australian celebration. It was certainly one in which the Irish, or Irish Australians, could be seen in a most favourable light. Thomas Moore, beloved by many throughout the civilised world, was in a sense providing a pathway for them towards full incorporation into colonial society.

The newspaper report of the day's proceedings would not have been complete without the inclusion of a poem composed for the occasion. 'Tom Moore' revealed just how well the poet, one Mona Marie, knew her *Irish Melodies*. Derivative phrases occurred line after line: 'Erin's dear harp', 'shrill'd its sweet strings', 'a race brave and free', 'yon isle of the sea', and so on, fitting homage to Moore and to Ireland.[10] The writing of such verses signified that Moore was not just an icon for Irish Australia in general but also for local poets who found in his lyrics sentiments and styles they wished to emulate. From the early years of white settlement until the late nineteenth century, Moore-inspired themes of remembrance of family and friends, of recollections of times past, and of Ireland and liberty were adopted by poets because of their appeal to the migrant psyche. It is their work and the role of Thomas Moore in interweaving the Irish element into the fabric of colonial society that are the subject of this chapter.

The initial appearance of Moore in Australian literature provides in an unusual manner an insight into the nature of early colonial society. The second song in the Seventh Number of the *Irish Melodies* (1818), 'As slow our ship', was printed virtually unchanged in the *Sydney Gazette* two years later with a new title, 'Song', and attributed to 'E'.[11] Plagiarism was not uncommon in the nineteenth century, but one might have expected the editor[12] to have been more circumspect about the origins of the poem, especially since 'E' never published any other poems. One might also have expected that at least one reader would have been sufficiently conversant with Moore's (comparatively) recent work to write in protest to the editor. But subsequent editions of the *Gazette*, Sydney's only newspaper at the time, were silent on the matter. While there were occasional letters, their subjects were unseemly behaviour at church services, dangers from prowling dogs or the like, not literary matters.

A question must therefore arise as to why this thoroughly British society seemed so ignorant about the work of a most popular poet. During the years when the *Irish Melodies* were published (1808–34), the two colonies in the antipodes, New South Wales and Van Diemen's Land, were not particularly rich in cultural matters. Until the mid-1820s, each colony had only one newspaper, and while original poems were occasionally published — nine in the *Sydney Gazette* for 1820–1 — the readership for such literary endeavours was very small. These were essentially garrison societies: convicts and their military gaolers formed the bulk of the population. There were few schools, no colleges or universities or theatres or cultural societies, and consequently, little opportunity to engage in literary discourse.[13] Moreover, that genteel, leisured society, to which Moore's melodies were addressed, was largely non-existent. In his 'Letter on Music' Moore had stated that the melodies were not composed for the general population; instead, 'it (the work) looks much higher for its audience and readers: it is found upon the piano-fortes of the rich and the educated'.[14] Few such people lived in the antipodes, and commentators did lament the absence of polite society. Peter Cunningham, for example, writing in 1827, complained, 'Agreeable amusements are still much wanted to relieve the full monotony of a town like Sydney . . . cut off, in a manner, from all communications with the other parts of the civilized world'.[15]

But, one may venture, surely there were some Irish readers in New South Wales who would have protested to the editor of the *Sydney Gazette* about the plagiarism of Moore's lyric. None did so, a principal reason being that there were few Irish readers of the *Gazette*. The vast majority of Irish were convicts. From the arrival of the *Queen* in 1791 until the 1850s tens of thousands were transported, some for political offences (especially after the 1798 rebellion), others, for various crimes.[16] At the first census in New South Wales in 1828, over 7,000 Irish-born residents were classed as convicts or emancipists (freed convicts) while only 500 or so were free settlers, and some of these were relatives of convicts.[17] As Patrick O'Farrell has indicated, many of these convicts had Irish as their first language while others were not literate.[18] Once freed, they tended to settle quietly in recently opened-up lands west of Sydney, often out of regular contact with the town. They were eager to melt into the emerging society and not arouse any suggestion that they still harboured rebel traits. They might have heard of Thomas Moore, but few would read the *Gazette*, and even fewer consider writing to the editor.

Certainly, Moore was at least a name to that small Irish group who did achieve prominence in the early decades of colonial society: bushrangers. Escaped convicts could achieve fame, or notoriety, by evading recapture, shooting at soldiers or robbing terrified settlers. Their methods were similar to those employed by the tories, rapparees and whiteboys who had long roamed the troubled districts of Ireland, the type commemorated by Moore in *Captain Rock*.[19] Like their Irish counterparts, they acquired a host of admirers. Peter Cunningham with righteous indignation, protested that songs were composed to record the deeds of such 'foolish fellows'; one, Michael Riley, for instance in 1821, 'vaunting that he should long be spoken of, . . . in fear by his enemies and in admiration by his friends'.[20] One song about Jack Donohoe became so popular among the 'lower orders' that its singing was banned in public houses, an indication that the authorities were frightened about the unsettling effect of such 'treason' songs on the lower classes.[21] The reasons for their appeal are not hard to establish. They celebrated in verse opposition to the colonial positives of resignation and acceptance of one's lot, as well as a victory even for a brief period against the hated penal system, and the achievement of a kind of independence in the wilderness. They naturally alluded to freedom from British oppression — an Irish ingredient added to the Australian adventure. Jack Donohoe, for example, 'scorn'd to live in slavery or be humbled to the Crown', while Francis MacNamara announced, 'I was convicted by the laws of

England's hostile crown'.[22] 'Tyrants', 'chains', 'oppressed' were terms that frequently surfaced in these ballads, terms with distinct Irish connotations, and not unknown in Moore's *Irish Melodies*. It is in one such ballad, on Jack Donohoe, that a reference to Moore occurs:

> I've left the old Island's hospitable shores,
> The land of the Emmets, the Tones and the Moores.

This ballad is reputed to date from the time of Donohoe's escapades in the late 1820s,[23] so Moore's association with Emmet and Tone indicates that within an Irish Australian rebel ethos he was acclaimed as pro-Ireland and pro-liberty.

This association would not have impressed the colonial garrisons, but such poems as 'As slow our ship' would not be considered offensive. On the contrary, the feelings of the poem's narrator as he is wrenched from family and friends would have appealed to many as they read the lines:

> As slow our ship her foamy track
>   Against the wind was cleaving,
> Her trembling pennant still look'd back
>   On that dear Isle 'twas leaving:-
> So loath we part from all we love,
>   From all the links that bind us;
> So turn our hearts, as on we rove,
>   To those we've left behind us.[24]

Looking back to the 'joy that's left behind us' became a recurring refrain for the Irish and others who saw themselves forever exiled in this remote southern continent. In his novel, *The Playmaker*, Thomas Keneally presents the isolation of early colonists in twentieth-century terms. He speaks of New South Wales as 'this penal planet' or 'convict moon', which is 'eight months travel in space' from England, an expressive metaphor of the psychological as well as physical distance all had travelled.[25] The awful realisation of the unlikelihood of return prompted some to pour forth their thoughts in verse, always derivative and often poorly written, but appealing to many who shared their *angst*. The exercise of writing was undoubtedly therapeutic. The restlessness induced by exile may have been abated, poetic reclamation of the past a way to assuage a dreary present or uncertain future. Specifically, this dabbling with words to express feelings towards a land now distant was a way of warding off, at least for a time, confrontation with a continent that seemed forbidding. Many would have agreed with a much later (and temporary) migrant, D. H. Lawrence, when he wrote: 'This land always gives me the feeling that it doesn't *want* to be touched, it doesn't *want* men to get hold of it'.[26] In the early decades of white settlement, such expressions of alienation were commonplace. Moreover, Barron Field in 1819 struck a typical note when he determined that, like America, this new land was bereft of material for literature:

> . . . (here) Nature is prosaic,
> Unpicturesque, unmusical, and where
> Nature reflecting Art is not yet born;-
> A land without antiquities . . .[27]

A view no doubt shared by many of the early newspaper poets who took comfort from the familiar rather than test their language on the unknown.[28]

Especially for such verse writers of Irish extraction, Thomas Moore provided themes and styles appropriate to their mood. The first to betray Moore's influence was Edward O'Shaughnessy. He was transported from Dublin in 1824 but due to his education, was assigned to work for the *Sydney Gazette* and some time after his release, became the editor.[29] In the late 1820s he began publishing lyrics, inspired by a girl left behind in Ireland. Past times with her are sweetly remembered and inevitably contrasted with present ennui. In suitably wistful tones she is admonished not to forget,

> That hour so sweet, when first we met,
> Those smiles and tears we've had together.[30]

Such vocabulary is everywhere employed; 'fondly cherished', 'warm blush of youth', 'flowers fade', 'bright scenes flown' and so on also owe a debt to Moore. In particular, his frequent reflections on the morning sunlight of youth and the evening clouds of age recall 'I saw from the beach' or 'Has sorrow thy young days shaded', and his dwelling on the memory of 'Affection's broken chain' contains echoes of 'Oft in the Stilly Night'.

Such unambiguously derivative verse was probably unavoidable from the pen of one who was more interested in the curative powers of writing than in developing an original style,[31] and a similar conclusion can be drawn about a more accomplished poet, Eliza Hamilton Dunlop. She had been born into an upper-middle-class Protestant family in County Armagh in 1796, but her sympathies were not Unionist.[32] Support for the aims of the Volunteers, concern for the decline of Gaelic culture and a knowledge of the Irish language are all evident in poems written before she migrated to Australia.[33] She arrived in Sydney with her husband, a magistrate, in 1838, and within months was contributing a series of exile songs to local newspapers. As with O'Shaughnessy, in the foreground of her verse was the trauma of separation from family and friends. She also summoned up childhood times, and indulged the pain of nostalgia by recalling landscapes, especially around Rostrevor, which were dear to her. Like Moore, who responded emotionally to landscape rather than delineating it, she experienced a *frisson* from summoning to her mind what now appeared idyllic scenes:

> 'Tis morning! from their heather bed
>   The curling mists arise
> And circling dark Slieve Donard's head
>   Ascend the drowsy skies.[34]

She did, however, go beyond Moore by juxtaposing the desert 'here' with the lush 'there'. In 'Tho the last glimpse of Erin' Moore vaguely envisaged 'the gloom of some desert or cold rocky shore',[35] but despite his own experience of exile in Europe, his imagination never left Ireland. His few exile poems seem written, as it were, on board ship, looking backwards.[36] He never explored the contrast between foreign places and those in Ireland. For Eliza Hamilton on the other hand, such a contrast was worth dwelling on:

> Away! these clustering grapes and olives ripening round,
> For the cloudless sky is brass, and she treads on iron ground
> The bright Azelia blushes on its bed of burning sand,
> But oh! the brook that gushes, in her own green land.[37]

A harsh land in which plants had to fight for survival, so unlike that soft Irish countryside with its gushing streams, seemed a suitable metaphor for a spirit now withering since removed from its native soil.

Despite an overwhelming longing for Ireland, she was not blind to future possibilities for this developing continent. So, she accepted an invitation from the composer, Isaac Nathan,[38] to write the words for a national song, 'Star of the South'. But her vision of 'Happy homes and free altars, broad land and bright skies' was hardly original, even in the 1840s, and a somewhat patrician image of Australia with 'soft flowing tresses' and 'proud eagle glance' annoyed local critics.[39] The poet defended her song, but its poor reception may have alerted her to an underlying philistinism in Australian society, which, I suspect, she would have treated with disdain.[40] She was also disturbed by the callous attitudes towards the Aborigines, and her sensitive poems on their culture met with hostility.[41] By the late 1840s, she seems to have abandoned poetry — she had exhausted her store of exile thoughts — and retreated instead to increasing her understanding of Aboriginal societies.[42]

Ironically, her transfer of scholarly interest from one indigenous culture in decline (Gaelic) to another (Aboriginal) reflected a measure of assimilation she would not have acknowledged. In Australia she did choose to write poems on Aboriginal issues rather than reviving topics such as the need to restore the minstrelsy of Gaelic Ireland. And she was not alone in avoiding Gaelic topics. A review of Australian poetry confirms that until the 1840s very few poems were published on Ireland's cultural and heroic past.[43] Some writers were surely familiar with 'Let Erin remember the days of old', 'The Harp that once', or similar Moore airs, yet few chose to imitate them. One, 'Eathlina's Lament', published in 1825, is a rare exception. The poet declaims on Irish heroes of former times and the harp, now broken, which once sang of their victories:

> Thro' thy halls Castle Connor, the harp once with pleasure
> Would tell all the battles my father had seen;
> Whilst princes have gather'd to list the soft measure,
> And recall with delight the days that have been.[44]

The narrator is depicted wandering, a lonely Romantic figure, along a desolate Sydney beach, an appropriate location for such sombre thoughts. There was probably a personal context here; the poet was the daughter of William Gore, an Anglo-Irish gentleman and senior official under Governor Bligh, but by the 1820s, financially disgraced and his family forced to live north of Sydney.[45] His daughter at least had developed an antiquarian interest in Gaelic society, and felt that its despair matched her own. But she wrote no further poems on this theme.

One can speculate on reasons for this neglect of Irish heroic themes. Moore himself admitted that some of the Melodies which touched on Ireland's 'national complaint' were regarded by some in England as treasonable: 'It has been accordingly said that the tendency of this publication is mischievous and that I have chosen these airs but as a vehicle of dangerous politics'.[46] While any censure was unlikely for long to outweigh popular acclaim in England, in penal colonies where a garrison mentality was never far beneath the surface, poetic attention to Irish heroes might be seen to have threatening implications for the present. The legacy of 1798 was difficult to live down and Irish emancipists and free settlers were barely tolerated by influential people who saw them as a threat to the 'British way of life'.[47] Secondly, the number of Irish people in the colonies with a scholarly interest in Gaelic society must have been pitifully small. The *Australian Dictionary of Biography* indicates that until the 1840s there were few educated colonists of Irish origins, and middle–class settlers were more likely to have a mercantile rather than a cultural disposition. Most significantly perhaps, the general reading public had no interest in Ireland's ancient past. Brian Boru, Malachi, Tara, Kinkora, were not only remote in time, but their society was totally foreign to most residents in the antipodes who looked to England for their culture.

Neglect, however, did not persist beyond the mid–century. As historians have noted, the composition of the Irish population changed considerably from around 1840 when free settlers began arriving in huge numbers.[48] Between 1851 and 1861, for example, over 100,000 migrants arrived from Ireland, and the majority were far from the stereotypical Irish migrant of the famine years: an illiterate peasant. Most were literate, though unskilled, and as Patrick O'Farrell has stated, 'particularly in the early forties, there was a leavening of the lower middle class and Irishmen of skill and attainment'.[49] These new migrants tended to be less integrationist and more assertive about Irish affairs than their predecessors. Australia might be a land of opportunity, and most would later integrate successfully, but they did seek to establish Ireland as an issue in colonial affairs. Daniel O'Connell was their hero, and Repeal of the Union their goal.

Newspapers sympathetic to Irish issues were launched: the *Freeman's Journal* (Sydney) in 1850, the *Catholic Tribune* (Melbourne) in 1853, the *Advocate* (Melbourne) in 1868 and *Irish Harp* (Adelaide) in 1869. Consequently, opportunities for publishing, and audiences for reading, poems with Irish themes increased. Whatever the subject of the poems, and they ranged from St Patrick's Day to the horrors of the famine to the death of O'Connell, images and motifs which owed a debt to Moore's *Irish Melodies* continually recur. Lines are filled with words and phrases such as 'Erin's isle', 'song of the harp', 'chains', 'brave chieftains', 'sighs', 'woes', 'light of liberty'; and those haunting cadences, so effectively used by Moore to emphasise a tone of lament, are frequently adopted. 'Lines on hearing of the death of O'Connell' is a typical example:

As Hibernia the woes of her sons sat bewailing,
Her heart steep'd in sadness, her eyes founts of tears,
On an emerald car thro' the air there came sailing
An angel, whose sad looks but heightened her fears . . .
As the voice of the tempest his words now resounded,
Till around Erin's isle the fell tidings had spread.
And the voices of millions in anguish resounded,
'Our Chieftain is gone — our O'Connell is dead'.[50]

One image, illustrated above, was prominent in these poems. Ireland was represented as woman, specifically as cherished mother with her children in these distant colonies distressed at her plight. The personification was hardly original in the 1840s, since Moore had popularised it in such lyrics as 'Remember thee' (1818), but it did promote a sentimental attachment to Ireland. Poets could share with their audiences an anxiety for a mother, perpetually sad having been deceived by a masculine and perfidious Albion. Erin, they protested, was long-suffering and worthy of unswerving loyalty from her children here in Australia who could still assist her in this hour of need. Although they were separated from their loving mother, affection and especially charity would increase, not diminish.[51]

Moore himself became identified with the image in the following poem written in Brisbane in 1879:

> True bard of our land, shall we ever forget
> The bright wreath on the brow of our mother thou'st set?
> In her chains and her grief she was dear to thy heart
> And thy glory shall still of her fame be a part.
>
> Farewell gentle minstrel! though far o'er the sea,
> From the land of thy love her true children are we;
> And as long as our race are brave, grateful and pure,
> Shall be honour and praise to the memory of Moore.[52]

Moore is proudly acknowledged as dutiful son paying respect to his grieving mother, a respect which enhances his reputation amongst Irish Australians who, the poet notes, still retain their attachment to Ireland.

The appeal of such verses, however, remained limited to Irish migrants or to those of Irish descent. As the century developed, all literature that owed its origins to migrant homelands had to compete with a movement to concentrate on indigenous subjects. An article in the *Australian Monthly*, for example, adopted a strongly nationalist line: — 'a young and new nation . . . should in literature fling off the trammels of the systems elsewhere adopted, and give to its actions and thinking a style. And in poetry this must be done by at once flinging aside recollections of other scenery, and selecting both imagery and subjects from our own climate, natural objects and population.'[53] Irish subject matter was clearly of the 'recollections' type, although, interestingly, some Irish issues could develop an Australian dimension. The pursuit of liberty was one such issue, taken up, for instance, by Charles Harpur.

Harpur, one of the major poets of the colonial period in Australia,[54] is never considered in an Irish context, despite the fact that his father, an Irish convict, was also his teacher and an influence on his republican politics.[55] Nor has any association been made between the nationalist element in his politics and his reading of Moore. Yet the second in a series of 'Rhymed Criticisms' was addressed to Moore, and opened with a flourish of praise:

> Bright, sparkling Moore! when first I heard him sing,
> How daring seemed his Muse! how sweetly wildering!
> Gods! what strong ecstasy my soul did seize
> When first I read his matchless Melodies![56]

Echoes of the *Irish Melodies* can be found in Harpur's work, especially in poems evoking places and friends from youth, but he did here admit that early enthusiasm waned when he judged that Moore's muse was more 'Of rhetoric than of true poetic lore'. Nevertheless, the poem concluded with an emotive endorsement of Moore's 'high and spirited praise of Liberty'. Commitment to liberty became the focus of Harpur's own political credo. Occasionally, he too declaimed on liberty for Ireland: his poem on Robert Emmet is presented as a riposte to 'Oh breathe not his name', the first stanza of which appears as an epigraph. Characteristically, Harpur is for thunderous protest:

Oh, why should the cold chain of silence be thrown
Round a name that must ever to glory belong?
Give me rather a war-trumpet's challenging tone
To enrap with that word the big feeling of wrong![57]

Liberty, he believed, could be achieved only through action, not what he saw as acquiesence. Perhaps, he had not recalled the second stanza of Moore's lyric where Emmet's memory is believed to be quietly keeping the revolutionary spirit alive. More likely, he was predisposed towards action; another poem on the Repeal movement speaks of 'crushed Ireland' summoning up 'retributive thunder'.[58]

The Emmet poem concluded with the claim that 'Liberty's tree shall find root in the blood of her martyrs', and this image of liberty as a tree was one that recurred in Harpur's major Australian poems. It seemed as appropriate for Australia as Moore's 'light of liberty' did for Ireland. For Moore, the 'light' might break through the gloom of oppression; for Harpur, the 'tree' would be planted and flourish in a new land. In one often quoted poem, 'The Tree of Liberty', he explored his belief that liberty was ever a rarity in the old world, its 'fruits' only for the few, but here in Australia the 'tree' would flourish and produce 'The fruit that blooms for all'.[59]

Harpur preferred to concentrate on this promise of the new world rather than on the oppression of the old. He was optimistic about Australia's social and political future, and at times aggressively presented his nationalist vision which did make him enemies in conservative circles.[60] But he was undaunted, and continually lauded Australia as the only land where equality for all would prevail. In 'The Emigrant's Vision', for example, he focused on an exile, presumably from Ireland, receiving a vision while on board ship. As in the Gaelic *aisling* tradition, the vision is a goddess, but representing Australia, not Ireland; she is beckoning the dispossessed or downtrodden to settle in this new land where Liberty can be found, and where settlers can find material Plenty, 'wedded to honest Endeavour'. When the dreamer awakes, he determines, 'Be the home of my hope then Australia'.[61] Unlike the exile in 'As slow our ship', he looks forward expectantly, not back.

Increasingly in the latter half of the century, Irish migrants adopted the decision of the dreamer in this poem. Looking forward meant getting a decent house, a steady job or piece of land, education and possible entry into the professions for the children, and taking an interest in local affairs. Funding of Catholic schools was an issue that linked many Irish to a common cause, but there were no distinct Irish communities, or ghettoes in cities, or Irish electorates.[62] Despite complaints from some quarters about Irish exclusiveness, integration was achieved remarkably quickly.[63] And with integration, active involvement in Irish issues was difficult to sustain, despite visits by Home Rule politicians and others in the final years of the century. Of course, migrants continued to look back. For a time, there was even a kind of dual allegiance in evidence, an attractive condition to many, including William Carleton jun., son of the novelist, who proclaimed it in a poem, 'The New Land and the Old':

> When Fortune's smile hath found us
>   And banished care and fear,
> When happy homes surround us
>   And those we love are near,
> The young shall pause and listen
>   To hear the story told
> How they should love the new land
>   But *doubly* love the *old*.[64]

Carleton was investing a natural stage in the integration of an Irish migrant with a romantic aura. He proudly displayed the achievement of material well-being, followed by domestic bliss, and time to relax from 'getting on', time to ensure that the young in particular did not lose touch with their cultural origins.

For Irish Australians looking back was characterised by sentimentality. And what better way to satisfy that nostalgia for the old country than by singing Moore's melodies. Evergreen favourites such as 'Oft in the Stilly Night' and 'Tis the last rose of summer' captured that mood which the migrant wanted to enjoy in reflective moments. These airs summoned up a moment of stillness, a moment for a wave of memories of childhood, of family forgotten or friendships decayed by long absence, to sweep over the listener. The elegaic tone was so captivating to many for whom Ireland was ever fixed in the mind as a place of happy childhood, soft evening light and sweet birds singing. Like the narrator, an individual could temporarily adopt a pose of loneliness and wistfulness before returning to the hurly-burly of daily life. Just such a migrant was Danny DeLacy, the central character in Miles Franklin's novel *All That Swagger*. A pioneer in the outback and eventually a patriarch of a large Australian family, he turns maudlin in his old age, and at any festivity breaks into singing Moore songs, especially 'Those Evening Bells':

> . . . this song suddenly struck a deep chord in his being, and filled him with wistfulness. He was startled to find that the glow of life, in which he had walked as in dawn light, had stealthily slipped behind him, and that he had to look over his shoulder to behold it as he went on into the night.[65]

That emotional jolt bringing with it an awareness of mortality was no doubt the experience of many Irish as they momentarily stepped outside their colonial lives to listen to Moore's lyrics.

Although no Irish occasion, especially St Patrick's day concerts,[66] was complete without the rendition of Moore's melodies, there was one local poet, firmly in his tradition, who achieved a measure of popularity. She was Eva Mary O'Doherty, or 'Eva of the *Nation*' as she was known, the wife of Kevin

Izod O'Doherty, a transported 1848 rebel who later became a highly regarded surgeon and public figure in Brisbane.[67] She was long renowned for her patriotic achievements — her stirring political contributions to the *Nation* had earned her the sobriquet long before she came to Queensland — and her highly publicised marriage to a hero of the 1848 rebellion stimulated interest in her poetry. An acquaintance, Spencer Browne, wrote in his memoirs that her work was 'viewed through glasses violet-hued by sympathy, and that tenderness coming from the old assessment of the world's love for lovers'.[68] Perhaps. Whatever the reason, her patriotic songs, exile lyrics and love poems according to one literary historian 'had an exceptional vogue during her lifetime'.[69]

A Queensland poet, George Vowles, in a paean to his native Brisbane paused to pay homage to Eva and her contribution to Queensland verse:

> Long may my country such high honour know!
>   And long may Eva live to tune her lyre
> And sing of Shannon's banks and Erin's woe,
>   A credit to her island and her sire.[70]

Vowles alluded to two separate aspects of Eva's verse: 'Shannon's banks' and 'Erin's woe'. Her thoughts on 'Erin's woe' had often produced poems of defiance against British oppression, poems with titles such as 'The Felon', 'The Men in Gaol for Ireland', 'National March',[71] which in strident tones called on the men and women of Ireland to cast off slavery and develop national self-esteem. But a more reflective mood was evident in 'The Fallen Queen', for instance, which in a style reminiscent of Moore, centred on a personification of Ireland as queen, once proud but now signified by ruin and decay. These poems were mainly written in Ireland, but those on 'Shannon's banks' date from her years in Australia. In these she concentrated on intensely-realised memories of Irish scenes, where glad times in childhood spent beside burbling streams were recalled and contrasted with migrant weariness:

> Still is the blackbird singing
>   The live-long day.
> Still are the waters ringing
>   This golden May.
> But ah! not for me that singing,
> Nor the stream with its silver ringing,
> Though my heart to that spot is clinging
>   Far, far away![72]

Such flourishes of emotionalism may strike a modern reader as overdone or even false, but one hundred years ago they were not so considered. On the contrary, that heart-rending rhetoric that pervades these verses partly accounted for her popularity amongst Irish Australians. Her recollections of Irish scenes with Moore-like fresh breezes, mellow light and summer evenings were often combined with an appealing sensuous element: 'We taste a beauty which is almost pain', for example. On occasion, she even indulged in a train of thought in which Ireland was enchanted, paradisal, almost a vision of Heaven itself. For Eva, the land possessed:

The choral strain of living waters,
  Pervading all the earth and air;
Mysterious music still that utters
  Eternal thoughts of praise and prayer![73]

In her best-known poem, 'Queensland', she turned to her adopted land but could not avoid implying a contrast between its barrenness and Irish richness. It was not just the harshness of the landscape, something that Eliza Hamilton complained of, but that the country was bereft of culture and history. Like other migrants, she could praise the bright, blue sky and benevolent climate, but essentially Australia was a *terra nullius* in terms of history and associations attached to place:

No poet-fancies o'er thy skies
Spread tints that hallow, live for ever;
No old tradition's magic lies
On mountain, vale and river.
There is no heart within thy breast,
No classic charms of memories hoary,
No footprint hath old time imprest
On thee of song or story.[74]

Few migrants shared Eliza Hamilton's interest in Aboriginal societies, and such thoughts as Eva's must have occurred to many. She was indeed repeating the views of Barron Field fifty years earlier: Australia lacked the stuff of poetry. Specifically however, she was tapping a wellspring of Irish feeling. With all the opportunities for material success accepted, the new country had not accrued those personal or cultural associations which were important for the Irish in signifying a particular location as 'home'.[75] That heritage extolled by Eva and by Moore was therefore attractive not just because it was Irish, but also because the Irish psyche could not for some time construct anything local to compare with it.

But this situation could not continue indefinitely. In Patrick White's *Voss*, a character comments, 'A pity that you huddle . . . your country is of great subtlety'.[76] Eva O'Doherty and others who indulged in the sentimental backward look were, metaphorically, huddling, refusing to consider the creative potential of the new land. In the final decades of the century, Australia forced itself on the consciousness of writers. The novelist Marcus Clarke developed those nationalist sentiments expressed in the *Australian Monthly* by requesting poets not to dwell on 'sunsets by some ruined chapel on the margin of an Irish lake' but to attend to the local:

. . . this our native or adopted land has no past, no story. No poet speaks to us. Do we need a poet to interpret Nature's teachings, we must look into our own hearts, if perchance we may find a poet there.[77]

Such advice was not ignored by Irish Australian poets, and as the interpreters of integration established themselves, the influence of Moore waned. For popular consumption, the ballad tradition, once associated with protest, took on more benign themes focusing especially on the trials and vagaries of life in the outback. John O'Brien's songs in *Around the Boree Log*, for example, with their humorous and quintessentially Australian evocations of Irish small settlers, in time became as widely performed as those of Moore.[78] More literary poets such as Victor Daley and Roderic Quinn[79] drew on contemporary Irish styles and motifs and gave them a local colouring. To these poets around the turn of the century, Moore was truly in the distant past, someone with no influence on an Australia asserting its identity.

However, this evolution in Australian poetry did not mean that the *Irish Melodies* ceased to find an audience among Irish Australians. On the contrary, popular admiration for Moore increased in the final decades of the century. Even those songs of liberty such as 'Let Erin remember' and 'The minstrel boy', which in earlier generations were unacceptable in colonial society, were now taken up not only by those asserting their Irish heritage but by many who supported liberty for Australia and a weakening of imperial ties.[80] It is possible to measure the acclaim accorded to Moore by comparing the centenary celebrations for his birth with those for another Irishman, Daniel O'Connell. O'Connell may have been a hero to the migrants of the mid-century, but his political methods had little influence on Irish Australia. At best he was a hero of the past, someone to place beside Emmet and Tone. At worst, his aggressive nationalism was seen as irrelevant for an Irish community that wished quietly to integrate into the evolving Australian society.[81] His centenary celebrations in 1875 were distinctly Irish and Catholic. J. T. Reilly's record of the O'Connell festival held in Perth is characteristic: 'Faith and Fatherland were pleasingly represented'; 'hundreds of patriotic individuals (attended) in honour of Ireland's great patriot', and so forth.[82] There was no mention of Australia. Very different, and much more successful, were the celebrations for Moore four years later. At concerts throughout the land, thousands of Irish people, together with English, Scottish and native-born Australians, gathered to listen to speeches eulogising a great lyric poet, and to hear once more a selection of those melodies.[83] Politicians, clergymen and people of all ranks were keen to pay homage to a poet whom everyone could praise. No one would deny that these were Irish occasions, another opportunity to grow nostalgic about the old country while listening to 'Tho' the last glimpse of Erin', for example; an opportunity too for local poets to reflect the general mood by composing verses in honour of Moore and attachment to Ireland. But the Irish could approve the Australian dimension to these celebrations. The melodies with their nostalgia for places far away and their muted demands for liberty had found a general audience. Indeed, it could be claimed they were even smoothing the passage of the Irish into these British colonies. Toasts to Moore and to Ireland were followed by 'The Land we live in' and 'Queen Victoria'; and 'God Save the Queen' concluded the evening's proceedings without a hint of incongruity. A speaker in Adelaide summed up the national approbation: 'We honour him . . . because we English, Irish, Scotch, Colonials, one and all uniting here beneath the Southern Cross, . . . are willing and proud to recognize genius, though it shines upon us rarely'.[84]

During his visit to Australia in 1885, the dramatist, Dion Boucicault, was fulsome in his praise for the achievements of Irish Australia: 'They were poor and unappreciated at home; but they came here, and what is the result? They prove themselves to be most valuable citizens — good, loyal, hard-working members of your great progressive communities'.[85] Words indeed that the Irish were delighted to hear, a confirmation that integration had been accomplished. Few Irish now felt themselves on the margins of this society, or concentrated their minds solely on the intricacies of Irish affairs. In those years of dual allegiance, most were Australian first and Irish second. Yet inevitably images of a green and pleasant land would continue to surface, especially when the Irish, on their own or with other migrants, paused to recall their past. Coming together for concerts in town halls or social 'occasions' in the outback meant singing, and singing meant Moore's *Melodies*. Moore was ever the poet of the public occasion. Local imitators such as Edward O'Shaughnessy, Eliza Hamilton, Eva O'Doherty and a host of anonymous poets might for a time reflect a sentimental longing, but their literary efforts could never replace the primacy accorded to Moore. And in time they were replaced by poets who would follow Harpur and focus on indigenous subject matter. But the wistful, nostalgic tones of Moore were not forgotten. Well into the twentieth century, Australians continued to be captivated by lyrics about a land most had never seen. Certainly, many would have applauded the claim of Kevin O'Doherty, speaking at the Brisbane centenary in 1879, that 'in the drawing rooms of the rich and the humble homes of the poor, the story of Ireland (would) be told and sung in Moore's glowing language to untold generations'.[86]

Notes

1. *Ulysses*, The Corrected Text, Penguin, Harmondsworth, 1986, p. 133.
2. For Joyce's admiration for Moore see Thérèse Tessier, *The bard of Erin: a study of Thomas Moore's 'Irish Melodies' (1808–1934)*, Institut Für Anglistik und Amerikanistik, Salzburg, 1981, pp. 147–52; Terence De Vere White, *Tom Moore: the Irish poet*, Hamish Hamilton, London, 1977, pp. 75–6. It is revealing of Joyce's knowledge of Moore that the first line from every song in the *Irish Melodies* is incorporated into *Finnegans Wake*.
3. See White, *Tom Moore*, pp. xi–xiii.
4. Information provided to the present writer by the Ballarat Library and Ballarat Historical Society, 4 October 1991. This was not the only statue outside Ireland; a bust of the poet was unveiled in Central Park, New York in 1880. See Tessier, *Bard of Erin*, p. 136.
5. The citizens of Ballarat later decided to erect a statue to Queen Victoria instead of one to Shakespeare. The positioning of the statues on Sturt Street has led to wry comments in recent years, especially among literary theorists who see special signification in Victoria facing Burns but with her back to Moore!
6. In a letter written from Cove Harbour in 1824, Captain Rock declared, 'For myself, I am grown old in the service — repose has at length become welcome, if not esential to me; and when all that a man wishes is to be able to say, "inveni Portum", Port Jackson [Sydney] perhaps will do as well as any other' (*Memoirs of Captain Rock: the celebrated Irish chieftain*, Longmans, London, 1874, p. 373). Clearly, Captain Rock, and perhaps his creator, knew little about the penal colony at Port Jackson; 'repose' is a word few would have used. For a study of this work see Patrick O'Sullivan, 'A literary difficulty in explaining Ireland: Tom Moore and Captain Rock, 1824' in

Roger Swift and Sheridan Gilley, (eds), *The Irish in Britain, 1815–1939*, Pinter, London, 1989, pp. 239ff.

7. See Douglas Pike (ed.), *Australian dictionary of biography*, Vol. 5, 1851–90, Melbourne University Press, Melbourne, 1974, pp. 364–66. O'Loghlen was a member of the Victorian parliament for many years and premier from 1881 to 1883.

8. Report in the *Ballarat Star*, 4 December 1889, p. 4.

9. *Ballarat Star*, p. 4

10. *Ballarat Star*, p. 4. At a concert held in the Academy of Music, Ballarat, on 3 December, an 'Ode to Tom Moore' by Denis Florence McCarthy was recited.

11. *Sydney Gazette*, 9 December 1820, p. 4.

12. George Howe worked on *The Times* before being transported in 1799. He was the first government printer in New South Wales and editor of the *Gazette* from its founding in 1803 until his death in 1821. In 1819 he published the first book of poetry in Australia, *First fruits of Australian Poetry*, by Barron Field.

13. For further information on the early history of Australia see C.M.H. Clark, *A history of Australia*, Vol 1, Melbourne University Press, Melbourne, 1962; Robert Hughes, *The fatal shore*, Pan Books, London, 1987, especially pp. 323–67; for a contemporary account of the society see W.C. Wentworth, *A statistical, historical and political description of the colony of New South Wales and its dependent settlements in Van Diemen's Land*, 1819, Griffin Press, Adelaide, 1978.

14. Reprinted in *Irish Melodies*, Longman, Brown, Green and Longmans, London, 1852, p. 153. All subsequent references in the chapter are from this edition. (The quotation in the chapter title is from 'Oh! blame not the bard', p. 29.)

15. *Two years in New South Wales*, 1827, Angus and Robertson, Sydney, 1966, p. 34. Visitors tended to criticise the quality of cultural life in particular. In the 1840s Louisa Meredith could still complain: '. . . not a question is heard relative to English literature or art; far less a remark on any political event, of however important a nature:- not a syllable that betrays *thought*' (*Notes and sketches of New South Wales during residence of that colony from 1839–1844*, 1844, Penguin, Ringwood, Vic., 1973, pp. 49–50.

16. See Con Costello, 'The convicts: transportation from Ireland' in Colm Kiernan (ed.), *Ireland and Australia*, Angus and Robertson, Sydney, 1984, pp. 12–22; Patrick, O'Farrell, *The Irish in Australia*, University of NSW Press, Sydney, 1987, pp. 22–53; Robert Hughes, *The fatal shore*, pp. 187–94.

17. For details of this census see M. R. Sainty, and K. A. Johnson (eds), *Census of New South Wales, November 1828*, Library of Australian History, Sydney, 1980. The vast majority of Irish convicts were sent to New South Wales; the Irish element in Van Diemen's Land was less than 10 per cent. See O'Farrell, *The Irish in Australia*, p. 36.

18. See Patrick O'Farrell, *Vanished kingdoms: Irish in Australia and New Zealand*, University of NSW Press, Sydney, 1990, pp. 1–21.

19. See P. Butterss, '"Convicted by laws of England's hostile crown": popular convict verse' in Oliver MacDonagh and W. F. Mandle, *Irish Australian Studies*, Australian National University Press, Canberra, 1989, p. 19. The following description of seventeenth-century tories is particularly apt for Australian bushrangers two hundred years later: 'The tories were outlaws whose natural taste for robbery was strengthened by resentment against the new settlers and the regime that supported them. In spite of their depredations, they acquired something of a patriotic character among the native Irish' (J. C. Beckett, *The making of modern Ireland 1603–1923*, Faber, London, 1966, p. 105.

20. *Two years in New South Wales*, p. 282.

21. A belief that 'Bold Jack Donahoe' was banned has long been held, but the evidence is now thought to be suspect. There may have been an unofficial suppression, but as

Phil Butterss has indicated, the *Historical records of Australia*, Series 1, Vol. XV, p. 906, do not clearly specify that the ballad was banned (Letter to the present writer, 11 November 1991).

22. The first quotation is from 'Bold Jack Donohoe', in D. Stewart and N. Keesing, *Old bush songs and rhymes of colonial times*, Angus and Robertson, 1957, p. 36; the second is from 'Labouring with the hoe', in John Meredith and Rex Whalan, *Frank the poet*, Red Rooster Press, Melbourne, 1979, p. 39. *Frank the poet* contains a biography of this, the best-known Irish writer of convict ballads.

23. From 'Jack Donahue and gang', in *Old bush songs*, p. 37. A comment on this ballad suggests it was composed by Donahue himself. Another version, entitled 'Old Ireland lies groaning', is printed in *Old bush songs*, pp. 38–9.

24. The version printed is from *Irish Melodies*, pp. 83–4. The plagiarised version in the *Sydney Gazette* substituted 'pendant' for 'pennant' (line 3), 'those' for 'all' (line 5) and 'when'er' for 'as on' (line 7).

25. Thomas Keneally, *The Playmaker*, Hodder and Stoughton, London, 1987, p. 3; p. 13.

26. D.H. Lawrence, *Kangaroo*, 1923, Penguin, Harmondsworth, 1950, p. 306.

27. Barron Field, 'On reading the controversy between Lord Byron and Mr Bowles', 1819, reprinted in Brian Elliott and Adrian Mitchell, *Bards in the wilderness: Australian colonial poetry to 1920*, Nelson, Melbourne, 1970, pp. 18–19.

28. The number of newspapers, and the number of original poems published in them, greatly increased from the mid-1820s. See E. Webby, *Early Australian poetry: an annotated bibliography*, Hale and Iremonger, Sydney, 1982.

29. See Douglas Pike. (ed.), *Australian dictionary of biography*, Vol. 2, 1788–1850, Melbourne University Press, Melbourne, 1967, pp. 304–5.

30. Edward O'Shaughnessy, 'Stanzas to——', *Sydney Gazette*, 6 January 1829, p. 4.

31. O'Shaughnessy was very limited in his subject matter and after a few years ceased writing verse.

32. See Margaret DeSalis, *Two early colonials*, n. p., Sydney, 1967.

33. Eliza Hamilton Dunlop's poems are available in manuscript, Mitchell Library, Sydney. A number of the early poems were published in Sydney newspapers.

34. 'Morning on Rostrevor Mountain', *The Atlas* (Sydney), 26 April 1845, p. 257.

35. *Irish Melodies*, p. 9.

36. See, for example, 'Farewell! but whenever you welcome the hour' (pp. 64–5), 'As slow our ship' (pp. 83–4); 'Come o'er the sea' (pp. 68–70); 'Sail on, sail on' (pp. 96–7).

37. 'Songs of an exile, No 7', *The Australian*, 11 April 1840, p. 4.

38. See Pike, *Australian dictionary of Biography*, Vol. 2, pp. 279–80.

39. See DeSalis, *Two early colonials*, p. 109.

40. *Sydney Morning Herald*, 30 August 1842, p. 3. Following Eliza Hamilton's request, the *Herald* published the words of the song.

41. Her interest in the plight of the Aborigines was aroused soon after her arrival in the colony by the publicity surrounding a massacre of natives at Myall Creek. She published what has become her best-known poem on this massacre, 'The Aboriginal mother', but at the time it was condemned in a patronising manner. Further poems on Aboriginal culture were also poorly received. See DeSalis, *Two early colonials*, pp. 102–8.

42. See L. E. Threlkeld, *Reminiscences*, cited in DeSalis, *Two early colonials*, pp. 106–8. Mrs Dunlop spent much of her time learning the language of the Aborigines in the district where she lived.

43. Webby, *Early Australian poetry*, *passim*.

44. *The Australian*, 8 September 1825, p. 3.

45. See Douglas Pike, *Australian dictionary of biography*, Vol. 1, 1788–1850, Melbourne University Press, Melbourne, 1966, pp. 459–60.
46. 'Letter on music', *Irish Melodies*, p. 153.
47. Chief proponent of an anti-Catholic/anti-Irish policy was Samuel Marsden, an influential evangelical clergyman. See A. T. Yarwood, *Samuel Marsden: the great survivor*, Melbourne University Press, Melbourne, 1977, pp. 70–2, 78–9, 98–100.
48. See O'Farrell, *The Irish in Australia*, pp. 54–114; J. O'Brien and P. Travers (eds), *The Irish emigrant experience in Australia*, Poolbeg, Dublin, 1991; C. McConville, *Croppies, Celts and Catholics: the Irish in Australia*, Edward Arnold, Melbourne, 1987, pp. 29–61.
49. O'Farrell, *The Irish in Australia*, p. 59.
50. Written by 'Celt', published in *The Sydney Chronicle*, 18 September 1847, p. 4.
51. A number of poems in the 1840s were pleas for assistance for the victims of the Famine.
52. Written by 'Thomasine' (Hope Connolly), published in the *Brisbane Courier*, 29 May 1879, p. 3.
53. Cited in E. Webby, 'Before the *Bulletin*: nineteenth-century literary journalism' in Bruce Bennett (ed.) *Cross currents: magazines and newspapers in Australian literature*, Longman Cheshire, Melbourne, 1981, p. 24.
54. Judith Wright said of Harpur: he 'was undoubtedly Australia's first poet of sustained significance, and in important respects he was also our most interesting nineteenth century poet'. See *Charles Harpur*, Oxford University Press, Melbourne, 1977, p. 3.
55. For Harpur's life see J. Normington-Rawling, *Charles Harpur: an Australian*, Angus and Robertson, Sydney, 1962.
56. 'Moore' in E. Perkins, (ed.) *The poetical works of Charles Harpur*, Angus and Robertson, Sydney, 1984, pp. 815–17.
57. Perkins (ed.), *Poetical works*, p. 770.
58. First published in *The Sydney Chronicle*, 23 December 1847, p. 4. A later version of the poem, included in Perkins (ed.), *Poetical works*, p. 422, substitutes Poland for Ireland. The original version is reprinted in M. Ackland (ed.) *Charles Harpur: selected poetry and prose*, Penguin, Ringwood, Vic., 1986, p. 73.
59. Perkins (ed.), *Poetical works*, pp. 9–10. On Harpur's use of the tree motif see M. Ackland, 'Charles Harpur's Republicanism', *Westerly*, Vol. 29, No. 3, October 1984, pp. 75–88.
60. See Normington-Rawling, *Charles Harpur*, pp. 194–218.
61. Perkins (ed.), *Poetical works*, pp. 448–9.
62. Anthony Trollope provoked outrage amongst Irish Australians when he claimed there was an Irish quarter in Melbourne. See *Australia and New Zealand*, 1873, University of Queensland Press, St Lucia, 1967, p. 375. For the Irish response see J. F. Hogan, *The Irish in Australia*, Ward and Downey, London, 1888, pp. 36–7. Hogan accused Trollope of 'lying and unblushing effrontery'.
63. See Hogan, *The Irish in Australia*, *passim*; O'Farrell, *The Irish in Australia*, pp. 247–8.
64. *Advocate* (Melbourne), 10 September 1870, p. 12. For information on Carleton see Hogan, *The Irish in Australia*, p. 337.
65. *All that swagger*, 1936, Angus and Robertson, Sydney, 1984, p. 214.
66. See Oliver MacDonagh, 'St Patrick's Day in Australia 1888' in Oliver MacDonagh, W. F. Mandle, P. Travers (eds), *Irish culture and nationalism translated 1750–1950*, Macmillan, London, 1983, pp. 76–80.
67. See Ross and Heather Patrick, *Exiles undaunted: the Irish rebels Kevin and Eva O'Doherty*, University of Queensland Press, St Lucia, 1989. Mary Anne Kelly, later

O'Doherty, is so thoroughly known to history as 'Eva' that I have decided that it would be pedantic to call her anything else in this Chapter.

68. *A journalist's memories*, Read Press, Brisbane, 1927, p. 109.
69. Morris Miller, *Australian literature 1795–1938*, Vol. 1, 1940, Sydney University Press, Sydney, 1973, p. 171.
70. 'A sketch', quoted by Henry Kellow, *Queensland Poets*, George G. Harrap, London, 1930, p. 102.
71. There were two published collections of Eva O'Doherty's poems, the first by Thomas, San Francisco, 1877; the second by M. H. Gill, Dublin 1909. Page references in this chapter are from the Dublin edition.
72. 'Glenmaloe', *Poems*, pp. 17–18.
73. 'A flight across the sea', *Poems*, pp. 63–4.
74. *Poems*, pp. 92–3, reprinted in Richard Jordan and Peter Pierce (eds), *The poets' discovery: nineteenth-century Australia in verse*, Melbourne University Press, Melbourne, 1990, pp. 201–2.
75. See O'Farrell, *The Irish in Australia*, p. 197: 'Irish immigrants came from a country in which primary loyalties had been to family, then clan, then town, region, or at widest, county'.
76. Patrick White, *Voss*, 1957, Penguin, Harmondsworth, 1960, p. 11. This novel is set in nineteenth-century Australia with Voss based on the explorer Ludwig Leichhardt.
77. Preface to Gordon's *Poems*, 1876, reprinted in John Barnes (ed.) *The writer in Australia: a collection of literary documents 1856 to 1964*, Oxford University Press, Melbourne, 1969, pp. 33–7.
78. See F. Mecham, *'John O'Brien' and the Boree Log*, Angus and Robertson, Sydney, 1981. *Around the Boree Log* was first published in 1921 and ran to many editions in Australia and later in North America.
79. For brief biographical information on these two poets see William H. Wilde *et al*, *The Oxford companion to Australian literature*, Oxford University Press, Melbourne, 1985, p. 201 and p. 574.
80. See, for example, the following from the popular magazine, the *Bulletin*: 'The policy of freedom is a policy which gives to a people . . . the direct government of its own land. Poland for the Poles, Egypt for the Egyptians, Ireland for the Irish and Australia for the Australians!' Cited in S. Lawson, *The Archibald paradox*, Allen Lane, Ringwood Vic, 1983, p. 129.
81. See Patrick O'Farrell, 'The image of O'Connell in Australia' in Donal McCartney (ed.), *The world of Daniel O'Connell*, Mercier Press, Dublin and Cork, 1980, pp. 112–24.
82. *Reminiscences of fifty years in Western Australia*, Sands and McDougall, Perth, 1903, pp. 138–9.
83. See reports in the *Brisbane Courier*, 29 May 1879, p. 5; *The Argus*, 29 May 1879, p. 6; *The Age*, 29 May 1879, p. 5; *Sydney Morning Herald*, 29 May 1879, p. 6; *Hobart Mercury*, 29 May 1879, p. 2; *South Australian Advertiser*, 14 June 1879, p. 11.
84. *South Australian Advertiser*, p. 11.
85. Quoted in Hogan, *Irish in Australia*, p. 342.
86. Report in *Brisbane Courier*, p. 5.

6 Hunting the fenians: problems in the historiography of a secret organisation

Patrick J. Quinlivan

Introduction

Many English historians have taken their revenge on the fenians by writing them out of the history books. The editors of *The Cambridge History of English Literature* follow the same line in stating that 'fenianism was unconnected with literary effort'.[1] The growth of interest in Anglo–Irish studies and in world-wide Irish history, heritage and identity has brought new life to the study of fenianism. Local history projects begin to show the extent of fenianism but there is still a lot to be done and many mysteries to be investigated.

My first teaching post was at Hugh Myddelton North School in London when Alfred Caiger was Headmaster.[2] He knew of my interest in local history and suggested a study of Clerkenwell starting with the school building. The Hugh Myddelton Schools in London were built on the site of the Clerkenwell House of Detention and parts of the prison were incorporated into the school buildings. Set in the school wall is a plaque[3] with the following inscription:

The Boundary Wall of the
'Hugh Myddelton' Schools
formerly enclosed the
MIDDLESEX HOUSE OF DETENTION
The portion of the wall where this tablet is
placed was destroyed by an explosion of
gunpowder on
Friday December 13th 1867
in an attempt to rescue certain prisoners who
were here awaiting their trial on a charge of
FENIAN CONSPIRACY
By this explosion nine persons were killed & forty
severely injured

The plaque was a useful point for local history studies. In the course of these studies I became aware of the lack of information about the incident and the misunderstanding and misinformation about the events leading to the Clerkenwell Explosion and resulting from it. Most history textbooks dealing with the period dismiss the incident with a brief reference or footnote to the effect that it was a futile gesture by mad Irishmen. Yet the British Prime Minister, William Gladstone, declared on more than one occasion that the Clerkenwell Explosion was one cause of his changing his mind about the 'Irish Question'.[4] The explosion helped to make Home Rule practical politics. It helped put Gladstone on to the path that led to the disestablishment of the Church of Ireland, and to the Land Acts and the Home Rule Bills, and thus it helped shape modern Irish history and Anglo-Irish relations.

The Clerkenwell Explosion shook Victorian England, causing alarm and despondency. It brought death, destruction and armed troops to the streets of London, and it led to the last public execution in Britain. Most important of all, at a time of crisis it quenched enthusiasm for the Irish Republican Brotherhood and stopped English working-class support for Irish political freedom.

Dr E. D. Steele has pointed out that the activities of the Irish Republican Brotherhood in Britain is a topic that awaits its historian, as indeed does fenianism in general.[5] The history student in Britain can be forgiven for thinking the fenians were never in England, so effectively have they been eliminated from the history textbooks. Within a few years of the events of 1867 an historian could write that children were asking 'Who or what were the fenians?' and that the subject was remote and unknown to the general public.[6] It took the centenary year of 1967 to bring new interest to the study of the fenians in Ireland and succeeding years have brought interesting papers on the IRB in England.

Historians and the fenians

Much of the 'history' of the fenians has been written from hostile sources. Slanted reports and errors of fact have accumulated and not all are as obvious as those of Michael Harrison, whose book *London by Gaslight* should be listed under fiction rather than history. He attributed the Clerkenwell Explosion to Jeremiah O'Donovan Rossa despite the fact that Rossa was in a British prison at the time and had been a prisoner for two years. Harrison stated that the explosion was caused by 'the Irish dynamiters, supplied with money and high explosives by O'Donovan Rossa, from his headquarters in New York'. Harrison then added 'having used up all their dynamite on the underground the fenians decided to use gunpowder'. The use of dynamite on the London underground of 1867 would have surprised the inventor who was still continuing his experiments with it![7] The reported killing of a police officer at the scene, mentioned by Harrison, likewise escaped the notice of the police and press as did the deaths of nineteen persons at the public execution of Michael Barrett for causing the explosion.[8] There are a number of other ludicrous statements matched only by the general inaccuracy of contemporary British press reports on the fenians in England.

When the name and pseudonym of one of the most active British secret agents against the fenians were made public they were reported on the same day as follows:

The Times	Thomas Willis Beach/Henri Le Caron
Standard	Thos. Phillip Beach/Henri Lecaron
Daily News	Thomas Miller Beach/Major Le Carom
Daily Telegraph	Thos. Philip Beach/Major Lecaron
Daily Chronicle	Thomas Philip Leach/Honore Le Carom
Pall Mall Gazette	Thomas Miller Beech/Major Le Carom
Star of the East	Thomas Bellis Peach/Henry McCaron
East Anglian Daily Telegraph	Thomas Billis Beach/Henry Le Caroni
Morning Post	Thomas Billis Beach/Henry Le Caron

Only the *Morning Post* had both names right[9] and various permutations of the other names have been in use ever since. Even in 1967 in Desmond Ryan's *The Fenian Chief* the spy is indexed as 'Beach, Thomas (Willis? or Miller?)'.[10]

Journalists writing under the pressure of deadlines have some excuse for errors of fact. There is less excuse for writers who purport to cover nineteenth-century Anglo-Irish history and yet unwrite the fenians or dismiss them in a few lines filled with contention and error. To say that the majority of British historians writing about Victorian Anglo-Irish history at any level are unbalanced and unreasonable may be unkind but hardly unfair. The organisation that brought a sense of insecurity to Britain, cost Britain millions of pounds to combat and which had a decisive influence on Anglo-Irish history is usually unspoken in a manner reminiscent of George Orwell's *Nineteen Eighty-four*. By 1884 the organisation had been dismissed as moribund and by 1934 even the word 'fenian' had been declared obsolescent.[11]

When the fenians are mentioned the references are almost all dismissive, contemptuous, facetious and factually highly erroneous. A. M. Newth reported in *Britain and the World, 1789–1901*, that the fenians failed to rescue Thomas Kelly and Timothy Deasy in Manchester in 1867.[12] R. J. Minney in *No. 10 Downing Street* referred to savage outrages by the fenians in England and stated 'in Manchester a dozen lives were lost'.[13] H. Bolitho in *Victoria the Widow* claimed 'the fenians blew up Clerkenwell Prison, rather incongruously, since two of their own "martyrs" were inside. How could the English understand these mad creatures who cut off their noses to spite their faces?'[14] R. Howe claimed in *The Story of Scotland Yard* that at Manchester in 1867 four fenians were arrested and later hanged.[15] A. G. Gardiner in his biography of *Sir William*

Harcourt accepted the usual figure of three public hangings in Manchester but unaccountably named the men as Allen, Larkin and Gill.[16] Y. Kapp in *Eleanor Marx* was more sympathetic to the fenians but followed a well-worn track in locating the Clerkenwell Explosion at the wrong prison.[17] P. M. H. Bell in *Disestablishment in Ireland* got the right prison but the wrong date.[18] G. Howard in *Guardians of the Queen's Peace* reported that the fenian ringleader Michael Bartlett was executed in 1864,[19] probably a garbled reference to the public execution of Michael Barrett in 1868. T. Burke in *The Streets of London* reported that Barrett was 'one of the fenians who blew up Clerkenwell Sessions House'.[20]

The report by L. Apjohn that 'in March 1868 the Duke of Edinburgh was shot in the back by an armed fenian in Australia, and was hung for the offence'[21] sounds like a grammatical outrage. The report that 'a body of fenians had been discovered drilling on the Kennington Oval Cricket Ground'[22] sounds like an Irish joke. R. S. Seth in *The Specials* claimed that the Young Ireland revolutionary movement of 1848 'actually sprung from another, known as the Fenian Society'[23] formed in 1858, which is absurd (as Joseph Casey used to say so often that James Joyce adopted and recorded the expression).[24] Two noted historians wrote of Michael Davitt that he 'lost an arm in an accident at work when he was 11. Not unnaturally the fenian revolutionary movement attracted him, and in 1870 he was sentenced to 15 years hard labour for collecting arms'.[25]

Even historians of the calibre of Edward Norman get strangely confused over fenians. He states in *A History of Modern Ireland* that 'Richard O'Sullivan Burke had been sentenced to death for his part in the 1867 rebellion, but, in some measure due to the personal intervention of Cardinal Cullen, he had been reprieved. In December the fenians tried to spring him from Clerkenwell Gaol by dynamiting a hole in the prison wall.'[26] It was Thomas Bourke (1840–89) who was sentenced to be hanged, drawn and quartered and who was reprieved through the intercession of Cardinal Cullen. It might be thought pedantic to point out that the prisoner in Clerkenwell was Ricard O'Sullivan Burke and not Richard. There was a Richard O'Sullivan Burke, brother of Ricard, living in Coachford, Co. Cork, at the time of the explosion and his descendents live there still, though even they are unable to explain what possessed Burke Senior to name one son Richard and the other Ricard.

P. Magnus in *Gladstone* reported[27] a previously unknown fenian bomb outrage in Manchester in 1867 that cost a dozen lives; perhaps this was linked with the savage outrage in Manchester that cost a dozen lives in the imagination of R. J. Minney. Another dozen fictitious deaths appear in *The Trouble with the Irish* by L. Wibberley. He reported 'twelve prisoners killed' at Clerkenwell.[28] H. L. Peacock's standard textbook (4th, corrected edn., London 1980)[29] still claims that the leaders of the 1866 fenian raid on Canada were executed and that the Clerkenwell Explosion took place in 1866; the explosion is said to have drawn 'attention to the desperate social and economic condition of the Irish people'. Robert Kee in his book and television film on Irish history oddly increased the number of dead at Clerkenwell from three to thirty: this was further increased by E. H. Hunt to fifty[30] (and by such progression the figure of one hundred should be reached soon).

One of the most widely accepted sources of fenian 'history' is John Rutherford's *The Secret History of the Fenian Conspiracy* (London, 1877). John O'Leary called it a horrible libel by a villain and Denis Dowling Mulcahy said it had ten lies in any twenty lines. A Unionist paper more kindly described it as a work of fiction. Robert Kee agreed it was 'full of small inaccuracies' but claimed it was not worthless.[31]

Political and religious emotional bias over the years has produced an erroneous history of ever-increasing myth. There can be errors, too, in non-controversial matters where the sources seem impeccable. For the 1967 fenian centenary celebrations the Irish Government produced well-designed stamps showing the stamps reported to have been issued by the fenians. Today the issue of stamps by governments in exile is a well-established practice; revolutionary organisations, including the provisional IRA, have issued stamps and ensured they were delivered through the normal mail. The original fenian stamp issue seemed genuine. The issue was widely reported[32] in 1866 and in Dublin yet another British police file was started.[33] The stamps were sought by collectors and by 1987 the price for a single set had reached £6,100.[34]

Daniel O'Sullivan of the Fenian Brotherhood Secretariat had disclaimed any connection with the issue as early as March 1866, but the stamps have gathered their own history[35] and authenticity[36] with the years and finally the accolade of Irish Government approval with the official issue of 1967. Keen philatelists have shown that the original fenian stamps (or rather proofs) were made in Boston in 1866 by a speculator.[37] The printer, S. Allan Taylor, had no connection with the fenian movement but he had a reputation for forgery.[38] A recent publication notes that the forged fenian stamps have proved so popular with collectors that there were abundant forgeries of the forgeries and even an 1893 reprint.[39]

Surprising inaccuracy is not confined to English historians. An Irish publication, *A Dictionary of Irish Biography* produced by H. Boylan in 1978, is remarkably deficient in information on the fenians. The fenian leader Thomas Kelly is omitted and so is his successor, Ricard O'Sullivan Burke, though half a page is given to William Burke, the Edinburgh murderer. Another half-page is devoted to James Carey, 'fenian and informer', and includes a claim that the British Government executed five fenians in public in 1883. The well-known names of William Allen, Michael Larkin and Michael O'Brien are grouped together in a general entry and dealt with cursorily in a few lines.[40] Even the well-documented book by Fr. William D'Arcy, *The Fenian Movement in the United States: 1858–1886*, nods on James Carey when it states that in 1882 'Carey was spirited aboard a ship bound for Capetown, South Africa. He was never seen again, disappearing when the vessel was a few days at sea'.[41] The shooting of Carey by Patrick O'Donnell was, in fact, followed by a much publicised arrest, trial and execution.

Many writers have tended to rely on the autobiographies of long-lived fenians. These useful primary sources are often marred by memories made even more selective by later dissensions. Personalities and hindsight cloud the accuracy of reports even from men present at the events they describe. Active fenians in the 1860s made a point of not keeping files, letters[42] or records of any sort. They also made a point of changing names and addresses frequently and were often successful in confusing the British police and military. The leading members were highly mobile and travelled to many parts of England and Scotland as well as to France and America.

Who were the fenians?

For this study there is the problem of definition. Not just what was a fenian but who was a fenian.

An active fenian might believe in universal suffrage, in one–man–one–vote, in votes for women, in paid Members of Parliament, in secret ballot, in the abolition of patronage, in competitive examinations for the Civil Service, and other such equalitarian notions thought to be radical and fenian in 1860, though within two generations such dangerous ideas would be accepted in England and proclaimed part of British democracy.

Fenians believed in the right of the Irish people to choose the form of government they preferred. They believed that the British Government denied Ireland this right by the use of force. They felt this justified their aim to obtain political freedom by the use of force against force. The English reaction to this claim was emotional and coercive. The fenians were castigated as criminals at best and murderers at worst.

I use the term 'fenian' to cover any person who took part in the work of the Irish Republican Brotherhood in the period 1858–68. This use agrees with John O'Leary's comment that the word, even when technically incorrect, saves 'one constantly from more or less periphrasis'.[43] Thomas Clarke Luby rightly forecast in 1890 that members of the organisation founded by James Stephens 'will be spoken of as fenians'.[44]

There were many 'cool' fenians, sympathisers who provided funds, accommodation and support for the IRB. They took part in constitutional activities but their participation in illegal activities was dependent on circumstances and their judgement of the particular situation. Often middle class, with family and business commitments, they had much to lose; their judgement could be swayed by dramatic incidents such as the public execution of Irish prisoners in Manchester or the killing of English civilians in Clerkenwell.

The term 'fenian'

The course of Irish history has given a number of new words to the world as well as new meanings to old words. The action against Captain Charles Boycott in Mayo is memorialised by such words as *boycottage* in French, *boykott* in German, *boycotteo* in Spanish, *boicottagio* in Italian and the even more musical *boikotti* in Finnish; perhaps only the official Irish *baghcat* is not immediately recognisable. The origin of the word 'boycott' is clear and well documented. In contrast, when John O'Mahony adopted the word 'fenian' he gave an old word a new life in the English language, though lexicographers have found difficulty in defining the word because of its obscure origin and changing meaning. O'Mahony also gave a new word to the Irish language, *finin*, tersely defined in Dineen's *Irish-English Dictionary* as 'a fenian, in the 1867 sense'.

The creation of the word 'fenian' has often been attributed to James Macpherson (1736–96), that ardent Scottish forger. He was not much of an Irish scholar and went to great trouble to decry anything Irish. He claimed that his epic poem[45] in English was based on ancient poems about Fingal, a great Scottish hero, who always came to the rescue of the mere Irish and was in every way their superior. In 1910 Douglas Hyde declared he had checked Macpherson and found no mention of fenians.[46] In 1979 I spent many hours going through the great collection of Macphersonalia at Aberdeen University and found no mention of a fenian. The staff at Aberdeen University were exceptionally helpful and pointed out 'falans' in the *Fingal* of 1762; they even found 'Fynnanum filium coeli (Fyn Mak Coul vulgari vocabulo) virum . . .' in a *History of Scotland* published by Hector Boethius in Paris in 1526, not to mention *Fhianuis*, a Glasgow magazine issued by Eaglais Saor na hAlba, 1845–50.

Hyde attributed the first use of the word to Charlotte Brooke and quoted from her translation of some Ossianic lines: 'He cursed in rage the fenian chief and all the fenian race'. He added 'who or what the fenians were has given rise to the greatest diversity of opinion'. Charlotte Brooke (*c.* 1740–93) in *Reliques of Irish Poetry* published in 1789 referred to the 'fenni', soldiers organised in groups of nine under one leader, who joined with other groups to make one hundred men under a senior officer. She also used the words 'fenii' and 'finian' and referred to finian tales and finian poems. On page 15 of her book[47] comes the statement 'The Irish in general were frequently called fenians, or phenians, from their great ancestor Phenius Farsa, or perhaps in allusion to their Phoenician descent'. Charlotte spoke some Irish but acknowledged her debt to other writers such as James Cooper Walker (1761–1810),[48] who in 1786 mentioned a 'finian' commander in his *Memoirs of Irish Bards*. Phenium or Fenius Farsa appears in a fabulous genealogical tree in *Chronica Scotorum*, an ancient Irish manuscript of uncertain origin; he is credited with creating the Irish language and founding a great school of languages in Scythia.[49]

The phenius theory was favoured by Charles Vallencey (1721–1812) and probably 'fenian' originated with him. He was certainly using the word in 1781.[50] The *Dictionary of National Biography* notes stuffily that Vallencey may be regarded as 'the founder of a school of writers who theorise on Irish history, language and literature, without having read the original chronicles, acquired the language or studied the literature, thus retarding real study'. Vallencey was the English-born son of a French admiral and is remembered for his enthusiasm for the Irish language and for his maps of Ireland. He became a general in the British Army and spent most of his service career mapping Ireland. He was convinced that 'Irish is a language of utmost importance and most desirable to be acquired'.[51] His remarkably inventive philology linked Irish with Arabic, Hebrew, Finno-Ugrarian, Persian, Kalmuck and other languages. Producing a new word would have presented no problem to him. His *Grammar of the Irish Language* of 1781 has 'phenian' and his friend, Charles O'Conor, used 'fenian' in 1782.[52]

The alternative forms of 'finian' or 'finnian' were popularised by Thomas Moore (1799–1852) in his melody 'The wine cup is circling in Almhin's Hall'. The Irish bulbul noted 'the finians or fenii were the celebrated national militia of

Ireland'.[53] He gave Edward Bunting (1773–1843) as the source[54] of many of his songs. 'Finnian' was used in *The Times* in 1863[55] and 'Fians' in a book title as late as 1891.[56] Strangely enough 'finian/finnian' is not mentioned in the *Oxford English Dictionary* even as an archaism.

The main English reference books and dictionaries provide examples of the querulous tone used by so many English writers when referring to the fenians. The entry in *The Dictionary of English History* is a prime example of the mixture of half-truth and innuendo. Listed under the heading of Fenian Conspiracy is a report that 'secret drillings in connection with this Society took place frequently in 1864, but the Society is supposed to have been formed as early as 1858 . . . on 15 September 1865 the Irish Government of Lord Wodehouse became possessed of information convincing them of the treasonable character of the proceedings . . . O'Donovan Rossa who was one of the conspirators, had his paper, the 'Irish People' confiscated. James Stephens was arrested but was enabled to make his escape . . . 1,000 men who held the market place in Drogheda fled at the approach of a few policemen . . . an attack was made on a police van at Manchester, and on 13 December followed an attempt to blow up Clerkenwell Prison . . . released prisoners were uproariously welcomed in the United States but the organisation of Irish sedition passed into different hands'. The description concludes 'The French Communist General, Cluseret, who had been in the fenian service says, most probably with truth: "their insurrection was foolishly planned, and still more foolishly executed"'. The dictionary also claims that the name fenian is 'derived from Fion or Finn MacCool, the Fingal of Macpherson's Ossian'.[57]

According to the *Oxford English Dictionary*, 'fenian' is formed from the Old Irish 'fene' and so derives from one of the names of the ancient population of Ireland. The dictionary gives the additional information that the word was 'confused in modern times with "fiann", feminine collective, the name of a body of warriors, said to have been the defenders of Ireland in the time of Finn and other legendary Irish kings'. The word is said to be obsolete except historically; obviously the editor was never in Belfast.[58] According to the OED the earliest reported use is from 1816 and the chosen illustrative quotation reads: 'Do you compare your psalms to the tales of the bare-armed fenians?'.[59] The next quotation is dated 1861 and refers to Goll MacMorna 'the great chief of the Connacht fenians'. The third citation in the section is from the 1879 edition of the *Encyclopaedia Britannica* and adds 'according to popular tradition the fians or fenians were mercenary tribes acting as a permanent military force for the support of the Ard Rig, or King of Ireland'. The dictionary seems on safer ground with the secondary definition that a fenian was a member of 'an organisation or "brotherhood" formed among the Irish in the United States of America for promoting or assisting revolutionary movements, and for the overthrow of the English Government in Ireland'. The inverted commas round the word brotherhood, the vagueness of the first aim and the imprecision of the second add to the reader's uncertainty.

The OED's first quoted use for this secondary definition of 'fenian' is from the *Leeds Mercury* of 11 March 1864, though many earlier examples are available. In 1861 for example, the *Universal News* of London included several references to fenians and their activities.[60] Possibly the OED Editor wanted to use the later quotation that 'Irish revolutionaries under the general name of fenians are regarded with no friendly eye by the Roman Catholic clergy in Ireland and America'. The dictionary's second example is from the *Saturday Review* of 4 March 1865, a short reference to 'Irish rebels of late called fenians'.

A clear definition is not to be found in the section dealing with the use of the word as an adjective. The fenian poems are mentioned as being attributable mainly to Oisin, apparently a different fellow from the Ossian mentioned a few lines above. Under 'Fenianism' the quotation used is from the *Spectator* of 1 December 1866 and includes the claim that 'the revival of fenianism is as formidable as its outbreak'; this predates the fenian rising by some months.

The *Oxford Dictionary of English Etymology* states that a fenian was a member of a 'mercenary tribe forming a military force for the support of the king of Eire'. It gives the same 1816 reference as the OED and the same warning that the word was 'confused in modern times with fiann', those warriors 'Said to have been the defenders of Ireland in the times of the legendary Irish kings'. The *Oxford Companion to the Camden History of English Literature* ignores the warnings of confusion and states firmly that fenian is derived from the Old Irish fene (Irishman) and fiann 'member of a legendary body of heroes, the bodyguard of the king'. It adds that the word was a 'common name of an Irish republican movement that found expression in the Fenian Brotherhood organised in Dublin in 1858 and among Irish immigrants in New York in 1859'.

The modern usage of the term originated in the mid-nineteenth century to describe Irishmen who supported the use of force to gain independence for Ireland. The organisation founded for that purpose by James Stephens in Ireland and England was the Irish Revolutionary Brotherhood, later renamed the Irish Republican Brotherhood. However, when the American arm of the organisation was formed in 1858 it took the name 'Fenian Brotherhood'. Within a few years the term fenian had become commonplace on both sides of the Atlantic.

The name was used with pride by most IRB members in the 1860s. However, after the failure of the 1865 Rising and of the Fenian Raids on Canada its use declined in popularity amongst the Brotherhood. A sometime member of the London IRB, John Boyle O'Reilly, was not alone in his thoughts when he wrote to John Devoy in 1871 that many Irishmen had grown sick of fenianism and asked 'Did I tell you how I hate the damned word?'[61]

In part, that revulsion may have reflected the adoption of the term by the movement's enemies. It was much used by British administrators of the time in expressions such as 'fenian conspiracy', 'fenian fire', and 'fenian prisoners'. The British press in particular and opponents of Irish independence in general used the word 'fenian' as a convenient catch-all term for many forms of Irish nationalism. By the 1880s it was being used in England to describe not only active members of the IRB, or of the linked but legal organisation, the Friendly Brotherhood of St Patrick, but any supporter of Irish independence and so, by analogy, those who showed the slightest sympathy with Irish nationalism.[62] Even rival revolutionary groups in violent opposition to the IRB were termed 'fenians' by the British press.

From the 1860s to the present day the word has been used in a derogatory sense by Ulster Unionists, and in rough speech it is usually qualified by a descriptive alliterative adjective. In English slang after 1867 a fenian meant a threepenny glass of Irish Whiskey and cold water. This and the allied expression 'three cold fenians' were linked with the execution of three fenians in Manchester.[63] The slang usage has not survived: perhaps whiskey drinkers declined to water the product to make a political point. The term 'fenian barracks' was used to describe any large block of apartment houses inhabited by Irish emigrants; the term does not appear to have survived outside Northern Ireland.

Slowly at first but more obviously after 1922 the word has again been used with pride. It is noticeable that many writers today claim that their ancestors were fenians. Some of the ancestors might have regarded the claims with mild surprise. Cecil King has stated that his grandfather was a fenian[64] even though he worked as a British colonial administrator in India. John Pope Hennessy has been claimed as a fenian though he was Governor of British Mauritius and in his day was regarded as a very moderate nationalist. Lord George Brown of the British Labour Party has noted that his grandfather was a fenian[65] and so have Denis Healey and Jim Callaghan.[66] Conversely, Brendan Bracken, Conservative Minister and confidant of Winston Churchill, concealed his fenian links for many years; he was the son of John K. Bracken, a leading IRB man from County Tipperary.

Signs of the increasing popularity of the word came when it was used in songs at public concerts. 'The Rising of the Moon' by fenian John Keegan Casey (1846–70) has been popular for over a century. In the 1860s, singing the song in public could lead to an entry in the British police dossiers[67] about yet another suspected fenian. The ballad inspired Lady Gregory's play of the same title (1906) and in 1957 it provided the theme music and title for a popular John Ford film. A glance at a list of record and cassette titles today shows that 'My Old Fenian Gun', while not top of the pops, does not stand alone. The 'Bold Fenian Men' remains an evergreen favourite. It was played by Irish troops in the United Nations service when they took over part of Cyprus and the significance of the song was not lost on the evacuating British regiment.

In the 1970s the word gained a new currency. It achieved some prominence in Spain when the Glasgow Rangers played a memorable match in Barcelona. In the evening, Glasgow fans, possibly with a little drink taken, used the expression 'fenian bastards' to the Spanish police who reacted in a manner that gave much satisfaction in the Falls Road area of Belfast. Despite the 1934 dictum of the *Oxford English Dictionary*, the word was not obsolete to the Shetland poet William Tait. He wrote in 1975 of 'knocking it back abuin the cloods, an aa yon fenian wogs tae bash yet . . . Jings!'[68] In 1978 the *Guardian* described Irish–American demonstrators in San Francisco as 'fenians'.[69] In true 'Grauniad' style the fenians were reported to have had a 'two–hour warm–up at an Irish pub' and to be allied with the local Nicaraguan community. These latter–day fenians were demonstrating against a British naval visit to San Francisco and were calling attention to the ill–treatment of prisoners in Northern Ireland.

In book titles the word has been increasingly used for identification of period and theme. *Fenian Chief, Fenian Fever, Fenianism in Canada, Fenianism in North*

America, The Fenians in Canada have appeared in recent years and show the revival of interest after a blank period between the two World Wars.

The headline 'Fenian Fairies' in *Hibernia* of 26 April 1979 did not describe an article on homosexuality in the IRB but a favourable review of the poetry of James Stephens (1880–1950), namesake of the fenian leader. Confusion of the names has led more than one researcher astray and caused annoyance to the two men during their lifetimes. The *Hibernia* article deals with ten stories in *Irish Fairy Tales*. It notes that in the first and last story appears St Finnian, Abbot of Moville in Donegal, and claims that all the stories are from the fenian sagas.

Sources

I have said that it took the centenary year of 1967 to bring new interest to the study of the fenians in Ireland.

The study of fenianism in England has much of the frustration and enjoyment experienced by students of Irish genealogy. Marcus Bourke has suggested that comparative success in fenian studies requires the patience of a Job, the cunning of a Machiavelli and the inscrutability of a Sphinx. British officials at the Public Record Office in London are still sensitive about Irish records and I have suffered the frustration of being refused certain files even though they were over a century old. The Special Branch and Secret Service files are not available and may never be available. Many of the records have been destroyed or are not available to the researcher; on the other hand, much information may be gained from sources other than archives and files.

Although the claims of oral historians are regarded with some suspicion by academic historians, there is still much to be gained from long-lived children of long-lived fenians. There is a pleasurable shock when a pensioner says 'You are speaking of my father and he told me . . .' The evidence may be helpful despite the inaccuracies of age and selective memory. My own father told me as a child that members of his family were fenians in the 1860s and smuggled guns for the organisation. I believed the story until, with teenage disbelief, I dismissed it as a family fable unbacked by documentary evidence and unknown to historians; at least unknown until 1967 when Breandan Mac Giolla Choille wrote 'Mourning the Martyrs', and there in his article were David and Edward and Thomas Quinlivan identified as fenians and reported to be under surveillance by the British police in Limerick. They were thus identified and documented from a hostile police source.[70]

Although, like other workers on fenian history, I have used hostile sources such as the police records, I have found it is now possible to supplement these to a certain extent and so gain a more balanced picture. Autobiographies and biographies fill in some of the gaps. No English fenian archives exist but material is available from widely separated sources. A Canadian writer[71] has declared that the fenian material is infinite; it is certainly widely distributed and diffused. Information from contemporary newspapers and registers, from miscellaneous collections in county record offices, from the oral traditions of certain families and from genealogical studies have helped to trace the world-wide story of the fenians between 1858 and 1868.

The largest available collection of documents relating to fenians is in the State Paper Office in Dublin.[72] The collection is in two parts. One part contains the correspondence of the Chief Secretary for Ireland and consists of nearly 4,000 cartons.

The constabulary section alone has fifteen sub-headings for 1867 and has many letters dealing with IRB members in England. Some files have only one tantalising letter while others are inches thick. For 1867 the number of individual registered files is over 22,000. References to individual fenians can be found but tracing them through the registers and indexes is a slow job made bearable by the extreme helpfulness of the staff. Some of the files were captured by the IRA in 1921, some were left by the British in the evacuation of 1922 and some were returned by the British Government in the 1930s. They have been pruned, sifted, mixed up and reformed. They are a rummager's delight and an archivist's nightmare.

The British police surveillance of the population was extensive, yet for over five years the British authorities did not know of the extent of the IRB in Ireland, much less in England. The police were aware of unrest and of small, local societies such as the Phoenix Society in Skibbereen but, judging from the files, they were unaware of the organisational strength of the movement founded by James Stephens, and of the close links with America, Britain and France. For this reason police references to IRB members or activities cannot be found under the title of 'fenianism' until the end of 1864. However, references to individuals can be found in the police reports to Dublin Castle which form part of the general surveillance of the population; for example, when James Stephens toured England and Ireland in 1856 the Kilkenny police reported to Dublin: 'It is expected he will return to this city as he has left his clothes at his brother-in-laws'.[73]

The second part of the collection owes its origin to Samuel and Robert Anderson. After the Clerkenwell Explosion of 1867, Robert Anderson was sent to Dublin to co-ordinate military, police and political action against the fenians.[74] A separate secret service department was set up to control this work and to provide information to the British Cabinet. The Dublin files made by the Andersons contain papers dating from 1857 to 1883 but the bulk of the material is from the 1866–74 period. The collection was taken to England and about 40 per cent was destroyed including the contemporary registers and indexes. Using these files is fascinating and frustrating. The work of Breandan Mac Giolla Choille in 'Mourning the Martyrs' and Léon Ó Broin in *Fenian Fever* shows what can be done with the material available. The sifting and indexing of the papers will take many years and there is abundant material for research.

One file, for example, contains some letters from C. C. Hoey to J. P. MacDonnel in Dublin. He mentions his travels through England and Scotland adding 'I have left no town without getting them to learn the soldier's trade. Our brothers understand us to mean something'. He refers to his meetings with James Maguire in Aberdeen 'the most influential Irishman in the town, a native of Fermanagh[75] . . . I have got hold of the trades here and will lecture to them next Friday night'. He had arranged for the *Glasgow Free Press*, a pro-fenian paper, to be sold by agents in London. He was guarded in his comments 'one has to be cautious in this country . . . there are matters I would like to tell you about but cannot mention until we meet'. He mentions 'a little opposition from interested parties' and adds 'betimes I feel lonely when I think of home'. His letters are next to a note to MacDonnel from Maria Shaw about a certain young lady: 'I told her how anxious you were to get an introduction and she seems just as anxious . . . ' This is a delightful human touch but it adds nothing to the Hoey information. Many of the letters have the injuncion 'burn this' and their survival must be due to human caprice, errors of judgement or unexpected arrest. These papers are invaluable but it must be remembered that they represent only a part of the Anderson collection, a collection that owes its origin to the Clerkenwell Explosion of 1867.

The State Paper Office files in Dublin are supplemented by the Home Office papers in the Public Record Office in London. There are copies of Dublin reports in the London collection and vice versa. Some of the gaps can be filled by using both collections. The police files in the PROL and in the County Record Offices are helpful but it is obvious that certain Irish files are not available to the researcher even now.

A most useful source for the student of fenianism is *Devoy's Postbag*, two volumes edited by William O'Brien and Desmond Ryan and issued in 1948. During his long life John Devoy (1842–1928) preserved nearly every letter sent to him; the two volumes contain nearly half a million words and illustrate the history of the Irish revolutionary movement between the 1860s and the 1920s.

A number of university theses have challenged the accepted mixture of stereotypes and misinformation from the nineteenth century. Work such as R. J. Cooter's *The Irish in County Durham and Newcastle 1840–1880* supplements and extends the revision of fenian history made by researchers like W. J. Lowe (*The Irish in Lancashire, 1846–71*), R. V. Comerford (*Irish Nationalist Politics, 1858–70*), A. J. Semple (*The Fenian Infiltration of the British Army in Ireland, 1864–71*), and J. Moloney (*The National Brotherhood of Saint Patrick*). The growing number of volumes of *Dictionary of Labour Biography* is helping to make easier · the task of tracing individual fenians in the radical movements of the nineteenth century.

Two other sources are the Cranbrook Collection in the East Suffolk Records Office and the Howell Collection in the Bishopsgate Institute in London. The Cranbrook Collection contains the diaries of Gathorne Hardy (1814–1906) from 1863 to 1870 and letters on the subject of fenianism from Queen Victoria, the Duke of Buckingham, the Duke of Cambridge, Lord Cairns, Lord Mayo, Lord Derby, Benjamin Disraeli and General Gray. Gathorne Hardy was a member of the British Government from 1866–8 and was Home Secretary at the time of the executions of William Allen, Michael Barrett, Michael Larkin and Michael O'Brien. The *Dictionary of National Biography* notes 'he faced the fenian conspiracy with courage. He refused to commute the capital sentence passed on the fenian murderers at Manchester, although a disorderly mob forced its way into the Home Office. His life was repeatedly threatened and warnings which he had received compelled him to impose special restrictions on Queen Victoria's movements. The intimate relations which he established with Queen Victoria at this critical period were maintained throughout her reign.'[76]

The Howell Collection contains the papers of George Howell (1833–1910) who took part in almost every phase of working–class activity from the decline of Chartism to the rise of the Labour Party. His correspondence and the records of the Reform League for the 1860s contain many references to fenianism in London and elsewhere.

The National Library of Ireland has an extensive collection of fenian material. It includes the Larcom papers, the Luby papers, the Samuel Lee Anderson papers, the Devoy papers, the Earl of Mayo papers and some correspondence of Alexander Sullivan. The Larcom collection is most useful for providing information on fenians in London; the collection of newspaper cuttings and photographs is extensive.

Fenians are mentioned in many memoirs of the 1860s but these recollections prove of small use. Benjamin Disraeli and Charles Bradlaugh are among the important figures who kept a strict control when writing about fenianism; they and others hinted they had amazing tales to tell when it would be politic to do so. By 1922 they were dead and the stories were never told. Other memoirs are so full of omissions and errors that they are valueless but in the course of time their errors have become accepted and embellished. Some errors of fact are over a century old and the modern historian is hard pressed to sort fact from fiction. Phantom fenianism is well fixed in the national mythologies of England and Ireland.

The Bow Street Police Museum appears to have nothing connected with fenianism and even Scotland Yard was unable to produce any photographs or items connected with the London fenians of the 1860s. However, I can record that a helpful police officer at Scotland Yard went to the Special Branch for me and came back with a bundle of original documents containing statements made in 1868 by James Mullany.

Another useful source of material is slowly becoming available through the publication in Cork of the John O'Mahony collection now in the Catholic University of America, Washington, DC. The collection consists of the account books and official papers of the Fenian Brotherhood, plus thousands of letters from the 1858–76 period. The entire collection was microfilmed and 4,600 negatives were presented to Cork County Council. About two-fifths have been calendared.[77]

The growing interest in Victorian studies and in local history in England has produced much information on the role of the fenian in English life.[78] The information is usually published in specialist periodicals and thus is not always readily available, even in universities. *Northern History* provides useful source references to fenians in Northern England. W. J. Lowe in the *Transactions of the Historical Society of Lancashire and Cheshire* has drawn attention to the many files on fenians in the Liverpool and Lancaster Records Offices.[79] Detailed information on *The Irish Liberator*, the London fenian newspaper, appeared in the *Clogher Record*, Fermanagh.[80]

The British Government had compelling reasons for not allowing everything to be published about their counter-fenian activities. Spies like Thomas Beach and F. F. Millen had to be left as sleepers in Irish revolutionary movements. In the event of a war between Britain and America (or France or Russia) they would have been men of tremendous importance to British military leaders. As late as 1878 Millen was in touch with Russian officials[81] and no doubt the British authorities were well informed of his part in the great game of world politics.

Desmond Ryan in his work on James Stephens and the Devoy correspondence seems to have been unaware of Millen's role as spy for Britain; so was Professor S. Pender in his centenary lecture[82] on fenianism and so were other speakers at the time of the centenary commemorations. Léon Ó Broin appears to be the first to note the significance of Millen's visits to the British Consul in Philadelphia.[83]

The need for secrecy by active members and discretion by former members in the period 1858–1922 meant that the study of fenianism was held back for decades by political considerations. The few autobiographies that were written were mainly by members whose first qualification was longevity; old men forget, and have selective memories. While working on the fenians I have met a number of professional writers who had given up work on the story of the IRB in England because of the difficulty of finding reliable information on individual members. Some members of the IRB in England were active for only a year or two before they left for America, often for a life unconnected with politics or secret organisations. A number of members have qualified for the title of the unknown fenian.

For example, very little is known of Michael Barrett (*c.* 1840–68) of Drumnagreshial, although his name appears in many history books as that of the last man to be publicly executed in England. His links with Fermanagh were unknown in the 1960s to writers like Cahir Healy of Enniskillen and James Hurley of Cork who were authorities on fenian history. Barrett's name appears on the National Monument in Cork and for many years a memorial service was arranged by Corkonians under the impression that he was a Corkman.

I was able to trace his family background through the *Irishman*, local newspapers, files in the Belfast PRO, files in the Dublin SPO, files in the London PRO, through the oral tradition in Drumnagreshial, Co. Fermanagh, and through correspondence with members of the Barrett family in America, Ireland and New Zealand. Yet the final picture of the man is far from complete. Perhaps in a record office or private home original papers are still awaiting the researcher; the British Home Secretary could examine Michael Barrett's notebook in 1868 but it is not available today.[84] By contrast, the life story of a fellow Ulsterman and fellow member of the IRB, John Denvir (1834–1915), is well known from his many publications and articles. He was born in Bushmills, County Antrim, but spent nearly all his life in England. He was an active member of the IRB and other Irish organisations. His autobiography shows his close links with many leading men of his day, but he is reticent when dealing with IRB membership and activities.[85] He lived a long life but it was not long enough for him to be able to write freely and fully about the fenians in England. John Denvir was certainly a fenian but the membership of Aylmer, Boucicault, Campbell and Le Fanu is less certain.

The Irish Republican Brotherhood was a secret society and did not keep a considerable body of documents for the historian to rummage through. Most of the documentary evidence about the organisation is from British police and judicial records and such evidence is patchy and occasional. A long and laborious process of accumulation and piecing together of scraps of evidence from scattered sources is necessary before the story of the fenians in Britain can emerge. As I have said, Henry Boylan's *Dictionary of Irish Biography* is notably reticent about membership of the Fenian Brotherhood or the Irish Republican Brotherhood. The researcher longs for a *Who Was Who of the IRB* as new names and details appear. Certain identification of James Murphy/George Jackson was not easy for the British Police in the 1860s and is not easy for the researcher today. Genealogists have difficulties in tracing a particular James Murphy or George Jackson even when the person concerned was not trying to keep his identity and movements secret; one of the leading London IRB members in 1867 was James Murphy and a popular pseudonym at the time, used by Michael Barrett and others, was George Jackson.

Some references are tantalisingly vague. A police report casually mentions that 'O'Connor the artist' was present at a fenian meeting in London in 1867. O'Connor was a popular patronymic and pseudonym in the fenian ranks. Luby mentions a Bernard O'Connor, artist, as attending meetings in Dublin in 1864. Four artists named O'Connor are listed[86] as exhibiting work at the Royal Society of British Artists in the 1860s and at least another two are noted[87] in general directories of Victorian London artists. The identity of O'Connor, artist and fenian, remains unproven. Fifty years ago an historian could still interview surviving members of the early IRB; today the positive statements of the police, exaggerating spies and self-important mercenaries are naturally suspect when they cannot be tested against other sources.

The fenians and the police agreed on two things; the organisation was important and it was secret. The fenian oath of secrecy prevented many members from ever speaking or writing about the organisation, though few would go so far as H. G. Castle who claimed 'the oath of secrecy taken by members of the Brotherhood was as binding as that taken by the Mau Mau. To break it meant certain death. No one did break it.'[88]

James Stephens was insistent on strict secrecy about the Republican Brotherhood even when members had left England or Ireland. When asked if he regarded the oath as being absolved on emigration to America he replied 'I believe the oath to be binding on the soul of the man who takes it until he dies or Ireland is free'.[89] The long wait for freedom thinned the ranks of fenian writers[90] and gave undue prominence to those who broke the oath or who lived to be octogenarians.

Conclusion

Historians today have a duty to separate myth from truth, prejudice from pertinence, fiction from fact. The revision of Irish history will lead to a revision of English history. Researchers working on the world-wide Fenian Movement have to deal with a mass of misleading evidence as well as coping with missing evidence. It will be no easy task to persuade academic historians, much less the general public, that their view of the fenians needs revising. It will be even less easy to persuade popular history writers, who generalise from false premises, based on false evidence, yet who help to shape attitudes and guide judgements on present–day Anglo-Irish problems. Many English historians have unwritten the fenians and established a convenient myth they defend and embellish almost as a patriotic duty. They write nostalgically of the great days of Empire. They write in neutral prose of revolutionary movements in former colonies but on the subject of fenianism they are silent when they are not abusive or facetious.

Earlier interpretations of the fenians are inadequate or false because they are based on inadequate or false information. A new view is needed. The fenians of 1867 may not have been successful but they altered the course of history in more than one country.[91] The ghosts of those notable adversaries, Benjamin Disraeli and James Stephens, in surveying Ireland today would surely agree that the aims of the fenians have been largely achieved while the aims of the nineteenth-century British Government are filed with those of Nineveh.

James Stephens would have enjoyed the irony of the existence of the Republic being internationally and officially confirmed in Canada first; he would have been flattered by the fulsome praise of the President of the United States, John F. Kennedy, who placed a wreath on the fenian memorial in Dublin and quoted fenian poets with much aplomb. Stephens would have enjoyed the sight of an Irish army group taking over British barracks in Cyprus and playing 'Out and Make Way for the Bold Fenian Men' as they marched in.

Fenians present at the public execution in London of Michael Barrett in 1868 could hardly have foreseen that less than a century later there would be an enthusiastic public ceremony in London's Trafalgar Square honouring the Fenian Rising of 1867. The fenian centenary was marked by celebrations and ceremonies all over the world. Only in Northern Ireland were such events banned and the ground prepared for the Civil Rights Movement. Perhaps Stephens and the fenians of 1867 would have wept to know that bombs would still be exploding in the streets of Belfast and London 125 years later and that men and women would be dying in Ireland for the republic they had deemed 'now virtually established'.

The tangible link of the fenians of old with events today is part of the vague picture of the Fenian Movement as seen through a very dark glass. Some events have been highlighted but the connecting facts and linking characters remain shaded and obscure. Research will deepen our understanding of the conditions that shaped the formation of the Fenian Movement and set it in its social and economic framework. Researchers will trace the ancestry of the Movement in Chartism, nationalism, republicanism and socialism; they will analyse its apparent defeat by imperialism and espionage, and then its phoenix rebirth and partial success.

Notes

1. A. W. Ward and A. R. Waller (eds), *Cambridge history of English literature*, Vol. 14, Cambridge University Press, Cambridge, 1916, p. 321.
2. Alfred Caiger, MC, was popular with staff and pupils. He was best known to the wider community for his conducting of the communal singing at the Wembley cup finals.
3. The origins of the plaque have not been discovered, despite extensive investigation and much help from London and Middlesex county officials.
4. Lord Eversley, *Gladstone and Ireland: the Irish policy of Parliament from 1850–1894*, Methuen, London, 1912, p. 17: 'These two violent acts [Manchester and Clerkenwell] for a time greatly exasperated public opinion in England against the Irish.

They had, however, the effect of bringing home to the English people the depth of discontent among Irishmen, and the necessity for probing its causes, and finding some remedy which should alleviate it. The best evidence is to be found in a passage of a speech delivered by Mr. Gladstone two years later, when speaking in the course of the debate on the Disestablishment of the Irish Church . . .'

5. E. D. Steele, 'The Irish presence in the North of England', *Northern History*, Volume XII, 1976, p. 229.

6. J. McCarthy, *History of our own times*, Volume 4, Caxton, London, 1896, p. 147.

7. The dynamite fable is still current. Grenfell Morton in *Home Rule and the Irish question*, Longmans, London, 1979, p. 13, refers to the 'callous brutality of the dynamite explosion at Clerkenwell Prison'.

8. Michael Harrison, *London by gaslight*, Davies, London, 1963.

9. *Essex County Standard*, 9 Feb. 1889.

10. Desmond Ryan, *The Fenian chief: a biography of James Stephens*, Gill, Dublin, 1967, p. 369.

11. *Oxford English dictionary*, Oxford University Press, Oxford, 1934.

12. Annie Munro Newth, *Britain and the world, 1789–1901*, Penguin, Harmondsworth, 1968, p. 30.

13. R. J. Minney, *No. 10 Downing Street*, Cassell, London, 1963, p. 272.

14. Hector Bolitho, *Victoria the widow*, Cobden & Sanderson, London, 1934, p. 70.

15. Reginald Howe, *The story of Scotland Yard*, Barker, London, 1965, p. 43.

16. A. G. Gardiner, *The life of Sir William Harcourt*, Constable, London, 1923, Vol. 1, p. 181.

17. Yvonne Kapp, *Eleanor Marx: Volume 1, family life*, Lawrence & Wishart, London, 1972, p. 85.

18. Philip Michael Hett Bell, *Disestablishment in Ireland and Wales*, SPCK for the Church Historical Society, London, 1969.

19. G. Howard, *Guardians of the Queen's peace*, Odhams, London, 1953, p. 217.

20. Thomas Burke, *The streets of London through the centuries*, Batsford, London, 1949, p. 126.

21. L. Apjohn, *The Earl of Beaconsfield*, Tyne Publishing, London, 1881, p. 210.

22. *Western Star*, 21 Dec. 1867.

23. Ronald Seth, *The Specials*, Gollancz, London, 1961.

24. James Joyce met Casey, the 'old rebel', in Paris. Joyce recorded and clearly relished the phrase, 'which is absurd': see Stuart Gilbert (ed.), *Letters of James Joyce*, Faber, London, 1957, p. 394.

25. J. L. Hammond and M. R. D. Foot, *Gladstone and Liberalism*, English Universities Press, London, 1952, p. 141. See also *The Times Educational Supplement*, 27 June 1980, p. 1.

26. Edward R. Norman, *A history of modern Ireland*, Allen Lane, London, 1971, p. 168.

27. Philip Magnus, *Gladstone: a biography*, Murray, London, 1954, p. 196.

28. Leonard Patrick O'Connor Wibberley, *The trouble with the Irish (or the English, depending on your point of view)*, Holt, New York, 1956, p. 178.

29. Herbert Leonard Peacock, *A history of modern Britain, 1815–1979*, Heinemann, London, 1980, p. 12.

30. E. H. Hunt, *British Labour history, 1815–1914*, Weidenfeld & Nicolson, London, 1981, p. 170.

31. John Rutherford, *The secret history of the Fenian conspiracy*, Keegan Paul, London, 1877. John O'Leary, *Recollections of Fenians and Fenianism*, Downey, London, 1896 [reprinted with an Introduction by Marcus Bourke, Irish University Press, Shannon, 1969], p. 67. Ryan, *The Fenian chief*, pp. 295–8. See *Irish Book Lover*, June 1910, for the background of John Rutherford and his small inaccuracies. Robert

Kee, *The green flag*, Weidenfeld & Nicolson, London, 1972, p. 783. The reference to the now more generally available 3-volume version is Robert Kee, *The green flag: Volume 2, The bold Fenian men*, Quartet, London, 1976, p. 278.

32. *The Stamp Collector's Magazine*, London, 1866, No. 4, p. 24; *The Collector's Guide*, Newport, R. I., 15 June 1866.

33. SPO Dublin, File F3308/66.

34. D. MacDonnell and I. Whyte, *Stamps of Ireland*, MacDonnell Whyte, Dublin, 1987.

35. A. P. Cohen, 'The Fenian Movement in the US — its philatelic and numismatic aspect', *The Essay Proof Journal*, New York, 1963, Vol. XX, pp. 147–56. Highly erroneous on fenian and on philatelic matters.

36. *Irish Independent*, 5 Jan. 1905, claims the stamps were approved by James Stephens.

37. J. E. Foley, *The Taylor-made Fenian essays*, Eire Philatelic Association, New York, 1971. See also *Fenian Rising centenary*, Department of Posts and Telegraphs, Dublin, 1967, p. 2.

38. F. J. Melville, 'The lives of the forgers' in *An anthology of papers read at the Philatelic Congress*, Blandford, London, 1953, p. 151.

39. M. Don. Buchalter, *Hibernian specialised catalogue of the postage stamps of Ireland*, Hibernian Stamp Co., Dublin, 1972, p. 148.

40. Henry Boylan, *A dictionary of Irish biography*, Gill & Macmillan, Dublin, 1978, pp. 45, 50, 218.

41. William D. D'Arcy, *The Fenian movement in the United States, 1858–86*, Catholic University of America Press, Washington, 1947, p. 405.

42. Luby MSS 331 in NLI: 'As much as practicable we tabooed letters'. Joseph Denieffe, *A personal narrative of the Irish Revolutionary Brotherhood*, Gael Publishing, New York, 1906, p. 109: he 'never kept anything on paper that could compromise' him. [Denieffe's *Narrative* has twice been reissued: Irish University Press, Shannon, 1968; Irish Academic Press, Dublin, 1978.]

43. O'Leary, *Recollections*, p. 92.

44. Luby MSS 331.

45. James MacPherson, *Fingal: an ancient epic poem*, Becket & de Hondt, London, 1762, and *The works of Ossian, the son of Fingal*, Becket & de Hondt, London, 1765.

46. Douglas Hyde, *A literary history of Ireland from the earliest times to the present day*, Unwin, London, 1899, p. 364.

47. For Charlotte Brooke see *Reliques of Irish poetry (1789) by Charlotte Brooke and a memoir of Miss Brooke (1816) by Aaron Crossley Hobart Seymour*, fascimile reproduction with an introduction by Leonard R. N. Astley, Scholars' Fascimiles and Reprints, Gainsville, 1970. This includes a fascimile of the original *Reliques of Irish poetry . . .* by Miss Brooke, George Banham, Dublin, 1789. Charlotte Brooke's book is noteworthy for being the first purely literary work containing printing in the Irish character to be published in Dublin. See E. W. Lynam, *The Irish character in print, 1571–1923*, Oxford University Press, Oxford, 1924, pp 19–21.

48. R. A. Breatnach, 'Two eighteenth-century Irish scholars', *Studia Hibernica*, Dublin, 1965, No. 5, p. 88.

49. The Phoenix Reading Circle of Skibbereen (1856–8) helped to confuse nomenclature for British politicians. Archibald William Montgomerie, 13th Earl of Eglinton and sometime Lord Lieutenant of Ireland, always referred to the early IRB members as 'Phoenicians': he was not alone in his confusion. See L. Ó Broin, 'The Phoenix Conspiracy', *Irish Sword*, Dublin, 1980, No. 55, p. 160. Mabel Gregory Ward, *The Fenian Movement* Ralph Myles, Colorado Springs, 1969, p. 9, deals briefly with confusion in the United States about the arrest of the Phoenix Reading Circle and mentions a short-lived newspaper called *The Phoenix*. Charles Townshend, *Political violence in Ireland: government and resistance since 1848*, Clarendon Press, Oxford,

1983, p. 25, seems to opt for 'Phoenixism' as a possible origin of 'fenianism'. The arrival of Sinn Fein brought even more confusion: you occasionally come across the abortive expression 'Sinn Finnian'.

50. Charles Vallencey, *Grammar of the Irish language*, Dublin, 1781.

51. Charles Vallencey, *Collectanae de rebus hibernicis*, Dublin, 1786, Volume 2, p. 251.

52. Vallencey, *Collectanae*, Vol. 4, p. 240. The term was well establishd when used by John Dunne: see 'The Fenian traditions of Slievenamon', *Transactions of the Kilkenny Archaeological Society*, 1851, pp 333–62.

53. Thomas Moore, *Poetical works*, Longmans, London, 1841, Vol. 4, p. 101. But you will find 'The wine cup is circling', in any full edition of the *Irish Melodies*.

54. Edward Bunting, *General collection of ancient Irish music* Volume 1, Preston & Son, London, 1796; Volume 2, Hime, Dublin, *c*.1798.

55. *The Times*, 23 October 1863.

56. J. G. Campbell, *The Fians*, D. Nutt, London, 1891.

57. S. J. Low, *Dictionary of English history*, Cassell, London, 1928. There are eight editions from 1884 to 1928, all misleading on fenian matters. On that last point see also 'Fionu and the Fenians', *The Times*, 11 October 1865.

58. *Oxford English Dictionary*, Clarendon Press, Oxford, 1961, Vol. 4, p. 157.

59. The 1816 reference is to Walter Scott, *The Antiquary*, Archibald Constable & Co., Edinburgh, 1816, and the quotation is described as 'A pretended translation from Ossian'. Though the word 'fenian' can be found in several eighteenth-century publications pre-dating the Walter Scott reference this 1816 date seems to have stuck and is repeated in many etymological dictionaries, e.g. E. Weekley, *An etymological dictionary of modern English*, Murray, London. 1921; C. T. Onions, *Oxford dictionary of English etymology*, Clarendon Press, Oxford, 1966; T. Finkenstedt, E. Leisi, D. Wolff *et al.*, *Chronological English dictionary*, Winter, Heidelberg, 1970.

60. *Universal News*, 2 February 1861.

61. William O'Brien and Desmond Ryan (eds), *Devoy's post-bag, 1871–1928*, 2 volumes, Fallon, Dublin, 1948, 1953, Vol. 1, p. 31.

62. *Everyman's encylopaedia*, Dent, London, 1978, Vol. 5, p. 83. This edition notes that 'fenian is still used in Northern Ireland as a term of abuse for an Irishman of republican tendencies'. Unfortunately the rest of the definition is a rehash of old innuendo.

63. Eric Partridge, *A dictionary of slang and unconventional English*, Routledge & Kegan Paul, London, 5th edition, 1961, Vol. 1, p. 271.

64. Cecil Harmondsworth King, *On Ireland*, Cape, London, 1973, p. 10.

65. *The Sunday Times*, 13 July 1980, p. 33.

66. Local historians have noted that Irish patriots seem popular ancestors. See D. J. Steel and L. Taylor, *Family history in schools*, Phillimore, London, 1973, p. 14; B. Murphy, 'History in the family', *Teaching History*, London, Vol. 2, No. 5, 1971.

67. *Nation*, 23 Feb. 1867.

68. W. Tait, 'Glesca Haiku' in *Scottish Poetry 8*, Edinburgh, 1975, p. 77.

69. *Guardian*, 29 Sept. 1978.

70. Breandan Mac Giolla Choille, 'Mourning the martyrs', *The North Munster Antiquarian Journal*, Volume 10, No. 2, 1967.

71. Hereward Senior, *The Fenians and Canada*, Macmillan of Canada, Toronto, 1978, p. 171.

72. See B. Mac Giolla Choille, 'Fenian documents in the State Paper Office', *Irish Historical Studies*, Vol. XVI, No. 63, March 1969, pp. 258–84.

73. SPO, file CSO Rp 1856/12589.

74. R. Anderson, *Sidelights on the Home Rule movement*, Murray, London, 1906.

75. SPO, file 373R. *The Aberdeen directory* for 1864 lists James Maguire as a tailor and cloth merchant. He lived at 51 Queen Street and had shops in Queen Street and Lodge Walk. His name appears in the directories from 1843 until 1880. He lived only nine doors from James Duthie, Superintendent of Police in Aberdeen.
76. *Dictionary of national biography*, 2nd. Supplement, Vol. 2, p. 189.
77. S. Pender, 'Fenian papers in the Catholic University of America', *Journal of the Cork Historical and Archaelogical Society*, 1969–78.
78. See, for example, Norman McCord (ed.), *Essays in Tyneside Labour history*, Department of Humanities, Newcastle upon Tyne Polytechnic, Newcastle, 1977, especially 'The Irish workers on Tyneside'.
79. See, for example, Steele, 'Irish presence', p. 229; W. J. Lowe, 'Lancashire Fenianism 1864–71', *Transactions of the Historical Society of Lancashire and Cheshire*, Vol. 126, pp. 156–85.
80. D. Bell, 'The Reverend David Bell', *Clogher Record*, Vol., 6, No. 2 (Monaghan), pp. 243–76.
81. Ryan (ed.), *Devoy's post-bag*, Vol. 1, p. 51, p. 209.
82. S. Pender, *Fenianism*, Cork University Press, Cork, 1967.
83. L. Ó Broin, *Fenian fever: an Anglo-American dilemma*, Chatto & Windus, London, 1971, p. 19; pp. 47–51.
84. The finding in 1974 of the diaries of Edward Henry Stanley (1826–93) during building operations at the Knowsley Social Club is a happy omen. Stanley (Lord Stanley, 1851–69; Earl of Derby, 1869–93) was for many years a member of British Cabinets. His diaries contain many references to fenians. The published version has been heavily pruned: see John Vincent, *Disraeli, Derby and the Conservative Party — journals and memoirs of Lord Stanley, 1849–1869*, Harvester, London, 1978.
85. John Denvir, *The life story of an old rebel*, Seacy, Bryers & Walker, Dublin, London, 1910; see also his *The Irish in Britain*, Kegan Paul, London, 1892.
86. Jane Johnson, *Works exhibited at the Royal Society of British Artists 1824–93*, Woodbridge, London, 1975.
87. A. Graves (ed.), *Royal Academy of Arts dictionary of contributors 1769–1904*, Vol. 3, Henry Graves, London, 1905.
88. H. G. Castle, *Case for the prosecution*, World's Work, London, 1956, p. 95.
89. G. W. Carleton [?], *A life of James Stephens*, New York, 1866, p. 116.
90. See, for example, the comments of F. MacDonald on the failure of Michael Davitt and J. J. O'Kelly to write a history of the fenian movement, *Irish Book Lover*, August 1917, Vol. IX, p. 13.
91. It is, for example, customary to dismiss the fenian raids into Canada as having had no real consequences. For an alternative interpretation see Peter Berresford Ellis, 'Ridgeway, the Fenian raids and the making of Canada' in Robert O'Driscoll and Lorna Reynolds, *The untold story: the Irish in Canada*, Celtic Arts of Canada, Toronto, 1988.

7 Story-tellers and writers: Irish identity in emigrant labourers' autobiographies, 1870–1970

Bernard Canavan

Working-class autobiographies have long provided an important source for the study of labour militancy, and in recent years the systematic study of large numbers of such works[1] has directed attention to the evidence they provide about other more elusive aspects of the lives of the poor, such as self-perception and migration. What appears most striking to commentators on these works is the absence of a sense of 'significant selfhood'[2] when compared with middle-class accounts. These life histories, it is said, have none of the assertive confidence, the well-rounded characterisation and above all the sense of ego found in middle-class literary works. While working-class autobiographies provide insights into the labour movement for the historian, their authors would appear unable themselves to locate their own experience in a wider social and historical setting. They express the suffering of their class but appear unable to conceptualise it. Gagnier in her study of the genre[3] identifies six different categories of narrative. They include accounts of religious conversion or cautionary, 'gallows' tales of misspent lives, usually written with the motive of saving their readers; commemorative narratives by itinerant artisans with a strongly picaresque anecdotal flavour; narratives in which the personal is transmuted into the political; confessional works of a sensational nature and works of intense self-examination, more therapeutic than genuinely revelatory.

Viewed against the paradigm of the middle-class literary autobiography, these works indeed appear limited and unsatisfying. But there was another starting-point for Victorian working-class autobiographies and that was the story-telling tradition, one where a developed literary concept of self is unnecessary since the speakers or authors are known to the audience. What these story-tellers have to say is an immediate expression of individual experience; no reflective space exists between voice and story. Walter Benjamin reminds us how central the story-telling tradition was to working-class life: 'If peasants and seamen were past masters of story telling, the artisan class was its university. In it was combined the lore of faraway place, such as a much travelled man brings home, with the lore of the past, as it best reveals itself to natives of a place'.[4] But Benjamin also reminds us that story-telling is becoming increasingly out of place in the modern world, where individual experience is everywhere contradicted by the expert and rendered insignificant by the infinite quantity of our knowledge of human life. The distant land is becoming ever more familiar, and the individual's experience is correspondingly devalued in the process. Once experience is displaced from the hearth-stone to the page it becomes problematic, and incomplete. Many of the nineteenth-century working-class authors were aware of how slight their story appeared when written down, and were appropriately apologetic about the fact. They also had to compete with fictionalised novels about the working class by professional authors that were far better realised and more imaginative than they could hope to produce. With every step in the modernisation process — the establishment of universal literacy, cheap newspapers and free circulating libraries — the oral tradition became more attenuated. And only a few working-class writers, those that had the time and inclination to master the craft, managed to learn the literary conventions of middle-class autobiography.

If we take the writings of Irish emigrants at the end of the nineteenth century as a case in point, we find examples of works from both the literary and the oral tradition. Ireland was one of the places in the British Isles where story-telling lasted longest, and it was most vital in the areas where traditional communities were strongest; the tales told, whether of foreign travel, the afterlife, or the peculiar nature of people's behaviour, helped to reinforce local values against the strangeness of the foreign world beyond. Migration weakened that tradition.

Those Irish labourers who came to Britain entered a culture where the literary models of autobiography had long been established. If those migrants who wrote autobiographies were to address the wider reading public in Britain, and thereby benefit from the commercial rewards such a market might provide, they had to abandon the story-telling tradition with its local defensiveness and unreflective qualities in favour of the more explicit and personalised tone of the literary tradition.

If the presentation of working-class experience was problematic, the ethnic dimension of these works was more straightforward. Irish middle-class writers had already marked out a space for material about Irish life in Britain during this period. During the twilight days of the Union a number of Irish writers were busy reclaiming and chronicling the existence of a long-standing Irish community in Britain, and stressing its achievements and integration.[5] John Denvir published his history of the *Irish in Britain*[6] in which he noted that the progress of the Irish migrant 'has been marvellous'; D. B. O'Sullivan wrote a laudatory account of *The Irish Intellect in England*;[7] and Elliot O'Donnell in his *Irish Abroad*[8] included an extensive chapter on Britain. Michael McDonough researched a work on *Irish Graves in London*[9] and Francis Fahy with D. J. O'Donohue wrote a work called *Ireland in London*.[10] It was also common for middle-class Irish exiles to reflect favourably in their autobiographies upon the period they spent in England, usually in London. Justin McCarthy recalled in his *Reminiscence*[11] how he had as a boy looked forward to coming to England; T. P. O'Connor in his *Memoirs of an Old Parliamentarian*[12] wrote of how he had been charmed by London, its 'Cockney accents' and 'the beautiful young goddesses' he met on the street.[13] The journalist William O'Malley wrote that during 'the fifty odd years he had lived in England (he) had never experienced anything but kindness in the hands of Englishmen'.[14] This positive presentation of Irish life in Britain was part of the general focus on the class content of their experience rather than on ethnic identity during this period.

Patrick MacGill's *Children of the Dead End*,[15] the work that usually comes to mind when working-class autobiographies are mentioned, does not belong to the story-telling tradition of old but is an example of the literary style of autobiography. MacGill makes a novel out of his life story: he refers throughout to himself as Dermot Flynn.

He was born in the Glenties area of Donegal in 1891. His schooling, such as it was, lasted until he was nine when he went to the hiring fair in Strabane,[16] where he was contracted for a season to a Protestant widow as a farm servant. He described in the book how he ran away when he was fifteen and joined a potato picking gang, part of the annual tide of agricultural labour that crossed to Scotland every year. The crossing to Britain is not presented as a particularly important divide in his own or his companions' lives: but it is none the less a rite of passage. On the boat over Flynn meets Norah Ryan, with whom he falls in love and so begins the relationship that provides the plot of the book. MacGill described the living conditions on the farms, and the 'shameless' language and behaviour of the older women from Glasgow who had joined the party. On finding Norah kissing the farmer's son he is overwhelmed with jealousy and disgust at what he regards as her fall and the two drift apart. Flynn leaves the group and becomes a railway navvy. He goes on the tramp with Moleskin Joe — one of the great literary creations of working-class fiction — and learns to fight and make do as an itinerant labourer; in his spare time he reads about socialism, history and literature and begins writing verse. Norah remains in his thoughts, however, and his search for her takes him to Glasgow where he finds she has become a prostitute.

He is offered a job as a journalist in London on the strength of some articles he wrote about navvying life; however before long he returns to Scotland to rescue Norah, only to find her on the point of death and there his story ends.

In spite of the melodramatic plot, MacGill's *Children of the Dead End* is an accomplished piece of literary work with none of the hesitation or deference noted by cultural critics of other working-class life stories. His skill in scene construction owes nothing to the self-referencing of the oral tradition. The book combines verisimilitude to life at the bottom with the moral freedom central to the characters of middle-class novels. *Children of the Dead End* is structured as a novel which, while lending the work readability, blurs the distinction between the factual and the imaginative. MacGill, aware of this, assures the reader that 'most of (the) story is autobiographical'. But we have difficulty in seeing in Flynn a typical migrant labourer. He is much more the aesthete, or free spirit, motivated by moral imperatives rather than economic need. It is the story of the artist as a young labourer rather than a work of proletarian literature, for the author was only 23 when the work was published, had abandoned the life of a labourer and was on his way to achieving his ambition of becoming a man of letters.[17] There is little about the responsibilities or ties of class in this work. It is true that MacGill mentions sending remittances home to his parents in Ireland, but from his remarks he leaves the impression that it was unlikely that his family depended upon him financially.[18]

MacGill rejects the social bonds of religion, nation and family in favour of the individualism and independence of a figure like Moleskin Joe.

The book points up the general difficulty of trying to reconcile the defensive working-class perspective of the period, with the moral perspective of the bourgeois autobiography. The more MacGill focused on the corrupting effect of the migrant's harsh conditions, the more difficult it was for him to explain how he had avoided this corruption himself. The deferential and egoless quality of the subject so common in Victorian working-class autobiographies was not MacGill's way round this difficulty. The authors of these works begged the reader's indulgence and presented themselves as little more than a cipher for their class. But in *Children of the Dead End*, where the protagonist, Flynn/MacGill, is drawn as a free agent in control of his life in the way the reader expects from the middle-class literary autobiographies, the tension between literary genre and class reality, between the author as the hero of the book and the victim of his environment, cannot be reconciled.

We can compare MacGill's work with that of another Irish migrant of the period, Ernest Acheson. His *Memoirs of a Motorman*[19] was written, according to his son's preface, as a kind of personal testament to the author's future wife. This writer is not addressing a socially superior reading public, but a working girl from a bakery who knew about the economic pressures of a migrant worker's life and he finds it unneccessary to stress the moral dilemmas of his experience or project his own self as the centre of the world. If the result can at times appear somwhat flat in comparison with MacGill's dramatic and decisive role in his book, Acheson's story gains its drama from being told to an audience who knows the author personally, where the understatement of events is as important as their dramatisation. In short, it is an autobiography that is closer to the story-teller's tradition.

Acheson was born in 1882 and his *Memoirs* begin with an account of the straitened circumstances of his childhood in a small cottage in Co. Fermanagh. He left school at an early age to become a grocer's apprentice in Belfast, and his experience belongs to a more structured, even genteel, strata of the working class than MacGill's. Not being happy with the grocery trade, he briefly changed to an engineering works where conditions were rougher and the attitude of the other workers more hostile, which led him to seek other, more casual, employment: he crossed to Scotland, where he joined his sister. His first job there was 'mucking out' a large stable, waiting each morning with groups of men in the hope of being selected for a day's work. After that he took employment with the Caledonian Railway Company, first as a carriage cleaner and later as brakes man, lighterman and conductor. He describes a succession of lodgings houses, most of them run by fellow Irish, where conditions varied. Some were overcrowded and filthy; others were run by homely and helpful landladies who provided him with decent meals. Like MacGill, he recounts a number of incidents which provide interest and variety for the reader — his own foolish involvement with religious cranks, his fights with other workers, his narrow escapes from injury or death in the shunting yards and an account of a melancholy visit he made to Ireland to see his dying mother. The book ends with an account of a period he spent on the trams in Newcastle where he met his future wife, and the two subsequent years he spent in New York, earning money to get married.

Acheson's autobiography is without the strong story-line of MacGill's. It is neither a campaigning, nor a deferential work, still less a revelation of life in the lower depths. There are accounts of fights, but if anything these incidents are understated. The book's Irishness is mute, but understood: there is a suggestion of a network of Irish employers, officials and friends who help Acheson occasionally with employment, support and companionship. Unlike MacGill, Acheson does not reject the social world of his childhood but is full of tender memories of his family and the community he left in Fermanagh.

'Ourselves alone': the migrant without a community

The links that connected Ireland and Britain were shattered by a decade of military conflict: the First World War, the Easter Rebellion, the War of Independence and the Irish Civil War that followed, which lasted into the mid-1920s and divided the cultural world of the Irish migrant. In the shadow of these events the migrants, whose numbers continued to remain high,[20] began to be perceived by nationalists in Ireland in a less favourable light. They were no longer seen as the victims of landlords or English misrule, but as self-centred individuals hostile to the aims of a new Ireland, 'cowards and traitors'[21] who were only interested in their own economic well being, or — more damaging still for their image — as part of the outgoing garrison.[22]

With the shift of the Irish government from London to Dublin the position of Irish immigrants in Britain also changed. There was no longer an Irish elite of lawyers, journalists and politicians connected to the Irish Parliamentary Party in Westminster, who looked upon the Irish in British cities as a part of their constituency, and who represented their interests. The leaders of the new political parties that emerged in Ireland after Independence tended not to visit England: after the fierce emotions stirred up by the Civil War few wanted to appear too culturally or politically identified with the old adversary. Whereas in the 1870s all members of the Irish Parliamentary Party were familiar with migrant life and nearly a third of the IPP's members were British-born,[23] by the 1930s few Irish politicians had any idea of the problems faced by Irish migrants, and the number of TDs born in England was less than five per cent.[24] The Irish state, together with the Catholic interests, banned much of the literature produced in England as being Godless, Communist or pornographic. After Independence a generation of Irish citizens grew up ignorant of the most basic aspects of their neighbour's culture, yet many were destined to have to make their lives there. Irish immigrants increasingly appeared in Britain as displaced people in a foreign country, without a voice or coherent identity.

But if the separation of the two cultures made the Irish migrant feel and perhaps appear more alien in Britain, changes in class structure and the representation of labourers in literature in the 1920s and 1930s made it easier for the migrant worker to enter the mainstream of British literature. MacGill's work was itself part of that change, but there were others such as Jack London, George Orwell, Robert Service and W. H. Davies who had discovered among the rootless poor an area of literary fascination for a wider reading public. Many of these writers were not themselves working class and felt no loyalty to it. In their search for more extreme forms of experience they wrote about the shiftless, the criminal, the drifter, and in so doing rendered the narrow, deferential respectability of Victorian working-class literature unnecessary.

Rearden Connor's neglected autobiography, *Plain Tale from the Bogs*,[25] was one of the most powerful works to emerge from this period. Connor was born in 1907, the only child of a member of the Irish Constabulary whose mother died when he was born. His autobiography opens with him as a small boy gazing at a dead soldier in the street during the 1916 Easter Rising. Physically frail, he suffered daily bullying from his schoolmates because his father was employed in the police force: eventually he was sent to school in Cork where his family was unknown. He described the violence of the Black and Tans during the War of Independence, and the atrocities carried out by both the Republicans and Free State troops during the Civil War that followed. When he finished school he realised that 'there is no work for such as (him) nowadays . . . the demobilised men from the Free State Army get what work is going . . . For them are picked the fat plums and the not so fat plums until the tree is bare'. He left Ireland for England, but experienced none of the elation felt by nineteenth-century exiles on arriving in London. For him the city sights were gloomy, if awesome, its people distant and strange. He sought office employment appropriate to his qualifications, but as his funds ran out he was eventually forced to seek work as a manual labourer, tramping the street, unable to afford fares. Thrown out of his lodgings, he became a *habitué* of the Embankment, living among down-and-outs and prostitutes whose lives he recorded with fascination. Eventually he secured employment as a door-to-door salesman for a photographer, and began the long struggle back towards a more stable and respectable existence. He became a coal canvasser, then a furniture remover. However, heavy work undermined his health and he was soon back to his former precarious existence. He described his morbid states of mind during this period: only the fortuitous offer of a gardening job in Hampstead saved his life and his sanity. During a brief visit to Dublin he met, fell in love and married, and a new more secure stage of his life began.

A Plain Tale from the Bogs is a remarkably frank account of life at the bottom. It is about the struggle of a solitary individual in an indifferent society. It is a study of individual loneliness, rather than a picture of a particular social class. During his bitter spiritual journey Connor, like MacGill before him, dispenses with those religious beliefs that no longer answer his emotional needs. But what sets Connor's work apart from MacGill's is his lack of moralising, his frankness and the sexual explicitness of his writing; his descriptions of the sexual longings he saw in others and felt himself bring him into the mainstream of British literary tastes of the period.

Another migrant of that period was Jim Phelan, and one who displays a similar sense of egotism in his autobiography *The Name's Phelan*.[26] This is an account of a young man from a Dublin background who becomes a writer. He was born in 1895 into a family whose origins he described as once comfortable, but which by the time of his birth was reduced to life in a Dublin tenement. Phelan ran away from home several times and was usually flogged on return.

His school, he observed, was a 'dreadful hole . . . completely worthless', and he abandoned it when he was ten years old to lead a kind of ragamuffin existence round the streets of Dublin as a telegraph boy and labourer in the Inchicore railway works. By the time he was sixteen he had more or less taken up an itinerant life-style leaving home regularly, and had been as far as Glasgow as a stowaway. By then he was big enough to stand up to his bullying father and 'beat him to pulp in a fair fight'; in a similar matter-of-fact tone he describes how he lost his virginity to a young Dublin prostitute. He completes an apprenticeship as a blacksmith and recommences what he calls his life of 'tramp-drifting' along the roads of Ireland, Britain and, for a brief period, France. During the 1913 Dublin Lockout he joined the Citizen's Army, and in the later Troubles he repaired and altered small arms for the IRA, though he played little part in the actual struggle itself. *The Name's Phelan* contains many references to political and cultural figures of the period, though he is uncharacteristically modest about his involvement in events. The book rather bizarrely ends with Phelan being sentenced to a ten-year period in jail as a result of what he describes as his involvement in a 'non-political' mail robbery in which a policeman is shot dead. His experiences of prison life are the subject of a number of later novels.

Phelan regarded his work as being like MacGill's — the authentic voice of the itinerant labourer and drifter; he was contemptuous of low life accounts by such writers as Robert Service which he regarded as middle class and unauthentic. He has no belief in working-class solidarity, and no compunction about rejecting the respectability of the poor. He drew a distinction between the 'proper tramps' with whom he identifies and what he called 'the mugs', the men who wander the roads looking for work. He admitted that he was 'too ignorant of Irish or any other politics to understand much, too self-centred and implacably logical to be urged illogically, anywhere'. What he enjoyed was being at the centre of a ferment, and in his search for adventure he deliberately sought out rather than avoided the dangerous and volatile in society.

A writer of that period who shared Phelan's life-style and to some degree his outlook was Bonar Thompson, the author of *Hyde Park Orator*.[27] In it he described his early years as the illegitimate child of a Presbyterian girl who belonged to 'the poorest Ulster peasantry'. His father, a neighbour, never acknowledged him and his mother abandoned him to go to England leaving him to be brought up by a God-fearing aunt. He described his schooling as 'unprofitable', with much of his childhood spent 'on loan' to neighbouring farmers for the sixpence-a-day wages he could earn. When he was fourteen years old he was reunited with his mother who had married and settled in Manchester. First as a messenger, then a greaser on the railway, he eventually earned sufficient wages to leave home and take lodgings. His landlord was a socialist and young Thompson became converted and joined the newly formed Labour Party. Like Phelan, he observes few of the social proprieties of Irish life and his description of his first sexual encounter with a young prostitute is similarly frank. Within a short time he abandoned conventional employment and became a public speaker, at first advocating socialism, but finding this 'too tame', he moved on to anarchism. At a demonstration he organised against unemployment — although he claimed that he 'didn't care a fig about the unemployed' at the time — some windows were broken and Thompson was arrested and jailed for twelve months. On his release he tramped to London and eventually established himself as a speaker in Hyde Park and other public places, affecting a cynicism about the world's affairs and existing on donations from his audience. The rest of the book is taken up with accounts of life on the road, alternating with periods of public speaking, and the occasional literary excursion into journalism.

These last three writers all wrote works that were intensely egoistical and sometimes sensational in character, addressed to a readership hungry for novelty. They present themselves as individuals outside society, uncommitted intellectuals whose poverty made them part of the traditional constituency of the Left, but who had themselves had little commitment to ideologies or organisations bent on improving their conditions. They were writers who had abandoned commitment, and for whom Ireland held no romantic attractions or memories.

Two writers whose works bring us back to the story-telling tradition as opposed to the literary one are Michael MacGowan, whose *Hard Road to Klondyke*[28] was taken down in Irish by his son-in-law, a professional folklorist, and Patrick Gallagher, who received assistance in writing *My Story*[29] from a neighbour who had 'heaps of education'. Both writers were returned migrants, who had spent part of their youth in the potato fields of Scotland and both framed their stories for a local audience where they were already well known.

MacGowan was born in 1865, which makes him the oldest of the group. His work contains an extended account of a poor but close community in Donegal where he spent his childhood and worked as a hired farm servant. He crossed to Scotland on St Patrick's Day 1880 and found employment in an Iron Works at Coatbridge where the wages and accommodation were better than on the potato farms. He described this period as comfortable, but lonely, and abandoned it when June came in order to join neighbours coming over from Ireland to go potato picking. Farm work was indeed rough: MacGowan often had to sleep out and, when work was scarce, he walked the roads from farm to farm in the hope of finding work. MacGowan spent five years crossing between Scotland and Donegal before deciding to emigrate to America, and the remaining two-thirds of his book is taken up with his life in the States.

Patrick Gallagher was also born in Donegal in 1871, the second eldest of a large family. When he was ten years old he, too, like MacGill and MacGowan, went to the hiring fair in Strabane. From his sixteenth year he went on annual trips potato picking to Scotland. Provident and hard working, he managed to improve his condition, and after he married, he and his young wife travelled together. He advanced from labouring to bricklaying, while his wife rented some rooms and provided accommodation for other labourers. When they had sufficient savings they returned and settled in Ireland and he set about establishing a farming co-operative operating on principles he had seen in Scotland. The remainder of this book by 'Paddy the Cope' (Co-op) tells the story of his struggle against merchants and others in the local town seeking to stop the project and of his eventual success.

Gallagher's picture of migrant Irish life in Scotland is very different from MacGill's. In contrast to MacGill's competitive and often brutal gangs,

Gallagher recalls the small convivial group of potato pickers with which he travelled, workers always willing to share what they had, and he describes the hospitality of the families of Scottish farmers even if they were not always able to offer employment. He remembers the songs they sang as they walked the roads, how they maintained their devotions and kept up their morale under difficult circumstances. Gallagher may have omitted some of the less attractive aspects of that life because in the tradition of the oral story-teller part of his aim was to present a positive view and reaffirm qualities such as endurance and cheerfulness which belonged to his own people. Gallagher the story-teller was distrustful of the written word; as he put it when recounting a story told to him by a Scottish woman: 'I cannot put in writing how I felt when I heard of the unjust treatment that charming woman got, but if you were near to me now I would whisper it to you'. The work of these last two writers belongs to the pre-First World War migrations of their youth when Ireland was still part of the Union: it has none of the alienation from society found in the works of Phelan, Thompson or Connor, nor yet the defensiveness about Irishness that became a hallmark of later writers.

The re-discovery of Britain: Irish migration in the 1950s and 1960s

Irish neutrality during the Second World War cast both Ireland and the Irish migrant in an unfavourable light in Britain. Irish individuals living in Britain who returned home to avoid conscription often faced hostility and were accused of cowardice by the British.[30] But, in spite of the dangers of coming to British cities during the Blitz, emigration from Ireland continued on a small scale even during the war. Between 1943 and 1945 some 40,000 Irishmen were issued with work permits,[31] mainly to fill the labour vacuum in factories and construction sites as the armed services absorbed British manpower. In the decade that followed 1945 the numbers arriving increased dramatically. About 352,000 Irish men and women came to Britain[32] during this period, released by farm mechanisation in Ireland and attracted by the employment opportunities offered in Britain by war reconstruction and development.[33]

Four migrants whose experience covers this decade published autobiographies. John O'Donohue was 43 when he came to England in 1943; his book, *In a Strange Land*,[34] is a continuation of an earlier volume about his life in Ireland.[35] Brian Behan's book *With Breast Expanded*[36] is a wry account of his youth in Dublin and his work as a union organiser and Communist party official in London. John B. Keane's *Self-Portrait*[37] is only partly about Irish life in Britain, covering the two years he spent in Northampton and London in the early 1950s. Donall Mac Amhlaigh's *An Irish Navvy*,[38] which was produced as a series of weekly articles written for an Irish language paper in his native Galway, also describes life in Northampton and London. With the exception of O'Donohue, all these writers were born after Irish Independence and came from a marginally more secure and better educated strata of Irish society than the majority of their fellow migrants.[39] O'Donohue had served as a member of the Garda Síochána and had studied for some years in a monastic order; Keane had received a secondary education; Mac Amhlaigh was literate in both Irish and English and had served in the Irish-speaking division of the Irish Army; while Behan belonged to one of the Dublin's best-known literary families. This educational advantage made them interpreters and often critics of the migrant community, about whom in the main they write, for unlike the majority of pre-war writers they show little curiosity about the wider intellectual life outside the exile community.

The appearance of four autobiographies by Irish migrant labourers written within such a short time of each other may not have been entirely coincidental. When they appeared in the mid-1960s, a profound change was occurring in British literary circles; the 'Kitchen Sink' school of novelists and dramatists such as Osborne, Wesker and Arden was replacing what had been a more middle-class literary tradition. Working-class literature during these years became mainstream literature. While the autobiographies of these Irish migrants (with the exception of Behan) did not share the radicalism of the new school — they were in fact unfashionably traditionalist for the 1960s in their social views and attitudes to sex — their writings were still undeniably about the working class and benefited from the publishing trends of the period.

John O'Donohue's autobiography, *In a Strange Land*, begins in Lincolnshire where he found work as a labourer on a wartime runway for the RAF. The work was tough and unhealthy from the cement dust, and O'Donohue was ill-equipped to deal with the rough world he found himself in. He is the most culturally inquisitive of this group of writers, and spent his spare time looking round the colleges in nearby Cambridge, talking to locals, teachers and dons about life, his discoveries tending to confirm rather than undermine his beliefs. He returned to Ireland for a time after the airfield was completed, but the threat of having to accept Irish government employment in the bogs sent him back to England, where he found a job as a labourer on the railway in Swanley, near Dartford. He took up writing after a letter he sent to the management of the railway company complaining about working conditions resulted in a request for him to rewrite part of a local guide book. He was paid three pounds for the project, but nothing further developed from this opportunity. After a period on the railway, he joined a fellow countryman repairing bomb damaged buildings in Poplar and went to live in a hostel at Bromley-by-Bow. Once again O'Donohue described how he found himself in the company of uncongenial fellow Irish labourers and switched jobs to a painting company run by a group of Yorkshire men to get away from them. He had to learn this trade from the start and the book ends with an account of his rather belated apprenticeship and subsequent employment in different parts of the country as a painter.

O'Donohue had much in common with John B. Keane. Both were sharp observers of the exiled Irish, and their work offered an interpretation and defence of the Irish migrant navvy to a wider general public. The main differences between the two accounts is that O'Donohue wrote mainly for a British and Keane for an Irish public. Keane's *Self-Portrait* was published in Ireland, where Keane's reputation as a dramatist at the time was already spreading. But neither wrote with a particular local community in mind. The defensiveness of the story-teller tradition with its locally based values had been passed, eroded and replaced by national identities.

John B. Keane was born in 1928, the son of a National School teacher in Listowel, Co. Kerry. After secondary school he took a job with a companion as a fowl buyer, touring the countryside in a van. He recalled that he decided to emigrate in order to earn sufficient money to marry and chose England in preference to America, arriving in Northampton in 1952. His first job was in a chemist shop, followed by a period as a road sweeper, and then as a factory worker with a firm that manufactured roller bearings. During the summer months the heat from the furnaces was too much and Keane took bar jobs in Leicester and London. He returned to the factory in Northampton with the coming of winter and remained there until his return to Ireland.

Donall Mac Amhlaigh's *An Irish Navvy* begins with his arrival in Northampton in 1951, where he got a job of ward orderly in a hospital. The pay was poor and he soon switched to the heavier, but better rewarded, labour of pipe laying. In making this change, he also left the comfort of hospital accommodation for the make-do conditions of overcrowded lodging houses. Mac Amhlaigh entered the spirit of building site communities with greater enthusiasm than O'Donohue, and his love of the Irish language brought him a network of Gaelic-speaking friends where he found a solidarity and friendship among his fellow migrants, whereas O'Donohue only found brutality and exploitation. The latter part of Mac Amhlaigh's book is an account of his time on building sites from Stanford on the Vale to London and the Kilsby tunnel near Daventry.

What strikes the reader about these autobiographies is that these writers are indeed coming to 'a strange land'. In the forty years after Irish Independence the culture of the two islands had diverged radically. Even before they reached England, departing Irish emigrants were painfully aware of this fact. 'All around us', John B. Keane wrote, 'as we left Dun Laoghaire, there was drunkenness. The younger men were drunk — not violently so but tragically so, as I was, to forget the dreadful loneliness of having to leave home . . . For us, as it was then, it was the brink of hell and don't think I use the word lightly!' O'Donohue, too, remembered the 'hundreds of people, young and old, with red eyes and lonesome faces'; while Mac Amhlaigh described how his heart felt like 'a solid black mass inside (his) breast'. The contrast between this experience and the crossings made by nineteenth-century migrants could hardly be more different.

The three authors with rural backgrounds, Keane, Mac Amhlaigh and O'Donohue, are united on a number of opinions. They strongly defend the Catholic Church and are profoundly suspicious of anything they suspect as Communist. They share a puritan outlook, which sets them apart from the mainstream of the British working class. Women in fact play a very small part in their descriptions of the exile community.[40] Both O'Donohue and Mac Amhlaigh express surprise at the social freedom women enjoyed in Britain and the high-handed way English women treat their husbands. It is interesting in the light of recent debate about anti-Irish racism that all these writers concur that the English are 'in no way prejudiced against the Irish',[41] though since they all express such antipathies towards sections of their own community, either because they belong to rival parts of Ireland, fail to speak Irish, or are wilder than themselves, anti-Irish prejudice might have been of little consequence in comparison. Of these writers only Keane mentions the existence of 'no Irish' notices on accommodation boards and he endorses the ban as justifiable given the behaviour of some Irish lodgers. He and his Irish colleague stayed with a landlady, who displayed such a notice after her husband had been attacked by some of her Irish lodgers, by pretending they were Scots. Their subterfuge was discovered when detectives called at the house to interview Keane and his colleague after the doorman of a local dance-hall had been kicked to death by 'a number of men who were allegedly Paddies'. In spite of their origins being made known, the landlady relented and continued to provide them with accommodation. This prohibition against the Irish mainly affected Irish labourers; Irish girls often came to employment where accommodation was provided. Accommodation of the period was crowded and usually meant 'full accommodation with meals', and landladies were engaged in a perpetual search to find 'guests' whose needs were minimal, whose habits were familiar and whose characters were pliant to the dictates of the house rules. Few Irishmen who worked on building sites met all these criteria, and from the activities of some of the lodgers described by these writers there were a number who met none of them.

In spite of their denial that they encountered anti-Irish feeling, all of the writers attempt to account for 'the bad reputation of the Irish over here'. O'Donohue believed that the roots of the problem sprang from the pre-war IRA bombing campaign in Britain, which led to every Irishman being taken for an 'irresponsible bomber', while Mac Amhlaigh believed that it was the tendency of the Irish labourers to indulge in drinking and fighting, and the fact that those Irish were high-spirited, country lads: 'it was a small wonder', according to Mac Amhlaigh, 'that the Irish were getting a bad reputation over here'.

Mac Amhlaigh mentions over a dozen fights. They include exchanges in dance-halls, in pubs, in lodging houses, on buses, on building sites and in village camps. A few were between English and Irish labourers, but most were between Irish workers themselves, caused by what Keane diagnosed as 'the age old hatred of the country for the town'.

Friction between different Irish regional groups also led to discussion about class status and national attitudes. English employers were universally pre-ferred to fellow Irishmen. 'Give me an English boss any day before an Irishman', one Irishman told O'Donohue, a preference endorsed by Mac Amhlaigh who felt that it was 'no wonder that Irish foremen have such a bad reputation over here when half of them haven't the manners of a dog'. The comments in these works suggest that Irish foremen of that period brought with them from Ireland a respect for social hierarchy that was on the wane in Britain. 'I can't get over how nice the doctors and other like them are in this country — quite different from at home', wrote Mac Amhlaigh. O'Donohue put this deference down to the fact that the Irish had 'to coax the powerful if we want a position: a roll of butter for the local doctor, a laying pullet for the priest', and what Keane called 'the frightening complacency at the same old indignities where married men . . . (were) forced to go cringing caps in hands to TDs and county councillors looking for jobs'.

Brian Behan's autobiography is the nearest in tone to the restless intellectual radicalism of Phelan and Thompson. He was born in 1926 into a well-known Dublin republican and left-wing family. Like Phelan, he spent his youth working in Dublin, as well as periods down the country, including a time in one of the turf camps so dreaded by O'Donohue, where conditions were 'dog-rough', before he came to London. His first job in Britain was as a pile driver on a building site in Southwark. Before long he had joined the Communist Party, married and became a full-time political organiser in the building trade. He was part of the first British delegation to Communist China, and achieved even more notoriety in 1959 for his role in organising a strike on the South Bank building site, where pickets clashed violently with police. In the latter part of *With Breast Expanded* he described his disillusionment with the Communist Party and a brief flirtation with the Trotskyites, and later the anarchists. He was eventually thrown out of his union and his story ends with an account of his employment as a bricklayer in Whitechapel.

Keane and Mac Amhlaigh, whose works were addressed to an Irish audience, were concerned to raise the status of the migrant back home where some regarded them as, in Keane's phrase, 'scruff'. To go to England was an admission of both economic and moral bankruptcy, and prejudice against the emigrant could be seen in a number of ways. Irish magistrates were known to dismiss cases where offenders made the plea that they were off to England in the morning.[42] Many in Ireland believed that emigration was, as one contributor to the Irish Commission on Population and Emigration expressed it, a means of releasing 'social tensions that might otherwise explode and makes possible the stability of manners and customs which might otherwise be the subject of radical change'.[43] In the light of these attitudes in Ireland it was understandable that those who left often brought with them a sense of guilt and failure, leading some in Ireland to speak of the 'inferiority complex'[44] of the Irish in Britain. In spite of the massive population transfer of the period, the values and perceptions of the two societies were very different. But that gap between the fragile moral superiority of comfortable Ireland and those Irish who came to Britain began to close in the late 1960s.

The causes of what one historian has referred to as the 'cultural homogenisation'[45] between Irish and British society that began in the 1970s are manifold, but not least among them was the existence of three-quarters of a million Irish in Britain who returned home twice, or three times a year, sent their children home during the school vacations, and in the late 1960s and 1970s returned home themselves with new expectations and experience to take advantage of the boom in Ireland during these years. The growth in Britain of a successful Irish business class and of an exile minority that were vocal in politics, the arts and literature in Britain provided a new — though not always welcome — perspective on the eighteenth and nineteenth-century cultural influence of Irish London, an influence which has begun to reassert itself again after an interlude of isolationism and 'little Irelandism'. British television channels, papers and magazines reintegrated Ireland into the wider world of the emigrant, where previously the lament was that those who departed from Irish shores also departed from Irish standards. The commercial opportunities across the water brought a rediscovery of Britain by Irish business classes and professions, while the 'Troubles' in Northern Ireland in their own grim way highlighted how much Irish politicians shared with their British counterparts.[46] And once the Irish middle classes began to return to Britain it became impossible for them to ignore the casualties among the Irish working–class in Britain, or to see in migrant failure only migrant flaws.[47] The academic links between the two cultures can be seen reflected in the number of studies of the Irish in Britain by historians both in Ireland and Britain during the 1980s, which brings us full circle to that other flourishing period of migrant studies a hundred years ago. The voices of those migrants who left accounts of their experience provide an illuminating commentary on changing conditions and identity in these intervening years.

Notes

1. Two studies in particular have helped this task: John Burnett, David Mayall and David Vincent, *The autobiography of the working class: an annotated and critical bibliography Vol. 1, 1790–1900* Harvester, Brighton, 1984; and Nan Hackett, *XIX century British working class autobiographies: an annotated bibliography*, AMS, New York, 1985.
2. Regienia Gagnier, 'Social atoms: working class autobiography, subjectivity and gender' in *Victorian Studies*, Spring 1987. David Vincent, *Bread, knowledge and freedom: a study of nineteenth-century working class autobiography*, Europa, London, 1981.
3. Gagnier, 'Social Atoms', p. 345.
4. Walter Benjamin, *Illuminations*, Fontana, London, 1970, p. 85.
5. Note the point made by David Fitzpatrick that the active minority has dominated the study of the Irish overseas and their experience may not have been the same as that of the mass of migrants. See *Irish emigration 1801–1921*, Studies in Irish Economic and Social History 1, Dublin, 1984, p. 36.
6. John Denvir, *The Irish in Britain, from the earliest times to the fall of Parnell*, Kegan Paul, Trench, Trübner & Co., London, 1892, p. 435.
7. D. B. O'Sullivan, *The Irish intellect in Britain, a talk given in Newcastle-on-Tyne*, Duffy, Dublin, 1871.
8. Elliot O'Donnell, *The Irish abroad*, Pitman, London, 1915.
9. Michael McDonough, *Irish graves in England*, *Evening Telegraph* Reprint, Dublin, 1888.
10. Francis A. Fahy and D. J. O'Donohue, *Ireland in London*, *Dublin Evening Telegraph* Reprint, Dublin, 1889.
11. Justin McCarthy, *Reminiscences*, Harpers, London, 1899, Vol. I, p. 4.
12. T. P. O'Connor, *Memoirs of an old Parliamentarian*, Ernest Benn, London, 1929.
13. O'Connor, *Memoirs*, p. 28.
14. William O'Malley, *Glancing back*, n.d., Wright & Brown, London, p. 64.
15. Patrick MacGill, *Children of the Dead End: the autobiography of a navvy*, Herbert Jenkins, London, 1914.
16. Contracted child labour was common in Ireland, particularly in the western counties in the late nineteenth century. See R. Breen, 'Farm servanthood in Ireland 1900–1940' *Economic History Review XXVI No. 1*, p. 89.
17. For a discussion of MacGill's development as a writer see Patrick O'Sullivan, 'Patrick MacGill; the making of a writer' in Seán Hutton and Paul Stewart (eds), *Ireland's histories: aspects of state, society and ideology*, Routledge, London, 1991.

18. Irish opinion tended to look unfavourably on MacGill's work in the 1950s. Patrick McGeown, a working-class admirer of MacGill described the unfavourable response his enquiries received when he visited MacGill's birthplace: "'He went away,' said one old man, "when he was just fourteen years old and he never came back. It was just as well, for his book were no good and there would be no welcome for him here."' And MacGill's nephew told McGeown that his books were never allowed into their house. Patrick McGeown, *Heat the furnace seven times more,* Hutchinson, London, 1968, pp. 174–5.

19. Ernest Acheson, *Memoirs of a motorman,* LIW, London, 1991.

20. Sean Glynn, *'Irish emigration to Britain 1911–1951',* Irish Economic and Social History, Vol. VIII, Dublin, 1981.

21. Terence J. MacSwiney, 'Education is desertion' in *The voice of Ireland: a memorial of Freedom's Day by the foremost crusaders,* Dublin, n.d., p. 598. The article went on: 'Emigration is desertion! Make this a battle-cry to hearten the waverer and scourge the coward who is ready to run away. Cowards should be scourged, for cowardice is a sin; it is a want of faith in God. Emigration is desertion! Repeat this, and cry it abroad as an article of faith, till it is written in every mind and stamped in every heart. It is our first principal of nationality of to-day; its command is explicit, emphatic, and final.'

22. The average annual net male migration for the census periods to 1926: 1881–91, 29,257; 1891–1901, 20,315; 1901–11, 11,764; and 1911–26, 13,068; (*Commission on emigration and other population problems 1948–1954,* Government Publications, Dublin, 1954). A discussion of the relationship between figures for Protestant decline and nationalism can be found in Robert E. Kennedy jun., *Irish emigration, marriage and fertility,* UCP, California, 1969.

23. A. O'Day, *The English face of Irish nationalism, Parnellite involvement in British politics 1880–5,* Gill & Macmillan, Dublin, 1977, p. 23.

24. Al Cohan discusses the background of Irish politicians and Civil Servants in *The Irish political elite,* Gill & Macmillan, Dublin, 1972, p. 27, and puts the figure of Irish-born Dáil deputies at 95 per cent.

25. Rearden Connor, *A plain tale from the bogs,* John Miles, London, 1937.

26. J. Phelan, *The name's Phelan: the autobiography of Jim Phelan,* Sidgwick & Jackson, London, 1948.

27. Bonar Thompson, *Hyde Park orator,* Jarrolds, London 1935.

28. Michael MacGowan, *The hard road to Klondyke,* taken down by Sean O hEochaidh, and translated from the Irish *Rotha Mór an tSaoil* by Valentin Iremonger, Routledge & Kegan Paul, London, 1962.

29. Patrick Gallagher (Paddy the Cope), *My story,* Templecrone Co-operative Society, Dungloe, 1945.

30. Marin Mitchell, *Back to England,* Frederick Muller, London, 1941, p. 194.

31. P. J. Drury, 'Migrants and labourers since Independence' in J. Drury (ed.), *Irish Studies 5; Ireland and Britain since 1922,* CUP, Cambridge, 1986, p. 126.

32. Stephen Glynn, 'Irish immigration to Great Britain, 1911–1951: patterns and policy', *Irish Economic and Social Review,* Vol. VIII, Dublin, 1981.

33. Kennedy, *Ireland,* Chap. V.

34. John O'Donohue, *In a strange land,* Batsford, London, 1958.

35. John O'Donohue, *In a quiet land,* Batsford, London, 1957.

36. Brien Behan, *With breast expanded,* MacGibbon & Kee, London, 1964.

37. John B. Keane, *Self-portrait,* Mercier Press, Cork, 1964.

38. Donall Mac Amhlaigh, *An Irish Navvy: the diary of an exile,* translated from the Irish by Valentin Iremonger, Routledge & Kegan Paul, London, 1964.

39. 82 per cent of Irish-born British residents in 1961 had left school at 15 or earlier according to *Investment in education*, Stationary Office, Dublin, 1966. This statistic covers both male and female emigration from Ireland and may not reveal the full extent of the educational disadvantage of labourers. Among the children of cottiers and small farmers, boys tended to be kept from school during sowing and harvesting periods, as labour was more critical for the family economy than education. Girls, on the other hand, were more likely to be encouraged to remain at school, usually the local convent, in order to improve their marriage prospects and, as one local study put it, to 'Speed their departure from home' (Limerick Rural Survey, *Social structure*, Limerick Rural Survey, Tipperary, 1962, p. 187). This gender imbalance in education, combined with need for nursing and office skills in the newly established welfare state in Britain, explains the higher status occupations of Irish women in comparison with Irish men in Britain.

40. Part of the reason why women featured so rarely in these accounts was the strong traditional division between male and female labour on small farms and the way that division continued in Britain where Irish men worked predominantly in male labour groups while Irish women went into hospitals and offices where employment was predominantly female. In spite of the fact that female outnumbered male migration from the late-nineteenth-century onwards comparatively few Irish women left accounts of their experience.

41. Mac Amhlaigh, *Navvy*, p. 113.

42. Several authorities mentioned this practice. Keane thought these 'rowdies and criminals' were responsible for giving the rest of the Irish communities a bad name in England. Keane, *Self-portrait*, p. 45.

43. 'Reservation No. 2' by Alexis Fitzgerald of *Irish Commission on Emigration*, p. 222.

44. Thomas Lane, *The Furrow*, April 1954, p. 229; and Revd M. D. Campbell, 'Irish Men and Women Going to England', *Christus Rex*, Vol. IX, No. 1, Jan 1955, The Christus Rex Society, Naas., p. 44.

45. M. A. G. O Tuathaigh, 'The historical pattern of Irish emigration: some labour aspects', . . . *the emigrant experience* . . . , Galway Labour History Group, Galway, 1991, p. 23.

46. Liam Ryan in 'Irish emigration to Britain since World War II', Richard Kearney (ed.), *Migrations: the Irish at home and abroad*, Wolfhound, Dublin, 1990, p. 59, quotes the remarks of Donough O'Malley, the Irish Minister for Health, to the members of the National University of Ireland Club in London in 1966 that they must play a fuller part in British political and social life. In the 1980s, the voice of the Irish community has played a greater cultural part in British life, but it probably has had an even greater effect on Irish life through the influence it has exerted in the media.

47. For over a decade now Irish governments have recognised a commitment to the Irish in Britain and have provided funds to assist migrant welfare groups.

8 The Irish migrant and film

Kevin Rockett

The history of the representations of the Irish migrant in the American cinema is a story of the gradual change from early crude stereotypes to the current state where 'Irish' representations are most likely only to be identified by the names of the characters. In this almost 100-year process lies a tale of the gradual assimilation of the Irish into the multi-faceted American culture.[1] Having its own peculiar qualities, cinema helped liberate the Irish from certain constricting representations, but it also displayed their relative lack of positive cultural power and influence in America. Cinema above all helped broaden the range of representations of the Irish as it successfully straddled class and gender differences, giving, for example, a more complex set of representations of Irish women than had previously been available. In large part these cinematic representations were made by non-Irish people and often drew, not on 'traditional' images of the Irish or literary conventions, but on evolving cinematic narratives.

Lacking capital and expertise, few Irish migrants or their descendants had control over the film images being produced. Unlike their literary predecessors, film production in America was rarely in the hands of Irish-Americans. True, many Irish performers and directors can be identified even in the early American cinema, and some film production companies have distinctly Irish names (for example, Powers, which made some Irish films as early as the 1900s). Nevertheless, the same applies as to other branches of industrial America: in general, the Irish lacked the capital and even entrepreneurial skills to form film production companies. This was especially true of Irish-born migrants in the USA. Only in the very early cinema, when all branches of the film industry could be entered with a minimum of capital, were the Irish reasonably well-represented. Once consolidation of the film industry began to occur in the 1910s, with a consequent need for greater capital, the Irish retreated almost exclusively to creative roles or worked in management.

The assimilation process, therefore, of the Irish via the cinema was mediated by other ethnic groups, such as Jews, who attained a degree of economic independence in Hollywood never achieved by the Irish, or by Anglo-Saxon producers. Neither of these groups was likely to produce films which would be directly critical of WASP attitudes to the Irish, one of the key issues for Irish-America. Nevertheless, the American cinema is a rich and complex source for representations of the Irish. As there are important social as well as cinematic distinctions between the silent and sound periods, with the exception of the discussion of the Irish–American films of John Ford, whose career straddled both periods, this chapter has been divided in two.

Silent cinema

At a time when Irish-American fiction writers were abandoning or reducing in importance their Irish backgrounds as central features of their work, early cinema brought to the fore a wide range of Irish themes unavailable in literature. Charles Fanning's 'Lost Generation' of Irish-American writers,[2] those writing during the first three decades of this century, precisely coincides with the most sustained and comprehensive presentation of the Irish in the American cinema. During the almost thirty-five years before 1929 of the silent period as many as 500 American films were made which had identifiable Irish themes or prominent Irish characters.[3] In assessing these films the researcher's task is made difficult by the small number of films extant. Nevertheless, it is possible to reconstruct those early crucial decades of the cinema as they tell us something qualitatively different about the Irish in America than is available in Irish-American writing.

During the silent period there were about 5 million Irish in America; one–fifth of them were Irish-born. Though only accounting for about 6 per cent of the American population, they were apparently concentrated in urban areas, and being overwhelmingly working class, were proportionately more important to film exhibitors than their numbers might suggest. It is this Irish-American constituency which the early cinema sought to bring to the cinema with images of themselves.[4] One of the most popular themes of that Irish-American cinema was the progress by the Irish from rural Ireland to urban America.

A useful point of departure for the Irish migrant and cinema, as indeed it is for the beginning of sustained film production in Ireland, is *The Lad from Old Ireland* (1910), which has the distinction of being the first American fiction film made in Ireland. In *The Lad from Old Ireland*, Terry, a labourer, who is played by the film's director, Irish-Canadian Sidney Olcott, leaves his poor rural environment, and his girlfriend, Aileene, and migrates to the USA. Promising to return when his fortune is made, he quickly rises from hod carrier to politician. Living amidst 'society' people, and receiving the attentions of an attractive woman, he forgets about Aileene until he receives a letter from home telling of her desperate plight. Poverty-stricken, she and Terry's mother are faced with eviction. Arriving in Ireland, Terry's American-earned money pays off the debt, with the result that the eviction is thwarted, and the lovers are reunited.[5] Implicit in this tale, one of the few 'Irish' films from this period to have survived, is the potential for material and social advancement in the USA, but there is also a warning of the potential loss of 'Irish' values there. This theme, of course, had been forcefully emphasised during the previous half century in the Irish-American Catholic propaganda tracts of such writers as Mary Anne Sadlier. Another film with a similarly named character, and on the same theme, was released earlier that year, but it had a markedly different slant.

The Irish Boy (1910) tells how a young Irish lad, Terence, who is dissatisfied with the poor economic conditions in Ireland, decides to migrate to the USA after his passage is paid for by Pat, a friend in America. Upon Terence's arrival in the USA, Pat immediately integrates him into American society by getting him 'less conspicious' clothes. Pat also finds him a job in the factory in which he works. Terence falls in love with Nora, who works in the factory's office. The foreman, jealous of this relationship, tries to frame Terence for theft. Nora, observing the foreman placing his own watch in Terence's pocket, reports the incident. The result is that the foreman is fired and Terence is promoted as his replacement. With a new-found position of relative wealth Terence is now not only able to marry Nora but can afford to bring his parents over from Ireland to attend the wedding. Irish customs are seen to be preserved in America when the old folks join in an Irish reel at the wedding.[6] By remaining honest and true to one's origins, the film suggests, the Irish, or any migrants, can become prosperous and happy in America. The film, like so many other Irish-theme films of this and later periods, was released to coincide with St Patrick's Day, which indicates that film distributors were well aware of the commercial value of Irish films at this time.

Not all migrant films were so sanguine about life in America. One film, *Far from Erin's Isle* (1912), which focuses on the role of women migrants, tells a cautionary tale. Kathleen migrates to the USA leaving her boyfriend, Brian, behind. Working in a sweatshop until a strike is called over a cut in wages, she then secures a job in a department store, suggesting a surprising ease of social class transition to white-collar employment. However, she becomes ill and is discharged. The doctor diagnoses homesickness as the cause of her illness. Returning to Ireland, she is reunited with Brian, to whom she promises never to leave Ireland again.[7] Contemporary evidence certainly shows that many Irish migrants, men as well as women, were unhappy in America, but, nevertheless, the vast majority of Irish migrants remained in the USA.

It seems that most migrants followed the pattern of gravitating to the established Irish neighbourhoods of the larger American cities, rather than, for example, attempting to make use of their farming backgrounds and continue on to rural areas. Lack of capital would have precluded them from entering agricultural production in America except as waged employees and this probably explains the relative lack of Irish characters in the cinema as either cowboys or ranchers. An environment markedly different from Ireland awaited them in the cities. The process of learning to cope with urban and industrial America had also been a feature of the Catholic tract propagandists. WASP social reformers also sought to guide them towards integration within American culture and society. Cinema brought a new dimension to this process and it was one, as noted, that the Irish only rarely had direct control over.

Kerby Miller's assessment of the letters and memoirs of working-class Irish migrants between 1870 and 1921 concludes that they 'reflect a pervasive dissatisfaction with urban industrial life in their adopted country'.[8] Part of that dissatisfaction may very well have been that by the late nineteenth century few Irish in America inhabited insular and ethnically homogenous neighbourhoods. This ethnic mix was one of the key features of the representations of the Irish during the early decades of cinema.

In part because of their longer tradition as migrants and, of course, their firsthand command of the English language, the Irish played a key mediating role between the dominant Anglo–Saxon culture of the establishment and the more recent Eastern and Southern European migrants. An early example of 'melting pot' disharmony is the 1907 film *Fights of Nations*. Drawing on a series of distinct vaudeville-type 'fights' ('Mexico versus Spain'; 'Our Hebrew Friends'; 'A Scottish Combat'; 'Sunny Africa'; 'Eight Avenue, New York'; and 'Sons of the Ould Sod'), it is significant that the Irish are the last to be stereotypically represented: a wife, her husband and another man fight as a result of a trivial incident, but their disagreements are soothed by beer. The final scenes show 'America, The Land of the Free' as a place of harmony, with Uncle Sam presiding over a Congress of Powers and proclaiming 'Peace'.[9]

In line with other social and cultural movements during the early decades of the century, cinema, too, expressed the importance of assimilating the huge numbers of new migrants into American society. Though principally producing entertainment narratives, cinema responded with a range of films which contained an underlying assimilative message. These films did not usually focus on a separate ethnic group, but explored inter-ethnic, and later, inter-class, harmony. The vehicle for this assimilative message was usually a love affair leading to marriage between the offspring of different migrant, or class groups. Generally, these films involved Irish and Jewish relationships on the one hand, and Irish women, but occasionally Irish men, marrying into upper–class WASP families, on the other. In the Irish-Jewish stories a frequent theme is that the young lovers are in conflict with their respective parents over their marriage, crossing as it does religious and occasionally class differences. One (comic) solution to this was to have two marriage ceremonies, one Catholic, one Jewish.

In the 1929 film version of the hugely popular 1920s' play, *Abie's Irish Rose*, Abie Levy secretly marries Rosemary Murphy in an Episcopal church. Abie then brings Rosemary, renamed for the occasion, Rosie Murpheski, to his home and they are married by a rabbi. Rosemary's father arrives just as the ceremony is ending, and a Catholic priest then marries them for the third time. Disowned by their respective families, it requires the rabbi and the priest to persuade the feuding parents to become reconciled with their offspring. This is successfully achieved when Rosemary produces twins, one of whom is named after Rosemary's father, the other after Abie's mother.

Often, though, the marriage alliance could serve to consolidate the business interests of the rival families. Two adjacent families, often rivals themselves, are brought together by the young lovers. In the first in a series which continued until 1933, *The Cohens and the Kellys* (1926), quarrelsome neighbours, shopkeeper Cohen and policeman Kelly, form a business partnership, which then lasts throughout the series.

Despite their comic format there lay a serious assimilative message beneath the banter: the need for even the most ethnically and religiously remote cultures to work together.

Social class differences were usually dealt with indirectly and satirically. This can be seen most forcefully when 'slummers' visit working-class districts or social reformers seek to improve working-class lives. In *Pat and the 400* (1910) pompous Mrs Bradley-Larkin and other members of the Four Hundred upper-class families visit Patrick Murphy and his family, having read that 'Slumming is Becoming Fashionable'. After giving the Murphys some luxuries, they reprimand Pat for his beer-drinking and complain to Mrs Murphy about dust on the mantlepiece. They leave contented with having done good. The following day Pat and his friends reverse the process and do their own version of slumming by visiting Mrs Bradley-Larkin's home during a musical recital. They end up dancing in the drawing room to Mrs Murphy's piano accompaniment of Irish tunes. Revenge satisfied, they leave the house. [10]

A variation on this theme is to be found in *Hell's End* (1918) when Irish self-made millionaire Flynn, who moved out of New York's tenement, Hell's End, goes on a slumming expedition with his sister, Mary, to visit an old friend, Jack, now a gang leader and associate of crooked politicians. Following a fight, Jack not only finds true love with Mary but abandons his old ways to work for the improvement of Hell's End. [11] This social reform message was also to be found in the anti-corruption film, *A Fighteen Colleen* (1919), when Alannah Malone, a recent immigrant, helps a district attorney secure proof that the mayor is collecting bribes. As a reward, Alannah and her boyfriend are appointed Superintendents of a municipal restaurant. [12]

The process, though, of moving from the working class to the middle class was far from an easy one. In what must have been a painful film to watch for Irish migrants, *Sweeney and the Million* (1913), seeks to ridicule that progression. Sweeney, a hod carrier, inherits a million dollars, but succeeds in squandering it on conspicious consumption, including giving a ball, and he then loses the remainder on a bet in a fashionable club, from which he is then thrown out. The next morning he returns to work as a hod carrier and is left only with the dress suit on his back. [13]

The process of social transformation was no less difficult for women. The main occupation for Irish women in America was that of domestic servant, where 54 per cent of Irish-born women were employed in 1900. [14] Another 6.5 per cent worked as laundresses. The Irish domestic servant was often the subject of unpleasant satire in the cinema. In *Bridget's Explanation* (1912), the servant accidentally breaks a precious Phoenician bowl at her employer's house. Asked how she broke the bowl, she picks up its companion and illustrates the accident by dropping the second one. [15] In *Bridget's Sudden Wealth*, also from 1912, Bridget O'Hoolihan, a domestic servant, inherits a small fortune. Abandoning her job and her boyfriend Pat, a policeman, she becomes a high-spending consumer. Arrested by Pat for speeding, Bridget and Pat's love is rekindled and Pat, resigning from the police force, marries the now wealthy Bridget. [16] Such a fantasy transformation of her lowly-economic position belied the real hardship of these workers. In an unusual reversal of this trend, the 1903 short comedy, *Lady Bountiful Visits the Murphys on Wash Day*, shows a well-dressed woman visiting Mrs Murphy, who is doing the washing. Mrs Murphy's son puts the lady's dress in the clothes wringer with the result that the washtub is overturned. As the film ends, Mr and Mrs Murphy are trying to extricate Lady Bountiful from the washtub and the dress from the wringer. [17]

As Irish-American women moved out of their working-class backgrounds more quickly than Irish men [18] it is not surprising to find, with the possible exception of the representations of Irish-American politicians, that women are seen most frequently integrated, often, though, with difficulty, within the Irish-American middle class or Anglo-Saxon worlds.

A good example of this trend was the hugely popular comedy, *Irene* (1926), with Colleen Moore, adapted from the 1919 James Montgomery play. In this film, Irene leaves her working-class Philadelphia background to work in New York. She meets a wealthy aristocrat, Donald Marshall, but their relationship is being thwarted by his WASPish mother. Though all works out well for the young lovers in the end, it requires Donald to seek her out in her own tenement dwelling after she runs away from the oppressive upper-class environment. Only by Donald accepting her social origins, and, though it is never explicitly stated, religious difference, is there any hope for their relationship.

While Irene transforms her social class position through love, the search for middle-class respectability, which was an important feature of the 'genteel' tradition in Irish-American literature in the late nineteenth and early twentieth century, was satirised in the *Bringing Up Father* newspaper cartoons of George McManus, which were cinematically adapted as *Jiggs in Society* and *Jiggs and the Social Lion*, both made in 1920. In the 1940s, there was another series of films based on McManus's drawings, including *Jiggs and Maggie in Society* (1947) and *Jiggs and Maggie Go West* (1950). This satirising of the 'lace-curtain', or upwardly-mobile, Irish was also seen in *Who's Who in Society* (1915). In this film, Mrs O'Brien aspires to social prominence, but her favoured suitor for her daughter, Mary Ellen, turns out to be a thief. As a result, Mrs O'Brien throws away her copy of *Who's Who* and Mary Ellen marries the man of her choice. In this film, as in the Jiggs and Maggie films, the mother is depicted as the social climber, while in *Who's Who . . .*, for example, Mr O'Brien prefers the saloon bar to the exclusive club.[19] In a more vicious comedy, aptly titled, *Breaking into Society* (1923), the O'Tooles, who inherit a fortune, alienate their society guests by their and their guests' uncouth manners.[20] Other films suggested that Irish-American parents were keen to see their daughters marry English lords, or anyone else, provided they could tranform their perceived inferior social status.

The contrast between the two generations of Irish-American women, the migrant mother and the first-generation Irish-American daughter, whether within the working or middle classes, is often quite striking. The mother is depicted well into the sound era as the matriarchial linchpin of the Irish family. The centrality of the Irish mother is reinforced by the representation of the Jewish mother, whose domineering presence and often stifling influence over her family echoes that of the Irish mother. Indeed, the encouragement of the Irish-Jewish films, from an establishment viewpoint, was undoubtedly related to how depictions of conservative family life were allied to an assimilative message.

With a conservative nuclear family ethos, the older generation was often in conflict with their American-born offspring. While the Irish-Jewish stories of social class transformation have at their core the mother, and her search for social advancement, for the young generation the concerns, while still with material and social improvement, are, however, also fuelled by sexual desire. The underlying concerns expressed by film-makers in these films, whether comedies or dramas, are not just about two implied different religions and social classes, but also with different conceptions of sexuality. In *Irene*, for example, Donald's snobbish and stilted upper-class girlfriend is contrasted with

Colleen Moore's exuberant and physically liberated flapper style. The fantasy of the free and easy sexuality of working-class people was a feature of Victorian literature and entered films almost from the beginning of cinema. The Irish were no less immune from this representation than others, at least in the cinema. Indeed, going against the perception of the supposed repressed Catholic sexuality of all Irish is the inclusion in a fictional instruction film, *The End of the Road* (1919), of an episode about how an Irish servant girl dies after her baby is born, as a result of contracting syphilis.[21]

The relative independence of (Irish) women in America was given a distinctly negative airing in the 1907 film, *When Women Vote*. In this anti-suffragette film, Mrs O'Brien is seen campaigning for elective office while her 'hen-pecked' husband looks after the baby and shines his wife's shoes. After impassioned campaigning, Mrs O'Brien is elected magistrate. One of her first cases involves Mr McGinnis, who is charged with kissing his wife. She sentences him to twenty years in prison.

Meanwhile, Mr O'Brien is supposed to be attending to the household duties. Returning home from court, Mrs O'Brien discovers that dinner is not ready, the baby is not washed and the rooms are not clean. The oppressed husband is forced to do his duties, but his efforts still prove inadequate for Mrs O'Brien. The husband is left hoping for a divorce but this reactionary film provides the final ironic twist by declaring that a divorce cannot be obtained while women vote.[22]

Male Irish-American politicians were not treated much better by the silent cinema. Politics was a means of non-traditional advancement for Irish people and by the turn of the century Irish political influence was widespread in city politics. However, representations of Irish-American politics on film tended to carry an air of corruption about them, both in the way politicians were elected and in their actions while in office. This is, perhaps, not surprising, given the relative lack of control Irish people had over film production. Nevertheless, it also reflected the sense of corruption which had surrounded the affairs of Tammany Hall since the late nineteenth century, when Irish politicians finally gained a considerable measure of control over the local Democratic Party.

Between 1892 and 1912 New York's electoral districts were identified with Big Tim Sullivan, even though Boss Croker and Charley Murphy were in the top positions. Sullivan became a state Senator and United States Congressman. Engaged in gambling and prize fighting, he also allegedly drew bribes from saloons, brothels, hotels and theatres on the East Side of Manhattan and the Tenderloin district. After Sullivan died mysteriously in 1913, he was the subject of a film, *The Life of Big Tim Sullivan* (1914). It traced his life from being born in New York, the son of Irish migrants, and his career as newsboy, his election as assemblyman in a district in which only four votes were cast against him, his work when elected and his death.[23]

The importance of the Irish vote in general elections was recognised even at the beginning of cinema. In *Irish Ways of Discussing Politics* (1900) Tammany Hall is ridiculed as two Irishmen discuss politics over a glass of whiskey, while in *Pat and the Populist* (1896) Pat drops a brick on the unwelcome Populist politician.[24] These anti-Democratic Party films testify to the clear public perception of Irish-American support for the Democrats, but they were also an early indication of where the power of film-making capital lay. Most of the films involving politicians, however, did not so explicitly address broader political questions. Town Hall corruption or political clientism were more likely to be depicted than questions of state or nation.

A good example is *Paddy's Political Dream* (1916). In this film, a labourer, Paddy, dreams that he is a political boss. He receives attention from cronies and hangers-on; he gives out money to a widow, has his henchmen break up a rival politician's rally, and then arranges with the police to free his own sympathisers and to jail his opponents. Indeed, the police are shown to be in league with Paddy to the extent of helping organise bribes from locals seeking political favours. These are channelled via the police station to the politician's next door office. Finally, on election day Paddy and his cronies are shown ballot-rigging. Just as he is gloating over his victory Paddy is rudely woken from his dream by the sound of the whistle summoning him back to work.[25] The dream technique and slapstick format of the film only served barely to disguise the anti-Irish message of the film.

One major concern of the Irish-American political leadership, if not the whole Irish-American community, was its commitment to Irish nationalism. As in Ireland, attitudes to Irish nationalism could level social class, if not religious, differences between the Irish. Indeed, Miller[26] goes so far as to assert that only 'the increasingly anachronistic rhetoric of Irish-American nationalism could unite and impel to concerted action Irish-America's diverse constituencies'. These, of course, were likely to exacerbate tensions between the Irish and the WASP establishment. In the years before the 1916 Rising, an event which not only alienated further many WASPs from Irish sympathies, but also disquieted middle-class Irish-Americans, political or 'rebel' films set in Ireland were fairly common.

In such films as *Rory O'More* (1911) and *Bold Emmet — Ireland's Martyr* (1915), both made in Ireland by the redoubtable Sidney Olcott, or *Ireland a Nation* (1914), which was made for an American company by Irish-born Walter MacNamara, anti-colonial feeling was given expression in historical tales usually set during 1798–1803. In *Rory O'More* the 1798 rebel escapes to the USA after being freed from the gallows by a sympathetic priest. In this film, and the longer *For Ireland's Sake* (1914), which has a similar story to *Rory O'More*, the rebel hero and his girlfriend are *en route* in the final scene to 'The Land of the Free'.[27] The 1916 Rising gave renewed, if temporary, impetus to the makers of radical nationalist films. Historical films set in Ireland continued to be made, such as *Brennon o' the Moor* (1916), about an adventurer/highwayman who escapes to America with his girlfriend, and *The Cry of Erin* (1916), the latest film adaptation of the poem, 'Shamus O'Brien', by Joseph Sheridan Le Fanu, which was written in 1840. Set in 1798 it tells how a captured rebel defends himself in court and when sentenced to death escapes the scaffold. Additional lines on migration to America were added to the poem by Samuel Lover while on a lecture tour of the USA in 1846: 'He has mounted his horse, on' soon he will be/ In America, darlint, the land of the free'.[28] These lines made it very popular amongst the Irish in America, and were used on at least one previous occasion when the film *Shamus O'Brien* was made in 1912.[29] A disguised version of the life of Sir Roger Casement, *Whom the Gods Destroy* (1916), which was banned in

Britain, and *The Irish Rebel* (1916), where the rebel escapes with his girlfriend to France, were also released in 1916. The latter film was probably a re-release of the 1912 film, *The O'Neill*.[30]

Most fighting in the Irish-American cinema did not involve the English but was between the Irish themselves. The largest number of films in which the Irish appeared in the early cinema was probably those where they were the butt of jokes and were caricatured in traditional stereotypical ways. These were often derived directly from vaudeville. Fighting was a regular feature of such films, and indeed continued to serve as the narrative resolution of many Irish-theme films well into the sound era. The donnybrook sequence in John Ford's *The Quiet Man* (1952) remains the classic example. The depiction of the Irish as professional fighters (and, indeed, in other sporting professions) was a major element of these films. Professional fighters John L. Sullivan and 'Gentleman Jim' Corbett were both the subject of biographical films, while the returned migrant, Sean Thornton (John Wayne), in *The Quiet Man* was also a fighter. It was a means whereby a member of the Irish-American working class (a foundry worker in Thornton's case) could improve on his lowly social status.

What many of the films of the silent era tend to demonstrate is that the Irish had little control over the content of the films made about them. By the mid-1910s new film production parameters and the changing nature of the Irish in America were reducing the number of specifically Irish ethnic films. With the release of *The Birth of a Nation* (1915), full-length and relatively costly feature films were firmly established. Many of the films released with Irish or ethnic backgrounds in the first half of the 1910s were shorts, less than fifteen or twenty minutes in length. The audience for these films was almost certainly first and foremost Irish. With a change in the means of film production larger budgets could only rarely be justified for specifically ethnic films. The main exceptions are the Irish-Jewish stories of the 1920s with a combined potential ethnic audience of almost ten millions.

Thus, we find that the total number of films centred on the Irish seems to decline as the 1910s wear on, though those made were longer, or feature-length films. Indeed, well before the end of the silent era the Irish become more integrated within narratives which do not have specifically Irish backgrounds, often as firemen, policemen, or boarding house keepers, or other professions deemed 'Irish'. As both film production and the position of the Irish in America altered, fewer films set in Ireland which lead to migration were made. In *How Molly Malone Made Good* (1915), for example, Molly's Irish origins are incidental to a story of how Molly is seeking to establish herself as a reporter. Indeed, the film was also referred to as *How Molly Made Good* indicating the relative unimportance of its Irish references.[31]

The end of the silent era in the late 1920s coincided with Irish migrants to the USA being reduced to about 1,200 per annum. As a result, sound cinema was to become almost exclusively concerned with second and third-generation Irish-Americans, or, in its reflections backwards, constructing an imagined history of the Irish in America.

Sound era

The sound era did not begin very auspiciously for the representation of the Irish migrant in the cinema. In *Smiling Irish Eyes* (1929), James Hall plays Rory O'More, an itinerant Irish musician who works in a peat bog. He leaves his girlfriend, Kathleen (Colleen Moore), behind when he migrates to the USA. During a theatrical production in which he is employed, he is seen kissing a girl by Kathleen, who has followed him to the USA. She then returns to Ireland in a huff. Rory and Kathleen are eventually reconciled when Rory arrives back in Ireland, and the whole family migrate to the USA. While this story may appear innocuous enough, its treatment was deemed repulsive, at least in Ireland.

Such was the negative impact of the film in Ireland, the first time 'Irish'-American voices could be heard in an American film, that a group of university students and others invaded the Dublin cinema where it was being shown and forced the cancellation of the rest of the film's run. Reflecting the widespread response in Irish reviews of the film, Mary Manning reported that when watching the film 'waves of nausea swept over me and the screen became a blur'. She added that Colleen Moore could be seen playing with pigs, a traditionally offensive Irish stereotype[32]. One wonders what might have been the audience response to some of the Irish-theme silent films when shown in America as well as in Ireland had sound cinema been available earlier in the century.

The sound era did continue with Irish themes, but because of the nature of sound itself, the hugely increased capitalisation of film production, and altering political and ideological concerns, some prominent Irish themes all but disappeared from the cinema. For example, Irish-Jewish films barely exist after 1933, while a repeat of the crudeness of *Smiling Irish Eyes*, itself probably a legacy of the silent period, was unlikely. In Depression-hit America of the early 1930s offence was to be avoided to any section of the cinema audience.

A barely perceptible theme during the silent era was the Irish gangster, but it was in this quintessentially early sound genre that the Irish made an immediate impact. During the Depression the gangster film, with its use of urban crime sounds — screeching car tyres and gun fire, for example — became instantly popular. Added to this new image of urban America was the rapid-fire, wise-cracking speech of Irish-American actor, James Cagney, who echoed on screen the popular anti-hero, but real crime, figures of the Midwest.

What *Little Caesar* (1930) did for the Italians, *The Public Enemy* (1931) did for Irish gangsters. It also made James Cagney a star in his portrayal of Tom Powers, a ruthless Prohibition-era Chicago gang leader. Almost all ethnic references in the film are Irish, though by 1931 Italian gangsters were effectively in control of the Chicago underworld following the St Valentine's Day Massacre of 1929, which all but eliminated Al Capone's Irish rivals, 'Bugs' Moran's gang. While *The Public Enemy* is often remembered solely for Cagney's infamous pushing of a half grapefruit into the face of his mistress, played by Mae Clarke, it does contain a theme which has recurred in both Irish-American literature and in earlier silent films: the centrality of the family to the Irish, and of the mother within that family.

Powers is shown early in the film as being from a poor, ordinary background. His life of crime is contrasted with his brother's pursuit of the work ethic. But, in choosing a life of crime, Powers 'violates the sanctity of the family'.[33] That criticism is strongly implied in the film's ending when Powers is expected home by his still devoted mother. Instead, his dead body is delivered to her, thus destroying the family unit. In choosing an Irish background for *The Public Enemy*, Warner Brothers were 'able to stress the warm extended family'[34] which was later to feature in many Cagney films, including *The Irish in US* (1935), a comedy about three Irish brothers, in which Cagney becomes a boxer, and features the 'mawkish sentimentality' of their mother.[35]

Cagney was to repeat his intense, staccato-voiced *Public Enemy* character in a number of other gangster roles, notably in his mother-fixated role in *The White Heat* (1949). The mixture of repressed sexuality and violent outpourings in these films was to be carried over into his role of IRA leader Sean Lenihan in the Irish War of Independence feature, *Shake Hands with the Devil* (1959). Cagney was also to prove a versatile actor, winning an Oscar for his portrayal of Irish-American song-and-dance man George M. Cohan in *Yankee Doodle Dandy* (1942). With the possible exceptions of Pat O'Brien, with whom he appeared in a number of films, and Spencer Tracy, Cagney, despite playing many mainstream non-Irish cinema roles, was the most identifiable 'Irish' actor in the USA.

Cagney played opposite O'Brien in one of the best-known transformations of the early 1930s gangster films, *Angels with Dirty Faces* (1938). In this film, Cagney and O'Brien share a similar Brooklyn Irish background, though they choose different careers: Cagney, a gangster, O'Brien, a priest. Seeking to reform young offenders, O'Brien tries to persuade Cagney to give up his life of crime, while recognising that he too might have taken that path. After Cagney is captured and sentenced to death, O'Brien seeks to convince him to die a coward's death, so as to de-glamorise himself in the eyes of the potential young hoods who idolise him. In the end, O'Brien gets his wish as Cagney appears to scream for forgiveness before his execution. While this outburst has the desired effect on the youngsters, the viewer is hardly convinced by this narrative response to censorship pressures.

Such endings, and the introduction to the screen in the 1930s of a strong role for a Catholic priest, were in large part a response to film censorship agitation, which had been orchestrated by the Irish-dominated American Catholic Church. Under pressure from the Catholic Church in the late 1920s, the film industry introduced a voluntary Production Code. It was written by a prominent Catholic layman and film trade publisher, Martin I. Quigley, and an influential Jesuit academic, Father Daniel Lord. It sought to 'establish once and for all a standard for moral values in a popular mass medium'.[36] However, with the film industry in a serious economic crisis during the Depression, the voluntary code was frequently broken with more films about sex, glimpses of nudity and *risqué* language than previously attempted.[37] The voluntary code, though, had led to a severe pruning of the script for *Public Enemy*.[38] In 1931 more stringent and binding enforcement of the Code was introduced. Nevertheless, still dissatisfied, in 1933 the Catholic Church decided to establish a nation-wide Legion of Decency which it was hoped would replace existing state and federal censorship authorities. It would organise boycotts of films which it deemed indecent or obscene. Launched in April 1934 and supported by other churches, the Legion's members were encouraged to sign a pledge which committed them to boycott films on the Legion's prohibited list. Within ten weeks of the pledge being launched it was claimed that as many as 11 million people had signed it.[39]

Fearful for their economic survival, the film producers announced that a Production Code Administration (PCA) would be set up, which would be headed by an Irish Catholic, Joseph Breen, who already worked for the Hollywood producers' own watchdog, the Motion Picture Producers and Distributors Association. At the PCA, Breen was to have complete authority in approving, censoring or rejecting films made or distributed by the Hollywood distributors. Supported by Quigley, Breen was interrogated and approved by the Catholic Bishops' committee concerned with the cinema. It was not until 1953, when distributor United Artists resigned from the PCA and released Otto Preminger's *The Moon is Blue*, despite Breen's refusal to approve it, that the PCA's power was effectively challenged. Breen retired shortly afterwards and the PCA was gradually dismantled and increasingly ignored as the decade went on.[40]

In the 1930s Catholic censors were further encouraged with the publication of the 1936 papal encyclical on the cinema, *Vigilanti Cura*, which was aimed at American Catholics in the first instance. The producers' response to these pressures is reflected in part by the introduction of the Irish-American Catholic priest as a screen character. He was played on a number of occasions by Pat O'Brien and Spencer Tracy. In addition to his *Angels* role, O'Brien played the Irish priest opposite Cagney in *The Fighting 69th* (1940) and in the title role in *Fighting Father Dunne* (1948), which is about a priest working in a slum, while Tracy played the real-life Catholic priest, Father Flanagan, in *Boys Town* (1938) and its sequel *Men of Boys Town* (1941). Barry Fitzgerald and Bing Crosby played Catholic priests in the Oscar-winning *Going My Way* (1944), while in its sequel, *The Bells of St Mary's* (1945), Crosby is joined by Ingrid Bergman as a nun.

While James Cagney and Pat O'Brien may have been the Irish-American film actors *par excellence*, John Ford was the Irish-American film director who towered above all American film-makers. Raoul Walsh, whose films are not discussed here, is perhaps the next most important American director from an Irish viewpoint, and John Huston, despite the infrequency of Irish resonances in his work, should also be acknowledged. While in Irish terms Ford is best known as the director of a series of sound films set in Ireland: (*The Informer* (1935), *The Plough and the Stars* (1936), *The Quiet Man* (1952), *The Rising of the Moon* (1957) and, partly, *Young Cassidy* (1964)), only two of these films even obliquely address migration to America. True, Sean Thornton leaves the USA to return to Ireland in *The Quiet Man* to escape both from his personal torment after killing a man in the ring and from money-obsessed America, and, conversely, Gypo Nolan's half-demented fantasy in *The Informer* is to get the money that will pay for his sea passage to America. However, neither film directly addresses the Irish in the USA.

Ford's first involvement in an Irish film story was in his brother, Francis's, film, *The Doorways of Destruction* (1915), in which he played the role of Frank Feeney, a member of an Irish Regiment in the British army in India, which succeeds in relieving the siege of a town after the English regiments fail to do so. He was also the film's assistant director. Ford's most extensive treatment of the Irish in America occurs during the 1920s. In 1920, when he was already a prolific director of westerns, Ford chose the cinematically popular topic of Irish-American politics as the subject of what is probably his first non-western film. *The Prince of Avenue A* (1920) concerns Boss Patrick O'Connor who has a favoured candidate for mayor, William Tomkins. However, O'Connor's son, Barry, (who is played by 'Gentleman Jim' Corbett), is thrown out of Tomkins's house for uncouth behaviour towards Tomkins's daughter, Mary. When Patrick O'Connor reacts angily to this, Tomkins, worried about his political future, goes with his daughter to apologise to O'Connor. She then consents to accompany Barry to a Grand Ball. There, Edgar Jones, O'Connor's political rival, insults Mary. Barry takes on Jones and his associates, and having defeated them, is happily reunited with Mary.[41]

Ford placed an Irish surveyor and foreman, Davy Brandon, played by George O'Brien, at the centre of *The Iron Horse* (1924), his first major western. He had made perhaps as many as 40 westerns before this film, though it is qualitatively different from any of these previous films. At its core is the successful completion in 1869 of the transcontinental railway enterprise which symbolically united the American nation. National unity is clearly signalled from the beginning of the film when the young Abraham Lincoln is introduced. Later Lincoln signs the bill to allow the project to proceed. In the film, Brandon, who is not as explicitly Irish as a trio of ex-soldiers, Sergeant Slattery (Francis Powers), Corporal Casey (J. Farrell MacDonald) and Private Mackay (James Welch), is in charge of a diverse group of ethnic workers: Chinese, Italians, Irish and others. The three Irish soldiers serve both as comic relief and as the one group whose identity is sympathetically presented as separate from the 'furriners', especially the Italians, whose refusal to confront hostile Indians is deemed cowardly, while their refusal to work without pay or food is ridiculed. Casey declares to one of his Irish colleagues that he 'knocked five down and still they won't work'. Brandon is also keen to promote the enterprise but has a more direct relationship with his WASP employer. In the process of aiding the project he overcomes a corrupt mining engineer and an unscrupulous landowner. In the end Brandon drives the last 'golden' spike to 'consumate' his father's dream of 'the buckle in a girdle of a continent'. Meanwhile, the ethnic tensions are resolved as an Italian announces: 'Me, Irish now, too — I marry Nora Hogan!', while Casey complains at the waste as a bottle of champagne is broken on the train.

Irish ambition in the film does not progress beyond assimilation into American society, which is represented in the film by Anglo leadership. To underpin this integration, the two rail crews join together in the final scene to celebrate the unity of the nation. One writer has observed that in *The Iron Horse* Ford places Irish values 'squarely in service to Anglo-American progress. Controlled labor and industrial development are finally more important than a multiethnic male community.'[42] Be that as it may, Ford's Irish films usually tended to be tinted green before all else. It may not be too far-fetched to speculate that Ford's promotion of the unity of the American nation in *Iron Horse* was connected to Ireland, released as it was the year after the Irish Civil War had ended, and set, of course, within four years of the ending of the American Civil War. When Cecil B. de Mille tackled the same key moment in

American history in *Union Pacific* (1939), the Irish dimension is largely confined to the railway's postmistress, Mollie (Barbara Stanwyck), who becomes involved with an heroic ex-soldier.

The post-American Civil War Irish soldiers are also a significant feature of other Ford westerns. This is unsurprising given that the Irish accounted for twenty per cent of the entire army, the force's largest ethnic group.[43] Besides celebrating the Irish military contribution to the Union and in the Indian wars through the roles of the ex-soldiers in *Iron Horse*, Ford also featured Irish soldiers in such key roles as Sergeant Mulcahy in *Fort Apache* (1948), Sergeant Quincannon in *She Wore a Yellow Ribbon* (1949) and *Rio Grande* (1950), all three played by Victor McLaglen. Irish involvement in the American military was also seen in Ford's 1926 film, *The Blue Eagle*, in which two groups of First World War Irish-American civilian rivals, led by D'Arcy and Ryan, continue their street rivalry in the Navy, until a submarine attack forces a truce. Civilians again, their rivalry is once more suspended when they unite to overcome a gang of drug smugglers. When this task is completed, they return to their previous behaviour: fighting each other.[44]

Almost thirty years later in *The Long Gray Line* (1955) Ford traced the career of an athletics trainer at West Point, Sergeant Marty Maher, who had migrated from Ireland as a young man, and had worked at the academy for fifty years. Initially unhappy with his role in the academy, 'his eventual assimilation is unconvincing'.[45] Indeed, as in *Fort Apache*, Ford's attempt 'to fuse the elitist traditions of the officer corps with the Irish-American experience doesn't work'.[46] Quite simply, the gulf between the two traditions was too great. Other film-makers also highlighted the Irish in the American military, most notably in *The Fighting 69th* (1940), about the legendary Irish-American regiment, and *The Sullivans* (1944), which was based on the true Second World War story of how five Irish-American brothers lost their lives at Guadalcanal.

During the 1920s Ford made two films set in both Ireland and America. *The Shamrock Handicap* (1926) concerns Sir Miles, a poverty-stricken Anglo-Irish landlord, who is forced to sell some of his horses to an American, who returns to the USA with them and an Irish jockey, Neil. Bringing a prize filly himself to the USA, Sir Miles, accompanied by his daughter, Sheila, who is in love with Neil, enters it in a race. The horse wins when ridden by Neil, and, financially solvent again, Sir Miles, Neil and Sheila return to Ireland, where the young couple plan to marry. *Mother Machree* (1928) begins in Ireland in 1899 when a widow, Ellen McHugh, and her son, Brian, migrate to the USA. When it is discovered that Ellen works as a fairground act, a 'half-woman', to pay for Brian's education, Brian has to be given up for adoption. Years later when Ellen has been the long-time servant of an upper-class couple, and having raised their daughter, Edith, Brian re-enters her life. He meets Edith and they fall in love, which in turn leads to mother and son being reunited. The film ends on the eve of war as Brian enlists in the army.

Ford made one notable sound film about the Irish in urban America. Adapted from Edwin O'Connor's novel, *The Last Hurrah* (1958) centres on Frank Skeffington, long-time mayor of a thinly-disguised Boston. A politician since the days of Al Smith in the 1920s, he is facing his last battle for re-election. The film, like the book, focuses on the operation of Democratic Party and ethnic working-class politics, and the relationship between Skeffington (Spencer Tracy) and his playboy and unsympathetically presented son. Representing a more hedonistic generation, the son has little time for the political shenanigans of his father. Yet Skeffington's life-long struggle against the WASP establishment continues, epitomised during the mayoral contest by his fight to gain financing for housing for low-income people. It is through the eyes of Adam, Skeffington's nephew, that the outsider's view of big city machine politics is viewed with an increasingly sympathetic eye. When Skeffington loses his final electoral battle, and, after suffering a heart attack is dying as the film ends, it is clear that an era in city politics has ended.

A decade before the release of *The Last Hurrah*, in 1948, *Up in Central Park* was made. It, too, concerned big city politics: this time, New York and the workings of Tammany Hall at the beginning of the century. It is a musical in which recently-arrived migrants, Rosie Moore and her father, are drawn into the Tammany Hall world of Boss Tweed and his cronies. Rosie falls for Tweed, who puts her father on the payroll. Matthews, a crusading reporter from the *New York Times*, who is seeking to expose the corruption at City Hall, falls in love with Rosie. Joined by the disillusioned Mr Moore, Matthews gets the vital evidence to expose Tweed and his associates. Rosie is then reunited with her father and with Matthews, a picture of Anglo uprightness and new migrant Irish values joining in harmony. *The Last Hurrah*, it can safely be said, represented a more accurate account of the tension between the Anglo and Irish political cultures.

The post-War years also brought a new sensibility to the cinema with realist productions shot on location such as Elia Kazan's *Panic in the Streets* (1950). Kazan's *On the Waterfront* (1954) applied the same treatment to a predominantly Irish milieu. In this realist account of trade union corruption and fear in New Jersey's docklands, Marlon Brando played Terry, the union strong man, who enforces the corrupt practices on the docks. When a docker is murdered, and a crusading Catholic priest is assigned to the docks, Terry's loyalty to the gang begins to waver. After he testifies against the racketeers to a state crime commission he is brutally beaten. By then, though, the gang's power has been broken and Terry leads the dockers back to work.

Other urban Irish communities were also introduced to the screen in the post-War years. In *A Tree Grows in Brooklyn* (1945), also directed by Elia Kazan, the trials and tribulations of a turn-of-the-century New York working-class Irish family are explored in the context of an alcoholic father and a mother seeking to improve her lowly economic and social status. The working-class world of the Chicago Irish in the 1920s was the centre of the disappointing 1960 feature-length adaptation of James T. Farrell's ground-breaking *Studs Lonigan* trilogy. The Bronx Irish were to be seen in *The Catered Affair* (1956). In this comedy, a mother, played by Bette Davis, wishes to invite hundreds to a wedding breakfast to celebrate her daughter's marriage. The event as perceived by the mother is to serve as a form of restitution for her daughter's frugal upbringing and also perhaps act as a means by which the estranged parents might be reconciled. The other family members determine that such expenditure of their hard-earned savings is a waste and the wedding proceeds in its original modest format. Nevertheless, the parents do find a new beginning and the hope of bridging their differences.

Though of a different social class, another dysfunctional Irish family was to be found in the adaptation of Eugene O'Neill's autobiographical play, *A Long Day's Journey into Night* (1962). Set in Connecticut during one day in 1912, Edmund, (O'Neill), a young writer, returns home ill having worked as a merchant seaman. His mother, recently returned from treatment for drug addiction, his actor-father and alcoholic brother, make up a family menagerie which leads to bitter quarrelling fuelled by alcohol. *The Subject was Roses* (1968), from Frank D. Gilroy's Pulitzer Prize-winning play, also explored Irish-American family disharmony. Set in the Bronx at the end of the Second World War, a young veteran, Timmy Cleary, returns home to find his parents' marriage in disarray. Failing to reconcile his parents, Timmy decides to leave in order to make a life of his own. With his parting at least a temporary family truce is achieved.

With such rare exceptions as *The Subject was Roses*, by the late 1960s little distinguished the cinematic representations of Irish-Americans from other groups. Certainly the icons could be different, and were more likely to be religious than national.[47] In *The Subject was Roses*, for example, Timmy's father becomes angry when he discovers that his son does not go to mass anymore. Nevertheless, the professions where the Irish had been most frequently represented, policemen and firemen, for example, were still seen as 'Irish' if only through the characters' names rather than through other distinguishing ethnic features. In *The French Connection* films, for example, the real-life 'Popeye' Doyle's Irish-American background is not alluded to. Only in the television biography, *Popeye Doyle* (1979), is there a reference to his Irishness, and then only in clichéd comments about his drinking habits. Similarly in *Backdraft* (1991), the two generations of the Irish-American family of firefighters and their colleagues could not be easily identified from the film's script. For many it is only in the names of the characters, the McCaffreys in particular, that their ethnic origin is known.

Nevertheless, interest in the Irish role in the formation of the American nation and its multiethnic identity has not disappeared. The release in 1992 of *Far and Away* reminds us of a potentially serious omission not just from this history of the Irish migrant and film but of Irish-American historiography in general. The researcher of the representation of the Irish in early American cinema in particular is confronted with a problem which has similarities with that facing other historians of Irish-America. It is how to weigh up the urban-rural balance of the Irish in America. While the Irish presence in certain urban locations is well documented, a universal urban profile of the Irish in the context of the rest of American society is lacking, let alone the more difficult task of profiling rural dwellers.[48] Similarly in the cinema. While the Irish in Manhattan's working-class districts, for example, are a regular feature of cinema in the 1910s, they *may* also be as prominent in rural dramas or 'westerns'. While the Irish in urban American silent cinema can be identified by the shorthand of inter-title Irish 'brogue' or characters' names, as well as film content and location, the same shorthand does not seem to apply to early cinema westerns. This tends, perhaps erroneously, to reinforce the view that the Irish were not prominent either in rural America in general or in the cinema of rural America at least until the films of John Ford. It is all the more intriguing, therefore, that the most prominent film so far of the 1990s of the Irish in America has been a migration story which begins in rural Ireland, has a central section amongst the Boston Irish, but unlike the vast majority of its predecessors continues its narrative route to the American West.

Far and Away, a $50 million romantic comedy, is set during 1892 and 1893 when Joseph (Tom Cruise) leaves his family home and small tenant farm following eviction, and emigrates to America. In one of the many narrative twists in the film, Joseph meets up with Shannon, played by Nicole Kidman, daughter of his father's landlord and the man untimately responsible for his father's violent death and the family's eviction. Arriving in Boston together, the young couple, separated by both class and religion, (chastely) share a room in a brothel. While Shannon, made penniless on her arrival in Boston as a result of theft, works in a poultry factory, Joseph proves adept with his fists, one of the many Irish stereotypes which the film reinforces. Another, and much more offensive stereotype, is seen early in the film when Joseph's brother, drunk and with a bottle of poteen in his hand, ridicules him as he is ploughing a field, a symbol of Joseph's determination to 'better' himself. At least Irish boxing heroes in America, such as John L. Sullivan and 'Gentleman Jim' Corbett, were symbols of native pride and helped define ethnic identity.

Joseph, though, has his boxing earnings stolen from him by his Irish mentors after his defeat by the Italian champion. Evicted from their room, Shannon and Joseph wander the city streets. Shannon is followed to America by her parents and her mother's preferred 'beau' for her, Stephen (Thomas Gibson), who is also Joseph's father's assailant. Shannon, wounded by a bullet as she and Joseph run from a house they have burgled, is reluctantly delivered by Joseph to her parents. He then abandons the hostile city and goes West. While working on building a railway he still dreams of his quest for land. He joins a wagon-train, and eventually arrives in Oklahoma where the film climaxes in the Cherokee Strip land rush of 16 September 1893. It only remains for Joseph and Shannon to be reunited, the film's final coincidence happening on the eve of the land rush. At the climax of the film's most spectacular scenes, the couple succeed in staking a claim to a favoured piece of land ahead of Shannon's abandoned fiancé. Simultaneously, and in keeping with the film's earlier anti-landlord rhetoric, Shannon's parents are seen staking a claim to their own patch of land. However, they are clearly cheaters ('Sooners' in contemporary parlance) as they have sneaked into the area ahead of the land rush. The film's final image showing Joseph and Shannon raise a green flag as they stake their plot of land summarises the overall ideological thrust of the film. With its obvious resonance back to Ireland, the denouement ensures the collapse of the film's range of Irish contradictions into young love: Catholic and Protestant; landlord and tenant; even nationalist and unionist are all subsumed in America's lush (and literally) green wilderness. It is not an image one readily associates with the majority of the Irish in America.

It is probably fair to say that no migration film has so shamelessly and directly strayed beyond the obvious material benefits of the USA for Irish migrants, as represented in, for example, the very first film in the genre, *The Lad from Old*

Ireland (1910). Despite the film's compressed and somewhat bizarre Irish periodisation,[49] *Far and Away* leaves behind both inhospitable rural Ireland and the brutal urbanism of East Coast ghetto life, to rediscover a supposedly socially, if not historically, free land. Native Americans are at least acknowledged as observers of the land rush that confiscated their territory. In this ironic twist the landless Irish tenant farmer and the daughter of his family's landlord combine to raise the green flag of Ireland above the new territory. It is a peculiar form of Irish imperialism. The beloved West of Ireland is deemed tainted by grubby materialism and alcohol, while American society with its 'democratic' grabbing of land is hailed as the new Arcadia. Perhaps the Irish in the American cinema are now so de-ethnicised (*Far and Away* and *Backdraft* director Ron Howard is of part-Irish extraction) that they can be interchangeable with other traditions, even WASPs, who of course can be said to have organised such western expansion. The Irish appear to be in command, even though social and economic power in America lies elsewhere. Such appearances, perhaps, reflect the actual reality of present-day Irish-America.

Notes

1. If this chapter focuses on the United States this is simply because there have been far more films made about the Irish migrant in the American cinema than in all other cinemas combined. A helpful early survey of the Irish in the American cinema is Roger B. Dooley, 'The Irish on the screen', Parts 1 and 2, *Films in Review*, Volume VIII, No. 5, May 1957, and Volume VIII, No. 6, June 1957. Though there are contextual limitations, both cinematic and Irish, in all three, the following books are worth consulting: Lee Lourdeaux, *Italian and Irish filmmakers in America*, Temple University Press, Philadelphia, 1990; James M. Curran, *Hibernian green on the silver screen: the Irish and American movies*, Greenwood Press, New York/Westport, Connecticut/London, 1989; and Anthony Slide, *The cinema and Ireland*, McFarland & Co, Jefferson, North Carolina/London, 1988.

   There is an interesting series of films concerning Americans and Irish-Americans visiting Ireland which are outside the focus of this chapter. Two in particular should be noted: *The Luck of the Irish* (1948), which is discussed in Kevin Rockett, Luke Gibbons and John Hill, *Cinema and Ireland*, Croom Helm, London, 1987; Syracuse University Press, Syracuse, New York, 1988; Routledge, London, 1988, pp. 227–8, and Neil Jordan's *High Spirits* (1989). This latter film concerns a group of Americans who are staying at a castle-hotel which has advertised for guests declaring that it is haunted. Their arrival, however, unleases supernatural powers and they then come up against some 'real' Irish ghosts in a *Ghostbusters*-type finale. The early part of the film, in which the guests arrive at the hotel, is an ironic reworking of the beginning of *The Luck of the Irish*.

   Irish Cinema has produced few fictional acounts of migration. A section of the feature-length adaptation of Charles Kickham's novel, *Knocknagow* (1918), is set in America when some of the protagonists are forced to migrate for economic reasons. See Rockett *et al.*, *Cinema and Ireland*, pp. 18–23, for a discussion of the film. A film version of Brian Friel's play, *Philadelphia Here I Come*, was made by an American company in Ireland in 1970.

   Britain and Australia in particular produced occasional films about Irish migration. In the case of Britain, much of its Irish-theme sound cinema was concerned with political or military events in Ireland, though the Irish were represented even more frequently in comic roles.

Irish migration, as such, rarely featured in the British cinema. In *Let's Be Famous* (1939), for example, Jimmy O'Dea plays an Irish postman whose vocal talent leads him to the BBC. *Another Shore* (1948) featured a feckless Irish civil servant, ironically named Gulliver, who fantasises about migrating to a South Seas island. Meeting a girl, he eventually settles for marriage, and goes back to work, with the result that he fails to leave Ireland. It was not until the 1960s, with the adaptation of Edna O'Brien's short story, 'A Woman by the Seaside', as *I Was Happy Here* (1965), that migration from rural Ireland to urban Britain was explored. In this film a young woman leaves her husband in London to return to the rural Irish environment of her childhood. Another British-made film about Irish migration was Irish-born Thaddeus O'Sullivan's formally innovative *On a Paving Stone Mounted* (1978). *Paving Stone* explored migrants' memory of home while in London, and examined the migrant's interactions on a visit to Ireland. O'Sullivan made an earlier short film, *A Pint of Plain* (1975), which also explored the lives of Irish migrants in London. For a discussion of both films see Rockett *et al.*, *Cinema and Ireland*, pp. 140–2. One film from the 1980s is worth noting: *No Surrender* (1985) is set in a Liverpool club where the conflicting religious and national allegiances of two elderly groups, one from the Orange Lodge, and the other from a Catholic Social Club, are brought out in a biting satire set on New Year's Eve.

The first major Australian film was *The Story of the Kelly Gang* (1906). This was also the first of many fiction films concerned with outlaw Ned Kelly, whose family background was Irish. Another important event involving the Irish in Australia was the Ballarat goldfields rebellion of 1854, which became a vehicle for the expression of Australian nationalism. Deriving their names from one of the rebellion's most famous incidents, the Eureka Stockade, two films with this title, made in 1907 and 1949, the latter an English production, depicted the events. A 16mm feature, *Stockade* (1971), also explored the rebellion. Probably the most widely seen film about the Irish in Australia is *The Irishman* (1978) from Elizabeth O'Conner's historical novel of the same name. Set in the 1920s, it explores the response to progress in a gold-mining region of Queensland by Paddy Doolan, who works with a team of Clydesdales, and his family. Resisting the transportation revolution, Paddy chooses to retire when his Clydesdales are no longer economically viable.

2. Charles Fanning in his *The Irish voice in America: Irish-American fiction from the 1760s to the 1980s*, University Press of Kentucky, Kentucky, 1990, Chapter 7, argues that there was a definite break between nineteenth and twentieth-century Irish-American writing during the first three decades of this century. As this coincides with the silent period, could cinema have been at least partly responsible for this? Fanning also usefully discusses 'slum fiction', or realist writing about the Irish-American working class during the late nineteenth and early twentieth centuries. This explores the terrain where some of the films made about the Irish are set (see especially pp. 176–97).

3. Lester D. Friedman in his *Hollywood's image of the Jew*, Frederick Ungar Publishing Co., New York, 1982, p. 9, reports that between 1900 and 1929 'approximately 230 films featured clearly discernible Jewish characters — a figure far surpassing the number of films featuring other ethnic types'. I beg to disagree with this assessment as I have identified for those years more than twice this number of films in which Irish characters are identifiable.

4. Before the rise of the five reel plus feature film, epitomised by *The Birth of a Nation* (1915), film producers made films targeted at specific ethnic audiences. However, with the transformation during the previous decade of the cinematic institution from an artisanal and small-scale production sector to an industry organised along

capitalist lines, with its attendant division of labour and greater capitalisation, there was a need to 'upgrade' the film product to attract the middle classes to the cinema while simultaneously squeezing out the 'rough trade' from cinemas and engaging in a form of 'ethnic cleansing' of the cinema product itself. The twofold result of this change was the creation of first-run cinemas (for the middle classes in business districts and near shopping arcades) and neighbourhood cinemas (in ethnic and working-class areas), while downgrading the importance of a specifically ethnic film-making practice. An ethnic cinema did continue to be produced but it tended to remain within the more modest production parameters of what would later be characterised as the 'B' film. For a selection from the recent rich scholarship on early cinema see the collection of articles edited by Thomas Elsaesser, *Early cinema: space, frame, narrative*, British Film Institute, London, 1990.

5. For a discussion of the films Olcott made in Ireland, see Rockett *et al.*, *Cinema and Ireland*, pp. 7–12.
6. *Bioscope*, 28 April 1910, p. 41; *Variety*, 26 March 1910.
7. *Moving Picture World*, 10 February 1912, p. 510.
8. Kerby A. Miller, *Emigrants and exiles: Ireland and the Irish exodus to North America*, Oxford University Press, New York/London, 1988, p. 502.
9. *Moving Picture World*, 9 March 1907, p. 10. Kemp Niver, *Library of Congress paper print collection*, 1985, p. 103.
10. *Moving Picture World*, 2 July 1910, p. 37.
11. *American Film Institute catalog of feature films 1911–1920*, University of California Press, Berkeley, 1989.
12. *American Film Institute catalog of feature films 1911–1920*.
13. *Moving Picture World*, 1 February 1913, p. 494.
14. Miller, *Emigrants and exiles*, 1988, p. 499.
15. *Moving Picture World*, 22 June 1912, p. 1156.
16. *Bioscope*, 21 November 1912, supplement, p. xxxvii.
17. Niver, *Library of Congress paper print collection*, 1985, pp. 177–8.
18. Miller, *Exiles and emigrants*, 1988, p. 494
19. *Moving Picture World*, 10 May 1915, p. 1168.
20. *American Film Institute catalog of feature films 1921–1930*.
21. *American Film Institute catalog of feature films 1921–1930*.
22. *Moving Picture World*, 22 June 1907, p. 252.
23. Kevin Brownlow, *Behind the mask of innocence*, Jonathan Cape, London, 1990, p. 214–5.
24. Charles Musser, *Before the Nickelodeon: Edwin S. Porter and the Edison Manufacturing Company*, University of California Press, Berkeley/Los Angeles/London, 1991, p. 69.
25. *Moving Picture World*, 26 February 1916, p. 1360.
26. Miller, *Exiles and emigrants*, 1988, pp. 494–5.
27. *Moving Picture World*, 17 January 1914, p. 526.
28. Quoted Carl Wittke, *The Irish in America*, Louisiana State University, Baton Rouge, Louisiana, 1956, pp. 242–3.
29. 'And soon we will be in America, the land of the Free', is how the final inter-title of the film expresses it.
30. See *Bioscope*, 22 February 1912, supplement, p. x, for an account of *The O'Neill*, and *Moving Picture World*, 10 June 1916, p. 1932, for a summary of *The Irish Rebel*. As the latter film was released one month after the 1916 Rising, it was probably intended to cash in on the effect these events had on Irish-Americans.
31. *Variety*, 22 November 1915, p. 21.

32. *Irish Statesman*, 22 February 1930, p. 497. For a detailed account of the controversy see Rockett *et al.*, *Cinema and Ireland*, pp. 53–5.
33. Nick Roddick, *A New Deal in entertainment: Warner Brothers in the 1930s*, British Film Institute, London, 1983, p. 106.
34. Roddick, *A New Deal*, 1983, p. 106.
35. *Monthly Film Bulletin*, 1935, p. 104.
36. Robert Sklar, *Movie-made America: a cultural history of American movies*, Chappell & Co, London, 1978, p. 173; orig. 1975.
37. Sklar, *Movie-made America*, 1978, p. 174.
38. See Henry Cohen (ed.), *The public enemy*, University of Wisconsin Press, Wisconsin, 1981, pp. 29–33. Attention should be drawn to *The Cotton Club* (1984) as it explores the milieu of New York's gangland during the same period. Real-life Irish gangster, Owney Madden, owner of the Cotton Club, is a central character in the film as he crosses paths with the rising Italian gangsters. More recently, Martin Scorsese's *Goodfellas* (1990), with its Irish-Italian narrator, Henry Hill, and Phil Joanou's *State of Grace* (1990), place the Irish in more contemporary gangster milieux. While *Goodfellas* has received much attention for its innovative style, *State of Grace* is set more firmly within an Irish environment.

   In this film Terry Noonan (Sean Penn) returns to Hell's Kitchen, one of New York City's original Irish ghettos, after many years' absence. 'The neighbourhood's disappearing in a tide of yuppies and dogshit', one of the characters declares, while another nostalgically complains that 'they could at least have left ten blocks for the Irish'. It is not just the neighbourhood which is changing, but ethnic loyalties as well. On his return, Terry meets an old friend, Jackie Flannery (Gary Oldham), who is one of the local Irish gangsters led by his brother, Frankie (Ed Harris). Frankie is trying to create an alliance with the local Italian Mafia but, unknown to the Irish gangsters, Terry is an undercover cop sent down from Boston to prevent the alliance. Turning on his own, indeed an 'informer', (as ultimately Henry Hill is in *Goodfellas*), and, ironically, on St. Patrick's Day, Terry walks into a bar and kills Frankie and his gang. This assault, though, is at least in part, revenge for Frankie killing his own brother to placate the irate Italians.

   Based loosely on the New York Irish gang, the Westies, the film features an array of Irish musical talent on the sound-track, but its cinematic resonances are Italian-American: Scorsese's *Mean Streets* (1972) and Francis Ford Coppola's *Godfather* films, an indication that the reworking of the gangster movie in the modern era did not come from the Irish. Indeed, while most contemporary gangster films still focus on the same ethnic groups as in the past, Italian, Irish, Jewish and WASP, as Mark Winkour points out, ('Eating children is wrong', *Sight and Sound*, p. 11, Vol. 1, no 7 (NS), November 1991), 'Perhaps the Coens' *Miller's Crossing* (1990), replete with Jews manipulating Irish who are killing Italians who are killing both Italians and Jews, is the best example of the resurfacing of traditional ethnic tensions'. However, *Miller's Crossing*, like *Goodfellas* and *The Untouchables*, takes place in the past and, as a result, does not engage with current ethnic or social tensions.
39. Sklar, *Movie-made America*, 1978, p. 173.
40. Sklar, *Movie-made America*, p. 295.
41. Peter Bogdonovich, *John Ford*, Studio Vista, London, 1967, p. 116.
42. Lourdeaux, *Italian and Irish filmmakers in America*, 1990, p. 98.
43. Edward Buscombe (ed.), *The BFI companion to the Western*, Andre Deutsch/BFI Publishing, London, 1988, p. 159.
44. See Lourdeaux, *Italian and Irish Filmmakers in America*, 1990, pp. 100–1.
45. Curran, *Hibernian green on the silver screen*, 1989, p. 82.

46. Curran, *Hibernian green on the silver screen*, p. 82. An argument could be made that all Ford's films are 'Irish' at some level, while John Wayne, especially in Ford's westerns, can often be regarded as 'Irish', notwithstanding the absence of an Irish name or specific reference to Irishness in his character.

47. The one notable exception to this is *The Outsider* (1979) in which an Irish-American, influenced by his grandfather's tales about the Black and Tans, goes to Northern Ireland to join the present-day IRA, where he is used for propaganda purposes.

    By way of contrast, *Patriot Games* (1992), from Tom Clancy's novel of the same name, turns such Irish-American support for Irish political violence on its head by having its central character, Irish-American, Jack Ryan (Harrison Ford), save Lord Holmes (James Fox), a cousin of the Queen (the Prince and Princess of Wales in the book) from kidnapping by an ultra-violent splinter group of the IRA. The group's motivations are then largely channelled into attempts to kill Ryan, who returns to work for the CIA to aid the destruction of the group. The book's often hostile view of matters Irish and Irish-American is reinforced by simple historical inaccuracies. For example, Clancy reports erroneously that the INLA, rather than the IRA, killed Lord Mountbatten. The film's ideological focus is on family values and the preservation of the family unit against the outside terrorist threat. The film, like the book, also serves as a vehicle for right-wing, and often ignorantly simplistic, views about political violence.

48. The problem is not confined to the urban/rural balance, but to the categories of professions of the Irish in rural America. For example, those who worked in building the transcontinental communications infrastructure, roads and railways especially, and those employed in coal-mining, can hardly be classified as rural dwellers as their life-styles and frames of reference probably had more in common with urban industrial workers than with 'farmers' or 'cowboys'.

    See Marjorie R. Fallows, *Irish Americans: identity and assimilation*, Prentice-Hall, Englewood Cliffs, N.J, 1979, especially pp. 68ff, for a discussion of social class variations and rural/urban differences amongst the Irish in America. See also D. H. Akenson, 'The historiography of the Irish in the United States', *The Irish World Wide*, vol. 2, chapter 4.

49. Amongst the features of *Far and Away* which do not ring true for an Irish viewer are the following: the eviction depicted is more akin to the violent phases of the 1879–82 Land War than events of 1892, by which time legislative provisions were already peacefully transferring land holdings to tenants, while the burning of the 'Big House' is most obviously associated with the Civil War of 1922–3 when almost 200 such houses were burned down by the anti-Treaty forces. The choice of 1892, a year many would associate with Douglas Hyde's cultural manifesto, 'The necessity for de-Anglicising Ireland', as the time when the Irish events take place was, no doubt, determined by the narrative's need to situate the film's climax in September 1893, when the Oklahoma land rush took place, rather than any concern with the contemporaneous accuracy of the Irish events depicted.

9 Irish dance world-wide: Irish migrants and the shaping of traditional Irish dance

John P. Cullinane

Early references to Irish dancing

'It may be candidly said that there are no allusions whatever to dancing either in old or medieval Irish literature.'[1] From this it could be concluded that the early Irish never danced, but that is extremely unlikely. It is possible that the term used in Old Irish literature to describe a dancer or dancing has not been recognised.[2] Alternatively, it could be that dancing was extremely popular with the ancient Irish but somehow little or nothing was written about it. Such is the case even today when Irish dancing is extremely popular world-wide and yet very little has been researched or written about the dancing in comparison to other aspects of Irish culture.

The invitation 'come and dance with me in Ireland' from the anonymous English poem (c. 1300–50) has become well known since being used by President Mary Robinson in her inaugural speech.[3] However, as a reference this poem is both vague and unreliable and can hardly be accepted as proof of Irish dancing in Ireland at that time.

O'Sullivan includes a mention of a dance performed by the O'Driscolls of Baltimore in the company of the Mayor of Waterford on Christmas Eve in 1413. Unfortunately he gives no further data nor does he state the source of this very early reference.[4]

It is not until the sixteenth and seventeenth centuries that references to Irish dancing are found in Anglo-Irish and English literature. The earliest definite reference dates from 1549 when the *Rinnce Fada* (long dance) was described as being danced both in Scotland and in Ireland.[5] Dineley in 1681 stated the Irish were addicted to dance and he briefly described an unnamed dance similar to the *Rinnce Fada*.[6] This dance was also performed for King James when he landed at Kinsale.[7] The *Rinnce Fada* continued to be performed up to the nineteenth century but is rarely danced nowadays.[8] It is currently included in the Irish Dancing Commission publication of thirty figure dances.[9]

It appears that the earliest dances were performed by long lines of dancers and probably to jig time. A letter written in 1569 to Queen Elizabeth by Sir Henry Sidney refers to Irish jigs danced by the ladies of Galway who were said to have been magnificently dressed.[10] No description of the dance was given but it was almost certainly a group or figure dance in jig time. Solo jig dancing evolved at a later date.

The round dances were probably introduced later than the long dances at the time of the Norman invasion.[11] At this time the Carol was a popular round song-and-dance in France. The earliest dances were all group or social dances with simple footwork.

The more intricate solo dances, e.g. reels, jigs, slip jigs, hornpipes and solo set dances, almost certainly originated from the travelling dance master early in the eighteenth century. The most comprehensive published account of the origins of solo Irish dancing is given in my own two books.[12] The earliest solo dances were probably jigs. The Neals' collection of dance music published in 1726 did not include any reels.[13] Young (1792) referred to jigs and minuets in Kerry but made no reference to reels.[14] O'Farrell's collection published in 1804 included three reel tunes.[15] It appears that the reel tunes/music were not introduced into Ireland until about 1800 and so the reel as a dance is likewise of relatively recent origin in Ireland. Nowadays it is by far the most popular solo dance. Since reel tunes and dances were known in Scotland as far back as 1598 it is most likely that the dances came to Ireland from Scotland.[16]

The late Nellie Sweeney of Derry informed me that there was a great Scottish influence in Donegal and Derry dancing where reels and flings were popular and where the hornpipes danced were the Lancashire hornpipes.[17]

Little or nothing has been written about the origins of the solo dances except for my own recent publication.[12] So little has been published that future scholars might possibly be led to believe that the present-day Irish did not perform solo dancing.

The travelling dance master

The travelling dance master emerged sometime in the early eighteenth century, possibly as a result of the relaxation of penal laws against Catholicism and Irish culture. Often in earlier times the dance master was associated with the hedge schools. He had no fixed abode but travelled around on a well-defined circuit teaching in each town and village in his territory. He was, however, found only in Munster, especially in Kerry, Cork and to a lesser extent Limerick. His influence maintained these three areas as the dominant schools of Irish dancing up to the first half of the twentieth century.[18]

The travelling dance master taught dancing to both peasant and gentry and his own social standing was somewhere in between. He was responsible for introducing not only the solo dances and social dances, but he also taught the dances popular in France, especially the 'Set of Quadrilles', known in Ireland as 'the sets'.[19]

The last of the great Kerry travelling dance masters, Jerry Molyneaux, died as recently as 1973.[20] He had learnt from a line of travelling dance masters traceable back to 1820. Molyneaux learned from Ned Batt Walsh who in turn had learned from a man named Moore (or Mooreen, the diminutive form of his name) who was teaching in Kerry about 1820. Many of Molyneaux's pupils emigrated to America. They included the legendary Professor James T. McKenna who taught Irish dancing to thousands of pupils in the New York area from 1910 onwards. So many present-day dancers and teachers in the New York area can trace their dancing lineage back through various travelling dance masters over 170 years to Moore, the Kerry dance master.[21]

Among Molyneaux's famous pupils was Phil Cahill.[22] He resides near Tralee in County Kerry and is now over 90 years old. I first met with and recorded Phil when he attended a workshop on Irish dancing in Killarney and at 80 years of age danced five different traditional settings of *The Blackbird*. He was born in 1900 and had assisted Molyneaux with his classes and so is a direct link with the travelling dance masters. Phil recorded for me the system operated by Molyneaux as he travelled around teaching for a six-week term in each location before moving to the next. A 'benefit night' was held after three weeks and after six weeks.

The early dancing masters were all men. Women began teaching Irish dancing as a profession only as recently as the 1930s. Among the earliest women teachers were Lily Comerford and Essie Connolly of Dublin.[23] Nowadays numerous women teach Irish dancing throughout eight different countries. Prior to the twentieth century the pupils were almost exclusively males and mostly adults. More recently, however, there has been a major shift not only to women teachers but also to a situation where the pupils are almost exclusively female. The world-wide problem is how to attract males into what has become a predominantly female art form.

There has been a major shift in the ages of the dancers, especially in solo dance competitions. It has changed from almost exclusively adults to almost exclusively teenagers and children. Many children nowadays commence lessons as young as four or five years of age. Whatever the merits or demerits of this shift in age bracket, the result has been an enormous increase world-wide in both the number of teachers and number of pupils of Irish dancing. Parallel with this increase in numbers, and indeed partly responsible for it, has been the enormous increase in dancing competitions and interest in competition.

Popularity of Irish dancing world-wide

The influence of the World Championships

Throughout the world, from New Zealand to Australia, North America, England, Scotland and Ireland, some 15,000 Irish dancers compete annually in their own area to represent their own region at the World Irish Dancing Championships held in Ireland every year at Easter time. About 2,500 finalists participate in this eight-day event, one of the biggest cultural events of its kind in the world.

For many of the overseas competitors, their participation in the World Championships often constitutes their first visit to Ireland, the home of their ancestors, but for the accompanying parents and teachers it has become part of the annual visit 'home'. While most overseas Irish dancers and teachers are first or second-generation Irish, many have no Irish connections. Often they are attracted to Irish dancing by the strong Irish influence in their neighbourhood or in the schools. Irish migrants have spread the love of Irish dancing as far afield as Africa, South America and the South Pacific Islands.

Popularity of Irish dancing in North America

In North America where it is most popular, some 50,000 pupils learn Irish dancing. Over 2,000 of these participate annually in the North American Championships. In the continent of North America there are now more qualified registered Irish dancing teachers than there are in Ireland itself.[24] Many of these teachers fly thousands of miles on regular dancing class circuits, often unaware that they follow the 250 years-old profession of the travelling dance master. They are simply using updated transport means and modern teaching techniques including videos and tape recorders to teach the art form. In 1992 there were over 120 Irish dancing events registered with the North American Feis Commission at venues as far apart as New York, Arizona, New Orleans, Toronto, Montreal, Vancouver, Houston and many more.[25]

It must be admitted that the motivating force for dancers to travel several thousands of miles a year is as much, if not more, a love of competition than a true appreciation of their heritage. Competition world-wide has been the driving motivating force that has made the dancing as popular as it is.

Lack of present-day publications on dancing

While Irish dancing is extremely popular world-wide the overwhelming emphasis is on competition. Little if any attention has been paid to publications or research on Irish dancing, especially in the last fifty years or so. Dancers and teachers of Irish dancing themselves possess little or no knowledge and express little interest in the origins and history of their heritage. While my own recent publications have done much to remedy the situation, O'Rafferty was largely correct when he wrote in 1953: 'No book has yet been written dealing exclusively with the history of Irish dancing and, except for an essay or two, only scattered often contradictory allusions to the subject are to be found'.[26] In addition, it should be said that many of those who have written about Irish dancing were not Irish dancers themselves and frequently they have somewhat ambiguously written more about the music than the actual dancing itself.

Influence of migrants

Irish migrants have popularised Irish dancing so much that there are now many more Irish dancers and teachers resident outside Ireland than within Ireland.[24] These migrants and their protégés have a very great influence on what is happening in Irish dancing world-wide as well as within Ireland itself. Legislation passed by the Irish Dancing Commission is often strongly influenced by overseas opinions, while dance movements and costume trends are frequently dictated by overseas influences as much if not more than by influence from within Ireland. However, Irish migrants always had a strong influence on Irish culture as was especially the case with the London Irish in the nineteenth century.

Influence of the London Irish migrants

The Gaelic League was founded in Ireland in 1893. It was a revival movement dedicated to all aspects of Irish culture. It achieved much and branches were rapidly established throughout the world. Shortly after its foundation, in an effort to establish an identifiable national costume, it adopted the kilt as everyday dress for those members of the League. The adoption of the kilt was apparently based on Joyce's claim that it had been worn by the Irish before the sixteenth century.[27] McClintock examined Joyce's evidence with a well-balanced approached and dismissed each of Joyce's claims in turn as being incorrect or even non-existent. Ironically, the non-endemic Irish kilt is nowadays the greatest deterrent to young boys becoming interested in Irish dancing.

The London Irish were very influential in the Gaelic Revival and in fact were among the first to wear the kilt at feiseanna in Ireland. Members of the London Gaelic League attending the Macroom Feis, 5 August 1900, were said to have been 'attired in an ancient Gaelic costume and attracted considerable attention'.[28] Apparently the people of Macroom (and probably many other parts of Ireland) saw the kilt for the first time when it was worn by the visiting London Irish.

At first kilts and shawls were worn by those identified with the Gaelic League and taking part in music or language competitions but not while dancing. The late Cork dance master, Cormac O'Keeffe, told how Dr Prionnsias Ó Suilleabháin, a vocational school inspector from Adrigole in West Cork, typically wore the kilt for everyday dress and for language and music competitions but he changed into knee breeches for the dancing competitions.[29]

The earlier kilts were too heavy and cumbersome for dancing. It was not until 1924 that Lily Comerford of Dublin adopted a scaled-down, less cumbersome version of the kilt and the shawl as a dancing costume for both her male and female pupils.[30] However, the kilt only became universally accepted as 'proper' dancing costume at a much later date, i.e. approximately in the 1950s. By that time the female costumes were already changing from the kilt. However, the kilt has been universally standardised as the male Irish dancing costume and remains so to this day.

The first Ceilí ever organised

Were it not for the work of the London Gaelic League and the assistance of a Kerry migrant named Reidy, the Ceilí as we know it might never have existed and Ceilí dances might have been lost completely. The London branch was the first to promote properly conducted Irish social evenings based on the format of the Scottish evenings being held in London in the 1890s.[31] The phrase *ceilí* (*le ceile* means together) was coined for the first such social evening held in Bloomsbury Hall in London on 30 October 1897. The 'ceilí' phenomenon grew rapidly throughout England and Scotland before reaching Ireland and spreading to America, Canada and Australia. The April 1916 ceilí in Melbourne was cancelled by the Irish National Association in sympathy with the patriots who had lost their lives in the Easter Rising.[32]

At the time of the first Ceilí those figure dances which have since become known as 'Ceilí dances' were not performed as they were almost unknown. Instead 'sets, quadrilles and waltzes' were danced. While visiting the Scottish social evenings the officers of the London Gaelic League became aware that the Scottish were performing figure dances similar to those being taught by Reidy, the London-based migrant dance master. Reidy was then employed by the League to teach these figure dances along with solo dancing and soon they were replacing the set dancing at the Ceilí evenings. So synonmous did they become with the social events that they became known as Ceilí dances.

Professor Patrick Reidy — father of Ceilí dancing: Patrick Reidy (Professor Reidy as he titled himself) was born in Castleisland, County Kerry, and was a well-known travelling dance master around north Kerry and west Limerick before he migrated to London sometime in the 1860s. He was familiar with the figure dances. It would appear that they were almost exclusively found in County Kerry where they were probably invented by the travelling dance masters. It was the great work of Reidy and the London Gaelic League that preserved Ceilí dances for posterity.

Controversy over Ceilí and set dances

The London branch of the League considered the newly discovered figure dances more suitable than the sets and quadrilles for their Ceilí evenings. The sets were performed without any prescribed footwork and a degree of frivolity and excessive enjoyment which led the League to fear that this might reflect badly on the Irish. They were extremely conscious of the rowdy image of the Irish created by some other Irish events held in London.

A strict, almost regimental, approach to the performance of the Ceilí dances was adopted, even to the extent where the strict basic solo dance movements (promenade and sidestep) as taught by Reidy were introduced into the Ceilí dances. Prior to that these dances were performed with more individual, non-prescribed spontaneous footwork such as still seen in the set dances.[33] Unfortunately, due to the recent introduction of competitions for the set dances, they too are in recent years being robbed of enjoyment and spontaneity and becoming regimental in both footwork and hand movements.

Prior to the first Ceilí it was the set dances that were performed world-wide at Irish social evenings. It was the London migrants' influence that changed the fashion from set dancing to ceilí dancing. This transfer of interest was aided by the spurious and unsubstantiated claim that the sets were introduced by the British soldiers.[34] If this was the case, how were the sets so popular at Irish socials world–wide? Outside Kerry, the Ceilí dances were almost unknown and they were in fact resisted when first introduced at the Oireachtas (the biggest feis in Ireland) in 1901. Following the recommendation of the Oireachtas Committee in 1903 these Ceilí dances were excluded from Oireachtas competitions in 1904 and were not readmitted until 1912.[35]

Early publication of Ceilí dances

The early works on the new Ceilí dances were all published outside Ireland. The first two books were published in London in 1902 by Sheehan and by O'Keeffe and O'Brien.[36] The latter was undoubtedly the most influential and was re-edited several times.

The authors, Seamus O'Keeffe and Art O'Brien, were members of the London Gaelic League. O'Keeffe was a migrant from Kanturk, Co. Cork, who taught solo dancing for the League. O'Brien was born in London but of Clare ancestry. They and other members of the League visited Ireland in 1899 and travelled to west Cork and Kerry. In Kerry they collected a number of these figure dances. Other dances they recorded from Irish migrants in London and Glasgow, especially from Patrick Reidy who was residing in London at that time. Their book not only recorded these figure dances but also gave an invaluable account of the history and origins of Irish dancing. Had it not been for their work we might never have known the origins of the different dances so popular at Ceilí nowadays.

In 1913, an American, Elizabeth Burchenal, visited Ireland for an International Folk Dance Institute meeting. With the assistance of J. M. Lang from Dublin, Burchenal recorded and described some 25 figure dances. These were published in New York in 1925.[37] This publication, complete with illustrations, diagrams and historically interesting photographs included the first record of several Ceilí/figure dances. The publication of this work was delayed due to the outbreak of the First World War.

Burchenal's book contains some of the best photographs of Irish dancers ever published, but it was not the first book to contain photographs. A book produced in London in 1914[38] contained a section on Irish dancing in America and included photographs of New York migrants performing both solo and figure dance movements. Included in the photographs is Tommy Hill, who was All Ireland Champion dancer in 1909, 1910 and 1911. He migrated in 1913 from his native Cork to New York, where his daughters and grandchildren still reside.[21]

It was almost 50 years after the foundation of the Gaelic League that the first Ceilí dance book was produced in Ireland. *Ar Rinncidhe Foirne*, Book 1, containing ten figure dances, was published by An Coimisiún le Rinncí Gaelacha (Irish Dancing Commission)[9] and it was strongly influenced by the earlier works, especially O'Keeffe and O'Brien's book. Prior to 1939 the Irish relied for published accounts of the Ceilí/figure dances on overseas publications and the work and influence of Irish migrants.

The feis

In 1899 the Gaelic League revived the 'feis'. In ancient Irish times the term 'feis' (feiseanna = plural) referred to a gathering of chiefs summoned by a king to review and enact laws. This political aspect was accompanied by a feast of Irish merriment. The feis as revived by the Gaelic League separated out the political aspects. It concentrated on the culture, namely language, music, song and dance, and promoted competitions in these skills.

The first feis was held in Macroom, Co. Cork in 1899[28] and was attended by visiting members of the influential London Gaelic League. By 1902 the Irish migrants in London and Glasgow had established their own feiseanna and the latter feis is still held annually. Feiseanna were organised in at least four major venues throughout America in the same year.[38]

The largest feiseanna in the world were probably those organised by Irish migrants in New York from the 1930s to the 1960s when crowds of up to 5,000 regularly attended feiseanna in Gaelic Park and the grounds of Iona College. The dancing was always the most prominent (numerically at least) section of these enormous social occasions and often up to 300 dancers lined up to take part in a single dancing competition.[39]

With the enormous increase in the popularity of Irish dancing throughout the world and a decline in the influence of the Gaelic League, the dancing became more isolated from other aspects of the culture. Festivals of Irish dancing competitions alone are nowadays more popular world-wide. These are commonly referred to as feiseanna but they are not so in the strict sense of the word.

In North America, where the Irish migrants still have a very strong influence, at least 200 true feiseanna are held annually, while ironically the true feis is almost extinct in Ireland.

The social aspect of the feis in North America

The feiseanna in North America are social occasions for the Irish community and are very much family-orientated affairs. While the dancing is the dominant feature at these feiseanna, all other aspects of the culture are catered for. Irish sporting events appeal more to the male members while the females become involved more in the dancing competitions. It is very much a family day and there is something for each member of the family, young or old, male or female.

Families drive or fly thousands of miles each year to attend these feiseanna, often competing at two feiseanna on a consecutive Saturday and Sunday. This helps to consolidate the Irish community and promote the culture. Friendships are made among the young Irish dancers that often last a lifetime and not infrequently lead to marriage.

The number of North American feiseanna has increased enormously. The past ten years or so has seen feiseanna organised in Florida, New Orleans, Atlanta, Houston, San Antonio, Calgary, Red Deer, etc. However, the increase in the number of events geographically and ease of travel has led to a decline in attendance numbers at individual events.

Festivals of Irish dancing

In Ireland and Great Britain the outdoor feiseanna with all their social implications have almost completely been replaced by indoor festivals of dancing competitions. This is due to two factors. The weather makes the outdoor event unreliable, while the Irish dancing community has become increasingly interested in the dancing only to the exclusion of the other aspects of the culture. The dancing competition festivals are attractive only for those members of the family that are willing to sit indoors in a hall and watch nothing but dancing all day. This does not usually appeal to all members of the family, and especially not to the male members, so the family social aspect is almost completely lacking as is the community spirit. No matter how great the increase in the popularity of the dancing, this isolation of the dancing from other aspects of the culture is regrettable.

The dancing class

In Ireland most dancing classes are conducted separately in a non-Irish cultural venue but in most overseas countries, where the Irish community is identifiable and the community spirit strong, the Irish dancing classes are often held in Irish club premises or even in Irish bars (especially popular in earlier times). In these latter venues there are usually additional side interests such as music and singing classes and language classes which may be of benefit to the non-dancing members of the family and so serve to strengthen the Irish community spirit. The dancing class is a venue where the Irish migrants meet on a weekly basis, if not more frequently, and where travel to feiseanna and even visits of the dancing school (including parents and family) to Ireland are planned.

The origins of Irish dancing overseas

North America

It is impossible to say when Irish dancing was first introduced into North America (or any other country). The earliest Irish migrants almost certainly brought some aspects of Irish dancing with them even if no records still exist, for it was the practice during long boring sea voyages for passengers and crew to exercise and socialise and pass the time by dancing up on deck. Indeed, most ships crews in early days included a musician or a dance master for the purpose of conducting such exercises, hence the popularity of the English sailor's hornpipe.

The earliest Irish migrants in North America travelled down the Appalachian Mountains to the states of Carolina, Tennessee and as far south as Florida. Their music and dancing blended with other forms, especially with the Scottish music and dance. The evolution of American square dancing was greatly influenced by Irish dancing. The figures and movements of American square dancing and/or country dancing are almost identical to those of both the Irish and Scottish Ceilí dances. In Florida in the remote areas the inhabitants, the swampies, have still preserved the *Kerry Four Hand Reel* as long as anyone can remember.[40] In keeping with the old Irish tradition, in Florida the *Four Hand Reel* is danced with the more American easy gliding footwork. The promenade and sidestep are not used in Florida since the migrants had presumably established these dances there before the promenade and sidestep were introduced back in Ireland in more recent times.

Irish dancing on the American stage

More recent Irish migrants, especially towards the end of the nineteenth century, tended to stay in the emerging settlements on the east coast, especially in Boston and New York. In these larger cities the migrant dance masters established classes where they taught the traditional solo and figure dances. The end of the nineteenth and start of the twentieth century were the most important years for the American stage. On stage dance acts were extremely popular and Irish dancing especially so. On stage, however, in response to audience appeal and away from traditional conservative constraints, Irish dancing evolved in many ways and gave rise to American tap dancing.[41] It was a great time for experimenting with stage dancing.

Irish jigs and clog dances were extremely popular. The clog dances gave rise to a faster variety which became known as buck dancing, which was performed in two-four time and got more beats by having less emphasis on the use of the heel than did the clog dances. The Irish expression, 'He's handy with the heel' referred to the clog or jigs performed on the stage by the Irish. The well-known American stage personality, the one and only George M. Cohan, specialised in Irish dancing in his earlier years and went on to become one of America's greatest stage dancers and composers. He was introduced to Irish dancing by his father Jerry, known as one of the best traditional Irish dancers in all New England, who specialised in working New World variations on standard Irish reels and jigs.[41]

Syncopated versions of Irish jigs were introduced by the Irish clog dancer Barney Fagan, while an Irish American, Kitty O'Neill, was the first to introduce a hard sole onto a soft shoe to get a distinctive sound. Nor was the influence of Irish dancing in America confined to tap dancing only, for as early as 1789 John Durang, an Irish American dance master from Philadelphia, performed Lancashire clog dances and Irish jigs and reels in a decidedly Negro manner. Durang's speciality was the hornpipe and a detailed description of Durang's own choreography of the hornpipe step by step *c*. 1789 has been recorded by Stearns.[42] He and many others to follow later wedded Irish and Afro-American steps and music to create the popular minstrel dances. The influence of Irish dancing in what has become American tap, jazz and stage dancing was very strong indeed, with such great American stage dancers as Barton, Primrose (real name Delaney), O'Connor, Durang, Kelly, Fagan, all being either Irish migrants or first-generation Irish.

Influence of stage dancing on Irish dancing

While in previous times Irish dancing had a great influence on American stage dancing, over the past decade or so traditional Irish dancing world-wide has become more tap-like in feature. This has been largely due to the influence of American migrants. There has been an increase, to an almost excessive level, in the amount of beats to the extent that Irish dancing is often accused of being tap dancing. Syncopated rhythm has become a feature of almost all modern heavy shoe Irish dancing world-wide since it was first introduced by Barney Fagan, the Irish clog dancer, almost 100 years ago.[43] For exhibition purposes many Irish dancing teachers have recently introduced stop-time dancing (i.e. where part of the dance is performed with and other parts without the accompanying music), almost certainly unaware that this has been common in American stage dancing since the early 1900s.[44] The dance routines performed, especially during exhibitions by some of North America's greatest solo Irish dancers, are frequently a stop-time routine of a hybrid of Irish step dancing and American-Irish tap dancing.

The fastest feet in the world belong to Irish-American Michael Flatley of Chicago, a qualified Irish dancing teacher and the first North American to win a World Championship in Irish dancing. He is recorded in the *Guinness Book of Records* as performing 28 beats per second. He is described as the world's fastest tap dancer who retains his love for Irish dance tradition but giving it a modern-day form.[45] He illustrates the fact that Irish American traditional Irish dancers have over the years, and to this day, had a great influence on American stage dancing (and vice versa).

American Irish dancing schools

Cork-Kerry influence

While on the stage Irish dancing merged with and influenced the development of tap and jazz dancing, there were many Irish dance masters who taught and preserved the traditional solo and figure dancing. Almost all of these great dance teachers in America early this century came from the great dancing schools of Cork and Kerry. Professor O'Mahony, a Cork migrant, taught dancing in San Francisco in about 1880 where one of his pupils was William P. Healy who founded his own dancing class in 1902. This tradition is still continued by the Healy family 90 years later.[46] Professor Harrington from Kenmare, County Kerry, taught dancing in Boston from the end of the nineteenth century. Josephine Moran was one of his pupils and she in turn has taught Irish dancing in Boston to several hundred Irish migrants.

In New York, Professor James McKenna from Castleisland, County Kerry, was almost certainly the most influential and legendary Irish dancing teacher. He was born about 1885 and migrated to New York in 1903 and started teaching about 1910. McKenna taught dancing to literally thousands of Irish in the New York area, among them some of the present-day's most famous teachers, including Kathleen Mulkerin, Peggy Smith, Peter Smith, Patsy McLoughlin-Early, to mention but a few. Other notable dance teachers in the New York area early this century included Cork migrants Tommy Hill, Bob Barrett and Dick Sisk.[21] It was the work of these and others that culminated in the enormous popularity of Irish dancing in the New York area and the thousands of dancers supporting the feiseanna in that area. In more recent years their pupils' pupils have returned to Ireland to compete successfully at the World Irish Dancing Championships.

The prominence of the Cork and Kerry migrants in the American Irish dancing scene reflected the fact that in previous centuries it was the Munster region exclusively that was the home of the travelling dance master and effectively the cradle of Irish step dancing. So it was the strong and fast Cork-Kerry style of dancing that was preserved, almost unaltered, in the New York area and throughout North America.

Introduction of Northern Ireland style to America

In Ireland the dancing style had been changing slowly and by the 1940s–50s the Northern Ireland style had become more dominant. This latter style was slower, more graceful and less aggressive and to some extent reflected the influence of the rising numbers of female teachers in Ireland.

In 1948 the famous Anna McCoy from Belfast and her troupe of dancers, singers and musicians made one of their first visits to America.[47] From then on the New York Irish dancing was influenced more by the Northern style than by the Munster style. The influence continued up to the 1970s which saw the introduction of the World Irish Dancing Championships and a universal homogeneity of style. During one of Anna's earlier American tours she met two young boys, Peter and Cyril McNiff, who had migrated to New York from Belfast. In Belfast they had been pupils of the Johnson School and so had the Northern style of dancing. The McNiff brothers started their own classes in New York as did Kevin McKenna, another Belfast migrant. They were very successful due to the newly awakened interest in this new style of dancing. Many dancers tried imitating the Northern style and even left the classes of the old Cork-Kerry dance masters to join the new classes and learn the 'new' northern style of dancing.[39]

Irish Dancing Teachers Commission of America — metronomic speeds

Conflict between the long established faster Cork-Kerry style of dancing and the slower Belfast style led to confrontation at feiseanna. This was resolved at a joint meeting in 1959 of the Irish Dancing Teachers Commission of America (IDTCA) (founded in 1953) and feis musicians. It was decided to introduce the use of a metronome: 'with this device the musician will merely have to set the dial to the desired tempo, turn it on, and play at that tempo'.[48] Two different metronomic speeds were introduced for the reel, jig and hornpipe. The North American teachers were the first to introduce the metronome for Irish dancing but it was not for another 30 years or so that the practice became universally accepted. The metronome only came into use in Ireland in the late 1980s. Since then its use is standard practice at World Championships and most other major dancing events.

Acceptance of Irish dancing in different countries

In overseas countries Irish dancing is most popular in Great Britain and the United States of America where it was always readily accepted. The Irish community has always been strong and influential throughout all parts of Great Britain largely due to the sheer number of Irish migrants over several centuries. Likewise the Irish were one of the largest and most influential sections of the American colonial population and were in the forefront in the American War of Independence. In America Irish music and dance were always readily accepted and freely practised, especially as the newly emerging country developed its own unique culture.

Irish dancing was not so readily accepted in other countries which remained under British rule, such as Canada, Australia, New Zealand. Although the early Irish migrants undoubtedly practised their dancing in these colonial countries it appears to have been overshadowed by the politically more accepted kindred, Scottish dancing. A major contribution to the lack of acceptability of the Irish culture was the Irish War of Independence from the oppression of the British empire. This led not only to discrimination against the Irish culture but also to the refusal of employment to Irish and Catholics.

Irish dancing in Canada

While Irish dancing was practised in some remote areas of Canada such as Nova Scotia, it appears not to have flourished in the larger cities until quite recently. When the legendary Mae Butler left her native Dublin and arrived in Toronto as recently as 1953 there was no one practising or teaching Irish dancing in that city.[49] Only the vulgar Scottish 'Irish jig' was performed at Scottish organised festivals at that time. Mae was a qualified Irish dance teacher before she left Dublin. She quickly organised a little dancing class of her own three children and two others and within two years of her arrival had replaced the farcical Scottish 'Irish jig' with competitions for proper Irish jigs.

Since then Mae has taught thousands of Irish dancers and some forty of her pupils have become qualified teachers and adjudicators with their own classes. Mae and her musical husband Paddy quickly set about organising Irish dancing feiseanna in the Toronto area. Today there are numerous such feiseanna and a very strong Irish dancing community in the greater Toronto area.

Mae Butler not only 'started' Irish dancing as we know it today in Toronto but her influence was also felt throughout the United States, especially in Chicago and Cleveland. Wherever Mae's pupils performed they aroused interest as she had a more up-to-date approach not only to the dancing style but also the evolutionary trends in costumes. In Chicago the dancing had been fostered first by Professor McNamara, a County Clare migrant who died in 1923, and then by Pat Roche, another Clare migrant who started teaching in Chicago in 1925 and was actively teaching when Mae arrived in Toronto.[50] Roche recorded how impressed he always was with Mae Butler's dancers as they brought new ideas and approaches to the dancing and the costumes.

Mae was one of the six founding members of the Irish Dance Teachers Association of North America (IDTNA) that met in New York in 1964 (along with Fidelmia Davis, Peter Smith, Cyril McNiff, Kevin McKenna and Anna O'Sullivan). This association organises Irish dancing throughout that continent including the North American Championships which are held in a different city each year. Mae is a Vice-President of the Irish Dancing Commission in Ireland and each year she brings groups of her dancers to Ireland for the World Championships. She is always conscious of and ever working towards maintaining and strengthening the links between Ireland and the Canadian Irish dancers.

Canadian dancers-musicians

Toronto is today not only the home of world champion Irish dancer Brian Grant, but it is also home to some of the best Irish dancing accompanists in the world, including Brian, his uncle-in-law Michael Woodgate and Pat King. All three play the accordion for Irish dancing competitions throughout North America all year round. Michael (Mike) and his wife Paula were both dancing pupils of Mae Butler and Paula is a qualified teacher and adjudicator herself and teaches classes in both Canada and the United States. Paula's sister-in-law, Brigid Grant (mother of Brian), is likewise a qualified teacher and adjudicator of Irish dancing. The dancing and musical accompaniment go hand in hand in Toronto nowadays and both serve to foster a strong Irish community spirit, a big difference from 1953 when Mae Butler and family arrived there.

Irish dancing in New Zealand

North Island

In New Zealand in both North and South Islands Scottish dancing seemed to have overshadowed Irish dancing. At least such was the case in North Island until Harry Whitty migrated from east Cork to Auckland in 1906. In Ireland he had learned dancing from Christy Murphy of Cork city, a three-times All Ireland Champion dancer. Harry won the New Zealand Championship at a St Patrick's Day sports event in Auckland in 1914. He taught his own five daughters Irish dancing and also had a class in the Convent School in Auckland.

Harry Whitty remained in regular contact with his teacher, Christy Murphy. Fascinatingly, the Whitty sisters learned much of their dancing from descriptions in letters sent from Ireland by Christie Murphy. They learned the dances and then made recordings on old 78 records of their performances which were sent back to Murphy for his comments. Elizabeth and Celia Whitty in turn took over the dancing classes founded by their father.

In 1923, a 14-year old Elizabeth (Lydia) Curran arrived in Auckland from Belfast. She was a niece by marriage of the well-known dance teacher and author of Irish dance books, Peadar O'Rafferty, and had learned dancing from him. Lydia's early attempt at dancing an Irish jig was rejected by the Scottish festival organisers who at that time ran almost all of the dancing competitions except those run at the St Patrick's Day sports. The Scots found Lydia's jig to be 'rather silly, being devoid of hand movements' and unfamiliar to them and they also refused to let Alice Whitty dance.

Lydia, at the request of Father O'Reilly, started a dancing class in the Good Shepherd's Hall in 1936. At that time Celia was teaching the Whitty class. Father O'Reilly organised the first true Irish dancing competitions in 1939 in which the two classes took part. This was a milestone in New Zealand Irish dancing.

In 1945 'Cecelia Whitty' received a telegram from Christie Murphy to certify that she was 'qualified to teach traditional Irish step, set and figure dances'. Her certification came from the Irish Dancing Commission, Cork. Cecelia (Celia) had learned her dancing from her father and from Murphy during her visits to Cork, 1939, and through correspondence with Murphy.[51]

When the first New Zealand National Feis was held in Christchurch in 1950, Lydia Curran (Mrs Scott) and Celia Whitty and dancers travelled by ship to South Island's Christchurch. Lydia judged at that feis and Celia's pupils competed at the feis. Lydia also judged the second National Feis in Wellington.

Although the earlier Irish migrants in North Island had almost certainly performed some dancing in previous centuries it was the work of the Whitty family and Lydia Curran that put the dancing on a more structured and sound footing. In the South Island this did not happen until a later period.

South Island

Scottish dancing and music were predominant in South Island and it appears that there are no records of Irish dancing there before 1950 (but more detailed research may reveal otherwise). About 1956, Mrs Kay, an Irish-Manchester migrant, arrived in Christchurch and began teaching Irish dancing. Her pupils included her daughter, the well-known Shealagh (Kay) Hallissey, who is still very actively teaching in Christchurch.

Phyllis Gale who was born in Christchurch of Scottish ancestry has over the last forty years promoted Irish dancing in South Island. Her introduction to Irish dancing was somewhat accidental. Phyllis had an interest in Scottish dancing and travelled to Scotland in 1948 to improve her Scottish dancing. However, during that visit she was exposed to Irish dancing for the first time and fell in love with it. She took lessons from Peggy O'Neill in Glasgow,[52] Charlie Smythe in London and Harry McCaffrey in Dublin and became a qualified Irish dancing teacher (TCRG).

From then on Phyllis (a Vice-President of the Irish Dancing Commission) dedicated all her work to promoting Irish dancing. Shortly after her return from Ireland she was deeply involved in founding the first National Feis in Christchurch.[53] This feis is still held annually in a different city in New Zealand. The National Feis and Irish dancing in general in New Zealand is well promoted and assisted by the Irish clubs and societies helping to promote the Irish community spirit.

The co-existence of Irish and Scottish dancing

Phyllis Gale had an uphill struggle to promote Irish dancing. Scottish dancing was very dominant and Scottish culture in general was accepted and promoted throughout New Zealand, whereas the Irish culture was not. Phyllis recalls how in the early days most of the dancers also danced Scottish dancing (as many still do to this day) and so she had a difficult task to try and preserve the correct style of Irish dancing. In the earlier days steps danced were often a blend of Scottish and Irish movements, often danced with the knees wide as in the Scottish style of dancing.

This struggle to establish Irish dancing as separate from the dominant Scottish dancing was not unique to Christchurch. As mentioned, it also occurred in Toronto and parts of Canada and also in parts of Australia. In some areas the struggle was a hard one, especially following Ireland's War of Independence. In other areas, the two dance forms not only existed side by side but often each depended for its survival on the other. Dancers sometimes learned both forms because competitions organised by either the Scottish or Irish depended numerically on entries from the two communities. This symbiotic relationship I have encountered in Hobart (Tasmania) and in many cities and towns in North Queensland (Townsville, Cairns, Mackay) during my visits to these areas.

Irish dancing in Australia

Early records

Early Irish migrants to the Australian colonies carried with them their love of Irish music and dance. Over the years the Irish tradition merged with the Scottish tradition. Recently, this hybrid form has become popular in New South Wales and Queensland, being described as Australian, indicative of a young nation endeavouring to establish a cultural identity. The social aspect of Irish dancing in Australia in previous centuries was probably fairly strongly developed, although it has not been well documented.

Prior to the establishment of the feis in Australia in the twentieth century, dancing competitions were held. These probably took the form of bouts of dancing where dancers challenged each other to see who could call themselves the state champion. These dancing competitions were frequently held in conjunction with St Patrick's Day festivities.

Photographs taken about 1915 show a man and a young girl dancing at a St Patrick's day event in Mount Morgan in Central Queensland.[54] Even earlier still many Queensland newspapers at the end of the nineteenth century advertised Irish dancing competitions.[55]

South Australia

In South Australia dancing competitions were held in Kapunda annually from about 1856 until 1865 when the acting parish priest suppressed them as a demonstration of Australian patriotism. However, dancing was well established by the end of the nineteenth century when migrant step dancers, such as

Martin Ryan and Martin Fox from Tipperary and Paddy Guinane and Paddy Clohesy from Clare, arrived in South Australia.[56]

As in other parts of Australia, in Adelaide dancing competitions and exhibitions were held as part of the St Patrick's Day festivities. To eliminate some of the abuses at these events the Irish Pipers Association founded their own dancing classes as early as 1912 with Bill (Patrick William) Doherty as tutor. Doherty had learned dancing in Melbourne from the County Limerick migrant Tim Downey and he also learned set dances from a sailor on the HMS Hood. Doherty was also an excellent tap dancer and clog dancer but was scrupulous about keeping the Irish step dancing separate and distinct.

Doherty is said to have taught about 1,000 children to dance a reel in groups as part of a welcome ceremony for a Duke who became a Governor General. Doherty died in 1950. By that time there were several dancing classes in Adelaide. At present there are some 20 qualified Irish dancing teachers certified with the Irish Dancing Commission in South Australia but it is extremely unlikely that there are 1,000 Irish dancing pupils.

Melbourne, Victoria

At the end of the nineteenth century Irish dancing was being fostered in Melbourne by two Irish migrants (possibly many more unrecorded), Tim Downey from Co. Limerick and James Patrick McCarthy, a dance master from Cork. At the end of the nineteenth century one of McCarthy's most famous pupils was Elsie Black.

About 1910 Duncan Conroy, aged ten years, commenced lessons with McCarthy and went on to become a legend in Melbourne Irish dancing. Conroy and his great colleague, G. P. Fitzgerald, worked hard. In 1936 Fitzgerald established the St Patrick's Dancing Class with Conroy as the dancing teacher.[57]

Anti-Irish feelings in Melbourne: In the 1930s there was a paucity of dancers in Melbourne and complaints that concert patrons were always seeing the same dancers, hence the establishment of the St Patrick's Dancing Class. This decline in Irish dancing popularity was part of the overall anti-Irish sentiments following the 1916 Rising and the Irish War of Independence. Conroy (pers. comm.) recalled how many shops in Melbourne would not employ any Irish Catholics and displayed signs to this effect. Many Irish nationalist organisations went out of existence.[57]

In the light of the anti-Irish feelings throughout Australia, Scottish dancing thrived and dominated even as late as 1945 when the Highland Dancing Association conducted both the Scottish and Irish dancing competitions at Fern Tree Gully (Melbourne suburbs) and elsewhere. According to G. P. Fitzgerald the Scottish section was run under idyllic conditions but the Irish section was a travesty, with the Scottish organisers paying no attention to the Irish dancing rule book. From then on every effort was made to separate the Irish dancing events from the Scottish events. Conroy and Fitzgerald dedicated themselves to the cause of re-establishing Irish dancing as a distinct and separate entity from Scottish dancing. Likewise, the Irish Pipers Association (IPA) kept the music and dancing alive during the rough anti-Irish period and indeed for many years after.

Melbourne was probably the first city in the world to draw up and publish a comprehensive book of rules and regulations for Irish dancing. In 1932 'The Irish National Dancing and National Dress Promoters Association of Victoria' (under the patronage of Archbishop Mannix) had its own 15-page printed book of rules for Irish dancers, dancing competitions and dancing dress, including photographs and descriptions of the compulsory 'dress for girls' and 'dress for boys', along with a breakdown of the allocation of marks for each dance (entrance 5, dress 15, deportment 20, execution 25, dance 30 and exit 5).[58]

Only as recently as 1931 the Irish Dancing Commission in Ireland had its rules approved by the Gaelic League at its Easter Congress and even then it is doubtful if their rules and regulations were as comprehensive as those drawn up in Victoria in 1932. On 2 May 1937 (in response to a newspaper advertisement in the *Advocate* of 22 April) a new Irish step dancing controlling body was formed to promote dancing along the same lines 'as the Academy of Irish Dancing in Dublin'. Before the year was finished the 'Rules of the Victorian Irish Dancing Association' were printed in booklet form.[58] The committee of the association was made up of 'four representatives of the Irish Pipers Association, two representatives each from other Irish societies and four representatives of the general public'. The objectives of the association were (a) registration of teachers, performers, musicians and judges; (b) examination to achieve certificates of efficiency. Note for the purpose of examinations for certificates of efficiency the association had a special examination committee and this consisted of recognised authorities on Irish dancing.

Prior to the 1937 meeting, Fitzgerald had written in 1935 to the recently established Irish Dancing Commission in Dublin for copies of its rules and regulations and a reply letter was received in 1936.[59]

Later on in 1944, following a meeting between Fitzgerald and the IPA, another booklet of 'Rules and Regulations of the Victorian Irish Dancing Committee' under the auspices of the IPA was produced. It legislated for many aspects of Irish dancing even to the number of steps to be danced in a competition.

Victoria was not only as up to date as Ireland in producing its first book of rules in 1932 but was, if one can judge from subsequent rule books, extremely well organised regarding all aspects of the dancing and was most likely the best organised area in the world.

Geraldine O'Shea (first Australian qualified teacher): In 1953 Geraldine O'Shea (a former pupil of Conroy) of Melbourne visited Ireland and became the first Australasian to qualify as a dancing teacher with the Irish Dancing Commission. Following her visits to Ireland she brought more up-to-date dancing to Australia, introduced the soft shoes for the first time, updated the dancing costumes and introduced kilts for the boys. Costumes in Australia had hardly altered since the 1920s and showed a very strong pipers and Scottish influence. In both America and Australia the Irish migrants had maintained Irish dancing in its more authentic form up to the early 1950s, whereas in Ireland Irish dancing had always been evolving. Coincidentally, it was the early 1950s that saw major updating of Irish dancing in both North America and Australia.

Australian Irish Dancing Teachers Association

In the early 1960s an Irish migrant, Sean Gilroy, arrived in Sydney. He was already a qualified Irish dancing teacher. He became a founder member of the present-day Australian Irish Dance Teachers Association (AIDA) and he established a strong and firm bond between AIDA and the Irish Dancing Commission in Ireland. Among other things, AIDA organises the Australian Championships in a different state each year, while each state holds its own championships which also serve as qualifying rounds for the World Championships in Ireland. Membership of AIDA is granted to those Australians who have qualified as teachers or adjudicators with the Irish Dancing Commission. Qualifying exams are now organised and controlled by the Irish Dancing Commission and held about every three years at the request of and in co-operation with AIDA.

Australian dancing and the Irish community

Through the work of AIDA Irish dancing is now very widespread throughout Australia in every state. While many of the dancers and teachers have Irish ancestors, in recent years many are attracted to Irish dancing as an art form rather than a part of their heritage. Some have no Irish background but were introduced to Irish dancing while attending Catholic (mostly Irish-run) schools. Just as in North America where one can find various nationalities, including full-blooded native American Indians, doing Irish dancing, so too in various parts of Australasia some of the dancers have aboriginal or Maori blood, or are of South Pacific Island or Japanese ancestry.

Many of the Australian Irish dancing classes have very strong links with the Irish organisations. Many dancing classes are held in Irish premises, thus contributing to the overall ethos of the Irish community, as for example in the Celtic Club in Melbourne, the Irish Club in Perth or Mount Isa. However, in Australia the outdoor feis catering for all aspects of the culture and for the family as a unit has almost been completely replaced by the indoor dancing-competitions-only type of event.

Irish dancing — world network

Irish dancing is extremely well structured throughout the world, either working through such national bodies as exist in North America, Australia and New Zealand or in Ireland, England and Scotland through 'regional councils'. These various bodies all function, with various degrees of autonomy, under the guidance of the parent body, the Irish Dancing Commission in Ireland. Thus, while allowing for some regional and geographical variation, the rules, guidelines and qualifications in Irish dancing are more or less universally standardised.

The Irish Dancing Commission organises examinations in the various countries for those wishing to become qualified as Irish dancing teachers (TCRG) and/or adjudicators (ADCRG). Those successful are then accepted as members of the various national bodies as well as being registered with the Irish Dancing Commission. The syllabus for these exams and standard required in the various sections of the exams is universal and controlled by the Irish Dancing Commission.

World uniformity

Uniformity of standard on a world-wide basis is desirable and it has contributed to raising the standard in many areas. However, as part of the exams all candidates world-wide have to pass a two-hour written test based on the thirty (Ceilí) figure dances in the Irish Dancing Commission publication, *Ar Rinncidhe Foirne*. Originally, the publication of these dances was meant to help popularise the Ceilí dances but now, due to the overemphasis put on them for exams and competitions, teachers and dancers world-wide know and perform only those dances. Dancers from Cork to New York to New Zealand perform the one and only version of the four-hand reel. The result is that numerous other local versions of fairy reels, four-hand reels, eight-hand reels, etc, have all been discarded. This uniformity is therefore endangering numerous traditional figure dances and many are for all practical purposes extinct.

World contacts

Ease of travel and affluence have increased contact between teachers and dancers internationally. Since the late 1960s, to an ever increasing degree, teachers and adjudicators from Ireland and Great Britain travel to North America and Australasia to conduct workshops for individual dancers, individual dancing classes or various groups of dancers and to adjudicate various competitions. Increasing numbers of dancers travel from all parts of the world to Ireland for such events as the All Ireland Championships and the World Championships. Adjudicators from all over the world travel to Ireland annually to judge at the World Championships. All of this has led to greater contact and greater familiarisation with Irish dancing world-wide.

World Championships and their effects

The World Championships, now in their twenty-fourth year in 1993, attract competitors, teachers and adjudicators from numerous countries to a single venue. While raising the standard of Irish dancing world-wide this event has greatly heightened the competitive aspect of dancing. In an effort to win, dancers go to extreme lengths to learn the approved material (dance steps and movements). To a large extent the World Championships set the trend for Irish dancing world-wide and this has led to a great homogeneity of style of dancing. This homogeneity is determined as much, if not more, by overseas Irish competitors as by the Irish themselves (the 1991 senior ladies' title was won by a Glasgow dancer and the men's title by a Coventry dancer).

Regretfully, this homogeneity of style of dancing means it is impossible to recognise a dancer's background, such as geographical location, teacher, etc, by their style of dancing. Gone are the days of the great distinctive Cork, Kerry, Limerick and Belfast styles. In the early years of the World Championships, North American and Australasian dancers were readily identifiable by their style of dancing which was somewhat old-style by comparison with that being performed by the Irish and English dancers. But these overseas dancers quickly bridged the gap and some (including American, Canadian and Australian dancers) became world champions themselves and were in turn the subject of imitation.

Changes in Irish dancing world-wide

Irish dancing is continuously evolving with the introduction of new movements, pieces of steps and ideas with ever-increasing emphasis on syncopation and balletic movements. The enormous amount of contact now in existence means that these evolutionary changes are popularised world-wide within weeks (if not days) of their introduction. In fact, the majority of these evolutionary changes originate outside Ireland. While maintaining its historical links, Irish dancing is continuously changing, and it is perhaps this that makes it more popular and widespread now than ever before. Competition offers that challenge which necessitates improvement, and more spectacular performances.

Influence on style, shoes and platforms: It is not just ideas alone that have contributed to the changes in Irish dancing. Dancing shoes and platforms have also contributed to these changes. The introduction of fibreglass toe and heel pieces allowed dancers to execute loud pistol-clear click sounds with the heels. The American dancers introduced a fibreglass protrusion (known as bubble heels) on the inside of the heels to produce these clicks. So numerous and widespread did these clicks become that legislation had to be passed to limit the number of clicks in an eight-bar step. Recently dancers have taken to splitting the sole of the hard shoes in order to perform a balletic movement on the extreme tip of the toes.

In earlier times Irish dancing was performed by necessity on a small area due to pressure of space in the small kitchens, etc. Dancers performed on top of a barrel to be seen, or on a single special hollow flagstone to bring out a better sound, or on the half door taken down and laid on the floor since the earthen floor was unsuitable, or dancers going out for the night brought their own small wooden platform. This obviously led to a close, tight-kneed style of dancing. Nowadays, dancers world-wide perform on large stages, especially at the indoor dancing competitions, and this has had a universal bearing on the style, allowing for much greater flow and movement.

Uniformity of dance costumes world-wide

Dancing costumes, like the style of dancing, had previously remained somewhat static in North America and Australia, while in Ireland they were continuously evolving. This perhaps reflected the Irish migrants' need to cling to their tradition and historical past and also the earlier lack of contact with evolving trends back in Ireland. This difference was very apparent in the costumes worn in Australia up to the mid-1950s. These were long, heavy and cumbersome, with a long shawl draped over the shoulders and hanging down to the tail of the dress, and a beret with a feather worn on the head. The costumes changed and became updated following the visits of Anna McCoy to New York, the visit of Geraldine O'Shea from Melbourne to Ireland and the arrival of Mae Butler in Toronto.

Since the introduction of the World Championships and especially during the last ten years or so there has been an enormous increase in the amount of embroidery used on the girl's costume. The embroidery often covers as much as 60 per cent of the entire surface of the costume. Extremely large, elaborate embroidery designs are used. *Diamanté* and rhinestones are used extensively to adorn the costumes and short white knee socks have become accepted in preference to the long black stockings. The dress is frequently of velvet, with black being the most popular colour, since often the dress material serves only as a background to the lashings of multi-coloured embroidery.

The style and type of dress has become universal. Dancers from different parts of the world are no longer identifiable by their dress. Solo or individual costumes are the order of the day. Gone are the days when all dancers from the same dancing class wore the same costume with a certain degree of identity of teacher and region. Both style and dress have universally become homogenised in the world of Irish dancing. The world-wide homogeneity of style and costume was perhaps best illustrated by the introduction of stone-studded metal tiaras as headgear. This trend started in England in late 1989. Less than six months later, at the 1990 World Championships, these tiaras were worn by a substantial number of competitors. Within days the fashion was introduced to North America. I am pleased to say that the Irish Dancing Commission reacted quickly (to my proposal) and banned the wearing of such elaborate (beauty-queen style) headgear world-wide. Some vestiges of our heritage and tradition must be preserved.

The role of the migrant in Irish dancing has changed somewhat over the years from just teaching and promoting the traditional style of dancing to that of trend-setters in both dancing style and costumes. They no longer anxiously wait to see what is happening in Ireland but in fact they dictate and influence what is happening in the world of Irish dancing as much if not more than the Irish themselves.

Notes

1. In a *Handbook of Irish dances* (first edn.: up to seven subsequent editions), O'Donoghue and Co., Dublin, 1902, the authors, J. G. O'Keeffe and Art O'Brien, on p. III, part 1, express dissatisfaction at not being able to find any reference to

dance in early Irish literature. Likewise, Peadar and Gerald O'Rafferty in *Dances of Ireland*, Max Parrish & Co. Ltd., London, 1953, on page 7 refer to lack of references in early literature and tell us that such well known investigators as Joyce (P. W. Joyce, *A social history of ancient Ireland*, 2 volumes, Longmans Greene, London, 1903) and O'Curry (Eugene O'Curry, *On the manners and customs of the ancient Irish*, 3 volumes, Williams, London, 1873) have searched the Gaelic literature in vain. Breandán Breathnach in *Folk Music and dances of Ireland*, Education Company of Ireland, Dublin, 1971, p. 37, refers to the lack of references.

2. O'Keeffe and O'Brien conclude that the term 'Fer Cengal' in an account of the Fair of Loc Carman (= Wexford) suggests an acrobat rather than a dancer and that the term 'cronan' mentioned in the sixth century by St Colman of Cloyne probably referred to a type of music probably made with the mouth closed. See also Breathnach, *Folk Music and dances*, pp. 37–8.

3. This short poem has also been quoted by P. and G. O'Rafferty, *Dances of Ireland*, p. 7.

4. Donal O'Sullivan, *Irish folk music, song and dance*, Mercier Press, Cork, 1952, p. 7, refers to both the anonymous English poem (note 3) and this reference, but says since both references are in English it is unsafe to base any firm conclusions on them. Breathnach, *Folk Music and dances*, p. 42, also points out that the description of the performance for King James was not given till *c*. 1780.

5. *Complaynt of Scotland* (sometimes written 'Complainte') was written anonymously to Wedderburn and Lindsay and was edited by J. Leydon, London, 1775–1811. In it, the Ring dance is stated to have been a favourite in the south of Scotland where it was performed at the grain harvest time and was said to be similar to the *Rinnce Fada*, Rinky or Field dance of the Irish. For a more detailed description see O'Keeffe and O'Brien, *Handbook*, p. xii, part 1.

6. Thomas Dineley, an English antiquary, toured Ireland in 1680/1681. His 'Journal' was published in the *Journal of the Royal Society of Antiquaries of Ireland* between 1856 and 1913. See the discussion in Constantia Maxwell, *The Stranger in Ireland*, Jonathan Cape, London, 1954, pp. 101–6. A selection from Dineley's 'Journal' was published in book form as Thomas Dineley, *Observations in a Voyage through the Kingdom of Ireland . . . in the Year 1681*, University Press, Dublin, 1870.

7. O'Sullivan, *Irish folkmusic*, p. 51, gives an account of the dances as performed at Kinsale on 14 March 1689 but cautions that the account is not contemporary and the description is somewhat different from that of the Scottish dance given by O'Keeffe and O'Brien.

8. Patrick Kennedy in *The banks of the Boro: a chronicle of the County Wexford*, Simpkin Marshall & Co., London, 1867, recalls having seen the *Rinnce Fada* performed in 1812 but he gives no description of the dance.

9. An Coimisiún Rinncí Gaelacha, Dublin (Irish Dancing Commission) have published three official handbooks of Irish figure dances. *Ar Rinncidhe Foirne*, Book 1, 1939, contained ten figure dances. Book 2, 1943, contained a further 10 figure dances and Book 3, 1969, included the dances published in Book 1 and 2 and an additional 10 dances, making a total of 30 figure dances. These books are now used universally as the compulsory texts for the Irish dancing teachers' and adjudicators' exams.

10. Sir Henry Sydney, 'State Papers 1569', in *Letters and memorials of the state in the reign of Queen Mary, Queen Elizabeth and King James*, 2 volumes, folio 1746.

11. For further details on the origin of the Carol and its introduction into Ireland by the Normans see both Breathnach, *Folkmusic and dances*, pp. 38–9 and also Sean ÓTuama, *an Grá in Amhráin na nDaoine*, An Clochomhar Tte, Dublin, 1960, which includes an entire chapter on 'An Carole': see pp. 205–17 and pp. 247–9.

12. John P. Cullinane, *Aspects of the history of Irish dancing in Ireland, England, New Zealand, North America and Australia*, Cork, 1987, deals not only with the origins of figure dances and ceilí dances but also with the travelling dancing master and the solo set dances; the second work by the same author (*Further aspects of the history of Irish Dancing*), Ballineaspig Publications, Cork City, 1990, includes numerous unpublished figure dances and a most comprehensive review of the origins of the solo dances, reels, jigs and hornpipes. These two works include a comprehensive list of 140 references to Irish dancing as well as being the only publications to deal with the Irish dancing phenomenon on a world-wide basis. They are essential reading for anyone researching any aspect of the history of Irish dancing.

13. John and William Neal published the earliest Irish collections in Christ Church Yard, Dublin in 1724, named *A collection of the most celebrated of Irish tunes* reissued by Irish University Press, Shannon, 1970. The Neals also published other collections, see Breathnach, *Folkmusic and dances*, p. 33, *Popular music in eighteenth century Dublin*, Folk Music Society of Ireland and Na Píobairí Uilleann, Dublin, 1985.

14. Arthur Young, *Tours in Ireland 1776–1779*, ed. A. W. Hutton, Bell, London, 1892. Young is quoted in *Popular music in eighteenth century Dublin*, p. 34, as making no mention to reels; however O'Keeffe and O'Brien, *Handbook*, page xvii, says Young mentioned country dances in addition to jigs and reels.

15. O'Farrell (no christian name), *National collection of Irish music for the union pipes*, Dublin, 1804.

16. The reel was known in Scotland and is referred to in an anonymous work, *News from Scotland*, 1598, in which it is said that 'Silas Duncan played this reel or dance' (see O'Keeffe and O'Brien, *Handbook*, page vi).

17. The late Nellie Sweeney started teaching Irish dancing in her native Derry around 1925 where her father had taught dancing before her. Interestingly, her father refused to teach her as a female the heavy dances (only in Cork did the women perform the same steps as the men). Miss Sweeney, as she was always referred to (pers. comm.), had very strong views on the popularity of the Lancashire hornpipe in N. Ireland and has no doubt but that it was from this dance that the Irish hornpipe originated. Her demonstration for me of the Lancashire 1, 2, 3, 4 and 5 steps of the hornpipe showed them to be identical with the basic steps of the Irish hornpipe. She also testified as to the very strong Scottish influence on Derry-Donegal dancing, especially in the form of the stratspeys and flings. Information gathered from her has been included in my own books. Most regretfully, very little of her knowledge of the history of Irish dancing has been recorded.

18. O'Keeffe and O'Brien, *Handbook*, p. xxii, verify that around 1800 the great dancing schools were those of Kerry, Limerick and Cork. The travelling dance master operated almost exclusively in these counties, making them the 'home' of Irish solo dancing.

19. For more on the dancing master, see my own book, *Irish dancing*, 1987; Breathnach, *Folk Music and dance*, 1971, has a chapter on the dancing master. See also William Carleton's account of Buckramback the dancing master, *The Autobiography of William Carleton*, with a preface by Patrick Kavanagh, MacGibbon & Kee, London, 1968, pp. 106–9.

20. Details of Jerry Molyneaux were given in the oration delivered by Dr. Bryan MacMahon on 17 June 1973, marking the unveiling of a memorial headstone over the grave of Jerry Molyneaux and reproduced in my own book, *Irish dancing*, 1987, pp. 29–32.

21. Unpublished notes on 'Aspects of the history of Irish dancing in the New York area' were produced by me as part of a lecture series I gave in New York to mark St Patrick's Day celebrations in 1991. The notes include accounts of such dance masters

as James T. McKenna, Bob Barrett, Tom Hill, Jerry Mulvihill, Kathleen Mulkerin, Peggy Smith and many others, along with accounts of the earliest exams held in North America in 1967, and history of various Irish dancing teachers' associations in America since 1964.

22. I have taped some three interviews with Phil Cahill and much of this data is recorded in my 1987 book. As a living connection with the travelling dancing masters of the nineteenth century he gave me a lot of valuable information on the traditional sets, the ceilí dances, etc. His recording is one of the rare firsthand accounts of the system operated by the Kerry travelling dance masters.

23. These two women were the first women to teach Irish dancing for a living in Dublin and as such were the prototypes of the hundreds of women who nowadays have taken up this profession. I have taped interviews with both of these women and much of the information I have published in my second book, *Further aspects*, pages 82–8 and 99–101. Lily died in 1969. She was the founder of the Irish Folk Dance Society and did trojan work to popularise Irish dancing at international folk dance festivals all over Europe. Her dancers, including the legendary Rory O'Connor, danced for Hitler in the early 1930s. Lily was the teacher responsible for the introduction of the kilt as standard costume for both male and female dancers. Essie Connolly, now approximately 90 years old, still resides in her native Dublin. Her taped interviews are a most interesting record of Irish dancing in Dublin. She recalls how she and Lily Comerford (rival dancing teachers) travelled to Cork to learn set dances such as *The Blackbird*, etc, as these solo sets originated in Munster and were unknown until these two pioneering women came to Cork to learn them and teach them in Dublin.

24. The Irish Dancing Commission publishes an annual list (*Liosta oifigiul na moltoirí claraithe agus na muinteoiri claraithe*) of registered qualified teachers and adjudicators. This list includes qualified teachers (TCRG) and adjudicators (ADCRG) in Ireland, England, Scotland, Wales, Canada, United States, New Zealand, Australia and occasionally in other countries.

25. 'Schedule of 1992 Registered Feiseanna', published by the North American Feis Commission; the list includes details of dates, locations, venues, organising secretary's name, address, etc, for all feiseanna throughout North America. It is produced annually by this body working in co-operation with the Irish Dancing Commission. For further details on the North American Feis Commission and the Irish Dance Teachers Association of North America see my own books cited in Note 12.

26. P. O'Rafferty and G. O'Rafferty, *Dances of Ireland*, Max Parrish & Co., London, 1953. Peadar O'Rafferty also wrote two books, *Irish Folk Dance Book*, Patterson's Publications, London. Book 1 was published in 1934 and contained a description of 12 figure dances, while Book 2 included 10 figure dances. Many of these dances were published for the first time ever in these works.

27. H. F. McClintock, in his work *Handbook on the tradional old Irish dress*, Dundalgan Press, Dundalk, 1958, pp. 23–5, tells us that the widespread belief that kilts were the national dress of men in Ireland in early times was first stated by Eugene O'Curry, Professor of Irish History in the Catholic University of Ireland, in his book *Manners and customs of the ancient Irish*, 1860. O'Curry's suggestion was reiterated strongly by P. W. Joyce in his book, *Social history of ancient Ireland*, 1903. This was the period immediately following the formation of the Gaelic League and the members of the movement were seeking a national costume with which they could identify. Joyce, who was President of the Royal Irish Society of Antiquarians, was extremely popular from his book, and his suggestion of the kilt as national costume was readily and without question accepted by the Gaelic League. McClintock, however,

states emphatically that there is no evidence that the kilt was ever worn in Ireland until modern times (*c.* 1900) and there is no historical basis for adopting the kilt as national costume. Joyce had claimed that some evidence exists that kilts were worn by the Irish before the sixteenth century and based his claim by making six references to ancient figures or paintings depicted on stone crosses or in old books. McClintock (*Old Irish dress*, Dundalk, 1943, 2nd edn., 1950) examined the original source of each of Joyce's six claims in detail and dismissed them as being entirely unfounded. McClintock was a most accurate research worker as shown by the detailed way in which he examined Joyce's claims. Those less experienced research workers would do well not to mistake drawings or sculptures depicting ancient Irish 'tunics' for 'kilts' as has been the case in some writings I have seen. The 'tunic' was, unlike the kilt, a full-length single garment from neck to knee gathered at the waist by a belt and roughly gathered but never pleated. The kilts, in contrast, consist of a single long partly pleated piece that is wrapped around the body from the waist down. It appears that even Joyce misinterpreted ancient drawings and sculptures of the Irish tunic for the kilt.

28. *An Claidheamh Solius*, Vol. 1, March 1899 and August 1900. This was a newspaper published weekly by the Gaelic League, Dublin. It is a very good source of information on advertisements and reports and results of the earliest feiseanna organised.

29. I have made many tape interviews with Cormac O'Keeffe and these and other memorabilia are in my private collection. My first book was dedicated to this man who taught my own mother Irish dancing. Cormac was fascinating in so many ways (see Cullinane *Irish dancing*, 1987, pp. 47–58). Born in 1896 he was a bridge between the travelling dance masters of the nineteenth century and the modern-day professional dancing teachers, of whom one of his pupils, Molly Hasson, was the first full-time professional female Cork dance master. Cormac not only learned the traditional sets from the great dance masters of the nineteenth century but he himself more than anyone else was responsible for the composing of many 'new' set dances for the first time. Among his most famous compositions were *The King of the Fairies*, *The Orange Rogue*, which he composed for Nellie Sweeney, and *Miss Brown's Fancy*, which he composed for me in 1954. Many famous dancing teachers from all over Ireland travelled to Cork to learn from him, including Brendan de Glin, Anna McCoy, Lily Comerford, Essie Connolly, etc.

30. Bridie Clements, a niece of Lily Comerford, in a personal taped interview recorded for me, told how she remembered herself and Rory O'Connor and other pupils of Lily's wearing the kilt as a new form of dancing costume, adapted and designed by Lily Comerford *c.* 1924.

31. I am grateful to Áine Ní Neachtáin, secretary of the London Gaelic League, who in 1980 sent me a copy of the minute book of the Gaelic League dealing with the organising of the first ceilí. This report was reproduced by me in *Notes on the history of Irish dancing*, produced for a workshop for teachers organised by me in Killarney in 1980, see also my 1987 book, *Irish dancing*, pp. 16–18.

32. Patrick O'Farrell, *The Irish in Australia*, New South Wales University Press, Kensington, NSW, 1986, p. 259.

33. According to Phil Cahill (pers. comm.), the ceilí dances in Kerry were always performed with spontaneous non-prescribed footwork and it was not until recent times that he saw the strict sidestep and promenade step being used. Likewise, Tomás Ó Faircheallaigh, who was largely responsible for compiling the dances in *Ar Rinncidhe Fóirne*, stated at the Killarney workshop that when he first saw the *Three Tunes* and other dances of South Armagh they were performed with individual

spontaneous footwork and the sidestep and promenade steps only became standard practice in these dances after he published them in *Ar Rinncidhe Fóirne*.

34. Until very recently, 'sets' were not allowed to be performed at ceilí functions. Nowadays, the 'sets' have undergone an unprecedented revival and are extremely popular world-wide. However, it is not uncommon to hear of people (including some of my own contemporary Irish dancing teachers and especially by members of the Gaelic League) refuse to perform the same or allow them to be performed on the grounds that they were brought to Ireland by the British soldiers. Yet such people are unable to substantiate this spurious claim. Such a claim would seem to be at variance with the facts that the 'sets' were performed at the first ceilí, and were accepted by the Gaelic League before the 'discovery of the ceilí dances'; the first president of the Irish Dancing Commission, Cormac MacFhionnlaoch, declared that he derived pleasure from the 'sets'; while my own parents (both of whom came from a nationalist background) bore witness to the fact that only the sets were performed in the Irish clubs in Cork in their days as was also verified by Cormac O'Keeffe. I can only surmise that the spurious claim that the sets were introduced by the British soldiers was introduced by the Gaelic League early this century in an effort to promote the newly discovered ceilí dances.

35. In an article on 'The beginnings of Ceilí dancing in London in the 1890s', *Céim*, Nicholas Carolan informs us that ironically the ceilí dances were excluded from the Oireachtas competitions for several years. Apparently the committee were unsure as to their origins and/or suitability. Carolan's article was published in *Céim*, Vol. 69, 1990, which is the official publication of the Irish Dancing Commission and contains numerous articles of interest to the Irish dance historian.

36. While the authors O'Keeffe and O'Brien are well known, little or no information seems to be available about J. J. Sheehan, who wrote *A Guide to Irish dancing*, John Denvir, London, 1902. This 48-paged very small-sized booklet includes descriptions of 4 Hand, 8 Hand, 12 Hand and 16 Hand dances and country dances, but is less well known than the more comprehensive work of O'Keeffe and O'Brien which was coincidentally also published in 1902. J. J. Sheehan's booklet was reprinted by Litho Press, Cork, for the Irish Traditional Dance Foundation (date not given, but *c.* 1987).

37. Elizabeth Burchenal, *Rinncí na hÉireann: National Irish Dances*, A. S. Barnes & Co., USA, 1925. The book is remarkable for its clear description and easy-to-follow diagrams for dances and numerous photographs of historical interest. Many of the dances were described for the first time, including the nowadays very popular *Gates of Derry*. Burchenal acknowledges the great assistance given to her by Lang.

38. T. Kinney and M. West (eds), *The Dance*, Heinemann, London, 1914, pp. 174–80.

39. Mr. James Early and daughter (well-known N. Jersey dancing teacher, Patricia Early McLoughlin) in a recorded interview recalled for me various aspects of the Irish dancing feiseanna in New York and the earlier dance masters in New York (see note 21 for further information) and also donated various memorabilia for my collection.

40. Bill (William) Haller of Gainsville, Florida, pers. comm.

41. Marshall and Jean Stearns book, *Jazz dance — the story of American vernacular dance*, Macmillan and Company, New York, Collier MacMillan Ltd., London, 1960. This book is essential reading for those interested in the origins of jazz dance and the contribution made by Irish dancers and dances, e.g. pp. 189–90: 'Tap dancing was evolving away from the original concept of the Irish jig, tap dancing began to utilise the entire body and open up more possibilities for expressiveness'.

42. Lincoln Kirstein in *The book of dance*, Garden City Publishers, New York, 1942, p. 342, refers to Durang being the first white person to blacken his face (some 30 years

before other whites adopted the fashion) while he danced Irish hornpipes as early as 1789 (see also Stearns, *Jazz dance*, p. 38).

43. Further information on Fagan, see Stearns *Jazz dance*, note 41, and Fagan's obituary, *New York Herald Tribune*, 13 January 1937.

44. J. Laurie, *Vaudeville*, Henry Holt and Co., New York, 1953, pp. 43–7, refers to Dave Montgomery and Fred Stone as performing stop time dancing in the 1920s (see also Stearns, *Jazz dance*, p. 56).

45. Donald McFarlane (ed.), *The Guinness Book of Records, 1990*, Guinness Publishing, Enfield, 1989, p. 177.

46. See 'San Francisco' dancing history pages 132–4 in my 1990 (*Further aspects*) book. This section was based largely on an 1989 interview with Ann Healy Curtin. Ann still has many of the old Cork steps taught to her father by Professor O'Mahony including *Moore's Dream*. In previous times, steps were much rarer and were only composed by the dance master and almost every step had a name (see p. 41, etc, in my 1987 book).

47. Anna McCoy (pers. comm.), tape-recorded interview in 1991.

48. Account taken from 'Minutes of a meeting of the Irish Dancing Teachers Commission of America' held in 1959. I am grateful to Peggy Smith for a copy of these minutes (see note 21).

49. Mae Butler (pers. comm.), tape-recorded interview, see pp. 120–28 in my 1990 book for a fuller account of Mae Butler's contribution to Irish dancing in Toronto.

50. Pat Roche (pers. comm.), tape-recorded interview, see also my own book, 1987, pp. 94–7.

51. During visits to New Zealand I met with and made tape-recordings of Lydia Scott Curran and members of the Whitty family and made copies of the correspondence between Christie Murphy and the Whitty family for my own collection.

52. Laureen O'Neill-James, personal communication referring to her mother Peggy O'Neill (see Cullinane, *Further aspects*, 1990). Peggy left her native Kildare in Ireland in 1936 and taught dancing in Glasgow for many years. She helped foster the very strong Irish dancing tradition in Glasgow. Among her pupils there was James McLoughlin who has produced several world champions in both solo and figure dancing. In 1964 Peggy arrived in Washington, DC. There she dedicated the remainder of her life to promoting Irish dancing. Her dancers performed for several US presidents. Her school is at present taught by her daughter Laureen.

53. Phyllis Gale, (pers. comm.); see also Cullinane, *Irish dancing*, 1987, pp. 108–10.

54. Photographs in the John Oxley Library, Brisbane.

55. *The Colonist*, a Queensland newspaper, 13.03.1872 issue, gives a report on the Hibernian Society of Queensland St Patrick's Day excursion to Moogell and sports events including Irish dancing competitions. *The Australian*, Queensland newspaper, 02.11.1878 issue, refers to Irish dancing competitions as part of the Prince of Wales birthday celebrations, while the 15.04.1879 issue refers to Irish dancing events at the St Patrick's Day sports at Ipswich and at Toowoomba.

56. Notes on Irish dancing in South Australia by the late Fr. Caoimhín Ó hAinniní (Fr. Kevin Hannon), see Cullinane, *Irish dancing*, 1987, pp. 105–7.

57. This dancing class was advertised in the *Advocate* Melbourne newspaper on 22.04.1937 and is also referred to in several letters written by G. Fitzgerald which were formerly in the possession of the late Duncan Conroy who donated them to me. I also have taped recordings of interviews with Duncan Conroy.

58. *Rules of the Irish National Dancing and National Dress Promoters' Association of Victoria* (Australia), 1932. This Association was under the patronage of Archbishop Dr Mannix. The 15-page booklet contains special rules for teachers, special rules for judges (and judging guidelines), rules for dancers, dancing competitions, and for

dress both for girls and boys, and photographs to illustrate the latter two. *Rules of the Victorian Irish Dancing Association*, 1937: similar in general to the previous. *Rules and Regulations of the Victorian Irish Dancing Committee (under the auspices of the Irish Pipers Association)*, 1944: Rule 1 states that 'the name of the committee shall be the Irish National Dancing Committee of Victoria' and Rule 2 'the members of the committee shall be appointed by the Irish Pipers Association'.

59. This reply letter was among the memorabilia given to me by Duncan Conroy and is possibly the earliest extant letter from the Irish Dancing Commission.

10 My love is in America: migration and Irish music

Graeme Smith

In the sleeve notes to the only commercial recording of the influential accordionist Joe Cooley, another player and commentator, Tony MacMahon describes the reel known as 'My Love is in America' as

> ideally suited to his style of playing and the long b flat note he makes in the first part has the same wild and haunted call in it that Johnny Doran had in his piping of that tune. Whether or not this music was made in the black famine times of death and the living death of emigration, nobody knows, but it has in it the lonesome cry of our people of those not too-long gone times.[1]

McMahon's is a conventional, if romantic, understanding of the social and historical context of Irish dance music. But though the namer of this reel did not intend its title to indicate a fondness for America, the ambiguity alerts us to alternative readings of the relationships between Irish dance music and migration.

In the late twentieth century Irish traditional dance music has a vigorous musical life. As well as continuing to attract performers and audiences in Ireland and abroad, it has a small but secure place in the burgeoning world music market, combining the aura of authenticity with the reach provided by the transnational recording giants. Although Irish traditional dance music has been much recorded, transcribed, lauded and loved, its relationship to Irish society has been scarcely investigated. Scholars have most often seen it as folklore, and so emphasised its survival and stylistic continuity. Their categories of tradition and authenticity are little help, however, in understanding the vitality of the music this century. That Irish dance music is still so vigorously performed and so popular cannot be understood in terms of the persistence of cultural forms and of 'traditions' proving resistant to the destructive forces of modernisation. The music continues to be played because Irish men and women have found it relevant to their experience of the modern world, and this relevance has been based in the music's long-standing accommodation with emigration. Paradoxically, emigration, that supposed destroyer of traditional, rural Ireland, has strengthened rather than eroded the music.

This chapter is mainly concerned with the social place of Irish dance music in the first half of the twentieth century, the musical ground which was the basis of the public revivals of interest of the 1960s — *Comhaltas Ceoltóirí Éireann*, the populist ballad revival and the Chieftains — and the subsequent folk revival of the 1970s and 1980s. When one examines the music's social meaning in this earlier period, particularly for its performers, what one finds, I will argue, is not a music tightly integrated into the social patterns of rural Ireland, but a music shaped by the integration of rural Ireland into the rest of the world through emigration.

Two musicians

Bill Moran was born into a musical family in Galway in 1930. He took up the melodeon in childhood, and the two-row accordion in his teens. By his late teens he was playing well enough to join the acclaimed Aughrim Slopes Ceilí Band, and his musical world quickly expanded beyond the limits of household and townland. He toured with the band through the lively Irish clubs of Britain in 1947, but declined the chance to go on to America, a decision he later regretted. Like many of his generation, he did not settle back long in Galway, but returned to Britain, playing there with men he described to me as 'the cream of Ireland', in the confident Irish musical subculture in English pubs and Irish clubs after the Second World War. From Britain he moved to Australia, where he has continued to play and has participated in the infusion of Irish traditional dance music into Australian popular folk music.

I interviewed Bill Moran in Melbourne in 1983 as part of a study of accordion-playing styles, and I will return to the interview at the end. During his life, music has provided a challenge of skill and craft, a social role and a source of sociability. It has also been a powerful personal expressive medium, in which individual performances, styles and aspects of the genre itself are joined in a complex network of meanings and connotations. In my discussion at the end I will contrast the meanings Bill attaches to Irish dance music with those of Martin Mulroe, another player of similar age also now living in Australia. For both these men the music they play contains contrasting attitudes to Irishness and emigration entwined with understandings of their own lives. I will argue that the music's capacity to carry individually nuanced meanings such as these is the basis of its continuing strength. But before doing this I wish to discuss the public meanings which have been associated with traditional Irish music in the projection of an Irish national cultural identity. The social meaning of the music emerges from both its public and private interpretations.

Irish music and national culture

Irish dance music first attained some cultural and political significance in the early nineteenth century, when antiquarian collectors were constructing a place for Irish music in their mythologised image of a Gaelic Ireland. Within this, dance music was included, although it was treated by collectors such as Edward Bunting and George Petrie as subordinate to the genre of song airs which had a more easily imagined relationship to a Gaelic past.[2]

Around the mid-century the 'Young Irelanders' began to espouse the idea of a *cultural* nationalism. The leading figure of this movement, Thomas Davies, who was explicitly influenced by the German romantic Herder, argued that a culturally defined nation was the necessary basis for an effective and legitimate political unit.[3] Though broken in their abortive uprising in 1848, the Young Irelanders left their imprint on the Irish nationalist movement. Henceforth distinctive Irish cultural activities were seen as an expression of an historically-based national culture, and such activities became an indispensable part of the struggle for political independence.

Irish dance music did not have a consolidated place in Irish national culture until the Gaelic revival movement of the turn of the century. This movement urged the maintenance and revival of the Irish language, of Irish sports and pastimes, and of Irish music and dancing, and spawned two organisations, the Gaelic Athletic Association (GAA) in 1884, and the Gaelic League in 1893. These organisations, although not overtly political, provided an intellectual focus for political activists.[4]

The two organisations, the Gaelic League and the Gaelic Athletic Association, appealed to different sections of the Irish population. The Gaelic Athletic Association gained the support of the rural masses, organising and promoting traditional Irish sports, primarily Gaelic football and hurling, and grew into a massive popular movement in Ireland. Its events and organisational bodies became a focus for many popular cultural activities beyond the games it championed and formalised. The Gaelic League drew a small number of middle-class city dwellers. The call for an 'Irish Ireland' in the abstract provided worthy goals for these followers — learning Irish, studying literature, promoting the historical tradition.

The Gaelic League was dedicated to the preservation and promotion of the Irish language as the corner-stone of a national culture, and it promoted associated activities, including Irish music and dance. When first formed, it espoused a secularist conception of Irish identity, a legacy of the Anglo-Irish cultural activists of the earlier part of the century, but as the nationalist movement developed a mass base, it became a militant Catholic organisation and a cultural focus for a new generation of radical nationalists and began to reject the attenuated policies of the Home Rule movement and call for full republican independence.[5]

In 1897 the Gaelic League held in Dublin its first *Feis Ceoil* or music festival. With the emphasis on 'competitions of archeological interest', the aims of the organisers were similar to those of the nineteenth-century collectors. They were a good deal more interested in the possibility of unearthing a player of the defunct wire-strung harp than in contemporary 'country fiddlers'.[6] The interest of the Gaelic League in the 'invented tradition' of the Irish war pipes also exemplifies its active attempts to guide Irish music into forms considered appropriate for the national culture. Pipe bands, with national costume and regalia, were better suited to the public display of Irishness, and more like the folkloric displays of European nationalisms than were the popular forms of entertainment provided by country musicians.

The most important musical initiative of the Gaelic League was the ceilí dance. The first of these was held by the London branch of the Gaelic League in 1897, in imitation of the dance meetings of Caledonian Societies. The ceilí dance seemed a possible public form for Irish music and dance, although the

League sponsored the resuscitation of defunct dance forms rather than commonly practised local forms of quadrille sets.[7] The respectable Irish bourgeoisie of the Gaelic Leagues, socially distant from the cottier musicians of Ireland, were proposing a new public role for Irish dance music, in which its national cultural status could be furthered. In the early part of this century, Gaelic League meetings established the ceilí dance as a social institution.

The Gaelic Athletic Association, with its sponsoring of Irish games, was much closer to the activities of the Catholic rural lower classes than was the language-centred Gaelic League. One of the most important achievements of the nationalist movement was to weld together these two groups of cultural activists.[8] While the Gaelic League established the national emblematic significance of Irish music, the Gaelic Athletic Association maintained and expanded its audience for Irish music through the organisation of dances, and through a conception of an Irish popular culture outside a literary, or at least verbal, tradition. The ban on its players participating in 'foreign sports' extended to attending 'foreign dances'. It was thus constrained to forbid 'foreign dances' at its social functions and became one of the most important promoters of Irish dance music in the countryside in the first half of the twentieth century.[9]

After the establishment of the Irish Free State, the demands of the Gaelic revival were constitutionally enshrined and the Irish language given official status. The ideology of the state, espoused by the victorious national populism of Prime Minister de Valera in the 1930s accorded Irish traditional music a special place. It was 'the musical equivalent of Irish thought and its modes'. It was also part of an idealised vision of social stability built on the small family farm, which was seen as the base of the national ideology vigorously promoted by de Valera's Fianna Fáil Party.[10] Tobin describes de Valera's vision of Ireland as

> a touching, idealistic and wholly fantastic piece of nonsense. But it did not seem like nonsense to a majority of Irishmen in 1943, or in 1950, or in 1955. In those years it enshrined a national ideal in which it was still possible for people to believe. It was the conventional wisdom.[11]

But the status of this ideology in the life of Irish country people was more complex than this quotation suggests; while it was widely assented to in the abstract, it was often rejected in actuality. Although the public ideology of national Irish culture plays an important part in the attitudes of musicians to their music, they also build their musical understanding on more personal understandings of their life experience; and although nationalist political ideologies have dominated the public meanings given to Irish experience, they do not necessarily dominate individuals' private interpretations of their experience. At the centre of the contradictions of the ideology of nationalism was its attitude to emigration.

Ireland and the emigrant

Joseph Lee suggests that the position accorded to emigration within Irish views of the social order remained essentially unchanged from the Great Famine till the late 1950s, and he emphasises the destructive social consequences of a public failure to face honestly the consequences of emigration.[12] Kerby Miller argues that the ideas of nationalism and emigration entwined to become the corner-stone of the Irish social consciousness created in the nineteenth century and 'on both general and individual levels, emigration and nationalism epitomised the oft times tortuous Irish efforts to resolve the tensions between tradition and modernity'.[13] But if nationalism and emigration are a pair linked in their contradictions they also reflect the difference between public and private understandings and actions. While nationalism is the main way in which Irish people are called upon to see their collective relationship with larger social structures, so emigration represents a private response, apparently individual and isolated, even if grounded in historical and economic circumstances. In the eyes of the nationalist movement, the church, and the post-independence state, emigration was a capitulation before the pull of the secular, materialist world epitomised by America, yet masses of Irishmen and women felt compelled to choose it. The emigrants were put into the position of feeling guilty for their emigration and the ideology of exile was defence against this guilt and ambivalence. The ideal of the sacralised family gave a personal focus to the guilt. For although a chosen emigration superficially implied a rejection of the authority of parents, the maintenance of the inviolable family farm and impartible inheritance was rigidly dependent on emigration.[14]

Ireland proved incapable of halting emigration after independence, in spite of nationalist hopes. The essential dilemma of the emigrants' appropriate attitude to their action remained: to what extent were they guilty of deserting their family, land and country, when that country had in fact proved incapable of adequately supporting them?

The contradictions of the emigrant's attitude were mirrored by those who stayed at home. In the 1950s, Meenan identified a popular contradiction in Irish consciousness: namely, that though emigration is seen in Ireland as a national problem and a weakness in the social fabric, individuals 'still congratulate themselves if their children obtain good employment abroad'.[15]

The act of emigration, with its attendant social complications and personal costs is of monumental significance to emigrants. But emigration also affected those who stayed in Ireland and its pervasive presence became part of the way in which they understood the relationship between themselves and the rest of the world.

Emigrants are unlikely to see themselves as a social problem. Though emigration has had a conventional representation as exile, there is always a gap between conventional cultural explanations and individuals' actions, where each life must create some resolution of the complexity of the dilemma which emigration presents.

The drift to the city has dominated rural communities all over Europe for the last two centuries. In Ireland, however, migration has been little directed to Irish cities. The Irish countryside is a hinterland to the large metropolitan centres of the world, to New York and London, as much as to the provincial cities and towns of Ireland. Since the mid-nineteenth century the social consciousness of Irish country people has been defined within this world, and a global metropolitan culture has continually been seen as an alternative to rural life. The existence of this alternative has meant that Irish countrymen and country-women have constructed systems of social meaning which comment on, explain and describe these alternative ways of life and their personal consequences. I will now elaborate this general argument in relation to Irish dance music.

Emigration and Irish dance music

Irish dance music has been seen as a traditional folk art, interpreted as inseparable from Irish cultural and national experience. Under such interpretations, performances by emigrants are likely to be read as conservative and backward-looking, and as attempts to keep tradition alive in greatly changed circumstances. Cut off from the source of the music's meaning, their fate is thus to become increasingly ossified and irrelevant. But such has not been the fate of Irish migrant players. Many have become key figures in the continuing development of the music. In numerous ways which will now be discussed Irish music has thrived on emigration.

The most significant and influential collector of Irish dance music was Francis O'Neill. O'Neill was born in West Cork in 1849, of a relatively prosperous family. He left Ireland in 1865, eventually settling in America in 1869, and rose to become chief of the Chicago Police Force. A traditional flute player and a man of irrepressible public spirit, he organised the Chicago Irish Musicians Association, gathering together scores of players in that city, dedicating himself to the study of Irish history and culture, and from Chicago carrying on correspondence with like-minded spirits around the world. Here he embarked upon collecting the tunes which he eventually published in a number of printed collections. O'Neill had joined the Chicago police force in 1873, and rose rapidly through its ranks to become Chief of Police from 1901 to 1905. His administration was lauded. O'Neill was able to use his social power to assist musicians, apparently guaranteeing to any musician employment in the police force he controlled. No doubt this contributed to his success as a collector. His published collections appeared from 1903 to 1922 and most of the tunes included were noted down from his fellow musicians in Chicago. The most important of his books was *Irish Dance Music: 1001 Gems*. Published in 1907 it became the most highly regarded collection of Irish dance music, the closest thing to a canon for the genre.[16]

The publication of his collections enabled a massive expansion in the repertoire of individual musicians. Other collections had appeared before O'Neill's, and a similar, but smaller series was published in Ireland around the same time by the Gaelic League enthusiast Francis Roche.[17] But O'Neill's was the only one to be widely used by traditional musicians, and to begin to consolidate relatively small local and personal repertoires of dance tunes into an impressive national genre. Although O'Neill's publications were used directly only by reading musicians, their effect filtered through to aural musicians. Versions of tunes which were assembled in his publications for the first time have become standard settings widely played by musicians within an aural tradition, and his *1001 Gems* is generally considered with veneration by performers, even if they do not use it.

Emigration presented many musicians with enhanced opportunities for demonstrating and developing their art. Most locally circumscribed musicians in rural Ireland, relying on a limited number of musical contacts, had a small repertoire of tunes. Emigration greatly expanded the opportunities of many for learning new tunes. Players from many areas, with many different styles, were 'now only a street-car ride away'. The most talented players could perform on public stages for general audiences, and within the Irish community music was appreciated, and 'even more significantly, paid for'.[18] Emigration, far from depleting a traditional form, enhanced the power of the genre enormously.

O'Neill's collections were an important initial stage in the consolidation of Irish dance music into a broadly available yet distinctive genre, but sound recording was more influential. The commercial recordings which appeared from the 1920s onwards were much better suited to the needs of performers than was notated music. Recordings of Irish dance music have been available almost since the beginning of commercial recording. Cylinder recordings of an anonymous Irish piper were issued in USA before the turn of the century.[19] The first important period of recording of Irish music was from the mid-1920s to the 1940s, during which the great majority of 78 r.p.m. recordings of Irish music was produced. Most of these recordings were of Irish–American players in America and were issued in the 1920s and early 1930s. Nicholas Carolan estimates that about three thousand Irish recordings were made on both sides of the Atlantic during this period, but the majority were from America.[20]

The Irish-American recording emerged as part of a new marketing strategy initiated by recording companies in the 1920s. In their attempts to tap new markets, American companies issued many recordings aimed at ethnic, racial and regional groups. This commercial tactic resulted in the genres of 'hillbilly' and 'race' recordings, which can be seen as instigating the two major forces in the subsequent development of popular music styles, Country and Western and Afro-American blues. As well as these now familiar musical styles, many 'foreign series' were included in the output of recording companies. It has been estimated that one of the major companies, Victor, issued more than 15,000 so-called 'foreign' records from the 1920s and 1930s, many recorded in the United States, ranging 'from Finnish fiddlers to Sicilian bagpipe players'.[21] Irish recordings were amongst these.

The Irish music recorded in this era included instrumental dance music, as well as a number of genres of vocal music. The most important of these were nineteenth-century genteel ballads of Irish origin or reference, Irish–American sentimental song, comic song, traditional ballads and rural narrative song, nationalist and political song and occasional religious songs. Recordings of Irish dance music from this period do not appear to have differed greatly from contemporary live performance. It seems that recording company executives did little more than call a performer or group into the studio and request them to play for three minutes as they would in a public live performance.

By far the most important players of this period to be recorded were a group of fiddle players from South Sligo, who all emigrated in the first twenty years of this century. Of these, the most influential were Michael Coleman, Paddy Killoran and James Morrison. They were all from around Ballymote and

Killavel in South Sligo, and born around 1890. Coleman emigrated to America around 1912, his musical compatriots a little later. These three players established publicly what is regarded as 'Sligo style' and their playing, particularly that of Coleman, has been regarded as the highest expression of Irish dance music. Their recordings sold widely, and they influenced the repertoire and style of almost all serious performers.

The three players probably had the same teacher and musical background. Although their playing techniques differed in some aspects of bowing style and degree of note separation and inequality, the features which they shared, however, were more prominent than the differences: a highly ornamented style, using a wide variety of fingered and bowed ornaments; a flexible and animated bowing style; and a relatively fast tempo with a tendency to use melodic variation. Their performances gave the impression of great virtuosity.[22] The Irish–American Sligo fiddlers were of unparalleled importance in delineating the position of Irish music in the twentieth century, not merely through their skill, but through the symbolic associations which were ascribed to their playing style.

Hall has indicated that Coleman's impact on Irish music might be read sociologically as well as musically. He compares him with the young Louis Armstrong:

> In another musical tradition, the New Orleans trumpeter, Louis Armstrong, was credited for his originality and ability to improvise when he was in fact playing common material from his hometown (there is evidence that he was playing a lot of Buddy Petit's music). I suspect Coleman drew on the common storehouse of music resting in the local fiddlers back home, like Jamesy Gannon, Phillip O'Beirne, John Dowd and Cipin Scanlon. Just as Armstrong was the down-home boy who made it in Chicago, Coleman symbolised the country Irish boy who found fame in America.[23]

Coleman's success and his impact on Irish music reflected contemporary Irish attitudes to emigration and the emigrant. Aspects of his musical style such as its great technical brilliance, its speed, and its spontaneous variations, could readily be interpreted by listeners as evidence of the best aspects of urbanisation. The undeniable musical ability of Coleman and his fellow Sligo players made bold statements about the social hierarchies of musical communities back home. The Sligo fiddlers were removed from the localised rural society and the social precedence of older teachers and players. From the emigrant perspective, the comparatively limited styles of most Irish playing could be seen as expressions of a limited, conservative traditionality which emigration could circumvent and ignore. The individual in the city stands on his own merit and ability.

Such urban emigrant players could have had little impact without widely disseminated recordings. The impact was enhanced by the suitability of recordings for the needs of performers. Irish dance music was often taught by painstaking imitation of another performer, and recordings substituted well for the teacher in this process. A recording could be played over and over again. One player has described how learning tunes from recordings in the 1930s he anticipated the techniques of ethnomusicologists, and would slow down the mechanical turntable with a finger to discern the details of ornamentation to imitate.[24]

Recordings, then, had a number of effects on Irish dance music. They stimulated a great increase in the size of individual repertoires. They elevated the individual player and brought great respect to technique and virtuosity. Ornamentation, now frozen in a recording rather than fleeting in its very execution, was probably elevated in importance. Playing for listening became firmly entrenched and the music grew as an autonomous expressive form independent of its use for dancing.

These musical modifications do not exhaust the role of recordings in reshaping the meaning of Irish dance music. The recording placed the musical sound within new social relations. Music played by friend or family was embedded in the relationships amongst the participants; the recording, by contrast, was a commodity. Its social significance lay in its economic origins, which were far from the family farm. Many recordings came directly to Ireland from the United States, gifts from emigrant relatives, and in Ireland the gift expressed the social relations between emigrant and sedentary in a way that echoed the cash remittance. The emigrant cash remittance, the focus of the relationship between the emigrant and the family farm, bore both obligation and guilt. As Brody points out, by reversing the relations of dependency between child and parent, it tended to erode and challenge the patriarchal power of the farm proprietor and family head, and to be a manifest example of the economic superiority of urban existence.[25] Similarly, the musical remittance, the recording, was both a masked criticism of Irish rural existence, and an attempt to redefine Irish music. A product of technology, recordings showed that the music could indeed take its place in the urban world. While on the one hand the recordings reassured the family back home that the symbols of Irish identity still survived vigorously in the corrupting city, on the other hand they challenged the backwardness and limitation of country life. Recordings brought friends and family still at home tunes they would never have heard from local musicians, and many recorded performances had a virtuosity and precision which challenged live performance. Just as the cash remittance disguised social criticism with dutiful filial obligation, the recording displayed the superiority of emigrant performance even as it affirmed a continuing commitment to Irish values. The power of recordings depended on their availability, their convenience as a source of tunes, and on the social meaning which they took on. They also showed that Irish music had a place in the modern world, and could take on a new, cosmopolitan meaning. In the broader context of cultural politics, the vitality of emigrant music undermined the socio-musical definitions of Irish music offered by Irish urban middle-class cultural activists, which limited the music to the role of a national cultural treasure, and ignored its value as entertainment.

The changes in Irish music wrought by recordings and by O'Neill's collections can be seen as part of the challenge which emigration presented to rural life. For the individual the recognition and freedom which awaited in America included enhanced possibilities of musical repertoire and experience. The new meanings for the genre did not confront or repudiate the music's place in rural Ireland, but modified and redefined it. They suggested how, even within the ideology of emigration, the rural and the metropolitan could be linked.

Emigration and music: structures of feeling

The effects of emigration in Irish dance music are not merely to be found in the repertoire and styles inspired by emigrant performers. As important is the way Irish people used the category of emigration to understand their lives and their music. Emigration was an issue for those at home as well as for those who chose to leave, and emigration has influenced the way in which all players and listeners understand Irish music.

To understand the significance of emigration in the consciousness of individual musicians, we must move beyond descriptions of broad historical effects such as those given above. These are the musical symptoms of emigration, general patterns which have emerged from the collective yet varied responses of individuals. To discuss these individual responses requires a change of perspective from a general social view to a detailed analysis of individuals.

The term 'structures of feeling' was coined by the English Marxist cultural critic Raymond Williams to counter the tendency in most cultural analyses to reduce the notion of the social to that which is fixed and institutional, with culture and society expressed 'in a habitual past tense'. This is not a consequence of the fact that we are studying the past, but of an attitude to social consciousness. That which refuses to be accommodated is regarded as personal; the personal becomes the category to which all that 'seems to escape from the fixed and the explicit' is consigned.[26] To understand consciousness as a lived process, whether past or present, Williams argues that we must move beyond such a reduction of the category of the social to the fixed and institutional.

The concept of the 'structures of feeling' of cultural acts attempts to bridge the gap between social structures and formations and individual consciousness. Even if consciousness is situated in material existence, it is believed, felt, and acted on, not simply determined by circumstance. The term 'structures of feeling' is internally contradictory, to capture the paradoxical nature of social action. 'Structures' suggests rigidity, determination and fixed relationships. 'Feeling' evokes the most personal, individual part of consciousness; that which seems to be immune from social constraint.

The historical developments already described and the socially constructed understandings of these constitute the structural framework of Irish music as a social phenomenon. The emigrant performer, the remitted record, O'Neill's collections and the understood institution of emigration are all part of a network of social meanings. In as much as these are consolidated into institutions, systems of ideas or patterns of actions, they contribute to the systematic beliefs about Irish dance music, what it is publicly held to mean and represent, and how it is played and used. But if we are 'concerned with meanings and values as they are actively lived and felt' by individuals, these meanings and values are not simply reducible to systematic beliefs. The relationship between lived meanings and public beliefs can vary 'from formal assent with private dissent to the more nuanced interaction between selected and interpreted beliefs and justified experiences'.[27]

Players do not simply adopt the publicly available theories of the nature of Irish dance music to explain the musical behaviour and attitudes of themselves or others. Rather, received knowledge provides possible patterns of social meanings from which they make their selection; and thus they participate in the continuing creation of meaning. The structures of feeling associated with emigration are central to the construction of the social meaning of Irish music. Emigration provides a central category for the understanding of a network of social and economic relations and experiences, including musical experience.

To illustrate and amplify this point, the musical opinions and attitudes of two emigrant Irish musicians now living in Australia, Bill Moran and Martin Mulroe, will be discussed. This discussion will show how attitudes to emigration organise their musical views on a range of questions, how they take certain institutional given understandings and mould them to their own requirements, and how their 'feelings' about Irish music are 'structured' through their understanding of emigration and its general social significance.

The construction of musical attitudes

Bill Moran and Martin Mulroe are men of about the same age, born around 1930, and from contiguous counties of Ireland, Galway and Mayo respectively. Both were raised in active musical families and had an early period of playing in Ireland. They emigrated to Britain around 1950, and then subsequently to Australia: Bill Moran in the 1950s, and Martin Mulroe in the late 1960s.

Though these men's childhood experiences of the music are similar, there are significant and symptomatic differences in their attitudes to the genre of Irish dance music. Close examination of the patterns of these differences reveals how, even in their divergence, they have been structured by shared experiences and understandings.

The differing attitudes of these two performers to the question of regional style are particularly illuminating. Regional, usually county, categories are often used by musicians and commentators to explain and discuss musical differences between players. In some cases the patterns of differences are elusive and subtle, and research suggests that even the most experienced listeners cannot consistently distinguish stylistic differences.[28] This does not imply that discussion of regional styles of playing is delusion or meaningless, but that more than merely musical sound is being discussed. When Bill Moran was asked about the difference between the musical environment of Galway and the England of the early 1950s, he commented:

> there was a lot more [music] in Ireland of course, but you got blokes from all the different counties coming to England, like they had a lot of different styles. Well, you could nearly tell any bloke where he came from the way he played. I could, anyway, and I think I nearly could now.[29]

When asked if the stylistic difference rested in differences of repertoire or in playing technique, he continued:

> It's the way they play. It's the style of their area, county. You can always tell anyone up around the Northern area, they have a different style to the Western, the West or the South.

He also used more localised categories. A player from only eight or nine miles away from where he was brought up would have 'a different style altogether'. Contrast these opinions with those of Martin Mulroe:

> Now, I've picked up records here, and the sleeve on the record says, somebody from, say, Meath or Offaly goes to America and gets in with the musicians there and he gets on a record, and then he describes himself as playing in 'Offaly style'. Now, another man will say Galway style, another man will say Waterford or Wexford style, something like that. Now to me, none of them are true. The whole thing is somebody's idea of his own value to Irish music and that doesn't ring true. To me there is only one style, and that is an Irish style of Irish music.

When further discussion focused on the possibility of regional differences in earlier times, when communication and travel between areas was more difficult, he continued:

> [there would be] different interpretations of the tunes. Say, like someone would play a different finish on it, or say, a different change over from the first sixteen bars to the second and so on. But this has been corrected by the likes of Joe Burke and Sean McGuire and Michael Coleman in particular and Paddy Killoran . . . They made it an international thing.

He went on to state that every player has his individual style, which is virtually impossible for another to emulate:

> every player puts his own, ah, flavour is the word I would say, more than say . . .[a county style] . . . I cannot see how there is a different county style, there isn't.

These players' differences of musical opinion on questions of regionality are in each case part of the way in which they imagine the relationship of the individual player to Irish music, and ultimately the relationship of Ireland to the rest of the world. Where Bill Moran wants to see differences in playing style between players in terms of differences of place and region, and so tie the music closely to the detail of Irish rural life, Martin Mulroe places Irish music on an international stage where the achievements of individual players are prominently displayed.

These two men diverge in similar ways on other related issues. Mulroe places great emphasis on the recordings of the Irish–American fiddle players such as Michael Coleman and Paddy Killoran, and thereby further emphasises the emigrant, international perspective of Irish music. By contrast, Moran was relatively dismissive of these players, seeing them in terms of the Irish-American cultural nexus exemplified in rural Ireland by the figure of the 'returned Yank'.

Mulroe and Moran also differ on another product of Irish emigrant experience, the tune collections of Francis O'Neill. O'Neill's collections are held in canonic status by some players, and Mulroe is one of these. Though he does not read music, Mulroe regards O'Neill's collections as authoritative versions:

> O'Neill's book, the 1001 tunes, that is, the original O'Neill's book, that was straight out Irish music . . . and anyone who picks up a tune out of O'Neill's book is picking the tune up straight as it should be . . . to me O'Neill's is the original, the best.

Moran has a different opinion. Though he also does not read music, he notes the inadequacy of printed versions for the transmission of the music, and stresses instead the importance of aural communication between players:

> I often heard fellows that was able to read it [O'Neill's collection] and in a couple of weeks time, you'd hear another fellow coming in who wasn't able to read a bit of music, with the same tunes that were completely different . . . he would listen to it . . . you know the ear, I think, is better than the mind . . . if you have the ear for music you can tell immediately whether it's a nice one or a nasty one anyway.

But emigration itself structures the understanding of the relationship between rural Ireland and metropolitan society. This can be seen in Mulroe's recollection of the circumstances under which he left Ireland.

> I'll tell you why I left. I was building houses with my father . . . the last job I did, I built the local dance hall for the priest and he said, 'I hope you'll play for me when we hold the first dance', but the week I finished the hall I left for England.
> And the reason I left Ireland was because all my mates, the fellows I grew up with, fellows who would have been 17, 18, 19 and 20 year olds, they'd all left and went to England.
> I was lucky. I was earning money, building houses with my father, but these fellows 3,4,5,6, or 7 in families, they just went to England to earn money . . . they could have gone to Dublin if they wanted to, but they decided to go to England.
> I went to a . . . dance hall and everyone was in my age group, and they all seemed to be . . . well built. If one wasn't tall he was broad. I was building a hall for a priest in another parish. I used to go to his dance more than anything else.
> (Later), I decided to find out what the local dance hall was like, so I went to the dance there one night, and I thought I was in school . . . it seem there everyone was a schoolkid, they all looked like that. Also all my friends, who hadn't married and settled down, they all had gone to England or gone to America, something like that, so I decided that I would go to England, all my friends were there, my brothers were there, so, that's why I left Ireland.

In this description of the experiences leading to his emigration, we see a rural society through the eyes of a young man. His was not the emigration of necessity, but one of dissatisfaction with his surroundings. He does not show a hatred or an active rejection of rural society, but a restlessness in a limited social environment. The central image of the restrictiveness of his own area is the perceived immaturity of his local peers. By contrast the lads in a neighbouring village hall dance are tall, well built: by extension, how much more so are the men of the diaspora. Home is small and limited. Emigration holds the hope of expansion and growth.

These social attitudes pervade his opinions about Irish music. In a sense, it is only 'grown up' when it can be seen from a global perspective. Local variations are not particularly valuable. Individual virtuosic performers have transformed the music from relatively trivial local entertainments to a respected and internationally recognised canon. Thus performers like Michael Coleman, Joe Bourke, Sean McGuire and Paddy Killoran have 'corrected' the idiosyncrasies in Irish dance music, and 'made it an international thing'. In different ways, the players named by Mulroe epitomise the importance of emigration and modernisation in Irish music. Coleman and Killoran are two of the famous

Sligo fiddlers. McGuire is a fiddle player of the next generation, whose recordings of the late 1950s and 1960s established widely his models of precise execution and his complex sets of variations. Joe Bourke is one of the main figures of the modern accordion style, which emerged in the 1950s and 1960s, largely in the attempt to emulate the virtuosity of Sligo fiddlers on the button accordion. From Mulroe's perspective, all these players represent the process of unifying and organising the public repertoire and its interpretation, and in so doing they demonstrate the power of individual skill and interpretation to move Irish dance music beyond localistic and limited contexts into an international cultural sphere. Martin Mulroe views Irish music from the perspective of the emigrant, rather than that of the resident of a local area or county. From this point of view, the national transcends the regional. The individual virtuoso, his importance emphasised by these basically metropolitan perspectives, provides the model for a theory of stylistic difference.

Bill Moran's attitude to the music could be regarded as 'localistic' by comparison. This is not to say that he is necessarily a more conservative character than Mulroe, nor that his attitudes are simply a reflection of his personal history. His early adulthood was marked by unsettled moving through a series of jobs in unskilled labouring, a pattern common to many Irish emigrant men of his generation. Within this social experience he had personal freedoms and a varied social life which were unobtainable at home. Though he sees his emigration as having provided expanded social possibilities, his musical focus is distinctly tied to his native place and the social circumstances which surrounded the music there, and he will not surrender this to a national conception of the music. Thus he has chosen to locate his music in a different place in a ideological system which he, none the less, shares with Mulroe.

The construction of the genre of Irish traditional dance music has a social history. On a public level, this is part of Irish social and political movements with wider goals and aspirations. The struggle for the definition of Irish music, for the assertion of its social, national and political significance, has been part of a general movement of cultural nationalism exemplified in organisations such as the Gaelic League, the Gaelic Athletic Association and the revivalist organisation *Comhaltas Ceoltóirí Éireann*, which through the 1960s, carried on the process of locating Irish traditional music within a changing cultural and political environment. Though these organisations have differed in focus and in the constituencies which they addressed, and have been influential in different periods, they have all placed Irish music in a national context. Music has been regarded as capable of speaking for *the nation*, rather than merely for the individuals who play or use it.

The foregoing discussion questions the exhaustiveness of national interpretations of Irish traditional dance music. Though formal public institutions and public ideologies have contributed to the construction of musical meaning, individuals, particularly players, modify and reinterpret the relatively rigid formulations which are publicly presented. Many of the social meanings for the music which they have created have been shaped by the place of emigration in their ideas and experience.

Emigrants have played a large part in Irish traditional dance music, but they have not merely preserved the genre, but reconstructed its meanings. Because they enabled the music to be tacitly associated with a cultural nexus of emigration and modernity, it could continue to speak to a broad constituency of players, both in and out of Ireland. Its vigorous existence today is attributable to this.

Notes

1. Tony McMahon, sleeve notes to LP recording *Cooley*, Gael Linn CEF 044 mono, Dublin, 1975.
2. Edward Bunting, *A general collection of the ancient music of Ireland*, Waltons, Dublin, 1969 (1796, 1809, 1840); George Petrie, *The Petrie collection of the ancient music of Ireland Vols 1&2*, Gregg Press, Farnborough, 1967 (1855), and *The complete Petrie collection of ancient Irish music. 3 Vols*, ed. Charles Villiers Stanford, Boosey & Co, London, 1905.
3. Conor Cruise O'Brien, *States of Ireland*, Pantheon, New York, 1972, pp. 74–84.
4. J. C. Beckett, *The making of modern Ireland*, Faber and Faber, London, 1966, p. 417.
5. Oliver MacDonagh, *States of mind*, George Allen and Unwin, London, 1983, pp. 104–25; O'Brien, *States of Ireland*, pp. 74–84.
6. Breandán Breathnach, 'The Feis Ceol and piping', *Ceol* 8, 1&2, 1986, pp. 13–16.
7. Barry Taylor, 'The Irish ceilidh band — a break with tradition?', *Dal gCais* 7, 1984, pp. 67–9.
8. O'Brien, *States of Ireland*, pp. 74–84.
9. 'The ban' was finally removed in 1971. See Fergal Tobin, *The best of decades: Ireland in the 1960s*, Gill and Macmillan, Dublin, 1984, p. 119.
10. Edward O. Henry, 'Institutions for the promotion of indigenous music: the case of Ireland's Comhaltas Ceoltoiri Eireann', *Ethnomusicology* 33,1, 1989 p. 69.
11. Tobin, *The best of decades*, p. 4.
12. J. J. Lee, 'Reflections on the study of Irish values' in M. P. Fogarty, L. Ryan and J. J. Lee, *Irish values and attitudes: the Irish report of the European values system study*, Dominican Publications, Dublin, 1984, pp. 114, 118.
13. Kerby A. Miller, *Emigrants and exiles: Ireland and the Irish exodus to North America*, Oxford University Press, New York, 1985, p. 3.
14. Miller, *Emigrants and exiles*: pp. 467–9, 482–92.
15. James Meenan, 'Some features of Irish emigration', *International Labour Review*, 69, 1954, p. 129.
16. Francis O'Neill, *The dance music of Ireland: 1001 Gems*, Waltons, Dublin, 1965 [1907].
17. Francis Roche, *The Roche collection of traditional Irish music, vols 1–3*. Ossian, Cork, 1982 (1927).
18. Barry O'Neill, sleeve notes to LP recording *The wheels of the world*, Shanachie, 33001, New York, 1974.
19. Reg Hall, 'Note', *Traditional Music* 2, 1975, p. 24.
20. Nicholas Carolan, 'A discography of Irish traditional music', *Ceol* 4, 2, 1984, p. 45.
21. Pekka Gronow, *The Columbia 33000-F series. A numerical listing*, John Edwards Memorial Foundation, Los Angeles, 1982, p. 1.
22. Lawrence McCullough, 'Michael Coleman, traditional fiddler', *Eire-Ireland*, 10, 1, 1975; and Katherine Potter and Daniel Michael Collins, sleeve notes to LP recording *The pure genius of James Morrison*, Shanachie 33004, New York, 1978.
23. Reg Hall, inserted notes to LP recording *Irish dance music*, FW 8821, Folkways, New York, 1973, p. 1.
24. Interview with Martin Mulroe conducted by Peter Parkhill, 1980, Parkhill collection, Oral History section, National Library, Canberra.

25. Hugh Brody, *Inishkillane*, Penguin, Harmondsworth, 1974, pp. 121–2.
26. Raymond Williams, *Marxism and literature*, Oxford University Press, Oxford, 1977, p. 128; see also Raymond Williams, *Problems in materialism and culture: selected essays*, Verso, London, 1980, p. 38.
27. Williams, *Marxism and literature*, p. 132.
28. Fionnualla Scullion, 'Perceptions of style amongst Ulster fiddlers' in *Studies in traditional music and dance: proceedings of the 1980 Conference of the UK National Committee (International Folk Music Council)*, UK National Committee (International Folk Music Council), London, 1980, pp. 33–46, 71–2.
29. The following quotations are taken from an interview conducted with Bill Moran by the author, 1983 (tape in possession of author) and from Mulroe and Parkhill, cited in note 24.

Index

The reader's attention is drawn to the indexer's note on page 222 of *Patterns of Migration* Volume 1 of *The Irish World Wide*.